BIOGRAPHICAL ESSAYS.

ESSAYS,

BIOGRAPHICAL AND CRITICAL;

OR,

Studies of Character.

BY

HENRY T. TUCKERMAN.

" All my life long
I have beheld with most respect the man
Who knew himself, and knew the ways before him;
And from amongst them chose considerately,
With a clear foresight, — not a blindfold courage;
And, having chosen, with a steadfast mind
Pursued his purposes." — TAYLOR, *Philip Van Artevelde.*

BOSTON:
PHILLIPS, SAMPSON AND COMPANY.
1857.

Stereotyped by
HOBART & ROBBINS,
New England Type and Stereotype Foundery,
BOSTON.

CONTENTS.

PAGE

THE PATRIOT.

GEORGE WASHINGTON.

The memory of Washington is the highest and most precious of national blessings, and, as such, cannot be approached by artist or author without reverence. To pervert the traits or to mar the unity of such a character is to wrong, not only his sacred memory, but the dearest rights of his countrymen. A poet once conceived a drama based on the fate of André; and, after striving to embody Washington in the piece, in a manner coincident with his own profound sense of his character, he found that the only way of effecting this, without detriment to his ideal, was to keep that august presence off the stage, and to hint its vicinity by the reverent manner in which the name and views of Washington were treated by all the *dramatis personæ.* This instinct of dramatic propriety is a most striking proof of the native sacredness of the subject. The more fertile it may be to the poet and philosopher, the less right has the biographer to interfere with, overlay, or exaggerate, its primitive truth, and the more careful should he be in adhering to the lucid and conscientious statement of facts, in themselves, and for themselves, immeasurably precious.

"You have George the Surveyor," said Carlyle, in his quaint way, to an American, when talking of heroes. Never had that vocation greater significance. It drew the young Virginian unconsciously into the best education possible in a new country for a military life. He was thereby practised in topographical observation; inured to habits of keen local study; made familiar with the fatigue, exposure, and expedients, incident to journeys on foot and horseback, through streams and thickets, over mountains and marshes; taught to accommodate himself to limited fare, strained muscles, the bivouac, the woods, the seasons, self-dependence, and effort. This discipline inevitably trained his perceptive faculties, and made him the accurate judge he subsequently became of the capabilities of land, from its position, limits, and quality, for agricultural and warlike purposes. A love of field-sports, the chief amusement of the gentry in the Old Dominion, and the oversight of a plantation, were favorable to the same result. Life in the open air, skilful horsemanship, and the use of the rifle, promoted habits of manly activity. To a youth thus bred in the freedom and salubrity of a rural home, we are disposed to attribute, in no small degree, the noble development of Washington. How naturally frank courage is fostered by such influences, all history attests. The strongest ranks in the old Roman armies were levies drawn from the agricultural laborers; the names of Tell and Hofer breathe of the mountains; and the English yeomen decided the victory on the fields where their kings encountered the French in the early wars. Political economists ascribe the deterioration of modern nations, in those qualities which insure fortitude and martial enterprise, to the encroachments of town life; and the greatest cities of antiquity fell through the insidious luxury of commercial success. Nor are these general truths inapplicable to personal character. In crowded towns artifice prevails. In the struggle for the prizes of traffic, nobility of soul is apt to be lost in thrift. The best hours of the day, passed under roofs and in streets, bring not the requisite ministry to health, born of the fresh air. It enlarges the mind to gaze habitually upon the horizon unimpeded by marts and edifices. It keeps fresh the generous impulses to consort with hunters and gentlemen, instead of daily meeting "the hard-eyed lender and the pale lendee." In a word, the interest in crops and herds, in woodland and upland, the excitement of deer-shooting, the care of a rural domain, and the tastes, occupations, duties, and pleasures, of an intelligent agriculturist, tend to conserve and expand what is best in human nature, which the spirit of trade and the competition of social pride are apt to dwarf and overlay. Auspicious, therefore, were the influences around the childhood and youth of Washington, inasmuch as they left his nature free, identified him with the least artificial of human pursuits, and nursed his physical, while they left unperverted his moral energies. He became attached to the kind of life of which Burke and Webster were so enamored, that they ever turned with alacrity from the cares of state to flocks and grain, planting and reaping, the morning hunt, and the midsummer harvest. There would seem to be a remarkable affinity between the charm of occupations like these and the comprehensive and beneficent mission of the patriotic statesman. To draw near the heart of Nature, to become a proficient in the application of her laws, to be, as it were, her active coadjutor, has in it a manliness of aim and a refreshing contrast to the wearisome anxieties of political life, and the sordid absorption of trade, which charm such noble minds, and afford their best resource at once for pastime and utility.

There were, too, in that thinly-peopled region over which impends the Blue Ridge, beside the healthful freedom of nature, positive social elements at work. The aristocratic sentiment had a more emphatic recognition there than in any other of the English Cisatlantic colonies; the distinctions of landed property and of gentle blood were deeply felt; the responsibility of a high caste, and of personal authority and influence over a subject race, kept alive chivalric pride and loyalty; and, with the duties of the agriculturist, the pleasures of the hunt and of the table, and the rites of an established and unlimited hospitality, was mingled in the thoughts and the conversation of the people that interest in political affairs whence arise public spirit and patriotic enthusiasm. Thus, while estates carelessly cultivated, the absence of many conveniences, the rarity of modern luxuries, the free and easy habits of men accustomed rather to oversee workers than to work themselves, the rough highways, the unsubstantial dwellings and sparse settlements, might not impress the casual observer as favorable to elegance and dignity, he soon discovered both among the families who boasted of a Cavalier ancestry and transmitted noble blood. The Virginia of Sir Walter Raleigh — a country where the most extravagant of his golden dreams were to be realized — had given place to a nursery of men, cultivators of the soil, and rangers of the woods, where free, genial, and brave character found scope; and the name of the distant colony that graced Spenser's dedication of the Faerie Queene to his peerless sovereign, instead of being identified with a new El Dorado, was to become a shrine of Humanity, as the birthplace and home of her noblest exemplar.

These advantages, however, Washington shared with many planters of the South, and manorial residents of the North, and they were chiefly negative. A broader range of experience and more direct influences were indispensable to refine the manners and to test the abilities of one destined to lead men in war, and to organize the scattered and discordant elements of a young republic. This experience circumstances soon provided. His intimacy with Lord Fairfax, who, in the wilds of Virginia, emulated the courteous splendor of baronial life in England, the missions upon which he was sent by the governor of the State, combining military, diplomatic, and surveying duties, and especially the acquaintance he gained with European tactics in the disastrous campaign of Braddock, — all united to prepare him for the exigencies of his future career; so that, in early manhood, with the athletic frame of a hunter and surveyor, the ruddy health of an enterprising agriculturist, the vigilant observation of a sportsman and border soldier, familiar alike with Indian ambush, the pathless forest, freshets and fevers, he had acquired the tact of authority, the self-possession that peril can alone teach, the dignified manners of a man of society, the firm bearing of a soldier, aptitude for affairs, and cheerfulness in privation. To the keen sense of honor, the earnest fidelity, the modesty of soul, and the strength of purpose, which belonged to his nature, the life of the youth in his native home, the planter, the engineer, the ambassador, the representative, the gentleman, and the military leader, had thus added a harmony and a scope, which already, to discriminating observers, indicated his future genius for public life, and his competency to render the greatest national services.

During these first years of public duty and private enterprise, it is remarkable that no brilliant achievement served to encourage those latent military aspirations which lurked in his blood. Braddock scorned his advice; Governor Dinwiddie failed to recognize his superior judgment; and he reached Fort Duquesne only to find it abandoned by the enemy. To clear a swamp, lay out a road through the wilderness, guide to safety a band of fugitives, survey faithfully the Shenandoah valley, treat effectively with Indians, and cheer a famished garrison, were indeed services of eminent utility; but it was only indirectly that they were favorable to his renown, and prophetic of his superiority. His apparently miraculous escapes from bullets, drowning, and the ravages of illness, called forth, indeed, the recognition of a providential care suggestive of future usefulness; but the perplexities growing out of ill-defined relations between crown and provincial officers, the want of discipline in troops, the lack of adequate provision for the exigencies of public service, reverses, defeats, physical and moral emergencies, thus early so tried the patience of Washington, by the long endurance of care, disappointment, and mortification, unredeemed by the glory which is wont to attend even such martyrdom, that he cheerfully sought retirement, and was lured again to the field only by the serious danger which threatened his neighbors, and the prompting of absolute duty. The retrospect of this era of his life derives significance and interest from subsequent events. We cannot look back, as he must often have done from the honorable retreat of his age, without recognizing the preparatory ordeal of his career in this youth and early manhood, wherein he experienced, alternately, the solace of domestic comfort and the deprivations of a border campaign, the tranquil respectability of private station and the responsibility of anxious office, the practice of the camp and the meditations of the council, the hunt with gentlemen and the fight with savages, the safe and happy hospitality of a refined circle and forest life in momentary expectation of an ambush. Through all these scenes, and in each situation, we see him preserving perfect self-control, loyal to every duty, as firm and cheerful during the bitter ordeal at Fort Necessity as when riding over his domain on a summer morning, or shooting game on the banks of the Potomac, ready to risk health, to abandon ease, to forego private interests, with a public spirit worthy of the greatest statesman, yet scrupulous, methodical, and considerate in every detail of affairs and position, whether as a host, a master, a guardian, a son, or a husband, as a member of a household or a legislator, as leader of a regiment or agent of a survey ; and, so highly appreciated was he for this signal fidelity within his then limited sphere, that his opinion in a social discussion, his brand on tobacco, his sign-manual to a chart, his report to a superior, and his word of advice or of censure to a dependent, bore at once and forever the sterling currency and absolute meaning which character alone bestows. In this routine of duty and vicissitude under these varied circumstances, in the traits they elicited and the confidence they established, it is impossible not to behold a school often severe, yet adequately instructive, and a gradual influence upon the will, the habits, and the disposition of Washington, which laid the foundations, deep, broad, and firm, of his character, and confirmed the principles as well as the aptitudes of his nature.

So intimately associated in our minds is the career of Washington with lofty and unsullied renown, that it is difficult to recall him as divested of the confidence which his fame insured. We are apt to forget that when he took command of the army his person was unfamiliar, and his character inadequately tested to the public sense. Officers who shared his counsels, comrades in the French war, neighbors at Mount Vernon, the leading men of his native State, and a few statesmen who had carefully informed themselves of his antecedent life and private reputation, did, indeed, well appreciate his integrity, valor, and self-respect ; but to the majority who had enlisted in the imminent struggle, and the large number who cautiously watched its prospects before committing either their fortunes or their honor, the elected chief was a stranger. Nor had he that natural facility of adaptation, or those conciliating manners, which have made the fresh leader of troops an idol in a month, nor the diplomatic courtesy that wins political allies. If we may borrow a metaphor from natural philosophy, it was not by magnetism, so much as by gravitation, that his moral authority was established. There was nothing in him to dazzle, as in Napoleon, nothing to allure, as in Louis XIV., when they sought to inspire their armies with enthusiasm.

The power of Washington as a guide, a chieftain, and a representative of his country, was based on a less dramatic and more permanent law; he gained the influence so essential to success,— the ability to control others,— by virtue of a sublime self-government. It was, in the last analysis, because personal interest, selfish ambition, safety, comfort, — all that human instincts endear,— were cheerfully sacrificed, because passions naturally strong were kept in abeyance by an energetic will, because disinterestedness was demonstrated as a normal fact of character, that gradually, but surely, and by a law as inevitable as that which holds a planet to its orbit, public faith was irrevocably attached to him. But the process was slow, the delay hardly tolerable to a noble heart, the ordeal wearisome to a brave spirit. In our view, no period of his life is more affecting than the early months of his command, when his prudence was sneered at by the ambitious, his military capacity distrusted even by his most intimate friends, and his "masterly inactivity" misinterpreted by those who awaited his signal for action. The calm remonstrance, the inward grief, the exalted magnanimity, which his letters breathe at this crisis, reveal a heroism of soul not surpassed in any subsequent achievement. No man ever illustrated more nobly the profound truth of Milton's sentiment, "They also serve who only stand and wait." His was not simply the reticence of a soul eager for enterprise, the endurance of a forced passivity, with vast peril and glorious possibilities, the spur of necessity, the thirst for glory, and the readiness for sacrifice stirring every pulse and bracing every nerve; but it was his part to "stand and wait" in the midst of the gravest perplexities, in the face of an expectant multitude, with a knowledge of circumstances that justified the "hope delayed," and without the sympathy which alleviates the restless pain of "hope deferred,"— to "stand and wait" before the half-averted eye of the loyal, the gibes of a powerful enemy, the insinuations of factious comrades,— with only conscious rectitude and trust in Heaven for support. How, in his official correspondence, did Washington hush the cry of a wounded spirit; how plaintively it half escapes in the letter of friendship; and how singly does he keep his gaze on the great cause, and dash aside the promptings of self-love, in the large cares and impersonal interests of a country, not yet sensible of its infinite need of him, and of its own injustice!

The difficulties which military leadership involves are, to a certain extent, similar in all cases, and inevitable. All great commanders have found the risks of battle often the least of their trials. Disaffection among the soldiers, inadequate food and equipment, lack of experience in the officers and of discipline in the troops, jealousy, treason, cowardice, opposing counsels, and other nameless dangers and perplexities, more or less complicate the solicitude of every brave and loyal general. But in the case of Washington, at the opening of the American war, these obstacles to success were increased by his own conscientiousness; and circumstances without a parallel in previous history added to the vicissitudes incident to all warfare the hazards of a new and vast political experiment. That his practical knowledge of military affairs was too limited for him to cope auspiciously with veteran officers,—that his camp was destitute of engineers, his men of sufficient clothing and ammunition,—that the majority of them were honest but inexpert yeomen,—that tory spies and lukewarm adherents were thickly interspersed among them,—that zeal for liberty was, for the most part, a spasmodic motive, not yet firmly coëxistent with national sentiment,—that he was obliged, month after month, to keep these incongruous and discontented materials together, inactive, mistrustful, and vaguely apprehensive,—all this constitutes a crisis like that through which many have passed; but the immense extent of the country in behalf of which this intrepid leader drew his sword, the diversity of occupations and character which it was indispensable to reconcile with the order and discipline of an army, the habits of absolute independence which marked the American colonists of every rank, the freedom of opinion, the local jealousies, the brief period of enlistment, the obligation, ridiculed by foreign officers but profoundly respected by Washington, to refer and defer to Congress in every emergency,—this loose and undefined power over others in the field, this dependence for authority on a distant assembly, for aid on a local legislature, and for coöperation on patriotic feeling alone, so thwarted the aims, perplexed the action, and neutralized the personal efficiency of Washington, that a man less impressed with the greatness of the object in view, less sustained by solemn earnestness of purpose and trust in God, would have abandoned in despair the post of duty, so isolated, ungracious, desperate, and forlorn.

Imagine how, in his pauses from active oversight, his few and casual hours of repose and solitude, the full consciousness of his position — of the facts of the moment, so clear to his practical eye — must have weighed upon his soul. The man on whose professional skill he could best rely during the first months of the war, he knew to be inspired by the reckless ambition of the adventurer, rather than the wise ardor of the patriot. Among the Eastern citizens the spirit of trade, with its conservative policy and evasive action, quenched the glow of public spirit. Where one merchant, like Hancock, risked his all for the good cause, and committed himself with a bold and emphatic signature to the bond, and one trader, like Knox, closed his shop and journeyed in the depth of winter to a far distant fort, to bring, through incredible obstacles, ammunition and cannon to the American camp, hundreds passively guarded their hoards, and awaited cautiously the tide of affairs. While Washington anxiously watched the enemy's ships in the harbor of Boston, his ear no less anxiously listened for tidings from Canada and the South. To-day, the cowardice of the militia; to-morrow, the death of the gallant Montgomery; now, the capture of Lee, and again, a foul calumny; at one moment a threat of resignation from Schuyler, and at another an Indian alliance of Sir Guy Johnson; the cruelty of his adversaries to a prisoner; the delay of Congress to pass an order for supplies or relief; desertions, insubordination, famine; a trading Yankee's stratagem or a New York tory's intrigue; the insulting bugle-note which proclaimed his fugitives a hunted pack, and the more bitter whisper of distrust in his capacity or impatience at his quiescence: these, and such as these, were the discouragements which thickened around his gloomy path, and shrouded the dawn of the Revolution in dismay. He was thus, by the force of circumstances, a pioneer; he was obliged to create precedents, and has been justly commended as the master of "a higher art than making war, the art to control and direct it," and as a proficient in those victories of "peace no less renowned than war," which, as Fisher Ames declared, "changed mankind's ideas of political greatness."

What, we are continually impelled to ask, were the grounds of hope, the resources of trust and patience, which, at such crises, and more especially during the early discouragements of the struggle, buoyed up and sustained that heroic equanimity, which excited the wonder, and finally won the confidence, of the people? First of all, a settled conviction of the justice of his cause and the favor of God; then a belief, not carelessly adopted, that, if he avoided as long as possible a general action, by well-arranged defences and retreats, opportunities would occur when the enemy could be taken at disadvantage, and by judicious surprises gradually worn out and vanquished. Proof was not wanting of a true patriotic enthusiasm,— unorganized, indeed, and impulsive, yet real, and capable, by the *prestige* of success or the magnetism of example, of being aroused and consolidated into invincible vigor. Scattered among the lukewarm and the inexperienced friends of the cause were a few magnanimous and self-devoted men, pledged irretrievably to its support, and ready to sacrifice life, and all that makes life dear, in its behalf. Greene and Putnam, Knox and Schuyler, Robert Morris and Alexander Hamilton, were names of good cheer, and reliable watchwords in the field and the council; Franklin and Adams were representatives of national sentiment rarely equalled in wisdom and intrepidity; the legislative body, whence his authority was derived, more and more strengthened his hands and recognized his ability; the undisciplined New Englanders hollowed a trench and heaped a mound with marvellous celerity and good-will; bushfighters from the South handled the rifle with unequalled skill; a remarkable inactivity on the part of the enemy indicated their ignorance of the real condition of the American army; and last, though not least, experience soon proved that, however superior in a pitched battle, the regular troops were no match for militia in retrieving defeat and disaster. The marvellous siege of Boston, the masterly retreat from Brooklyn Heights, the success at Sullivan's Island, and the capture of the Hessians at Trenton, made it apparent that vigilant sagacity and well-timed bravery are no inadequate compensation for the lack of material resources and a disciplined force.

Everything combines, in the events of the war and the character of the man, to deepen moral interest and extinguish dramatic effect. In the absence of "the pomp and circumstance" of war, and the latent meaning and grand results involved, the chronicle differs from all other military and civil annals. The "lucky blows" and "levies of husbandmen," the poorly clad and grotesquely armed patriots, were as deficient in brilliancy of tactics and picturesque scenes, as was the bearing and aspect of their leader in the dashing and showy attractions of soldiership. "His eyes have no fire," says the Hessian's letter. An adept in the school of Frederic could find scarcely a trace of the perfect drill and astute combinations which were, in his view, the only guaranties of success in battle. The arrogant confidence of Marlborough, the inspired manœuvres of Napoleon, ordered with the rapidity of intuition beside a camp-fire and between pinches of snuff, the theatrical charge of Murat, the cool bravery of William of Orange,— all that is effective and romantic in our associations with military heroism gives place in this record to the most stern and least illusive realities. The actors are men temporarily drawn from their ordinary pursuits by a patriotic enthusiasm which displays itself in a very matter-of-fact way. The only sublimity that attends them is derived from the great interest at stake, and the deliberate self-devotion exhibited. Patience far beyond action, caution rather than enterprise, faith more than emulation, are the virtues demanded. What of poetry lies hidden in the possibilities of achievement is solemn rather than chivalric; endurance is the test, perseverance the grand requisite, indomitable spirit the one thing needful; and in these conditions, the restless, ambitious, and mercenary, who form the staple of armies, can find little scope or encouragement. It is neither the land nor the era for laurel crowns and classic odes, for orders and patents of nobility. If the volunteer falls, his only consolation is that he fills a patriot's grave, while some rude ballad may commemorate the victim, and the next Thanksgiving sermon of the pastor of his native hamlet may attest his worth. If he survives, a grant of land, where land is almost worthless, and an approving resolution of Congress, are the only prizes in store for him,—save that greatest of all, the consciousness of having faithfully served his country.

The *tableaux* of Washington's life, however inadequately represented as yet in art, are too familiar to afford room for novel delineation to his biographer; and they differ from the prominent and dramatic events in other lives of warriors and statesmen in a latent significance and a prophetic interest that appeal to the heart more than to the eye. When we see the pyramids looming in the background of Vernet's canvas, the imagination is kindled by the association of Napoleon's victories with the mystical and far-away Egyptian land; but the idea of a successful hero, in the usual meaning of the term, of a distant campaign, of the spread of dominion, is dwarfed before the more sublime idea of a nation's birth, a vindication of inalienable human rights, a consistent assertion of civil freedom and the overthrow of tyranny, suggested by the successive portraits so dear to the American heart; — first, the surveyor guiding his fragile raft over the turbulent Alleghany; then the intrepid *aide-de-camp*, rallying the fugitive army of Braddock; next the dignified commander, drawing the sword of freedom under the majestic shadow of the Cambridge elm; the baffled but undismayed leader, erect in the boat which shivers amid the floating ice of the Delaware, his calm eye fired with a bold and sagacious purpose; cheering his famished and ragged men in the wintry desolation of Valley Forge; then receiving the final surrender of the enemies of his country; in triumphal progress through a redeemed and rejoicing land; taking the oath as first President of the Republic; breathing his farewell blessings and monitions to his countrymen; dispensing, in peaceful retirement, the hospitalities of Mount Vernon; and at last followed to the tomb with the tearful benedictions of humanity! It is the absolute meaning, the wide scope, the glorious issue, and not the mere pictorial effect, that absorbs the mind intent on these historical pictures. They foreshadow and retrace a limitless perspective, fraught with the welfare, not only of our country, but of our race. In comparison with them, more dazzling and gorgeous illustrations of the life of nations are as evanescent in effect as the *mirage* that paints its dissolving views on the horizon, or as a pyrotechnic glare beside the stars of the firmament.

As we ponder the latest record of his life,* its method and luminous order excite a new conviction of the wonderful adaptation of the man to the exigency; and it is one of the great merits of the work that this impressive truth is more distinctly revealed by its pages than ever before. Not a trait of character but has especial reference to some emergency. The very faults of manner, as crude observers designate them, contribute to the influence, and thereby to the success, of the commander-in-chief. A man of sterner ambition would have risked all on some desperate encounter; a man of less self-respect would have perilled his authority, where military discipline was so imperfect, in attempts at conciliation; a man of less solid and more speculative mind would have compromised his prospects by inconsiderate arrangements; one less disinterested would have abandoned the cause from wounded self-love, and one less firm, from impatience and dismay; one whose life and motives could not bear the strictest scrutiny would soon have forfeited confidence; and moral consistency and elevation could alone have fused the discordant elements and concentrated the divided spirit of the people. Above all, the felicitous balance of qualities, through a moderation almost superhuman, and never before so essential to the welfare of a cause, stamped the man for the mission. Not more obviously was the character of Moses adapted to the office of primeval lawgiver for the chosen people,—not more clearly do the endowments of Dante signalize him as the poet ordained to bridge with undying song the chasm which separates the Middle Age from modern civilization, than the mind, the manner, the disposition, the physical and spiritual gifts, and the principles of Washington proclaimed him the Heaven-appointed chief, magistrate, man of America. In the very calmness and good sense, the practical tone and moderate views, which make him such a contrast to the world's heroes, do we behold the evidence of this. What does he proclaim as the reward of victory? "The opportunity to become a respectable nation." Upon what is based his

* Irving's Life of Washington.

expectation of success? "I believe, or at least I hope, that there is public virtue enough left among us to deny ourselves everything but the bare necessaries of life to accomplish this end." What are his private resources? "As I have found no better guide hitherto than upright intentions and close investigations, I shall adhere to those maxims while I keep the watch." This moderation has been fitly called *persuasive*, and this well-regulated mind justly declared "born for command." His reserve, too, was essential in such an anomalous condition of social affairs. Self-respect is the keystone of the arch of character; and it kept his character before the army and the people, his brother officers and his secret foes, the country and the enemy, firm, lofty, unassailable, free, authoritative,—like a planet, a mountain, a rock, one of the immutable facts of nature,—a Pharos to guide, a sublimity to awe, and an object of unsullied beauty to win by the force of spontaneous attraction. It is his distinction among national leaders, as has been well said by our foremost ethical writer, to have been "the centre of an enlightened people's confidence." The nature of the feeling he inspired among the troops may be inferred from the expression in a letter from the camp at White Plains, preserved in a gazette of the times: "Everything looks very favorable; a fine army of at least twenty thousand men in remarkably good health and spirits, *consummate wisdom, centred in a Washington*, to direct them, and *a determined spirit with the whole body* to die or carry our purpose into effect." His relation was obviously representative; he incarnated the highest existent patriotism. His wisdom, not his genius, is thus recognized as the grand qualification. His own remark concerning Hamilton is singularly applicable to himself,—"His judgment was intuitively great;" and this was the intellectual endowment which justified to the good sense of the people the confidence which his integrity confirmed.

Another secret cause of this remarkable personal influence was self-restraint. There is no law of nature more subtle and profound than that whereby latent power is generated. The silent weight of the distant lake sends up the lofty jet of the fountain; and the clouds are fed by innumerable particles of aëriform moisture. The electric force generated amid the balmy quietude of the summer noon, the avalanche slowly conglomerated from the downy snow-flakes, the universal process of vegetation, the vast equilibrium of gravity, the irresistible encroachment of the tide, and all broad and grand effects in the universe, are the reverse of violent, ostentatious, and fitful. By gradual development, harmonized activity, regular and progressive transitions, are enacted the most comprehensive functions of the physical world. A similar law obtains in character. The most expressive phrases in literature are the least rhetorical; the noblest acts in history are performed with the least mystery; true greatness is unconscious; "life," says the wise German, "begins with renunciation;" silence is often more significant than speech; the eye of affection utters more with a glance than the most eloquent tongue; passion, curbed, becomes a motive force of incalculable energy; and feeling, subdued, penetrates the soul with a calm authority and the manner with an irresistible magnetism. Our instinct divines what is thus kept in abeyance by will with a profounder insight than the most emphatic exhibition could bring home through the senses. The true artist is conscious of this principle, and ever strives to hint to the imagination rather than to display before the eye. The poet, aware by intuition of this law, gives the clew, the composer the key-note, the philosopher the germinal idea, rather than a full and palpable exposition. In the moral world latent agencies are the most vital. If Washington had been the cold, impassive man those whom he treated objectively declared him to be, he could not have exercised the personal influence which, both in degree and in kind, has never been paralleled by merely human qualities. It was not to the correct and faithful yet insensible hero that men thus gave their veneration, but to one whose heart was as large and tender as his mind was sagacious and his will firm; the study of whose life it was to control emotion; to whom reserve was the habit inspired by a sublime prudence; whose career was one of action, and over whose conscience brooded an ever-present sense of responsibility to God and man, to his country and his race, which encircled his anxious brow with the halo of a prophet rather than the laurel of a victor. He who knelt in tears by the death-bed of his step-daughter, who wrung his hands in anguish to behold the vain sacrifice of his soldiers, who threw his hat on the ground in mortification at their cowardly retreat, whose face was mantled with blushes when he attempted to reply to a vote of thanks, whose lips quivered when obliged to say farewell to his companions in arms, who embraced a brother officer in the transports of victory, and trembled with indignation when he rallied the troops of a faithless subaltern, — he could have preserved outward calmness only by inward conflict, and only by the self-imposed restraint of passion have exercised the authority of principle. When the cares of public duty were over, and the claims of official dignity satisfied, the affability of Washington was as conspicuous as his self-respect, his common sense and humane sentiments as obvious as his modesty and his heroism. The visitors at Mount Vernon, many of whom have recorded their impressions, included a singular variety of characters, from the courtier of Versailles to the farmer of New England, from the English officer to the Italian artist; and it is remarkable, that, various as are the terms in which they describe the illustrious host, a perfect identity in the portrait is obvious. They all correspond with the description of Chief Justice Marshall: —

"His exterior created in the beholder the idea of strength, united with manly gracefulness. His person and whole deportment exhibited an unaffected and indescribable dignity, mingled with haughtiness, of which all who approached him were sensible; and the attachment of those who possessed his friendship and enjoyed his intimacy was ardent, but always respectful. His temper was humane, benevolent, and conciliatory; but there was a quickness in his sensibility to anything apparently offensive, which experience had taught him to correct."

To a reflective mind there is something pathetic in the gravity so often noticed as a defect in Washington. It foreshadowed, in his youth, the great work before him, and it testified, in his manhood, to his deep sense of its obligations. It betokened that earnestness of purpose wherein alone rested the certainty of eventual success. It was the solemnity of thought and of conscience, and assured the people that, aware of being the central point of their faith, the expositor of their noblest and best desires, the high-priest of national duty, it was not with the complacency of a proud, or the excitement of a vain, but with the awe of a thoroughly wise and honest man, that he felt the mighty trust and the perilous distinction. Let it never be forgotten that it was his task to establish a grand precedent, untried, unheralded, unforeseen in the world. Such experiments, in all spheres of labor and of study, lead the most vivacious men to think. In science, in art, and in philosophy, they breed pale and serious votaries. Such an ordeal chastened the ardent temper of Luther, knit the brow of Michael Angelo with furrows, and unnerved the frame of the starry Galileo. It is but a pledge of reality, of self-devotion, of intrepid will, therefore, that, with a long and arduous struggle for national life to guide and inspire, and the foundations of a new constitutional republic to lay, the chief and the statesman should cease even to smile, and grow pensive and stern in the face of so vast an enterprise, and under the weight of such measureless responsibilities.

The world has yet to understand the intellectual efficiency derived from moral qualities, — how the candor of an honest and the clearness of an unperverted mind attain results beyond the reach of mere intelligence and adroitness, — how conscious integrity gives both insight and directness to mental operations, and elevation above the plane of selfish motives affords a more comprehensive, and therefore a more reliable view of affairs, than the keenest examination based exclusively on personal ability. It becomes apparent, when illustrated by a life and its results, that the cunning of a Talleyrand, the military genius of a Napoleon, the fascinating qualities of a Fox, and other similar endowments of statesmen and soldiers, are essentially limited and temporary in their influence; whereas a good average intellect, sublimated by self-forgetting intrepidity, allies itself forever to the central and permanent interests of humanity. The mind of Washington was eminently practical; his perceptive faculties were strongly developed; the sense of beauty and the power of expression, those endowments so large in the scholar and the poet, were the least active in his nature; but the observant powers whereby space is measured at a glance, and the physical qualities noted correctly, — the reflective instincts through which just ideas of facts and circumstances are realized, — the sentiment of order which regulates the most chaotic elements of duty and work, thus securing despatch and precision, — the openness to right impressions characteristic of an intellect, over which the visionary tendencies of imagination cast no delusion, and whose chief affinity is for absolute truth, — these noble and efficient qualities eminently distinguished his mental organization, and were exhibited as its normal traits from childhood to age. To them we refer his prescience in regard to the agricultural promise of wild tracts, the future growth of localities, the improvement of estates, the facilities of communication, the adaptation of soils, and other branches of economics. By means of them he read character with extraordinary success. They led him to methodize his life and labors, to plan with wisdom and execute with judgment, to use the most appropriate terms in conversation and writing, to keep the most exact accounts, to seek useful information from every source, to weigh prudently and decide firmly, to measure his words and manner with singular adaptation to the company and the occasion, to keep tranquil within his own brain perplexities, doubts, projects, anxieties, cares, and hopes enough to bewilder the most capacious intellect and to sink the boldest heart. His mental features beam through his correspondence. We say this advisedly, notwithstanding the formal and apparently cold tenor of many of his letters; for so grand is the sincerity of purpose, so magnanimous the spirit, so patient, reverent, and devoted the sentiment underlying these brief and unadorned epistles, whether of business or courtesy, that a moral glow interfuses their plain and direct language, often noble enough to awaken a thrill of admiration, together with a latent pathos that starts tears in the reader of true sensibility. The unconsciousness of self, the consideration for others, the moderation in success, the calmness in disaster, the singleness of purpose, the heroic self-reliance, the immaculate patriotism, the sense of God and humanity, the wise, fearless, truthful soul that is thus revealed, in self-possessed energy in the midst of the heaviest responsibilities that ever pressed on mortal heart, with the highest earthly good in view, and the most complicated obstacles around, serene, baffled, yet never overcome, and never oblivious of self-respect or neglectful of the minutest details of official and personal duty, — is manifest to our consciousness as we read, and we seem to behold the benign and dignified countenance of the writer through the transparent medium of his unpretending letters. Compare, as illustrations of character, the authenticity of which is beyond dispute, the correspondence of Washington and that between Napoleon and his brother Joseph, recently published at Paris. All the romance of spurious memoirs, all the dazzling *prestige* of military genius, fails to obviate the impression the emperor's own pen conveys, in the honest utterance of fraternal correspondence, of his obtuse egotism, arrogant self-will, and heartless ambition. In Washington's letters, whether expostulating, in the name of our common humanity, with Gage, striving to reconcile Schuyler to the mortifications of a service he threatened to quit in disgust, freely describing his own trials to Reed, pleading with Congress for supplies, directing the management of his estate from amid the gloomy cares of the camp, acknowledging a gift from some foreign nobleman, or a copy of verses from poor Phillis Wheatley, the same perspicuity and propriety, wisdom and kindliness, self-respect and remembrance of every personal obligation, are obvious.

The eloquent biographer of Goethe has aptly compared the agency of strong passions to the torrents which leave ribs of granite to mark their impetuous course, and significantly adds: "There are no whirlpools in shallows." How much nobler the sustaining and concentrative result of these turbulent elements becomes when they are governed and guided by will and conscience, the character of Washington singularly illustrates; and "passion, when in a state of solemn and omnipotent vehemence, always appears to be calmness." These considerations enable us to reconcile what is apparently incongruous in the reports of different observers who have attempted to describe Washington's manner, aspect, and disposition. Thus we are told by one of his intimate companions, that he was "more free and open in his behavior at levee than in private, and in the company of ladies than when solely with men;" and by another, that "hard, important, and laborious service had given a kind of austerity to his countenance and reserve to his manner, yet he was the kindest of husbands, the most humane of masters, the steadiest of friends." One speaks of his large hand, the token of practical efficiency; one, of his personal attention to an invited guest; one, of his sagacious observations, in travelling, upon the facilities for internal communication or agriculture, suggested by the face of the country; and another, of his avoidance of personal subjects in conversation. But, in our view, some of the most striking tributes to the gradual but absolute recognition of his character are to be found in the contemporary public journals. Thus a London paper of February, 1784, says: "His circular letter to the army was read at a coffee-house not very distant from the Royal Exchange; every hearer was full of the writer's praises; in composition it was said to be equal to anything of ancient or modern date." Subsequently, another popular English journal holds this language: "Whenever the shock of accident shall have so far operated on the policy of America as to have systematized and settled her government, it is obvious that the dictator, protector, stadtholder, or by whatever name the chief magistrate so appointed shall be called, will be General Washington." His retirement established the purity of his motives; and a Dublin print, dated the same year with our first extract, said: —

"There are few so blinded by prejudice, as to deny such a degree of merit to the American general as to place him in a very distinguished point of view; but even those who have been accustomed to view him as the most illustrious character of this or any other age, will be astonished by the following instance of his integrity, which we give from the most unquestionable authority. When General Washington accepted the command of the American army, he rejected all pecuniary reward or pay whatever, and only stipulated for the reimbursement of such sums as he might expend in the public service. Accordingly, at the conclusion of the war, he gave in to Congress the whole of his seven years' expenditure, which only amounted to sixteen thousand pounds Pennsylvania currency, or ten thousand pounds sterling. In the eyes of our modern British generals the above circumstance will appear totally incredible; at least, they will deem Mr. Washington little better than a fool; for, if we judge from certain accounts, ten thousand pounds would scarcely have answered the demands of a commander-in-chief at New York a single month."

These items, taken at random from the newspapers of his day, serve to make us understand how the man whose cautious generalship provoked the ridicule of Lord Howe's soldiers at the opening of the war, and whose firmness in resisting the French alliance awoke a storm of detraction from the Jeffersonian democracy at a later period, lived down aspersion, and became, by the evidence of facts, the acknowledged exemplar of human worth and wisdom described by his last and best biographer.

His moral serenity, keeping reflection intact and forethought vigilant, is nobly manifest in the deliberate process through which, by gradual and therefore earnest conviction, he came to a decision when the difficulties between the mother country and her colonies were pending. Not one of the leading patriots of the Revolution ranged himself under its banner with more conscientious and rational motives. The same disposition is evident in his hesitation to accept the command, from that self-distrust which invariably marks a great and therefore modest soul, in his subsequent calmness in defeat and sobriety in victory, in the unexaggerated view he took of the means and his disinterested view of the ends of the momentous struggle, in the humility of spirit with which he assumed the reins of government when called to do so by the popular suffrage, in his uniform deference to the authority of all representative assemblies, in the prescient warnings of his parting address, in the unostentatious and simple habits that followed him into retirement, and in the unfaltering trust which gave dignity to his last hour. This normal characteristic of his nature, this being ever "nobler than his mood," is what preëminently distinguishes him from the galaxy of patriots, statesmen, and warriors, whose names are blazoned in history; for the copious rhetoric of modern republicans, the fiery and yet often compromised pride of Paoli, the selfish instincts of Marlborough, the heartless ambition of Napoleon, were never long concealed, even from the eye kindled with admiration at their prowess. Washington seems not for a moment to have forgotten his responsibility to God and his fellow-creatures; and this deep sentiment permeated his whole nature,—proof against all excitement, illusion, and circumstance. When he overheard a little boy exclaim, as the procession in his honor passed through the streets, "Why, father, General Washington is only a man!" the illustrious guest paused in his triumphal march, looked with thoughtful interest on the child, and, patting him on the head, replied, "That 's all, my little fellow, that 's all." He was, indeed, one of the few heroes who never forgot his humanity, its relations, obligations, dependence, and destiny; and herein was at once his safeguard and his glory.

These facts of character were viewed by distant and illustrious men in relation to their own experience; yet, diverse as may be the inference of each, a like feeling of admiration, and a testimony equally sincere and emphatic, signalize every tribute to the unparalleled and inestimable worth of Washington in the annals of humanity. The popular statesman, who had become familiar with the deadly aspersions of party hatred, wondered that so many inimical eyes intent upon a career exposed to the keenest personal criticism failed to discover and fix one stain upon the reputation of the man, the statesman, or the soldier. This "excites astonishment," said Fox. The splendid advocate, who knew how the spell of official dignity was broken to the vision of those near the sceptre and the ermine, recorded, as an isolated fact in his knowledge of mankind, that Washington alone inspired him with the unmodified sentiment of veneration. "For you only," writes Erskine, "do I feel an awful reverence." The incident of his career which impressed the most renowned soldier of the age was characteristic at once of the limited scope and the enthusiasm of military genius. The bold and successful passage of the Delaware, and the surprise of the Hessians, awakened in Frederic of Prussia the sympathy and high appreciation which he manifested by the gift of a sword, with an inscription exclusively in praise of Washington's generalship. The moderation of his nature, the heroic balance of soul, whereby elation was kept in abeyance in the hour of success, not less nobly than despair in the day of misfortune, attracted the French philosopher, habituated as he was in the history of his own nation to the association of warlike and civic fame with the extremes of zeal and indifference, of violence and caprice. In his estimation, the good sense and moral consistency of Washington and his compatriots naturally offered the most remarkable problem. Accordingly, Guizot bears witness chiefly to this unprecedented union of comprehensive designs and prudential habits, of aspiration and patience, in the character of Washington, and, doubtless through the contrast with the restless ambition which marks the lives of his own illustrious countrymen, is mainly struck with the fact, that, while "capable of rising to the level of the highest destiny, he might have lived in ignorance of his real power without suffering from it." The Italian patriot, obliged to vent his love of country in terse dramatic colloquies and through the lips of dead heroes, is thrilled with the grand possibilities of action, through the realization of his sentiments by achievement, opened to Washington. "*Felice voi,*" exclaims Alfieri, in his dedication of Bruto Primo to the republican chief, — "*felice voi che alla tanta gloria avete potuto dare base sublime ed eterna, — l'amor della patria dimostrato coi fatti.*" Even the poor Indians, so often cajoled out of their rights as to be thoroughly incredulous of good faith among the pale-faces, made him an exception to their rooted distrust. "The white men are bad," said an aboriginal chief in his council speech, "and cannot dwell in the region of the Great Spirit, *except Washington.*" And Lord Brougham, in a series of analytical biographies of the renowned men of the last and present century, which indicate a deep study and philosophical estimate of human greatness, closes his sketch of Washington by the emphatic assertion, that the test of the progress of mankind will be their appreciation of his character.

Is not the absence of brilliant mental qualities one of the chief benefactions to man of Washington's example? He conspicuously illustrated a truth in the philosophy of life, often appreciated in the domestic circle and the intimacies of private society, but rarely in history, — the genius of character, the absolute efficiency of the will and the sentiments independently of extraordinary intellectual gifts. Not that these were not superior also in the man; but it was through their alliance with moral energy, and not by virtue of any transcendent and intrinsic force in themselves, that he was great. It requires no analytical insight to distinguish between the traits which insured success and renown to Washington, and those whereby Alexander, Cæsar, and Napoleon, achieved their triumphs; and it is precisely because the popular heart so clearly and universally beholds in the American hero the simple majesty of truth, the power of moral consistency, the beauty and grandeur of disinterestedness and magnanimity, that his name and fame are inexpressibly dear to humanity. Never before nor since has it been so memorably demonstrated that unselfish devotion and patient self-respect are the great reconciling principles of civic as well as of social and domestic life; that they are the nucleus around which all the elements of national integrity, however scattered and perverted, inevitably crystallize; that men thus severely true to themselves and duty become, not dazzling meteors to lure armies to victory, nor triumphant leaders to dazzle and win mankind to the superstitious abrogation of their rights, but oracles of public faith, representatives of what is highest in our common nature, and therefore an authority which it is noble and ennobling to recognize. The appellative so heartily, and by common instinct, bestowed upon Washington, is a striking proof of this, and gives a deep significance to the beautiful idea, that "Providence left him childless, that his country might call him — Father."

THE MAN OF THE WORLD.

LORD CHESTERFIELD.

THERE is an epithet, of frequent occurrence in the writings of Philip Dormer Stanhope, Earl of Chesterfield, which suggests the nature of his philosophy of life; it is the word *shining*, which he applies to oratory, character, and manners, with an obvious relish. We have the greatest faith in the significance of language, especially in regard to the habitual use of certain adjectives as illustrative of individual opinions, temperament, and disposition. Brief sentences thickly interspersed with the first person singular form a style indicative of egotism; dainty verbal quibbles, of effeminacy; and a copious, prolonged, and emphatic combination of words seems equally native to a full and earnest mind. It may be a fanciful idea, — but this our experience frequently confirms, — that the constant use of the word designating a quality is an instinctive sign of its predominance in character. Chesterfield's ideal of excellence was essentially superficial; for his praise of solid acquirement and genuine principles is always coupled with the assertion of their entire inutility if unaccompanied by grace, external polish, and an agreeable manifestation. He omits all consideration of their intrinsic worth and absolute dignity; their value to the individual, according to him, is wholly proportioned to his skill in using them in a social form. It is seeming, not being, he extols; rhetoric, in his view, far transcends reflective power; manners have more to do with human welfare than sentiment, and tact achieves more satisfactory conquests than truth; it is not depth, elevation, or extent, the permanent qualities, but those of a temporary kind, that belong to the surface of life, upon which he relies. Accordingly, to shine in oratory, conversation, and behavior, is to realize the highest points both of nature and study; the casual scintillation of reflected light is more attractive to him, because more dazzling to the eyes of the world, than that which is evolved from primal and indestructible sources.

The eulogy of his biographer has, therefore, a literal justice when he says that Chesterfield was one of the most shining characters of the age. Thus we might be content that it should pass in a mere gallery of traditionary portraits. But the theory upon which it was based, and the system according to which it was formed, have been elaborately unfolded by Chesterfield himself with epistolary art; and, although he never designed publicly to advocate them, yet the fact that his letters have been not only for many years a manual of deportment, his name a synonym for attractive elegance, and his writings, within a short time, revised and edited by an English historian,* is sufficient reason for applying to him, and the school he proverbially represents, the test of that impartial scrutiny, challenged by whatever practically acts upon society, and exercises more or less prescriptive influence. Character may be divided into two great classes — the one based upon details, and the other upon general principle; and all history, as well as private experience, shows that elevated harmony and permanent influence belong only to the latter. And this is true of the various forms as well as the essential nature of character. The philosopher differs from the *petit-maître*, and the poet from the *dilettante*, by virtue of the same law; the view of the one being comprehensive, and the other minute. In art, also, we recognize true efficiency only where general effects are aptly seized and justly embodied; the artist of mere detail ranks only as a mechanician in form and color. But the most striking truth involved in these distinctions is, that the greater includes the less; the man of great general principles in literature, art, or life, is, in point of fact, master of all essential details; he combines them at a glance, or, rather, they insensibly arrange

* Lord Mahon.

themselves at his will; he can afford to let them take care of themselves. The great sculptors and painters busied themselves only about the design and finish of their works, for intermediate details were wrought by their pupils; and if the overseer, whether of domestic or public affairs, establish order and integrity as the principles of his establishment, he need not give his time or thoughts to the minutiæ of finance.

If we apply this principle to social life, the sphere which Chesterfield regarded as the most important, a similar result is obvious. No one, even in that artificial world called society, ever achieved a satisfactory triumph by exclusive mastery of details. All that is involved in the term manners is demonstrative, symbolic — the sign or exponent of what lies behind, and is taken for granted; and only when this outward manifestation springs from an inward source — only when it is a natural product, and not a graft — does it sustain any real significance. Hence the absurdity of the experiment of Chesterfield to inculcate a graceful address by maxims, and secure a winsome behavior by formal and minute directions; as if to learn how to enter a room, bow well, speak agreeably to a lady, dispose of unoccupied hands, and go inoffensively through the other external details of social intercourse, were to insure the realization of a gentleman. That character — as it was understood in chivalry, by the old English dramatists, and according to the intelligent sentiment of mankind everywhere — is as much the product of nature as any other species of human development; art modifies only its technical details; its spirit comes from blood more than breeding; and its formula, attached by prescription to the body without analogous inspiration of the soul, is as awkward and inefficient as would be proficiency in military tactics to a coward, or vast philological acquisitions to an idiot. Yet Chesterfield, with the obstinacy that belongs to the artificial race of men, persisted in his faith in detail, would not recognize the law from which all genuine social power is elaborated, and apparently lived and died in the belief that the art of pleasing was the great interest of life, and an absolute means of success and personal happiness. All his views, habits, and career, were impregnated with this artificial creed; phrenologically speaking, he was an incarnation of approbativeness; his zest of life came through this his predominant organ; and, judging from consciousness, he believed it to be the only one in others which could be universally appealed to. Unblinded by self-love, he had but to reflect upon his own experience to realize the fallacy of his doctrine. Everywhere, and always, he consulted explicitly the oracle of public opinion, and conformed to it with a fanaticism unworthy his intelligence. He confesses to the very son whom he strove with such zeal to make the "glass of fashion," that in college he was an absolute pedant, and thought great classical knowledge the test of all excellence; that, emancipated from the atmosphere of learning, and thrown among young men of fashion, he led a life of slavery by conforming to habits which were alien not only to his constitution and tastes, but even to his desires; and that, in mature years, the requisitions of the *beau monde* held him in equal vassalage; while his old age, we are told, "was cheerless and desolate."

There are men who regard the artificial as a necessary evil in social life, while they repudiate it altogether elsewhere; but, in the case of Chesterfield, it was deliberately advocated as a general principle; it influenced not only his theory of manners, but his literary taste, political opinions, and entire philosophy. Thus he laid aside the Anglo-Saxon direct and robust temper, and gave in so completely to French manners and superficiality, that, in Paris, he was considered one of themselves, and prides himself upon the distinction. In literature, the only branch which he thoroughly appreciated was oratory, and that chiefly for the rhetorical artifice to which it gives scope. Not as a noble inspiration founded on loyalty to instinctive sentiment, or urged for the cause of humanity, but as an elegant accomplishment whereby to exercise influence and gain applause, did Chesterfield cultivate oratory. It seems perfectly natural that he should excel in its studied graces, and equally so that such a cold virtuoso as Horace Walpole should have preferred him to Pitt. It is, too, not less characteristic of such a man that he should choose diplomacy as a profession. Believing, as he did, only in elegance and cunning, in politic self-control, veiled with agreeableness, the "smooth barbarity of courts" was admirably fitted at once to employ his ingenuity and gratify his refined selfishness. Thus devoid of earnestness on the one hand, and wedded to artificial graces on the other, we cannot wonder that, in his view, Dante, the most intensely picturesque of poets, could not think clearly; and that Petrarch, the beautiful expositor of sentiment, should appear only a love-sick rhymer; nor can we reasonably feel surprise that he quoted Rochefoucault and Cardinal de Retz with emphatic respect, while he could be only facetious in his allusions to Milton and Tasso. Macaulay, in alluding to Chesterfield's estimate of Marlborough and Cowper (the lawyer), says: "He constantly and systematically attributed the success of the most eminent persons of his age to their superiority, not in solid abilities and acquirements, but in superficial graces of diction and manner." Among the books he most cordially recommends his son, are a treatise on the Art of Pleasing, and the "Spectacle du Nature"—the very titles of which reveal his dominant ideas; for the end of being, in his opinion, was to please, at whatever sacrifice of honesty, comfort, or truth; and nature to him was but a spectacle, as life itself was a melodrama. He distrusted the motives of Fenelon, and thought Bolingbroke admirable. Even in more highly prized classical attainments, which we should imagine were endeared by personal taste, the same reference to external motive appears. He advises the study of Greek chiefly because it is a less common acquisition than Latin; and the translation of striking passages of eloquence, as a means of forming style, and storing the mind with desirable quotations. Indeed, in his view, the process of culture, instead of an end, was a means, not to perfect or enrich the individual character, but to obtain the requisites of social advancement. It is true he includes truth as essential to a gentleman; but this was the instinctive sentiment of his nation, whose manly energy and commercial probity alike repudiate falsehood. In accordance with his faith in the details of outward conduct, and obtuseness to the influence of the great natural laws of character in their social agency, Chesterfield advocated power over others as the lever by which to move away the impediments to personal success; not that legitimate power decreed by original superiority, and as certain in the end to regulate society as gravitation the planets; but a studious, politic, and artificial empire, won by dissimulation and attractiveness. In urging this favorite theory upon his son, he seems to have been unconscious of the painful discipline involved in the process, the long and weary masquerade, and the incessant danger of losing, in a moment, the influence gained by months of sycophancy; neither does he take into view the wholly unsatisfactory and untrustworthy nature of the relations thus established; and he fails to see the inevitable result of the short-sighted policy of detail, in the temporary sway thus acquired; the permanent is sacrificed to the immediate, and, by addressing the most insatiable and capricious of human propensities, his system entails not an hour, but a life, of social fawning. He recommends the study of character in order to discover the ruling passion, and then a skilful use of its key-note in order to play upon the whole for private benefit; forgetting that, as in the case of the indignant prince, a suspicion of such base friendship will lead to scorn and rejection: "Do you think I am easier to be played upon than a pipe?"

To this watchful observation he would have united a power to conceal our own emotions in order to give no advantage to our companion, and a facility in appealing to self-love as the best means of throwing him off his guard. The temper, the opinions, the tastes, and even the most gentle and noble sentiments, are to be kept in uniform abeyance; self-possession and adroit flattery are the two great requisites, in his view, for success in life; distrust of others, the guarantee of personal safety; and the art of pleasing, the science of the world. History, philosophy, and the prevailing instincts of enlightened humanity, teach another lesson. These maxims, so often quoted as sagacious, are, in fact, extremely shallow; instead of seeing more deeply into human nature, Chesterfield only saw its superficial action. If there were no sphere for character but promiscuously filled, elegant drawing-rooms, no more stable law operating on society than fashion, and no method of acting on human affairs but that of diplomacy, such advice would have a higher degree of significance. It applies to but few of the actual exigencies of life, and has reference only to partial interests. All men should be social adventurers, and all women aim exclusively at social distinction, to give any general utility to precepts like these. They are essentially temporary and occasional even when true, and utterly false when elevated into principles of action. Hence we deny Dr. Johnson's assertion that, setting the immorality of Chesterfield's letters aside, they form the best manual for gentlemen. The character repudiates the term; its elements are no more to be "set in a note-book" than the spirit of honor or the inspiration of art. The views of Chesterfield, practically carried out, would make a pedantic courtier or a courteous pedant; they trench too much upon the absolute qualities of manhood to leave substance enough in character upon which to rear enduring graces; they omit frankness and moral courage,—two of the most attractive and commanding of human attributes,—and substitute an elegant chicanery, incompatible with self-respect, upon which the highest grace of manner rests; their logic is that of intrigue, not of reason; their charms are those of the dancing-master, not of the knight. Their relation to a true philosophy of life is no more intimate than the *concetti* of the Italians to the highest poetry, or the scenery of a theatre to that of nature; for to cultivate grace of manners is not to supersede, but only to give expression to nature in a certain way; it is not imitation from without, but development from within.

"For God's sake," writes Chesterfield, "sacrifice to the graces; keep out of all scrapes and quarrels; know all ceremonies; maintain a seeming frankness, but a real reserve; have address enough to refuse without offending; some people are to be reasoned, some flattered, some intimidated, and some teased into a thing." By his own statement, this course secured him only a life of refined servitude and a desolate old age, for the official dignity he enjoyed was pettishly abandoned from disappointment as to its incidental benefits. It is not, however, in a moral, but in a philosophical view, as a question of enlightened self-interest, that we demur to the authenticity of his doctrine. Its real defect is narrowness, the exaggeration of certain principles of action, an inharmonious view of the relation between character and behavior, an undue importance attached to secondary interests — in a word, an artificial system in absolute contradiction to prevalent natural laws; and it is chiefly worthy of refutation, because, instead of being advanced as a judicious formula in specific instances, or details of conduct to be acquired once and habitually exercised afterwards, it is presented as a great leading principle, and a regular system altogether expedient and universally applicable; which can be true of no theory either in literature, art, or life, which is based on mere dexterity and address; for Jesuitism can no more permanently advance the interests of society than it can those of religion, science, or any real branch of human welfare.

Chesterfield's editor dwells upon his classical learning, and his benevolent policy while Lord Lieutenant in Ireland, where his rule is declared to have been second only, in its benign influence, to that of Lord Ormond; but neither of these graces seems to have originated in a disinterested impulse. His acquisitions were chiefly valued as a means of display, and sources of an efficient culture; and he advocated schools and villages to civilize the Highlands after the rebellion, instead of more cruel measures, because, on the whole, clemency was the most politic course to pursue. It was this barrenness of soul, this absence of manly enthusiasm, and fanatical reliance on the technical facilities of society, that deprive both the career and the precepts of Chesterfield of all claim to cordial recognition. A friend may have spoken of him with literal truth when he declared that he possessed "a head to contrive, a tongue to persuade, and a hand to execute" in masterly style what he attempted; but the beauty and desirableness of these endowments are much lessened when we perceive that the exquisite machinery was set in motion by motives so entirely selfish, and its action regulated by views destitute of intellectual scope and generous sympathies; when we hear the man thus gifted declare that "a never-failing desire to please" is the great incentive of his mind, and that the finest mental and moral qualities cannot win his love to one awkward or deformed.

Chesterfield, like all votaries of detail, repeats himself continually; he announces, with oracular emphasis, in almost every letter, proverbs of worldly wisdom and economical shrewdness, with an entire confidence in their sufficiency worthy of old Polonius, of which character he is but a refined prototype. The essence of these precepts is only a timid foresight utterly alien to a noble spirit. What, for instance, can be more servile than the maxims, never to give the tone to conversation, but adopt it from the company, and that no business can be transacted without dissimulation? Conformity and adaptation were his avowed means of success, the alpha and omega of his creed; both useful and sometimes necessary alternatives in social intercourse, but always inferior and secondary, never primal and enduring. When allowed to supersede the loftier and more genuine instincts, they not only fail of their end, but are absolutely incompatible with the character of a gentleman. Not by such a course did Sidney, Raleigh, Mackintosh, Robert Burns, or any one of nature's nobility, impress and win their fellow-creatures, but rather by ingenuous self-assertion, mellowed and harmonized by kindly and sympathetic feelings, that gave a grace "beyond the reach of art" to their conversation and manners.

But Chesterfield's disloyalty to nature and devotion to artifice are more signally betrayed in his views of the two great sources of actual refinement in social life, music and women. The first may be considered as the natural language of the soul, the cultivation of which is one of the most available means of acquiring that harmonious development and sense of the beautiful, which round her angles and elicit the gentle influences of human intercourse. Chesterfield peremptorily forbade his son to cultivate music, at the same time that he strove to preach boorishness out of him by rules of breeding; a process which might have been vastly facilitated by the study of any one of the fine arts for which he had the least tendency. But even in gallantry, — not to profane love by thus designating his idea of the relation of the sexes,— even in that which owes its zest and utility to gratified sympathies, he leans on the broken reed of prescription and expediency, counselling his son to choose a fair companion, not as a being to inspire, through natural affinity, his sentiments and conduct, but as an approved model and guide in fashionable life. How little did this shrewd man of the world know of the benefit, even to the manners of an intelligent youth, derivable from even one reality in his social relations! Indeed, from the affectionate disposition that appears to have belonged to Philip Stanhope, his good sense and general acquirements, the only chance for him to have realized his father's hopes, in point of expression, bearing, costume, address, and all the externals of character, would seem to have been a genuine attachment. He was so organized as to be unable to attach that importance to the graces his father adored, which would lead him to court their favors; for this he needed the stimulus of a powerful motive, and such a one would have been naturally supplied by real devotion to a fine woman; or the effect of such a feeling would have gradually softened and elevated his tone and air so that he would have become as insinuating as his elegant parent desired, and that, too, from instinct, and not by rule. The great evil of teaching the details of behavior is that, even when acquired in all their perfection, there is a want of unity in the result; they are exercised without the crowning grace of all manner, from the rhetorician's gesture to the courtier's salutations — unconsciousness. There is no happy fusion between manhood and manner; the one hangs objectively on the other, like two parts of an ill-adjusted machine.

Nature is apt to vindicate herself upon the ultra-conventional by entailing disappointment upon their dearest hopes. Her laws are as inexorable as they are benign. Chesterfield seems to have been more in earnest in the education of his son than in any other object in life; but true parental affection had little to do with this assiduity; he constantly reminds him that he has no weak attachment to his person, that his pecuniary supplies depend upon the respect paid to the instruction he receives, and that the estimation he will hereafter enjoy from his father, will depend upon the degree in which he realizes the expectations formed of him. In all this we see only a modification of self-love, but no true parental feeling. The object of all this solicitude well repaid the care lavished upon his mental cultivation, but he never became either elegant or fascinating; his good qualities were solid, not shining, and his advancement was owing to his father's personal influence. The latter's will is characteristic; he provides that, if his son ever engages in the vulgar amusement of horse-racing, he shall forfeit five thousand pounds to the Dean of Westminster, who is satirized in the compliment; for Chesterfield thought himself overcharged by him in a pecuniary transaction, and wished to leave this evidence of his reliance upon his grasping disposition.

During his life, a high position and good sense enabled Chesterfield to reap advantages from polished and sagacious urbanity, which naturally led to an exaggerated estimate of its value under less auspicious circumstances. Having studied with marked success at Cambridge, through the influence of a relative, he was appointed gentleman of the bedchamber to the Prince of Wales, and afterwards elected to Parliament by the borough of St. Germain in Cornwall. His first speech established a reputation for oratory, and is described as quite as remarkable for able reasoning as for elegant diction. He seems to have retained the good opinion thus acquired while in the House of Lords; to his father's seat in which assembly he duly succeeded. His judicious management while ambassador to Holland, in 1728, saved Hanover from a war, and, for this service, he was made knight of the Garter. Subsequently he filled, with apparent success, the offices of Lord Steward of the Household in George the Second's reign, Lord Lieutenant of Ireland, and Secretary of State. Upon resigning the seals, he retired from public life, and deafness soon confined him to books and a small circle of acquaintance. The *prestige* of official rank, and the allurements of an elegant address, having passed away with his life, we must turn from the orator and statesman to the author for authentic evidence of his character. His fate in this regard is somewhat curious. The elaborate speeches and sketches of character which he gave to the public have, in a great measure, lost their significance. The style of writing has so much advanced since his time that we recognize in him no such claims to literary excellence as his cotemporaries awarded. His name is now almost exclusively associated with his letters to his natural son — letters written in the most entire parental confidence, and with the vain hope of converting, by specific instructions, an awkward and apparently honest-hearted and sensible fellow into an accomplished, winsome, and shrewd man of the world. It has been said, in excuse for the absolute stress laid upon external qualities in these letters, that the youth to whom they were addressed was lamentably deficient in these respects; but there can be no doubt that they form the most genuine expression of Chesterfield's mind — the more so that they were never intended for the public eye. By a not uncommon fortune in literary ventures, these estrays and waifs of private correspondence alone keep alive the name and perpetuate the views of Chesterfield.

It would be unjust not to ascribe the worldly spirit and absence of natural enthusiasm in these epistles, in a degree, to the period that gave them birth. It was an age when intrigue prospered, and wit, rather than sentiment, was in vogue. There was a league between letters and politics, based wholly on party interests. It was the age of Swift, Pope, and Bolingbroke. The queen governed George the Second, Lady Yarmouth the queen, and Chesterfield, for a time, Lady Yarmouth. Agreeable conversation, an insinuating manner, and subtlety of observation, were then very efficient weapons. High finish, point, verbal felicity, the costume rather than the soul of literature, won the day. Neither the frankness and undisguised overflow of thought and feeling that mark the Shakspearian era, nor the earnest utterance and return to truth ushered in by the first French Revolution, existed; but, on the contrary, that neutral ground between the two periods, whereon there was the requisite space, leisure, and absence of lofty purpose, to give full scope to the courtier, the wit, and the intriguante. It was, comparatively speaking, a timid, time-serving, partisan, and showy epoch. The spirit of the times is caught up and transmitted in Horace Walpole's letters, and quite as significantly embodied, in a less versatile manner, in those of Chesterfield.

Instead, therefore, of regarding courteous manners as a mere necessary appendage to a man,— a convenient and appropriate facility, like current coin, or the laws of the land,— Chesterfield attempts to elevate them into the highest and most comprehensive practical significance. He would have manner overlay individuality, and goes so far as to declare that a soldier is a brute, a scholar a pedant, and a philosopher a cynic, without good breeding. If, for the latter term, feeling were substituted, those and similar broad inferences would be far more correct. Some of the greatest brutes, cynics, and pedants, we encounter in the world, are perfectly well-bred; they refuse an act of humanity with a graceful bow, smile good-naturedly while exposing the ignorance of a sensitive companion, and engross, with an affable and even respectful air, all the privileges at hand. It is common to see a Frenchman salute, in the most polite manner, those who enter a public conveyance, pass round his snuff-box, and entertain the company with agreeable remarks; but, if it suits his pleasure, he will, at the same time, gormandize a reeking *paté*, put on his nightcap and snore, or refuse to yield his seat to an invalid, with a complacent egotism that would astonish an American backwoodsman, who, without a particle of monsieur's external courtesy, obeys the laws of chivalric kindness from instinct and habit. "The understanding is the voiture of life," says Chesterfield, and, apparently, he infers that it is to be put at random on any track, and to move at any speed, which the will of the elegant majority dictate; an axiom wholly at variance with that independence which some one has nobly declared to be the positive sign of a gentleman. Absence of mind in company, so often the indication of superiority, he considered only as evidence of weakness; and so enervated was his taste that he preferred the cold proprieties of the artificial French stage to the violated unities of robust English tragedy. It is characteristic of such a man to believe in chance more than truth; and his unconquerable love of play accords with the blind philosophy that controlled his life. His conceit of knowledge of human nature was based upon the most inadequate and one-sided observation; he associated chiefly with women of fashion and men of state, and, therefore, saw the calculating and vain, not the impulsive and unconscious play of character. For the game of conventional life, therefore, are the best of his maxims adapted. In that latent sphere of truth and nature, familiar to more ingenuous and genial spirits, where candor, intelligent sympathy, and spontaneous taste luxuriate, they are as irrelevant as they are unnatural.

THE PIONEER.

DANIEL BOONE.

THERE hung, for many months, on the walls of the Art-Union gallery in New York, a picture so thoroughly national in its subject and true to nature in its execution, that it was refreshing to contemplate it, after being wearied with far more ambitious yet less successful attempts. It represented a flat ledge of rock, the summit of a high cliff that projected over a rich, umbrageous country, upon which a band of hunters, leaning on their rifles, were gazing with looks of delighted surprise. The foremost, a compact and agile, though not very commanding figure, is pointing out the landscape to his comrades, with an air of exultant yet calm satisfaction; the wind lifts his thick hair from a brow full of energy and perception; his loose hunting-shirt, his easy attitude, the fresh brown tint of his cheek, and an ingenuous, cheerful, determined, yet benign expression of countenance, proclaim the hunter and pioneer, the Columbus of the woods, the forest philosopher and brave champion. The picture represents Daniel Boone discovering to his companions the fertile levels of Kentucky. This remarkable man, although he does not appear to have originated any great plans, or borne the responsibility of an appointed leader in the warlike expeditions in which he was engaged, possessed one of those rarely balanced natures, and that unpretending efficiency of character, which, though seldom invested with historical prominence, abound in personal interest. Without political knowledge, he sustained an infant settlement;

destitute of a military education, he proved one of the most formidable antagonists the Indians ever encountered; with no pretensions to a knowledge of civil engineering, he laid out the first road through the wilderness of Kentucky; unfamiliar with books, he reflected deeply, and attained to philosophical convictions that yielded him equanimity of mind; devoid of poetical expression, he had an extraordinary feeling for natural beauty, and described his sensations and emotions amid the wild seclusion of the forest as prolific of delight; with manners entirely simple and unobtrusive, there was not the least rudeness in his demeanor; and, relentless in fight, his disposition was thoroughly humane; his rifle and his cabin, with the freedom of the woods, satisfied his wants; the sense of insecurity, in which no small portion of his life was passed, only rendered him circumspect; and his trials induced a serene patience and fortitude; while his love of adventure was a ceaseless inspiration. Such a man forms an admirable progenitor in that nursery of character, the West; and a fine contrast to the development elsewhere induced by the spirit of trade and political ambition. Like the rudely sculptured calumets picked up on the plantations of Kentucky, — memorials of a primitive race, whose mounds and copper utensils yet attest a people antecedent to the Indians that fled before the advancing settlements of Boone, — his character indicates, for the descendants of the hunters and pioneers, a brave, independent, and noble ancestry. Thus, as related to the diverse forms of a national character in the various sections of the country, as well as on account of its intrinsic attractiveness, the western pioneer is an object of peculiar interest; and the career of Boone is alike distinguished for its association with romantic adventure and historical fact.

A consecutive narrative, however, would yield but an ineffective picture of his life as it exists in the light of sympathetic reflection. The pioneer, like the mariner, alternates between long uneventful periods and moments fraught with excitement; the forest, like the ocean, is monotonous as well as grand; and its tranquil beauty, for weeks together, may not be sublimated by terror; yet in both spheres there is an under-current of suggestive life, and when the spirit of conflict and vigilance sleeps, that of contemplation is often alive. Perhaps it is this very succession of "moving accidents" and lonely quiet, of solemn repose and intense activity, that constitutes the fascination which the sea and the wilderness possess for imaginative minds. They appeal at once to poetical and heroic instincts; and these are more frequently combined in the same individual than we usually suppose. Before attempting to realize the characteristics of Boone in their unity, we must note the salient points in his experience; and this is best done by reviving a few scenes which typify the whole drama.

It is midnight in the forest; and, through the interstices of its thickly-woven branches, pale moonbeams glimmer on the emerald sward. The only sounds that break upon the brooding silence are an occasional gust of wind amid the branches of the loftier trees, the hooting of an owl, and sometimes the wild cry of a beast disappointed of his prey, or scared by the dusky figure of a savage on guard at a watch-fire. Beside its glowing embers, and leaning against the huge trunk of a gigantic hemlock, sit two girls, whose complexion and habiliments indicate their Anglo-Saxon origin; their hands are clasped together, and one appears to sleep as her head rests upon her companion's shoulder. They are very pale, and an expression of anxiety is evident in the very firmness of their resigned looks. A slight rustle in the thick undergrowth, near their camp, causes the Indian sentinel to rise quickly to his feet and peer in the direction of the sound; a moment after he leaps up, with a piercing shout, and falls bleeding upon the ground, while the crack of a rifle echoes through the wood. In an instant twenty Indians spring from around the fire, raise the war-whoop, and brandish their tomahawks; but three or four instantly drop before the deadly aim of the invaders, several run howling with pain into the depths of the forest, and the remainder set off on an opposite trail. Then calmly, but with an earnest joy, revealed by the dying flames upon his features, a robust, compactly-knit figure moves with a few hasty strides towards the females, gazes eagerly into their faces, lifts one in his arms and presses her momentarily to his breast, gives a hasty order, and his seven companions with the three in their midst rapidly retrace their way over the tangled brushwood and amid the pillared trunks, until they come out, at dawn, upon a clearing, studded with enormous roots, among which waves the tasselled maize, beside a spacious log-dwelling surrounded by a palisade. An eager, tearful group rush out to meet them; and the weary and hungry band are soon discussing their midnight adventure over a substantial breakfast of game. Thus Boone rescued his daughter and her friend, when they were taken captive by the Indians, within sight of his primitive dwelling; — an incident which illustrates, more than pages of description, how closely pioneer presses upon savage life, and with what peril civilization encroaches upon the domain of nature.

It is the dawn of a spring day in the wilderness. As steals the gray pearly light over the densely-waving tree-tops, an eagle majestically rises from a withered bough, and floats through the silent air, becoming a mere speck on the sky ere he disappears over the distant mountains; dew-drops are condensed on the green threads of the pine and the swollen buds of the hickory; pale bulbs and spears of herbage shoot from the black loam, amid the decayed leaves; in the inmost recesses of the wood the rabbit's tread is audible, and the chirp of the squirrel.

As the sunshine expands, a thousand notes of birds at work on their nests invade the solitude; the bear fearlessly laps the running stream, and the elk turns his graceful head from the pendent branch he is nibbling, at an unusual sound from the adjacent cane-brake. It is a lonely man rising from his night slumber; with his blanket on his arm and his rifle grasped in one hand, he approaches the brook and bathes his head and neck; then, glancing around, turns aside the interwoven thickets near by, and climbs a stony mound shadowed by a fine clump of oaks, where stands an humble but substantial cabin; he lights a fire upon the flat stone before the entrance, kneads a cake of maize, while his venison steak is broiling, and carefully examines the priming of his rifle. The meal despatched with a hearty relish, he closes the door of his lodge, and saunters through the wilderness; his eye roves from the wild flower at his feet, to the cliff that looms afar off; he pauses in admiration before some venerable sylvan monarch; watches the bounding stag his intrusion has disturbed, or cuts a little spray from the sassafras with the knife in his girdle.

As the sun rises higher, he penetrates deeper into the vast and beautiful forest; each form of vegetable life, from the enormous fungi to the delicate vine-wreath, the varied structure of the trees, the cries and motions of the wild animals and birds, excite in his mind a delightful sense of infinite power and beauty; he feels as he walks, in every nerve and vein, the "glorious privilege of being independent;" reveries, that bathe his soul in a tranquil yet lofty pleasure, succeed each other; and the sight of some lovely vista induces him to lie down upon a heap of dead leaves and lose himself in contemplation. Weariness and hunger, or the deepening gloom of approaching night, at length warn him to retrace his steps; on the way he shoots a wild turkey for his supper, sits over the watch-fire, beneath the solemn firmament of stars, and recalls the absent and loved through the first watches of the night. Months have elapsed since he has thus lived alone in the wilderness, his brother having left him to seek ammunition and provision at distant settlements. Despondency, for a while, rendered his loneliness oppressive, but such is his love of nature and freedom, his zest for life in the woods, and a natural self-reliance, that gradually he attains a degree of happiness which De Foe's hero might have envied. Nature is a benign mother, and whispers consoling secrets to attentive ears, and mysteriously cheers the heart of her pure votaries who truthfully cast themselves on her bosom.

Not thus serenely, however, glides away the forest life of our pioneer. He is jealously watched by the Indians, upon whose hunting-grounds he is encroaching; they steal upon his retreat and make him captive, and in this situation a new phase of his character exhibits itself. The soul that has been in long and intimate communion with natural grandeur and beauty, and learned the scope and quality of its own resources, gains self-possession and foresight. The prophets of old did not resort to the desert in vain; and the bravery and candor of hunters and seamen is partly the result of the isolation and hardihood of their lives. Boone excelled as a sportsman; he won the respect of his savage captors by his skill and fortitude; and more than once, without violence, emancipated himself, revealed their bloody schemes to his countrymen, and met them on the battle-field, with a coolness and celerity that awoke their intense astonishment. Again and again he saw his companions fall before their tomahawks and rifles; his daughter, as we have seen, was stolen from his very door, though fortunately rescued; his son fell before his eyes in a conflict with the Indians who opposed their emigration to Kentucky; his brother and his dearest friends were victims either to their strategy or violence; and his own immunity is to be accounted for by the influence he had acquired over his foes, which induced them often to spare his life — an influence derived from the extraordinary tact, patience, and facility of action, which his experience and character united to foster.

Two other scenes of his career are requisite to the picture. On the banks of the Missouri river, less than forty years ago, there stood a few small rude cabins in the shape of a hollow square. In one of these the now venerable figure of the gallant hunter is listlessly stretched upon a couch; a slice of buck, twisted on the ramrod of his rifle, is roasting by the fire, within reach of his hand; he is still alone, but the surrounding cabins are occupied by his thriving descendants. The vital energies of the pioneer are gradually ebbing away, though his thick white locks, well-knit frame, and the light of his keen eye, evidence the genuineness and prolonged tenure of his life. Overmatched by the conditions of the land law in Kentucky, and annoyed by the march of civilization in the regions he had known in their primitive beauty, he had wandered here, far from the state he founded and the haunts of his manhood, to die, with the same adventurous and independent spirit in which he had lived. He occupied some of the irksome hours of confinement incident to age in polishing his own cherry-wood coffin; and it is said he was found dead in the woods at last, a few rods from his dwelling.

On an autumn day, but a few years since, a hearse might have been seen winding up the main street of Frankfort, Kentucky, drawn by white horses, and garlanded with evergreens. The pall-bearers comprised some of the most distinguished men of the state. It was the second funeral of Daniel Boone. By an act of the legislature, his remains were removed from the banks of the Missouri to the public cemetery of the capital of Kentucky, and there deposited with every ceremonial of respect and love.

This oblation was in the highest degree just and appropriate, for the name of Boone is identified with the state he originally explored, and his character associates itself readily with that of her people and scenery. No part of the country is more individual in these respects than Kentucky. As the word imports, it was once the hunting and battle ground of savage tribes for centuries; and not until the middle of the eighteenth century was it well known to Anglo-Saxon explorers. The elk and buffalo held undisputed possession with the Indian; its dark forests served as a contested boundary between the Cherokees, Creeks, and Catawbas, of the South, and the Shawnees, Delawares, and Wyandots, of the North; and to these inimical tribes it was indeed "a dark and bloody ground."

Unauthenticated expeditions thither we hear of before that of Boone, but with his first visit the history of the region becomes clear and progressive, remarkable for its rapid and steady progress and singular fortunes. The same year that independence was declared, Virginia made a county of the embryo state, and forts scattered at intervals over the face of the country alone yielded refuge to the colonists from their barbarian invaders. In 1778, Duquesne, with his Canadian and Indian army, met with a vigorous repulse at Boonesborough; in 1778, occurred Roger Clark's brilliant expedition against the English forts of Vincennes and Kaskaskias; and the next year, a single blockhouse — the forlorn hope of advancing civilization — was erected by Robert Patterson where Lexington now stands; soon after took place the unfortunate expedition of Col. Bowman against the Indians of Chillicothe; and the Virginian legislature passed the celebrated land law. This enactment neglected to provide for a general survey at the expense of the government; each holder of a warrant located therefore at pleasure, and made his own survey; yet a special entry was required by the law, in order clearly to designate boundaries; the vagueness of many entries rendered the titles null; those of Boone, and men similarly unacquainted with legal writing, were, of course, destitute of any accuracy of description; and hence, interminable perplexity, disputes, and forfeitures. The immediate consequence of the law, however, was to induce a flood of emigration, and the fever of land speculation rose and spread to an unexampled height; to obtain patents for rich lands became the ruling passion; and simultaneous Indian hostilities prevailed — so that Kentucky was transformed, all at once, from an agricultural and hunting region, thinly peopled, to an arena where rapacity and war swayed a vast multitude. The conflicts, law-suits, border adventures, and personal feuds, growing out of this condition of affairs, would yield memorable themes, without number, for the annalist. To this epoch succeeded "a labyrinth of conventions."

The position of Kentucky was anomalous: the appendage of a state unable to protect her frontier from savage invasion; her future prosperity in a great measure dependent upon the glorious river that bounded her domain, and the United States government already proposing to yield the right of its navigation to a foreign power; separated by the Alleghany Mountains from the populous and cultivated East, and the tenure by which estates were held within its limits quite unsettled, it is scarcely to be wondered at that reckless political adventurers began to look upon Kentucky as a promising sphere for their intrigues. Without adverting to any particular instances, or renewing the inquiry into the motives of prominent actors in those scenes, it is interesting to perceive how entirely the intelligence and honor of the people triumphed over selfish ambition and cunning artifice. Foreign governments and domestic traitors failed in their schemes to alienate the isolated state from the growing confederacy. Repulsed as she was again and again in her attempts to secure constitutional freedom, she might have said to the parent government, with the repudiated "lady wedded to the Moor" —

> "Unkindness may do much,
> And your unkindness may achieve my life,
> But never taint my love."

Kentucky was admitted into the Union on the fourth of February, 1791.

From this outline of her history we can readily perceive how rich and varied was the material whence has sprung the Western character. Its highest phase is doubtless to be found in Kentucky; and there, perhaps, best illustrates American in distinction from European civilization. In the North this is essentially modified by the cosmopolite influence of the seaboard, and in the South, by a climate which assimilates the people with those of the same latitudes elsewhere; but in the West, and especially in Kentucky, we find the foundation of social existence laid by the hunters, whose love of the woods, equality of condition, habits of sport and agriculture, and distance from conventionalities, combined to nourish independence, strength of mind, candor, and a fresh and genial spirit. The ease and freedom of social intercourse, the abeyance of the passion for gain, and the scope given to the play of character, accordingly developed a noble race.

We can scarcely imagine a more appropriate figure in the foreground of the picture than Daniel Boone, who embodies the honesty, intelligence, and chivalric spirit of the state. With a population descended from the extreme sections of the land, from emigrants of New England as well as Virginia and North Carolina, and whose immediate progenitors were chiefly agricultural gentlemen, a generous and spirited character might have been prophesied of the natives of Kentucky; and it is in the highest degree natural for a people thus descended, and with such habits, to cling with entire loyalty to their parent government, and to yield, as they did, ardent though injudicious sympathy to France in the hour of her revolutionary crisis. Impulsive and honorable, her legitimate children belong to the aristocracy of nature; without the general intellectual refinement of the Atlantic states, they possess a far higher physical development and richer social instincts; familiar with the excessive development of the religious and political sentiments, in all varieties and degrees, their views are more broad, though less discriminate, than those entertained in older communities. The Catholic from Maryland, the Puritan from Connecticut, and the Churchman of Carolina, amicably flourished together; and the conservative and fanatic are alike undisturbed; the convent and the camp-meeting being, often within sight of each other, equally respected.

Nature, too, has been as liberal as the social elements in endowing Kentucky with interesting associations. That mysterious fifteen miles of subterranean wonders known as the Mammoth Cave, — its wonderful architecture, fossil remains, nitrous atmosphere, echoes, fish with only the rudiment of an optic nerve, its chasms and cataracts, — is one of the most remarkable objects in the world. The boundaries of the state are unequalled in beauty; on the east the Laurel Ridge or Cumberland Mountain, and on the west the Father of Waters. In native trees she is peculiarly rich; the glorious magnolia, the prolific sugar-tree, the laurel and the buckeye, the hickory and honey locust, the mulberry, ash, and flowing catalpa, attest in every village and roadside the sylvan aptitudes of the soil; while the thick buffalo grass and finest crown-imperial in the world clothe it with a lovely garniture. The blue limestone formation predominates, and its grotesque cliffs and caverns render much of the geological scenery peculiar and interesting.

The lover of the picturesque and characteristic must often regret that artistic and literary genius has not adequately preserved the original local and social features of our own primitive communities. Facility of intercourse and the assimilating influence of trade are rapidly bringing the traits and tendencies of all parts of the country to a common level; yet in the natives of each section, in whom strong idiosyncrasies have kept intact the original bias of character, we find the most striking and suggestive diversity. According to the glimpses afforded us by tradition, letters, and meagre biographical data, the early settlers of Kentucky united to the simplicity and honesty of the New York colonists a high degree of chivalric feeling; there was an heroic vein induced by familiarity with danger, the necessity of mutual protection, and the healthful excitement of the chase. The absence of any marked distinction of birth or fortune, and the high estimate placed upon society by those who dwell on widely-separated plantations, caused a remarkably cordial, hospitable and warm intercourse to prevail, almost unknown at the North and East. Family honor was cherished with peculiar zeal; and the women, accustomed to equestrian exercises, and brought up in the freedom and isolation of nature,—their sex always respected, and their charms thoroughly appreciated,—acquired a spirited and cheerful development, quite in contrast with the subdued, uniform tone of those educated in the commercial towns. Their mode of life naturally generated self-reliance, and evoked a spirit of independence.

Most articles in use were of domestic manufacture; slavery was more patriarchal in its character than in the other states; the practice of duelling, with its inevitable miseries, had also the effect to give a certain tone to social life rarely witnessed in agricultural districts; and the Kentucky gentleman was thus early initiated into the manly qualities of a Nimrod, and the engaging and reliable ones of a man of honor and gallantry in its best sense. It is to circumstances like these that we attribute the chivalric spirit of the state. She was a somewhat wild member of the confederacy — a kind of spoiled younger child, with the faults and virtues incident to her age and fortunes; nerved by long vigils at the outposts of civilization, — the wild-cat invading her first school-houses, and the Indians her scattered corn-fields, — and receiving little parental recognition from the central government, yet, with a primitive loyalty of heart, she repudiated the intrigues of Genet and Burr, and baptized her counties for such national patriots as Fulton and Gallatin.

Passing through a fiery ordeal of Indian warfare, the fever of land speculation, great political vicissitude, unusual legal perplexities, imperfect legislation, and subsequently entire financial derangement, she has yet maintained a progressive and individual attitude; and seems, in her most legitimate specimens of character, more satisfactorily to represent the national type than any other state. Her culture has not been as refined, nor her social spirit as versatile and elegant, as in older communities, but a raciness, hardihood and genial freshness of nature have, for those very reasons, more completely survived. As a region whence to transplant or graft, if we may apply horticultural terms to humanity, Kentucky is a rich garden. Nor have these distinctions ceased to be. Her greatest statesman, in the nobleness of his character and the extraordinary personal regard he inspired, admirably illustrates the community of which Boone was the characteristic pioneer; and the volunteers of Kentucky, in the Indian wars, under Harrison, and more recently in Mexico, have continued to vindicate their birthright of valor; while one of her most accomplished daughters sent a magnificent bed-quilt, wrought by her own hands, to the World's Fair.

A Pennsylvanian by birth,* Boone early emigrated to North Carolina. He appears to have first visited Kentucky in 1769. The bounty lands awarded to the Virginia troops induced surveying expeditions to the Ohio river; and when Col. Henderson, in 1775, purchased from the Cherokees the country south of the Kentucky river, the knowledge which two years' exploration had given Boone of the region, and his already established reputation for firmness and adventure, caused him to be employed to survey the country, the fertility and picturesque charms of which had now become celebrated. Accordingly, the pioneer, having satisfactorily laid out a road through the wilderness, not without many fierce encounters with the aborigines, chose a spot to erect his log house, which afterwards became the nucleus of a colony, and the germ of a prosperous state, on the site of the present town of Boonesborough.

While transporting his family thither, they were surprised by the Indians, and, after severe loss, so far discouraged in their enterprise as to return to the nearest settlements; and on the first summer of their residence in Kentucky occurred the bold abduction of the two young girls, to which we have previously referred. In 1778, while engaged in making salt, with thirty men, at the lower Blue Licks, Boone was captured, and, while his companions were taken to Detroit on terms of capitulation, he was retained as a prisoner, though kindly treated and allowed to hunt. At Chillicothe he witnessed the extensive preparations of the Indians to join a Canadian expedition against the infant settlement; and, effecting his escape, succeeded in reaching home in time to warn the garrison and prepare for its defence. For nine days he was besieged by an army of five hundred Indians and whites, when the enemy abandoned their project in despair.

* In a paper recently presented to the Pennsylvania Historical Society, Mr. John F. Watson demonstrates that Daniel Boone was a native of Pennsylvania, and that his family were Quakers. Several of its members were "read out of meeting" in consequence of marrying outside the pale. The fact of Daniel's place of birth is now doubly settled, by a veritable chronicler, and by Sparks' American Biography. Mr. Watson makes the county Berks, and Sparks names it Bucks — both of which are in the same state.

In 1782 he was engaged in the memorable and disastrous battle of the Blue Licks, and accompanied Gen. Clark on his expedition to avenge it. In the succeeding year, peace with England being declared, the pioneer saw the liberty and civilization of the country he had known as a wilderness, only inhabited by wild beasts and savages, guaranteed and established. In 1779, having laid out the chief of his little property in land warrants, on his way from Kentucky to Richmond he was robbed of twenty thousand dollars; wiser claimants, versed in the legal conditions, deprived him of his lands; disappointed and impatient, he left the glorious domain he had originally explored and nobly defended, and became a voluntary subject of the King of Spain, by making a new forest home on the banks of the Missouri. An excursion he undertook, in 1816, to Fort Osage, a hundred miles from his lodge, evidences the unimpaired vigor of his declining years.

So indifferent to gain was Boone that he neglected to secure a fine estate rather than incur the trouble of a visit to New Orleans. An autograph letter, still extant, proves that he was not illiterate; and Governor Dunmore, of Virginia, had such entire confidence in his vigilance and integrity, that he employed him to conduct surveyors eight hundred miles through the forest, to the falls of the Ohio, gave him command of three frontier stations, and sent him to negotiate treaties with the Cherokees. It was a fond boast with him that the first white women that ever stood on the banks of the Kentucky river were his wife and daughter, and that his axe cleft the first tree whose timbers laid the foundation of a permanent settlement in the state. He had the genuine ambition of a pioneer, and the native taste for life in the woods embodied in the foresters of Scott and the Leather-stocking of Cooper. He possessed that restless impulse,— the instinct of adventure,— the poetry of action. It has been justly said that "he was seldom taken by surprise, never shrunk from danger, nor cowered beneath exposure and fatigue." So accurate were his woodland observations and memory, that he recognized an ash-tree which he had notched twenty years before, to identify a locality; and proved the accuracy of his designation by stripping off the new bark, and exposing the marks of his axe beneath. His aim was so certain, that he could with ease bark a squirrel, that is, bring down the animal, when on the top of the loftiest tree, by knocking off the bark immediately beneath, killing him by the concussion.

The union of beauty and terror in the life of a pioneer, of so much natural courage and thoughtfulness as Boone, is one of its most significant features. We have followed his musing steps through the wide, umbrageous solitudes he loved, and marked the contentment he experienced in a log hut, and by a camp-fire; but over this attractive picture there ever impended the shadow of peril, in the form of a stealthy and cruel foe, the wolf, disease, and exposure to the elements. Enraged at the invasion of their ancient hunting-grounds, the Indians hovered near; while asleep in the jungle, following the plough, or at his frugal meal, the pioneer was liable to be shot down by an unseen rifle, and surrounded by an ambush; from the tranquil pursuits of agriculture, at any moment, he might be summoned to the battle-field, to rescue a neighbor's property, or defend a solitary outpost. The senses become acute, the mind vigilant, and the tone of feeling chivalric, under such discipline. That life has a peculiar dignity, even in the midst of privation, and however devoid of refined culture, which is entirely self-dependent both for sustainment and protection. It has, too, a singular freshness and animation, the more genial from being naturally inspired. Compare the spasmodic efforts at hilarity, the forced speech, and hackneyed expression, of the fashionable drawing-room, with the candid mirth and gallant spirit born of the woodland and the chase, — the powerful sinews and well-braced nerves of the pioneer with the languid pulse of the metropolitan exquisite, — and it seems as if the fountain of youth still bubbled up in some deep recess of the forest. Philosophy, too, as well as health, is attainable in the woods, as Shakspeare has illustrated in "As You Like It," and Boone by his example and habitual sentiments. He said to his brother, when they had lived for months in the yet unexplored wilds of Kentucky, "You see how little human nature requires. It is in our own hearts, rather than in the things around us, that we are to seek felicity. A man may be happy in any state. It only asks a perfect resignation to the will of Providence." It is remarkable that the two American characters which chiefly interested Byron were Patrick Henry and Daniel Boone, — the one for his gift of oratory, and the other for his philosophical content, — both so directly springing from the resources of nature.

There is an affinity between man and nature, which conventional habits keep in abeyance, but do not extinguish. It is manifested in the prevalent taste for scenery, and the favor so readily bestowed upon its graphic delineation in art or literature; but, in addition to the poetic love of nature, as addressed to the sense of beauty, or that ardent curiosity to explore its laws and phenomena which finds expression in natural science, there is an instinct that leads to a keen relish of nature in her primeval state, and a facility in embracing the life she offers in her wild and solitary haunts; a feeling that seems to have survived the influences of civilization, and develops, when encouraged, by the inevitable law of animal instinct. It is not uncommon to meet with this passion for nature among those whose lives have been devoted to objects apparently alien to its existence. Sportsmen, pedestrians, and citizens of rural propensities, indicate its modified action, while it is more emphatically exhibited by the volunteers who join in the caravans to the Rocky Mountains, the deserts of the East, and the forests of Central and South America, with no ostensible purpose but the gratification arising from intimate contact with nature in her luxuriant or barren solitudes.

To one having but an inkling of this sympathy, with a nervous organization and an observant mind, there is, indeed, no restorative of the frame, or sweet diversion to the mind, like a day in the woods. The effect of roaming a treeless plain, or riding over a cultivated region, is entirely different. There is a certain tranquillity and balm in the forest, that heals and calms the fevered spirit, and quickens the languid pulses of the weary and the disheartened with the breath of hope. Its influence on the animal spirits is remarkable; and the senses, released from the din and monotonous limits of streets and houses, luxuriate in the breadth of vision, and the rich variety of form, hue, and odor, which only scenes like these afford. As we walk in the shadow of lofty trees, the repose and awe of heart that breathes from a sacred temple gradually lulls the tide of care, and exalts despondency into worship. As the eye tracks the flickering light glancing upon herbage, it brightens to recognize the wild flowers that are associated with the innocent enjoyments of childhood; to note the delicate blossom of the wild hyacinth, see the purple asters wave in the breeze, and the scarlet berries of the winter-green glow among the dead leaves, or mark the circling flight of the startled crow, and the sudden leap of the squirrel.

We pause unconsciously to feel the springy velvet of the moss-clump, pluck up the bulb of the broad-leaved sanguinaria, or examine the star-like flower of the liverwort; and then, lifting our gaze to the canopy beneath which we lovingly stroll, greet, as old and endeared acquaintances, the noble trees in their autumn splendor, — the crimson dogwood, yellow hickory, or scarlet maple, whose brilliant hues mingle and glow in the sunshine like the stained windows of an old gothic cathedral; and we feel that it is as true to fact as to poetry that "the groves were God's first temples." Every fern at our feet is as daintily carved as the frieze of a Grecian column; every vista down which we look wears more than Egyptian solemnity; the withered leaves rustle like the sighs of penitents, and the lofty tree-tops send forth a voice like that of prayer. Fresh vines encumber aged trunks, solitary leaves quiver slowly to the earth, a twilight hue chastens the brightness of noon, and all around is the charm of a mysterious quietude and seclusion that induces a dreamy and reverential mood; while health seems wafted from the balsamic pine and the elastic turf, and over all broods the serene blue firmament.

If such refreshment and inspiration are obtainable from a casual and temporary visit to the woods, we may imagine the effect of a lengthened sojourn in the primeval forest upon a nature alive to its beauty, wildness, and solitude; and when we add to these the zest of adventure, the pride of discovery, and that feeling of sublimity which arises from a consciousness of danger always impending, it is easy to realize in the experience of a pioneer at once the most romantic and practical elements of life. In American history, rich as it is in this species of adventure, no individual is so attractive and prominent as Daniel Boone. The singular union in his character of benevolence and hardihood, bold activity and a meditative disposition, the hazardous enterprises and narrow escapes recorded of him, and the resolute tact he displayed in all emergencies, are materials quite adequate to a thrilling narrative; but when we add to the external phases of interest that absolute passion for forest life which distinguished him, and the identity of his name with the early fortunes of the West, he seems to combine the essential features of a genuine historical and thoroughly individual character.

THE MAN OF LETTERS.

ROBERT SOUTHEY.

THE character of Southey, as revealed in his biography, is essentially that of a man of letters. Perhaps the annals of English literature furnish no more complete example of the kind, in the most absolute sense of the term. His taste for books was of the most general description; he sought every species of knowledge, and appears to have been equally contented to write history, reviews, poems, and letters. Indeed, for more than twenty years his life at Keswick was systematically divided between these four departments of writing.

No man having any pretension to genius ever succeeded in reducing literature to so methodical and sustained a process. It went on with the punctuality and productiveness of a cotton mill or a nail factory; exactly so much rhyming, collating, and proof-reading, and so much of chronicle and correspondence, in the twenty-four hours. We see Robert Southey, as he paints himself, seated at his desk, in an old black coat, long worsted pantaloons and gaiters in one, and a green shade; and we feel the truth of his own declaration that this is his history. Occasionally he goes down to the river-side, behind the house, and throws stones until his arms ache, plays with the cat, or takes a mountain walk with the children. The event of his life is the publication of a book; his most delightful hour that in which he sees the handsomely printed title-page that announces his long meditated work ready, at last, to be ushered in elegant attire before the public; his most pleasing excitement to read congratulatory letters from admiring friends, or an appreciative critique in a fresh number of the "Quarterly." *

Minor pastimes he finds in devising literary castles in the air, projecting epics on suggestive and unused themes, giving here and there a finishing touch to sentence or couplet, possessing himself of a serviceable but rare tome, transcribing a preface with all the conscious dignity of authorship, or a dedication with the complacent zeal of a gifted friend. From the triple, yet harmonious and systematic life of the country, the study, and the nursery, we see him, at long intervals, depart for a visit to London, to confabulate with literary lions, greet old college friends, make new bargains with publishers, and become a temporary diner-out; or he breaks away from domestic and literary employment in his retreat among the hills, for a rapid continental tour, during which not an incident, a natural fact, an historical reminiscence, a political conjecture, or a wayside phenomenon, is allowed to escape him. Though wearied to the last degree, at nightfall he notes his experience with care, as material for future use; and hurries back, with presents for the children and a voluminous diary, to resume his pencraft; until the advent of summer visitors obliges him to exchange a while the toils of authorship for the duties of hospitality.

To these regularly succeeding occupations may be added the privileges of distinction, the acquisition of new and interesting friends, of testimonies of respect from institutions and private admirers; and inevitable trials, such as occasional assaults from the critics, or a birth or bereavement in the household. Sequestered and harmless we cannot but admit such a life to be, and, when chosen from native inclination, as desirable for the individual as can be imagined, in a world where the vicissitude and care of active life are so apt to interfere with comfort and peace. At the age of thirty-two, when thus settled at Keswick, Southey gratefully estimated its worth in this point of view: "This is my life, which, if it be not a very merry one, is yet as happy as heart could wish."

* Coleridge once said, "I can't *think* of Southey without seeing him either mending or using a pen."

Southey left a somewhat minute and very graphic sketch of his childhood, parts of which are written in his happiest vein. Some of the anecdotes are significant, but more as illustrations of character than genius. He was bookish, moral, and domestic, inquiring, and observant; but seems not to have exhibited any of that delight in the sense of wonder that kept the boy Schiller rocking in a tree to watch the lightning, or the generous ardor that made Byron a schoolboy champion, or the oppressive sensibility that weighed down the spirit of young life in Alfieri's breast. His autobiography, not less than his literary career, evinces the clever man of letters rather than the surpassing man of genius. It is characteristic of this that, between the ages of eight and twelve, he expressed the conviction that "it was the easiest thing in the world to write a play." Such is the natural language of talent; that of genius would be, "it is the greatest thing in the world."

The most effective portrait in the part of his memoirs written by himself is that of his Aunt Tyler. It is evidently drawn from the life, and would answer for a character in the very best class of modern novels. As a revelation of himself, the most excellent traits are the disposition, spirit, and state of feeling displayed. Southey obviously possessed steady affections, self-respect, and a natural sense of duty. The embryo reformer is indicated by his essay against flogging in school; and no better proof of his reliability can be imagined than the fact that several of his earliest friendships continued unabated throughout life. His sketches of teachers, classmates, and the scenes of boyhood, are pleasing, natural, and authentic.

Like most literary men, Southey in youth took an interest in science, and dabbled in botany and entomology; but he soon abandoned insects and flowers, except for purposes of metaphor. His education, too, like that of the majority of professed authors, was irregular, versatile, and unexact, vibrating between the study of text-books in a formal, and the perusal of chosen ones in a relishing manner. His love of the quaint in expression, his taste for natural history, church lore, ballads, historic incident, and curious philosophy, are richly exemplified in the specimens of the "Common-place Book," recently published, and especially in that fragmentary, but most suggestive work, "The Doctor;" and these but carry out the aims and tastes foreshadowed in his youthful studies.

Marked out by natural tastes for a life of books, we recognize the instinct in the delight he experienced when first possessed of a set of Newberry's juvenile publications, the zest with which he wrote school themes, invented little dramas, and fraternized with a village editor, not less than in its mature development, when taking the shape of beautiful quartos with the imprimatur of Murray or the Longmans. The sight of a fair finished page of his first elaborate metrical composition, "Joan of Arc," he acknowledges infected him with the true author mania, and henceforth he was only happy over pencraft or typography.

In his memoirs we find new evidence of the laws of mind and health, and the fatal consequences of their infringement. To Southey's kind activity we are indebted for a knowledge of the most affecting instance in English literature of early genius prematurely lost, that of Kirke White; and two other cases of youthful aspiration for literary honor blighted by death were confided to his benevolent sympathy; but the great intellectual promise, rapid development, and untimely loss of his son, is one of the most pathetic episodes of his life. His correspondence at the period explains the apparent incongruity between occasional evidences of strong feeling and an habitual calmness of tone. His nature was so balanced as to admit, as a general rule, of perfect self-control. He repeatedly asserts that the coldness attributed to him is not real. In this great bereavement, he seems to have perfectly exercised the power of living in his mind, and finding a refuge from moral suffering in mental activity. But one of the most impressive physiological as well as intellectual lessons to be drawn from Southey's life is in his own personal experience.

We have a striking example of the need of a legitimate hygiene for the assiduous writer, and the fatal consequence of its neglect. To his scholar's temperament and habits may be, in a measure, ascribed Southey's conservatism; and it is equally obvious how the same causes gradually modified his physical constitution, and, through this, the character of his mind. We believe it is now admitted that, where the temperament is not indicated with great predominance, it may be almost entirely changed by diversity of circumstances and habits. The influence of the brain and nervous system is so pervading that, where the vocation constantly stimulates them, and leaves the muscles and circulation in a great degree inactive, remarkable modifications occur in the animal economy; and so intimately are its functions associated with mental and moral phenomena, that it is quite unphilosophical to attempt to estimate or even analyze character without taking its agency into view. The sedentary life and cerebral activity of Southey seem to have very soon subdued his feelings. We perceive, in the tone of his letters, a slow but certain diminution of animal spirits; and, now and then, a prophetic consciousness of the frail tenure upon which he held, not his intelligent spirit, but his mental machinery, the incessant action of which is adequate to explain its melancholy and premature decay. The time will come when his case will be recorded as illustrative of the laws of body and mind in their mutual relations,— a subject which Combe, Madden, and other popular writers, have shown to be fraught with teachings of the widest charity for what are called "the infirmities of genius."

How many pathetic chapters are yet to be written on this prolific theme, before the world is sufficiently enlightened to know how to treat her gifted children! We need not go to Tasso's cell to awaken our sympathies in this regard; from the fierce insanity of Swift and Collins, to the morbid irritability or gloom of Johnson, Pope, and Byron, and the imbecile age of Moore and Southey, the history of English authorship is replete with solemn warnings to use even the noblest endowments of humanity with meek and severe circumspection. God is not less worshipped by select intelligences, through fidelity to the natural laws, than by celebrating his glory in the triumphs of art.

In a letter to Sharon Turner, in 1817, Southey remarks: "My spirits rather than my disposition have undergone a great change. They used to be exuberant beyond those of every other person; my heart seemed to possess a perpetual fountain of hilarity; no circumstances of study, or atmosphere, or solitude, affected it; and the ordinary vexations and cares of life, even when they showered upon me, fell off like hail from a pent-house.

That spring is dried up. I cannot now preserve an appearance of it at all without an effort, and no prospect in this world delights me except that of the next." Although he often attributed this change to special causes, and particularly to the bereavement which bore so heavily on his heart, he was, at the same time, soon aware that the recuperative energies of his nature were essentially impaired. "It is," he writes to another friend, "between ourselves, a matter of surprise that this bodily machine of mine should have continued its operations with so few derangements, knowing, as I do, its excessive susceptibility to many deranging causes." These shadows deepened as time passed on, and found him intent upon mental labor, when nature imperatively demanded freedom, variety, the comedy of life, and the atmosphere of a serene, cheerful, and unhackneyed existence.

There was nothing, however, in the native hue of Southey's mind that betokened any tendency to disease. On the contrary, his tone of feeling was singularly moderate, his estimate of life rather philosophic than visionary, and, for a poet, he scarcely has been equalled for practical wisdom and methodical self-government. Instead of wishing newly-married people happiness, which he considered superfluous, he wished them patience; in travelling, he was remarkable for making the best of everything; he cherished a tranquil religious faith; he systematized his life, and, instead of lamenting the dreams of youth as the only source of real enjoyment in life, he says, "Our happiness, as we grow older, is more in quantity and higher in degree as well as kind."

Another wholesome quality he largely possessed was candor. He bore with exemplary patience, as a general rule, the malevolence of criticism, suffered with few murmurs the indignity of Gifford's mutilations of his reviews, and seemed to exhibit acrimony only when assailed by a radical, or when he alluded to Bonaparte, whose most appropriate situation, through his whole career, he declared to have been when sleeping beside a fire made of human bones in the desert. He had the magnanimity at once to confess the genuine success of the American navy, at a time when it was common in England to doubt even the testimony of facts on the subject. "It is in vain," he writes, "to treat the matter lightly, or seek to conceal from ourselves the extent of the evil. Our naval superiority is destroyed." Of American literature, at an earlier period, he declared, with more truth than now could be warranted, that "the Americans, since the Revolution, have not produced a single poet who has been heard of on this side of the Atlantic." Subsequently, he was, however, the first to do justice to the poetical merits of Maria del Occidente, and numbered several congenial literary friends among her countrymen. A more versatile course might have contributed greatly to Southey's sustained vigor of mind. His early life was, indeed, sufficiently marked by vicissitude; he was successively a law-student, lecturer, private secretary, traveller, and author, and thought of becoming a librarian and a consul; but the result was a firm reversion to his primary tastes for rural life and books.

It is curious, as a psychological study, to trace the lapse of youth into manhood and senility, as indicated in the writings of men of talent, and observe how differently time and experience affect them, according to the elements of their characters. Some have their individuality of purpose and feeling gradually overlaid by the influences of their age and position, and in others it only asserts itself with more vehemence. There is every degree of independence and mobility, from the isolated hardihood of a Dante to the fertile aptitude of a Brougham. It was the normal condition of Southey to be conservative; taste and habit, affection and temperament, combined to reconcile him to things as they are, or, at least, to wean him from the restless life of a reformer. An intellectual friend of mine, noted for his love of ease, and whose creed was far more visionary than practical, surprised a circle, on one occasion, with his earnest advocacy of some political measure, and sighed heavily, as he added, "Vigilance is the eternal price of liberty." "But why," asked a companion, "do *you* put on the watchman's cap?" The inquiry was apposite; he had no vocation to fight in the vanguard of opinion. And this seems to us a more charitable way of accounting for Southey's change of views, than to join his opponents in ascribing it to unalloyed selfishness.*

* "In all his domestic relations Southey was the most amiable of men, but he had no general philanthropy; he was what you call a *cold* man. I spent some time with him at Lord Lonsdale's, in company with Wordsworth and

To the secluded *littérateur*, watching over his gifted invalid boy amid romantic lakes and mountains, the calm and nature-loving Wordsworth was a more desirable companion than Godwin, to whom, at a previous era, he acknowledged himself under essential intellectual obligations. His wife, the gentle and devoted Edith, might have objected to such an inmate as Mary Wolstonecraft, whom her husband preferred to all the literary lions during his early visits to London; and it was far more agreeable to "counteract sedition" in his quiet studio at Keswick, than to roughly experience *Pantisocracy* in America; while a man of sterner mould might be pardoned for preferring a picnic glorification over the battle of Waterloo, on the top of Skiddaw, to a lonely struggle for human rights against the overwhelming tide of popular scorn, which drove the more adventurous and poetic Shelley into exile. All Southey's compassion, however, so oracularly expressed for that sensitive and heroic spirit, derogates not a particle from the superior nobility of soul for which generous thinkers cherish his memory. We can, however, easily follow the natural gradations by which the boy Southey, whose ideal was the Earl of Warwick, and the youth Southey, intent upon human progress and social reformation, became the man Southey, a good citizen, industrious author, exemplary husband and father, and most loyal subject. Indeed, the conservative mood begins to appear even before any avowed change in his opinions. Soon after his return from the first visit to Lisbon, while hesitating what profession to adopt, and while his friends were discouraged at the apparent speculative recklessness and desultory life he indulged, we find him writing to Grosvenor, one of his most intimate friends, "I am conversing with you now in that easy, *calm, good-humored state of mind* which is, perhaps, the *summum bonum;* the less we think of the world the better. My feelings were once like an ungovernable horse; now I have tamed Bucephalus; he retains his spirit and his strength, but *they are made useful*, and he shall not break my neck."

This early visit to Lisbon, when his mind was in its freshest

others; and, while the rest of the party were walking about, talking and amusing themselves, Southey preferred sitting *solus* in the library." — *Rogers' Table Talk.*

activity, attracted him to the literature of Spain and Portugal; and the local associations, which gave them so vivid a charm to his taste, imparted kindred life to his subsequent critiques and historical sketches devoted to these scenes and people. They furnish another striking instance of the felicitous manner in which the experience of foreign travel and the results of study coalesce in literary productions.

Authorship, indeed, was so exclusively the vocation of Southey that his life may be said to have been identified with it; yet pursued, as we have seen, in a spirit often mechanical, we are not surprised that, while he felt himself adapted to the pursuit, he was sometimes conscious of that mediocrity which is the inevitable fruit of a wilful tension of the mind. Thus, while to one friend he writes, "One happy choice I made when I betook myself to literature as my business in life;" to another, in 1815, he declares, "I have the disheartening conviction that my best is done, and that to add to the bulk of my works will not be to add to their estimation." Yet Southey, like all genuine authors, cherished his dream of glory, and probably anticipated enduring renown from his poetry. The mechanical spirit of his literary toil, however, was carried into verse. He set about designing a poem as he did a history or a volume of memoirs, and proceeded to fill up the outline with the same complacent alacrity. Many of these works exhibit great ingenuity of construction, both as regards form and language. They are striking examples of the inventive faculty, and show an extraordinary command of language; in this latter regard, some of his verses are the most curious in our literature; — the "Fall of Lodore" is an instance. But it is obvious that, unless fused by the glow of sentiment, however aptly constructed, elaborate versified tales can scarcely be ranked among the standard poems of any language. The best passages of his long poems are highly imaginative, but the style is diffuse, the interest complicated, and there is a want of human interest that prevents any strong enlistment of the sympathies. They have not the picturesque and living attraction of Scott, nor yet the natural tenderness of Burns; but are melo-dramatic, and make us wonder at the author's fertility of invention, rather than become attached to its fruits.

One of the most striking instances of want of discrimination in the critical tone of the day, was the habit of designating Coleridge, Wordsworth, and Southey, under the same general term. The only common ground for calling them the Lake School was the fact that they each resided among the lakes of Cumberland at one and the same time. The diffuse, reflective, philosophic muse of Wordsworth is as essentially different from the mystic and often profoundly tender sentiment of Coleridge, as both are from the elaborate chronicles and rhetorical artifice of Southey. His "Pilgrimage to Waterloo" is an apt and clever journal in verse, occasionally, from its personal style and simplicity, quite attractive; his laureate odes have a respectable sound, and frequently a commendable sense, but rarely any bardic fire or exquisite grace. In a word, although there is much to admire in Southey's poetry as the work of a creative fancy and the result of research and facility, as well as invention in the use of language, we seldom find, in perusing his works, any of those "Elysian corners of intuition," where Leigh Hunt speaks of comparing notes with the reader. The amplitude, variety, and tact of constructive talent, and not the glow and mystery of genius, win us to his page. It informs, entertains, and seldom offends; but rarely melts, kindles, or nerves the spirit.

His most obstinate admirers cannot but admit that, as poems, "Joan of Arc," "Madoc," and "Roderic," have many tedious passages. They are fluent, authentic chronicles, recorded in a strain that so often lapses from the spirit and dignity of the muse as to read like mere prose. Here and there, a graphic descriptive sketch or felicitous epithet redeems the narrative; but no one can wonder that, in an age when Byron individualized human passion in the most kindling rhyme, when Crabbe described so truthfully humble life, and Shelley touched the ideal spirit with his aërial fantasy, a species of poetry comparatively so distant from the associations of the heart should fail to achieve popularity. Indeed, Southey recognized the fact, and seemed not unwilling to share the favor of a limited but select circle with Landor and others, who, instead of universal suffrage, gain the special admiration of the few. No author, however, cherished a greater faith in literature as a means of reputation. "Literary fame," he says, "is the only fame of which a wise man ought to be ambitious, because it is the only lasting and living fame. Bonaparte will be forgotten before his time in purgatory is half over, or but just remembered, like Nimrod or other cut-throats of antiquity, who serve us for the commonplaces of declamation. Put out your mind in a great poem, and you will exercise authority over the feelings and opinions of mankind as long as the language lasts."

The two poems upon which Southey evidently most genially labored are "Thalaba" and "The Curse of Kehama." They bear the most distinct traces of his idiosyncrasies as evinced in boyhood, when a translation of the "Jerusalem Delivered" seems to have first directly appealed to his poetic instinct. The scenes of enchantment particularly fascinated him; then came "Ariosto" and "Spenser." The narrative form, and the imaginative and romantic character of these works, harmonized with Southey's mind, and they continued his poetic vein after the taste of the age had become wedded to the natural, the human, and the direct, in poetry. His tone and imagery were somewhat modified by Bowles and Coleridge; but he remained essentially in the class of romantic and narrative bards, in whose productions general effects, vague dramatic and supernatural charms, and heroic chronicles, form the pervading traits. Another characteristic of the modern poetry he lacked was concentration. One concise, vivid, and inspired lyric outlives the most labored epic. Sterling's brief tribute to "Joan of Arc" brings her nearer to us than Southey's quarto.

As works of art, the varied rhyme and rhythm, and prolific fancy, won for Southey's long poems a certain degree of attention and respect; but he is remembered more for certain fine passages than for entire compositions. In these, his claim to the title of poet, in the best sense of the word, asserts itself; and, but for these, he would rank only as a clever improvisatore. Learning, indeed, overlays inspiration in his long poems. He faithfully explored Welsh annals for the materials of "Madoc," Hindoo mythology and Asiatic scenery for the "Curse of Kehama," and Gothic history for "Roderic." All narrative poems are somewhat indebted to external materials; but these must be fused, as we have before hinted, into a consistent and vital whole by the glow of some personal sentiment, ere they will find universal response. Thus, the intense consciousness of Byron, the chivalric zeal of Campbell, and the amorous fancy of Moore, give a life and significance to their stories in verse that invest them with a sympathetic atmosphere and unity of feeling. There is little of this in Southey's narratives; they are more ingenious than glowing, more imaginative than natural; and they entertain more than they inspire. He seems destitute of that sacred reserve which renders manners so efficient, deepens love's channel, and hallows truth to consciousness; that instinctive suggestiveness, which is a great secret of Dante's power, giving sublime intimations of Tennyson's exquisite sentiment, vaguely hinting the inexpressible, and of Wordsworth's solemn mysticism, as in the "Ode on the Prospect of Immortality." To such lofty and profound elements the poetry of Southey has no claims; but, in descriptive aptitude, and especially in rhetorical effect, he is sometimes remarkable. Occasionally, in these qualities, in their simplicity, he reminds us of the old dramatists; thus, in Madoc:

"The masters of the song
In azure robes were robed — that one bright hue,
To emblem unity, and peace, and truth,
Like Heaven, which o'er a world of wickedness
Spreads its eternal canopy serene."

And again, in the same poem:

"'T is pleasant, by the cheerful hearth, to hear
Of tempests and the dangers of the deep,
And pause at times and feel that we are safe,
Then listen to the perilous tale again,
And with an eager and suspended soul
Woo terror to delight us."

In Roderic is a fine and characteristic image:

"Toward the troop he spread his arms,
As if the expanded soul diffused itself,
And carried to all spirits with the act
Its affluent inspiration."

The description of moonlight in this poem, so justly admired, we perceive, by one of the author's letters, was drawn from an actual scene, which evidences the absolute need of strong personal impressions even for an imaginative poet. The description of the ruins of Babylon, in Thalaba —

"The many-colored domes yet wore one dusky hue" —

is one of the happiest examples of Southey's powers of language, and musical adaptation of rhythm to sense. To one having a natural feeling of wonder and fine elocutionary powers, it is susceptible of the most solemn recitative effect. The beautiful passage in his "Curse of Kehama," commencing, "They sin who tell us love can die," the ballads of "Mary of the Inn" and "The Battle of Blenheim," the "Verses to a Dead Friend," and "The Holly Tree," are among the fugitive pieces, written from actual emotion, which illustrate Southey's affections, and have endeared him as a lyrist.

He remarks, in one of his letters, that he most nearly resembles Chiarbrera, an Italian bard of the fifteenth century, who enjoyed high honors for his verses, and died at a prosperous old age. His works are comparatively neglected at present; but Maffei, the literary historian, ascribes his success to merits very similar to those we have recognized in Southey. According to this critic, it was a saying of Chiarbrera that he wished to follow the example of Columbus and discover a new world, or perish, and that poetry should "lift the eyebrow;" thus declaring surprise to be the great effect, and novelty the great means, of poetic excellence. Accordingly, his verse was prized chiefly for its style, which innovated greatly upon familiar models, and for its erudition, which was remarkable for that day. Thus his renown was gained by ingenuity and scholarship, rather than through intense natural sympathy or genuine inspiration. We therefore find Southey's own estimate of his poetry, in a great degree, confirms our own. But this coincidence is as clearly, though less directly, suggested by his casual observations on the art, in his letters to cotemporary writers, and his advice to young poets who sought encouragement from his counsel.

It is obvious, from the incidental views thus honestly

expressed, that he had not a vivid and permanent consciousness of a poet's birthright; that the art was too much a branch of authorship, and too little a sacred instinct, in his estimation; and that the more erratic versifiers of the age, less elaborate, but far more intense and genuine, won their larger popularity on legitimate grounds. He tells one of his correspondents, who had solicited his opinion of a poem, that his friends reckon him "a very capricious and uncertain judge of poetry;" and elsewhere, in speaking of the error which identifies the power of enjoying natural beauty with that of producing poetry, he says, "One is a gift of Heaven, and conduces immeasurably to the happiness of those who enjoy it; the second has much more of a knack in it than the pride of poets is always willing to admit." If Southey's poetic faculty and feeling had been equal to his "knack" of versifying, he would have been quite as reluctant to ascribe to ingenuity what was consciously derived from a power above the will. Perhaps he was chagrined into this commonplace view of the art by the fact that, while Scott was receiving three thousand guineas for the "Lady of the Lake," the "Curse of Kehama" was going through the press at the expense of Landor.

The professional character of Southey's life is almost incompatible with the highest literary results. His great merit as a writer consists in the utility of a portion of his works, and their unexceptionable morality and good sense. The most surprising quality he exhibited as an author was industry. His name is thoroughly respectable in literature as it was in life; but it would be unjust to the chivalric and earnest genius of the age, elsewhere manifested in deeper and more significant, though less voluminous records, to award to Southey either the title of a great poet or a leader of opinion. His career, in regard to the latter, is clearly explained in his biography. We perceive that, even in boyhood, the intellect predominated in his nature. In the heyday of his blood, the companionship of bolder spirits and less chastened enthusiasts, the infectious atmosphere of the French Revolution, and the activity of the poetical instinct, not yet formalized into service, made him, for a while, the independent thinker in religion and politics, and induced visions of social equality which he hoped to realize across the sea. But early domestic ties and a natural love of study won him gradually back to conservative quietude. More than either of his brother poets, Southey had the temperament and taste of a scholar. He neither felt as deeply nor dreamed as habitually as Coleridge. The sensuous and the imaginative were not so united in his being with the intellectual. He needed less excitement; his spirit was far less adventurous; and life did not press upon and around him with such prophetic and inciting power.

It is needless to ascribe the change in his views altogether to interest; this may have had its influence, but the character of the man yields a far more natural solution of the problem. He was doubtless as sincere when he accepted the laureateship as when he wrote "Wat Tyler;" but, in the latter case, his "blood and judgment were not well commingled." Southey, the Bristol youth, penniless, aspiring, and fed with the daily manna of poetic communion, looked upon society with different eyes than Southey, the recognized English author, resident of Cumberland, and father of a family. He knew how to use materials aptly, how to weave into connected and intelligible narrative the crude and fragmentary data of history and memoirs. In this manner he greatly served all readers of English. His "Life of Wesley" is the most authentic and lucid exposition of an extraordinary phase of the religious sentiment on record. Of Brazil and the Peninsular War he has chronicled memorable things in a perspicuous style. Few pictures of British life are more true to fact and suggestive than "Espriella's Letters." The "Life of Nelson" is a model of unaffected, direct narrative, allowing the facts to speak for themselves through the clearest possible medium of expression; and yet this most popular of Southey's books, far from being the offspring of any strong personal sympathy or perception, was so entirely a literary job, that he says it was thrust upon him, and that he moved among the sea-terms like a cat among crockery. For a considerable period after the establishment of the "Quarterly," he found reviews the most profitable labor. Many of these are judicious and informing, but they seldom quicken or elevate either by rhetorical or reflective energy, and are too often special pleas to excite great interest. Those on purely literary subjects, however, are agreeable.

If we were to name, in a single term, the quality for which Southey is eminent, we should call him a verbal architect. His prose works do not open to our mental gaze new and wondrous vistas of thought; they are not deeply impressive from the greatness, or strangely winsome from the beauty, of their ideas. Their rhetoric does not warm and stir the mind, nor is their scope highly philosophic or gracefully picturesque. But their style is correct, unaffected, and keeps that medium which good taste approves in manners, speech, and costume, but which we seldom see transferred to the art of writing. For pure narrative, where the object is to give the reader unalloyed facts, and leave his own reflection and fancy to shape and color them, no English author has surpassed Southey. He appears to have been quite conscious of the moderate standard to which he aspired. "As to what is called fine writing," he says, "the public will get none of that article out of me: sound sense, sound philosophy, and sound English, I will give them." There is no doubt, in so doing, he consulted the Anglo-Saxon love of regulated and useful principles and hatred of extravagance, and was thus an admirable type of the modern English mind; but such an ideal, however praiseworthy and respectable, scarcely coincides with the more noble and inspired mood in which the permanent masterpieces of literary genius are conceived and executed.

THE MODERN KNIGHT.

SIR KENELM DIGBY.

One of the most attractive figures visible on that imaginary line where the eve of chivalry and the dawn of science unite to form a mysterious yet beautiful twilight, is that of Sir Kenelm Digby. To our imagination he represents the knight of old before the characteristics of that romantic style of manhood were diffused in the complex developments of modern society, and the philosopher of the epoch when fancy and superstition held sway over the domain of the exact sciences. Bravery, devotion to the sex, and a thirst for glory, nobleness of disposition and grace of manner, traditional qualities of the genuine cavalier, signalized Sir Kenelm, not less than an ardent love of knowledge, a habitude of speculation, and literary accomplishment; but his courage and his gallantry partook of the poetic enthusiasm of the days of Bayard, and his opinions and researches were something akin to those of the alchemists. High birth and a handsome person gave emphasis to these traits; and we have complete and authentic memorials whereby he is distinctly reproduced to our minds. These, however, do not consist of those elaborate treatises which, doubtless, cost him severe application; his views of the nature of corporeal and spiritual laws are quite obsolete,— learned and ingenious, perhaps, but not of present significance. The criticisms that beguiled his imprisonment evince his taste and mental aptitudes by their subjects — Sir Thomas Browne and Spenser; two authors who include that wide range of sympathy that lies between fancy and reason. The events of his life, although remarkable, do not unfold the individuality of the man to the degree requisite for a genial impression. The offices he held imply no special interest of character; others have enjoyed royal favor, suffered persecution, and gone through all the phases of the courtier and scholar, without leaving behind them any fragrant memories. It is not, therefore, as gentleman of the bed-chamber to Charles I., as naval commissioner, as an exile for his religion, or as the eccentric devotee of science, that Sir Kenelm Digby claims our notice; but it is in his character of an adventurous gentleman and brave lover, as combining the loyalty and the aspiration of the knight with the graces of the man of the world and society, and thus giving us one of the last warm reflections of a departed era, which invests his name with a peculiar charm. The relics which bring him at once and vividly before us are his portrait by Vandyke, and the unique piece of autobiography he left; the former is in the Bodleian gallery at Oxford, and the latter is preserved in the Harleian collection of the British Museum. These are genuine records; they had a vital origin, and are caught from reality; whereas the more ostentatious traces of his life are lost in the obscurity of an antiquated style and foreign associations. All that is beautiful in Sir Kenelm's career originated in his love, which, like a thread of gold, interlaces and redeems his experience. Around the name of his wife are clustered the trophies of his fame. Sentiment elicited and glorified the elements of his character, which, uninfluenced by such a principle, would, in all probability, have diffused themselves in the blandishments of pleasure, or the career of ambition.

A mournful historic interest attaches to his name; for he was the eldest son of the most gentle in lineage and the most pure in motive of the conspirators who suffered death for the Gunpowder treason. Probably no victim of a cause so unrighteously supported ever more thoroughly atoned for his error with his life; the sacrifice of his existence and his estates appeared to silence forever the voice of reproach; he was soon regarded as unfortunate rather than criminal — a fanatic, not a traitor; and the memory of his patience, meekness, and fortitude, survived that of his conspiracy. With such a heritage of gloomy distinction, his son entered life; and there was that in his very blood which prompted, on the one hand, to honor, and, on the other, to mental cultivation and domestic peace. Educated a Protestant, he early commenced those travels abroad then deemed essential to a gentleman; and the first inkling of scientific zeal and public spirit appears in the recipe he brought home (which soon became famous), for making a "sympathetic powder," by applying which to anything that had received the blood of the wounded, instant relief was thought to be afforded, even if the patient was not present. This idea was never abandoned; it was one of the results of the occult studies then in vogue; and the "sympathetic powder" is as intimately associated with Sir Kenelm Digby's name, as tar-water with Bishop Berkeley's.

An old English writer mentions having seen, in the window of a brazier's shop in London, a mutilated bust, which he recognized as that of Venitia Stanley. It once surmounted the costly tomb, erected by Sir Kenelm Digby for her remains, in Christ Church, near Newgate; and bore the marks of the conflagration that nearly destroyed the monument in 1675–6. Such is the poor memento of one of the most celebrated beauties of her time. A descendant of the Percies of Northumberland, she was educated by one of her father's relations in the immediate neighborhood of the Digby manor; and hence occurred the childish intimacy between her and the boy Kenelm. When taken to court in her girlhood, Venitia became, at once, the object of universal admiration; and, as so often happens to ladies thus distinguished, rumor, never however authenticated, was soon busy with her fame. She was abducted by one impassioned suitor, but made her escape; was rescued from a wild beast by another, and induced, after a long persecution, on the report of Digby's death, to betroth herself to her preserver; this apparent disloyalty was, perhaps, encouraged by the strenuous opposition of Sir Kenelm's mother to his proposed alliance, occasioned by the malicious reports circulated to Venitia's prejudice. In the mean time her absent lover had won no little reputation as an accomplished gentleman. He stood high in the favor of the queen of France, when he first sojourned abroad, and reäccompanied a kinsman, who had been sent to negotiate the marriage of Prince Charles in Spain, to Madrid; and, on the way, killed two bandits who waylaid them. As attaché to the prince's suite, he soon became useful and a favorite at court, where he attracted a lady of the royal family; and his early love alone prevented an eligible marriage. We can readily imagine the feelings with which Digby, full of anxiety from the report of Venitia's engagement, disembarked with his royal friend at London, on his return from Spain. On the first day of his arrival he caught a glimpse of the fair object of his devotion; and it soothed his lover's heart to observe that "she sat so pensively on one side of her coach." An explanation followed. It appeared that their letters had been intercepted, and that the new aspirant for her hand had already been dismissed for his infidelity. A new prospect of happiness was thus opened; but Sir Kenelm was invited to accompany the Duke of Buckingham to Paris, to arrange the nuptials between Prince Charles and Henrietta Maria. Two evidences of the chivalric spirit of these lovers occurred at this epoch. Digby was solicited by a friend, who was ignorant of his relations with Venitia Stanley, to intercede for him with her; and this he felt bound in honor to do, although he "would rather have died than seen her in any other man's possession." Nor was she wanting in generosity; for, Sir Kenelm being too much impoverished to equip himself for the honorable expedition in view, Venitia pawned all her jewels to obtain the requisite funds. The arguments of his mother and friends were no longer allowed to influence his heart; he fought a duel with one of her traducers, and forced him to confess the baseness of his slanders; he obtained back her picture from his discarded rival; and they were privately married. Digby had been knighted on his return from Spain; and he was blest with the love and companionship of her whose image had never grown dim in his breast, from the time he sported with her in childhood, until that which made her his bride. His was not a spirit, however, to rest contented without crowning love with glory, and proving its inspiration by great deeds; he wished to show that it "had not lessened the nobleness of his mind, nor abated the edge of his active and vigorous spirits;" he desired, therefore, "to undertake something which should tend to his own honor and the king's service."

A great favorite at Whitehall, and naturally gay, he yet cheerfully embarked in a maritime expedition, and gained a naval victory at Scanderoon over the Algerines and Venetians. It was during his sojourn at an island, awaiting his fleet dispersed by a storm, that he became the object of interest to the ladies of his host's acquaintance, and to avoid even the appearance of forgetfulness of Venitia, he retired under pretence of writing despatches, and then composed the piece of autobiography to which we have alluded. In the quaint elegance of its style, and the lofty ardor of its sentiments, this curiosity of literature is a gem of its kind. Under fictitious names he describes himself, his mistress and friends, the course of his love, its origin, consummation, and philosophy. A few extracts will give an idea of the whole:

* * * * * * *

"At such times then as my soul, being delivered of other outward distractions, hath summoned all her faculties to attend to this main business, the first consideration that hath occurred to me hath been that the peace and tranquillity of the mind ought to be aimed at; the obtaining of which is an infallible token that one is in the right way of attaining to perfect happiness; or rather these two have so straight and near a relation, as that one cannot be without the other."

* * * * * * *

"And, besides, because that in exact friendship the wills of the two friends ought to be so drowned in one another, like two flames which are joined, that they become but one, which cannot be unless the faculties of the understanding be equal, they guiding the actions of a regulated will, it cometh to pass for the most part that this halteth on the woman's side, whose notions are not usually so high and elevated as men's; and so it seldom happeneth that there is that society between them in the highest and deepest speculations of the mind, which are consequently the most pleasing, as is requisite in a perfect friendship."

* * * * * * *

"But at length I perceived that that infinite light which illuminateth all things, is never wanting to illustrate such a mind as with due humility and diligence maketh itself fit to receive it; for it was not long before such an example occurred to me, as satisfied me that in this life a man may enjoy so much happiness as without anxiety or desire of having anything besides what he possesseth, he may, with a quiet and peaceable soul, rest with full measure of content and bliss, that I know not whether it be short of it in anything but the security of continuance. It was the perfect friendship and noble love of two generous persons, that seemed to be born in this age by ordinance of Heaven to teach the world anew what it hath long forgotten, the mystery of loving with honor and constancy between a man and a woman: therefore this is the true happiness that a wise man ought to aim at, since that himself is master of it, and he can give it to himself when he list. I hope, therefore, then, that you will no longer call that the weakest of all the passions which produceth so noble effects."

To a mind strongly alive to the beautiful there is a peculiar charm in traditional loveliness; and the effect of this is increased when such attractions are made known to us by the influence they exerted upon contemporaries, rather than by details of feature. The constancy which the graces of Venitia Stanley enforced upon Sir Kenelm, under circumstances of great temptation of fickleness; the faith she inspired in his soul notwithstanding the sneers of his comrades, the whispered innuendo, and some indiscretion on her part, and the entire satisfaction he found in her love, as well as his devotion to her memory, give us a deeper impression of her charms than the mere fact that she was universally admired. And then, too, there is an appeal to our best feelings in the very idea of beauty unjustly associated with shame; the readiness of the world to derogate from charms that excite envy, the liability, in one beloved and flattered, to forget circumspection, and a thousand other arguments at once suggest themselves in defence of the assailed. In the case of Lady Digby, her chief accuser was proved to be both false and malicious, and the consistent happiness of their married life soon justified the loving choice of Sir Kenelm.

On the first of May, 1633, he sustained the loss of this endeared and beautiful woman; and instantly retired to Gresham College, and there wore a "long mourning cloak, a high-cornered hat, and his beard unshorn." Ben Jonson eulogized her under the name of Eupheme; her husband raised the monument already mentioned, and her face is perpetuated in numerous busts and portraits.

The remainder of Sir Kenelm's life was given to travel and study. He endured persecution for his Catholic sentiments to which he had been converted in France, where, upon his return, he was regarded as a great acquisition to the court; visited Descartes, and wrote his treatises. At Rome he is said to have quarrelled with the pope. On the breaking out of the civil war with England, the queen mother of France, always friendly to him, successfully interceded in his behalf; and when, soon after the dissolution of the Long Parliament, he returned home, to the surprise of all, the Protector befriended him; an anomaly twice explained by the supposition that he endeavored to bring about a combination between the enemies of the monarchy and the Catholics.

The public spirit of Sir Kenelm Digby was never inactive. He fitted out the squadron he commanded at his own expense, and went on several embassies with little or no remuneration; he bequeathed the valuable collection of works inherited from his old tutor to the Bodleian library; and was constantly engaged either in the acquisition or the diffusion of knowledge. He expended over a thousand pounds for historical manuscripts relating to his family. While at Montpelier and other seats of learning, on the continent, he was intimate with the eminent men of science and letters. After the Restoration he was nominated to the Council. His last years were passed at his house at Covent Garden, in the study of philosophy and mathematics, and in the best social intercourse. He was a great sufferer from the same disease that afflicted Montaigne; and died, by a remarkable coincidence, on his birthday, which was also the anniversary of his naval triumph, in 1665, at the age of sixty-two.

Sir Kenelm was a thorough gentleman, and, although the genial dignity of that character was somewhat tinctured by a harmless vanity, his gifts of mind and grace of person and manner prevented any compromise of his self-respect. Lord Clarendon says that his conduct, which would have been considered affectation in the majority of mankind, "seemed natural to his size, the mould of his person, the gravity of his motion, and the tone of his voice and delivery." It is curious to imagine him in the various phases his character offers — the elegant courtier, moving with dignified pleasantry amid the nobles of England, France, and Spain; the credulous philosopher, consulting an Italian friar about the sympathetic powder, and a Brahmin as to the destinies revealed by the stars; the brave soldier, placing his ship alongside of the enemy's admiral, and cheering on his men to victory; the exile for religious opinion, the ambassador of his country, the scholar closeted with the most learned of his day; and all these, we must remember, are but the episodes in the love-poem of his life. Eccentric, wanting in steadiness of aim, both practical and speculative, yet learned, brave, and, though often accused, never found unworthy — faithful in love and war, and noble in spirit — the knowledge, weaknesses, aspirations, the manly beauty and chivalric passion of his times, found in Kenelm Digby an illustrious embodiment.

THE FINANCIER.

JACQUES LAFITTE.

In the majority of cases large fortunes are gained and preserved through careful attention to details — a habit which is supposed to militate with comprehensive views and liberal sympathies. It is, therefore, common to regard the acquisition of money and elevation of taste and character as essentially incompatible; and this consideration gives peculiar interest and value to the few noble exceptions to a general rule which reveal the sagacious financier as a patriot and philosopher. Prejudice, and the narrow ideas usually cherished by the devotees of trade, have caused the whole subject of money — its acquisition, preservation, and use — to be consigned to the domain of necessary evils, or the study of the political economist. It is, however, an interest too vital, and too inextricably woven into all the relations of modern society, not to have claims upon the most reflective minds, independent of all personal considerations.

The actual theory of an individual in regard to money is no ordinary test of character; the degrees of his estimation of it as a means or an end, and as a source of obligation and responsibility, are graduated by the very elements of his nature, and become a significant indication of his tone of mind and range of feeling. In its larger relations — those of a national kind — history proves that finance is a vast political engine, intimately connected with the freedom, growth, and civil welfare, as well as external prosperity, of a country. The traveller far removed from his native land, at a period of great financial distress, is made to realize the importance of credit, its moral as well as pecuniary basis, when he hears the character and means of all the prominent bankers in the world freely canvassed in some obscure nook of the earth, only connected perhaps with the civilized world by this very recognition of pecuniary obligation.

It is at such crises, bringing home to his own consciousness the vast and complicated relations of money to civilized life, that the individual becomes aware of the extensive social utility of those principles of financial science to which perhaps, in less hazardous exigencies, he has given but listless attention. The same broad views of the subject are forced upon a nation's mind in the junctures of political existence, and all great revolutions alternate from the battle-field and the cabinet to the treasury, — the state of public and private credit being, as it were, a scale that truly suggests the condition of the body politic, — like the pulse of a nation's life. Besides its attraction as a study of character, therefore, the life of one of the most illustrious of modern financiers possesses great incidental interest; and its unadorned facts yield the most impressive illustration of the relation of money to society and government.

The vicinity of the Pyrenees and the Bay of Biscay renders Bayonne a favorable site both for inland and foreign trade; and her commerce with Spain on the one side and her lucrative fisheries on the other, as well as the large amount of ship-timber annually exported to Brest and other parts of France, amply vindicate her claim to commercial privileges, which are still further secured by the enterprise of the Gascon character. That it is an excellent mercantile school is evident from the proverbial success of her inhabitants elsewhere.

It was from this old city that a youth of twenty, breaking away from his mother's tearful embrace, one night in the year 1787, departed for Paris, with no guarantee of a prosperous experience except that derived from an ingenuous disposition, enthusiasm, ready intelligence, and great natural cheerfulness. He became a clerk to the banker M. Perégaux; and soon after, by his own obvious merit, book-keeper, then cashier, and finally the exclusive director and indispensable man of business of the establishment. Such was the origin of Jacques Lafitte's career. The qualities which thus advanced him in private life soon inspired public confidence, and gradually led to his honorable and progressive activity in the national councils. Financial ability of a high order, combined with noble traits of character, thus identified him with the best interests of his country, and enrolled his name among her most efficient and illustrious citizens. One of ten children, his first object was to provide for his family, which he did with characteristic generosity. In 1809 the son of the poor carpenter of Bayonne was the president of the Chamber of Commerce, regent of the Bank, and master of a princely fortune. Thenceforth we trace his agency, more or less distinctly, in the wonderful series of events that succeeded the first revolution; now providing funds for a royal exile, now coming to the rescue of a bankrupt nation, and again lying wounded on his sofa, advising, ordering, and invoking the chief actors in the events of the three days in July, — his court-yard a barrack, and his saloon an impromptu cabinet, where a provisional government was organized and Louis Philippe proclaimed.

It was standing between Lafitte and Lafayette that the new king first ventured to show himself to the people. For many years the patriot-broker was the centre of a gifted society, the arbiter of pecuniary affairs, the coadjutor of monarchs and men of genius, of the working classes and political leaders. Surrounded by luxury, he never became indolent; with absorbing duties, he atoned by study for a neglected education; the possessor of immense wealth, he never forgot the responsibility it involved; a zealous partisan, and of so conciliatory a temper as to have the reputation of caprice in opinion, he preserved unbroken a moral consistency that won universal respect.

To this special insight of a financier Lafitte added genuine public spirit; he fully realized the social claims incident to his wealth and financial knowledge; and accordingly never hesitated to sacrifice personal interest to the general welfare, whenever circumstances rendered it wise and benevolent so to act. When governor of the Bank of France, he relinquished his salary of a hundred thousand francs in its favor, on account of the poverty of the institution; in 1814, when the directors assembled, after the entrance of the foe into Paris, to raise funds, he proposed a national subscription, and munificently headed the list. When the allies were at the gates of the city, he steadily refused to endanger the credit of the bank by a forced loan; and, to avert the horrors of civil war, placed two millions of his own property in the hands of the Minister of Finance. After the events of the three days, he resigned his coffers to the provisional government: his hotel was the rendezvous of the chief actors, his party installed Lafayette at the head of the troops, and it was he that sent word to the Duke of Orleans to choose between a crown and a passport, and subsequently caused him to be proclaimed.

Thus Lafitte thrice gave a safe direction to the chaotic elements of revolution, and came bravely and successfully to the rescue of his country in great emergencies. Nor was his action in behalf of individuals less noble and prompt. When Louis XVIII. was exiled, he sent the royal fugitives four millions of francs; when the Duke of Orleans offered large though doubtful securities to various commercial houses in vain, Lafitte accepted them at par value, uncertain as they were. When Napoleon departed for St. Helena, Lafitte became the repository of the remainder of his fortune; when General Foy experienced a reverse of fortune, and imprudently sought relief in stock speculations, the generous banker confidentially arranged with his broker to enrich the brave and proud officer, and, when he died, subscribed a hundred thousand francs for the benefit of his family. These are but casual instances of his private liberality. It was a habit as well as principle with him to afford pecuniary relief whenever and wherever real misfortune existed; to cherish, by the same means, industry, letters, art, and benevolent institutions, with a judgment and delicacy that infinitely endeared his gifts. It is not surprising that both people and rulers were, at times, impelled by grateful sympathy to recognize the noble spirit of such a financier; — that the Emperor Alexander placed a guard at his door when his liberty was threatened by the invaders; — that Napoleon expressed his confidence by saying, as he left the remnant of his fortune in his hands, "I know you did not like my government, but I know you are an honest man;" and that France herself, when his own fortune was wrecked by his devotion to the bank and the country, was moved at the remembrance of his sacrifices, would not permit the first asylum of the revolution to be sold, and, by a national subscription, redeemed it for Lafitte.

It is, however, to be regretted that he ever interested himself actively in politics, except as they were directly related to his peculiar sphere. When called upon to bring financial means to the aid of government or people, in their exigencies of civil life, we have seen his exemplary wisdom, integrity, and generous spirit; when he addressed the Chambers upon any question of debt, credit, loans, or currency, his superior intelligence and practical genius at once won respectful attention; his lucid and able reports, while governor of the bank, indicate his accurate knowledge of the principles of public credit; the remarkable speeches in which he revealed a project for resuscitating the nation's treasury,— the originality of his ideas, his colloquial eloquence, and the manner in which he made a dry subject, and even figures themselves, interesting and comprehensive,— amply prove his remarkable adaptation to the domain of social economy and political action he illustrated. Appointed by the king in 1816 as one of the Committee of Finance, with the Duke of Richelieu at its head, he contested the system of forced loans as identical with bankruptcy. In 1836 he demanded the reimbursement of the five per cents. His theory was founded essentially on the conviction that the way to diminish the burdens of the people is to diminish the expenses of the state.

Had Lafitte thus strictly confined himself to the subject of which he was master, it is probable he would have escaped, in a great degree, the blind prejudice of his opponents. As it was, however, his career as a deputy, to the view of an impartial spectator, reflects honor upon his character. Here, as in private life, he was eminently distinguished by moral courage. On one occasion he boldly proposed the impeachment of ministers. During the hundred days he was one of the intrepid minority that sought to preserve France from a second invasion. In opposing the system of forced loans, his noble hardihood induced the king to invest him with the legion of honor. "I have," he said to the Duke of Richelieu, his most formidable antagonist on this occasion, "bound myself to speak my mind; if the plan I propose is salutary, it is for the king to decide whether he will sacrifice the Chambers to France, or the country to the Chambers."

On the celebrated twenty-eighth of July, accompanied by his friends, he traversed the scene of hostilities to the Carousel,—the quarters of Marshal Marmont,—and adjured him to put a stop to the carnage. "Military honor," said the commander of Paris, "consists in obedience." "Civil honor," replied the brave deputy, "consists in not slaughtering the citizens to destroy the constitution." At the funeral of Manuel he arrested with his eloquence the outbreak between the military and the people. He was in the front rank of the defenders of the charter, the stanch advocate of the freedom of the press; and, when he saw the revolution of July approaching, effectually and at great personal risk strove to make it as useful and bloodless as the nature of things would permit. "My conscience," he said, "is without reproach. I founded, it is true, a new dynasty, but I found something in it legitimate. Posterity will judge me. I hope the loyalty of my intentions will find me grace in the eyes of history. I never deceived any one. My principles never changed. I believed in 1830 that France could only be republican through monarchy. I was wrong, and I repent with all my heart." For half a century he defended the rights of the people, and never ceased to preach moderation, but "a moderation compatible with liberty and national honor."

In the war of opinion and the strife of party Lafitte suffered the inevitable caprices of popular favor. Even his opponents, however, considered what they deemed his faults to arise from the strength of his affections, rather than the perversion of his will. His official life ruined his private fortunes; and the bitterness of his disappointment at the apparent inefficacy of the revolution in which he had taken so prominent a part, may be inferred from the memorable fact that he ascended the tribune, and, with much solemnity, asked pardon of Heaven for having contributed to its success. He seems at last to have become thoroughly aware of the limits of his natural vocation, and expressed himself as content when, free once more from the trammels of state, he began to retrieve his fortunes as a banker.

The views of Lafitte, however, on all subjects which he investigated, were remarkable for sound reason and moderation. He was no fanatic in politics, and understood the character of his nation. Louis XVI., he thought, aimed at a moral impossibility in attempting to retain all his prerogatives, without which the eclat of his office would be lost, while he knew the complaints of his people to be just. To the vacillation incident to this double view of the case, and the consequent indecision of a naturally good heart, he ascribed his course, which abased royalty while making sincere concessions. He believed, too, that the monarch owed his downfall more to injudicious friends than real enemies. The Girondists, he considered, tried the fatal experiment of attempting to reconcile people and court, and were too timid for the first and too advanced for the last; he regarded the irresolution of Lafayette as the flaw in his excellent nature; Danton, Robespierre, and Marat, he viewed as victims of the *fiévre revolutionnaire*, and, therefore, not to be jùdged in the same manner as men in a healthful condition. Indeed, he declared that no one could safely predict his own conduct under the influence of great political excitement. "I have," he said, "made the sad experiment; it is best not to enter the vortex; if you do you are borne on blindfolded." He always insisted that the great results of the French Revolution could have been attained by less terrible means. He recognized fully the reforms of Napoleon, and, with the acumen of a political economist, watched the growing prosperity of the nation; but none the less lamented the decadence of freedom with the grief of a patriot. He recoiled from the duplicity of the emperor, and grieved at the subserviency of the senate. What most surprised Lafitte, in Bonaparte, was his fortune; and he deemed his fatal error the attempt to impose on France a continental system wholly incompatible with the age. In a word, he honored Napoleon as a soldier, and despised him as a ruler. The office of the press he seems to have thoroughly appreciated; "*j'ai toujours pensé*," he says, "*que la presse est dans un état, l'unique moyen de retenir le pouvoir dans les bornes de la moderation et de l'empêcher de se livrer a l'arbitraire.*"

Although, when elected to the Chamber of Deputies, Lafitte immediately took his place on the benches of the opposition, and subsequently attained the presidency of the cabinet, and in 1817 was the only name deposited in the urns of twenty sections of the electoral college, by supporting the reduction of the rents and the creation of the three per cents, he alienated many of his party. Indeed, such was his political eclecticism, that a democratic writer says "he lost his popularity by his monarchical affections,"—alluding to his personal attachments to members of the royal family; and a monarchist attributes it to his democratic attachments; thus justifying the inference of his biographer, that he was "too much a man of heart to be a statesman." In the sphere of his individual ambition, however,—in his financial opinions and career, as well as in the tone of his character,—Lafitte was remarkably consistent; sagacious, upright, benevolent, and patriotic. He completely refuted the base charge, suggested by partisan animosity, of having sold his vote to the minister; and whatever popular favor he may have lost as the member of a faction, he amply regained as a man. This is evident from the universal sympathy awakened by his loss of fortune, and the confidence and gratitude with which the people rallied to his call when he established his famous *Caisse d'escompte*, now the memorial of his useful and honorable career. By means of this institution the poorest artisan has a safe and profitable investment for his earnings.

In 1837, having thus settled his affairs and reëstablished his credit, he thus addressed the shareholders: "It is not without emotion that I find myself restored to these labors, and about to crown, with an undertaking worthy of my best efforts, a career in which I have perhaps done some good. I forget many past mishaps, and all the bitterness of political life, which promised nothing to my ambition, and the burden of which I only accepted from devotion to my country. The future had compensation in reserve for me; and the second of October, 1837—the day on which I resume my business—consoles me for the nineteenth of January, 1831—the day on which I left it." Thus opening a credit to the humbler branches of industry, Lafitte rescued many a victim from the extortions of the usurer.

The financial services of Lafitte in France vividly recall those of Robert Morris in America. At the commencement of the

American Revolution he was more extensively engaged in commerce than any of his fellow-citizens, and was one of the first Philadelphians irretrievably to commit himself in behalf of the colonies at a great pecuniary sacrifice; thus inspiring the same unbounded confidence in his patriotism which his integrity and wisdom had long before gained for him as a man of business. He was on every committee of ways and means appointed by the legislature of his native state, and, from the outbreak of hostilities, devoted all the force of his talents, the influence of his name, his credit and fortune, to his country; and these seldom failed in the hour of need. When his official resources were inadequate he pledged his individual credit. Like Lafitte, he was exposed to misrepresentation, and, like him, triumphed over calumny. All the requisite means for Washington's expedition against Cornwallis were furnished by him; and his own notes, to the amount of four hundred thousand dollars, thus fearlessly given, were all finally paid. While invested, as he long was, with the entire provision, control, and expenditure, of the public finances, the history of his difficulties and expedients would fill a volume. When the imminent danger that originally induced him to accept this responsible office had passed away, he gladly resigned.

His resemblance to Lafitte was increased by a natural urbanity, vigor of action, broad views, rigid justice, strict method, and also by the eventual loss of his own fortune, and the establishment of an excellent system of finance. He founded the Bank of America, the first institution of the kind in that country, upon principles the utility of which time has fully proved. In patriotic zeal, and in the respect of his illustrious contemporaries, he also offers a parallel to the renowned French banker. He was the friend of Washington, and justly regarded as "the soul of the financial concerns" of the nation. "No one," it has been said, "parted more freely with his money for public or private purposes of a meritorious nature." When Hamilton became Secretary of the Treasury, no statistics of the country had appeared; her resources were only surmised; and, after holding the office for five years, he left it at an unprecedented height of reputation. By these two acute and zealous patriots the foundation of American prosperity was laid; and the identity of their opinions with those of Lafitte is remarkable. "The whole business of finance," they thought, "was comprised in two short but comprehensive sentences. It is to raise the public revênue by such modes as may be most easy and most equal to the people, and to expend it in the most frugal, fair, and honest manner."

The personal tastes of Jacques Lafitte were characterized by the same moderate tone. He loved elegance, and surrounded himself with all those brilliant resources that wealth so abundantly supplies in the French metropolis; but they did not enervate or bewilder his mind; he continued his daily toil with unremitted zeal; casting aside, however, with the greatest facility, the severe concentration of the financier, to mingle, with the *abandon* of the joyous south, at his own splendid fêtes, with the brave, the wise, and the lovely. Even his literary predilections were characteristic; he ignored the romantic and loved the classic writers of his country, while the *bonhommie* and patriotism of Beranger made him a favorite guest at his reünions, and he knew Molière by heart. His first discourse as deputy made a great impression, both on account of its style and ideas. It is curious that the sensation, if we may so call it, of wealth, is so independent of its possession. Lafitte declared that he never felt himself rich except when his appointments, under Perégaux, reached the sum of three thousand francs; an indirect but striking proof of his consciousness of the relations to society incident to fortune. His credulous faith in the integrity of others presents a striking contrast to his sagacious insight as regards affairs. When the Duke of Orleans said to him, "What shall I do for you when I am king?" his reply was, "Make me your fool, that I may tell you the truth;" yet he entertained such implicit confidence in the promises of the royal candidate, that he received his embrace upon his accession with fraternal trust. Calm, serene, industrious as a financier, generous and honest as a man, gay and kindly as a companion, after forty years of riches and honor, Lafitte found himself poor and unpopular; and perhaps no portion of his career is more suggestive of energy of character and elasticity of temper than the last epoch, wherein he retrieved both his fortune and his glory.

The power of money, thus illustrated, as a means of political and social influence, is not less obvious in ordinary experience. Recall the scene of morbid excitement, and its infinite probable consequences, which a single midnight hour offers at Frascati's; "the hard-eyed lender and the pale lendee" visible on the Exchange; the serene unity of life achieved by the philosopher satisfied with the freedom from care incident to a mere competency when attended by intellectual resources; the "weary hours" of the millionaire; the exalted aspect of human nature in the person of the man of fortune whose means are rendered absolutely subservient to taste and philanthropy; the comfort of households upheld by honest industry; the sublime results of genius when exempted from want and the baffled spirit of the persecuted debtor; the absorption of time, intellect, and feeling, in sordid pursuits; — let the imagination follow to their ultimate issues the various incidental fruits of these several conditions upon the individual and society, and we have a glimpse of the vast agencies involved in the use and abuse of money.

From the Bureaux du Monte de Pieté to the halls of a national bank, from the luxurious saloon to the squalid hovel, from the dashing spendthrift to the wretched miser, through all the diagnoses of usury and beneficence, we can trace the fluctuations of human passions and the assertion of human character in their most vital development. Accordingly, it is impossible to over-estimate the value of wisdom, integrity, and kindness, in pecuniary affairs. A high example in this regard is of boundless practical worth; and there is no social interest so universal and significant as that which relates to the acquisition, distribution, and maintenance of wealth. The morals and science of finance, rightly understood, embrace the principles of all ethics.

The "unfortunate compliances" which marred the unity of his political life; the indifference that settles on the public mind in regard to a fallen minister; the bitterness of partisan hostility, and the capricious alienation of popular favor, were all forgotten in tearful and affectionate memories, when, on the night of the 26th of May, 1843, it was announced in Paris that Lafitte was no more. He died as he had lived, amid noble and generous thoughts, affectionate ministrations, calm resolutions, and holy sentiments. The immense procession that followed to

Père la Chaise, and the sad group of brilliant statesmen, authors, and military officers, of poor and grateful recipients of his bounty, of loyal citizens and intimate friends, that saw his remains deposited in the tomb prepared for them, between those of Foy and Manuel, evidenced the ultimate appreciation of his character, which became more eloquently manifest in the tributes which Arago and the leading public men of the day spontaneously offered to his memory.

THE ACTOR.

EDMUND KEAN.

THE great moral trait in Kean was a certain spirit, tenacity of purpose, and lofty confidence in himself, which differed widely from presumption or conceit—a kind of instinctive faith, that no force of circumstances or prescription ever quenched. This quality, more easily felt than described, seems the prerogative of genius in all departments of life, and is often the only explicable inspiration that sustains it amid discomfiture and privation. It runs, like a thread of gold, through the dark and tangled web of Kean's career; lends something of dignity to the most abject moment of his life, and redeems from absolute degradation his moments of most entire self-abandonment. Thus, when an obscure and provincial actor, performing Alexander the Great, he replied indignantly to the sarcasm of an auditor in the stage-box, who called him Alexander the Little, "Yes, sir, with a great soul!"—and exultingly told his wife, after his first great success in London, in reply to her anxious inquiry what Lord Essex thought of him, "D—n Lord Essex; the pit rose to me!" He felt that the appeal of genius was universal, and that which stirred in his blood demanded the response of humanity. This consciousness of natural gifts made him spurn the least encroachment upon his self-respect, however poverty weighed him down, and long before fame justified to the world his claims. He rushed forever away from the house of his earliest protector, because of a careless remark of one of the company that disavowed his equality with the children of the family. Whenever an inferior part was allotted him, he fled to avoid the compromise of his feelings; and, after his triumph was achieved, poured a bowl of punch over the stage-manager's head at Drury Lane, to punish his impertinent criticisms at the first rehearsal. The same proud independence led him to avoid the social honors of rank. He liked professional and literary men because he thought they truly relished and understood his art. The restraints, the cold uniformity, and the absence of vivid interest, in the circles of the nobility, either oppressed or irritated him; and he chafed until free to give vent to his humor, passion, and convivial tastes, among boon companions.

A fine audacity, and that abhorrence of the conventional we find in hunters, poets, and artists, — the instinctive self-assertion of a nature assured that its own resources are its best and only reliable means of success and enjoyment,— thus underlaid Kean's wayward and extravagant moods; and, while it essentially interfered with his popularity as a man, it was a primary cause of his triumph as an actor; for no histrionic genius more clearly owed his success to the will. In this regard he was a species of Alfieri. The style he adopted, the method he pursued, and the aim he cherished, were neither understood nor encouraged, until their own intrinsic and overwhelming superiority won both the critics and the multitude. The taste in England had been formed by Kemble and his school; dignity, correctness, grave emphasis, and highly-finished elocution, had become the standard characteristics. Kean was a bold innovator upon this system; he trusted to nature more than to art, or rather endeavored to fuse the two. Thus, while carefully giving the very shades of meaning to the words of Shakspeare, he endeavored to personify the character, not according to an eloquent ideal, but with human reality, as if the very life-blood of Othello and Lear, their temperaments as well as their experience, had been vitally transferred to his frame and brain. He seemed possessed with the character he represented; and, throwing mere technical rules to the winds, identified himself through passional sympathy, regulated by studious contemplation, with the idiosyncrasies of those whose very natures and being he aspired to embody and develop.

Kean obeyed the instinct of genius, when, in opposition to the management at Drury Lane, arranging his débût, he exclaimed, "Shylock or nothing!" In that part there was scope for his intellectual energy, opportunity to give those magical shades of intensity, and throw into those dark, acute features the infinite power of expression for which he was distinguished. A few weeks before that memorable evening, his first-born son had died in a provincial town, and in all the agony of his bereavement he had been obliged to act, to gain money to defray the funeral expenses. Thence he had gone up to town, and, owing to a misunderstanding of the contract, for months endured the pressure of actual want, and the heart-sickness of hope deferred. The season was unpropitious; his spirits and energy were depressed by fasting, affliction, and neglect. While he was at rehearsal, his wife sold one of her few remaining articles of apparel to obtain him a dinner, fortified by which he trudged through the snow to the theatre. The series of triumphs succeeding this memorable night are well known. The overpowering reality of his personation gave Lord Byron a convulsive fit, caused an actress to faint on the stage, and an old comedian to weep, replenished the treasury of Drury Lane, electrified the United Kingdom, ushered in a new theatrical era, and crowned him with sudden prosperity and fame. His star, however, set in clouds. His last appearance in London was as melancholy as his first was brilliant. Alienated from his family, the victim of excess, — proud, sensitive, and turbulent, — his domestic troubles were only reconciled just before his death, which came as a relief to himself and those with whom he was connected.

While the histrionic achievements of Kean identify his name with the progress of dramatic art, his actual life and habits pertain rather to a sphere without the limits of civilization. A wild vein belonged to his very nature, and seemed indicative of gypsy or savage blood. It gleamed sometimes from his extraordinary eyes, when acting, so as to appal, startle, and impress, every class of observers. A man once cried out in the pit at the demoniacal glare of his optics, as Shylock meditating revenge on his creditor, "It is the devil!" His poet-biographer compares him to the van-winged hero of Paradise Lost; and West, the painter, declared he had never been so haunted by the look of a human face as by that of Kean. Something of this peculiar trait also exhibited itself in his action and tones, and made his audience thrill with the fierce energy of his soul. But while it thus subserved the purposes of art, and was, in fact, an element of his genius, it infected his private life with a reckless and half-maniacal extravagance, that was fostered by his addiction to stimulants, an unprotected infancy, and the precarious and baffled tenor of his youth and early manhood.

When we bring home to ourselves this erratic behavior, combined with extreme vicissitudes of fortune, the career of Kean, as a man, seems almost as remarkable as it was as an actor. A stage-Cupid at two years of age, a circus-rider and harlequin, then an infant prodigy reciting Rolla; his very origin disputed; now the slave of a capricious, ignorant, and selfish woman; and now the wayward protégé of a benevolent lady; arranging Mother Goose for one manager, and taking the part of a supernumerary for another; reduced to such poverty as to travel on foot, his wife trudging wearily at his side, and his boy clinging to his back; at one time swimming a river with his theatrical wardrobe in a bundle held by the teeth, and, at another, for whole days half famished, and his wife praying at her lonely vigils for a speedy release by death from hopeless suffering; to-day dancing attendance, for the hundredth time, at Drury Lane, to gain the ear of the director, and known among the bystanders only as "the little man with the capes;" and to-morrow the idol of the town, his dressing-room besieged by lords, — few chronicles in real life display more vivid and sudden contrasts than the life of Kean. The mercurial temper that belonged to him was liable, at any moment, to be excited by drink, sympathy, an idea, or an incident. One night it induced him to disturb the quiet household where he lodged by jumping through a glass door; another, to seize the heads of the leaders attached to his majesty's mail-coach, and attempt a wrestling-match. In Dublin, it winged his flight for hours through the dusky streets, with a mob of screaming constables at his heels. It inspired him to engage in midnight races on horseback. In more quiet manifestations, it induced him to make a pet of a lion, and a sacred relic of the finger-bone of Cook; and prompted him, to his wife's extreme annoyance, to retire to bed in the costume of a monkey. At one time it led him to muse for hours in a churchyard; and, at another, to try a country-life on his estate at Bute, or haunt the "Red Lion" and the "Coal-Hole." In England it made him a volunteer jockey at a race; in Italy, a fascinating story-teller and mimic to the monks of road-side convents; and in America, caused him to be duly inaugurated chief of a tribe of Indians.

There is no actor of whom such instances of arrogance toward the public and individuals are related; but it is to be observed that they generally originated in exasperated feeling, caused by undeserved neglect or gross misappreciation; and charity will ever make allowance for the inevitable results of an incongruous and homeless childhood. Kean's father nearly ruined his son's physique by employing him, at a tender age, to figure in pantomime; timely surgical aid having only saved his limbs from utter deformity. The redeeming influences of his early years were the benevolent intervention of Dr. Drury, who, recognizing his promise, sent him to Eton; and the patient teachings of Miss Tidswell, an actress of Drury Lane. That he was born with a genius for the stage is evinced by the fact that at the age of thirteen his Cato and Hamlet satisfied provincial audiences; and his recitation of Satan's Address to the Sun, from Paradise Lost, won royal approbation at Windsor. His talent for feigning served him occasionally more practical benefit than that derived from its entertaining quality; as, when he was released from a rash engagement on board ship as cabin-boy, for pretended deafness, and escaped the indignation of a London audience, he wantonly disappointed, by a well-acted dislocation of the shoulder.

If Kean's early circumstances were adverse to his moral, they were, in many respects, highly favorable to his professional development. The long apprenticeship he served to the stage, embracing every grade of character, and almost all functions of a player, made him thoroughly at home on the boards, and induced much of his ease, tact, and facility; his circus experiences and habits of active life gave both vigor and suppleness to his frame; while the vagrant career he led brought him in view of all kinds of character and phases of life, by which he observantly profited to a degree that only those intimate with him fully realized. While in this country his genius excited the intelligent admiration, and his recklessness the benevolent care, of a professional gentleman, Dr. J. W. Francis, who became his constant associate and friend. From him I learn the versatility of Kean's accomplishments was quite as remarkable as the intensity of his acting and the extravagance of his moods. He would often enchain an intellectual circle, at a fashionable party, by his exquisite vocalism, —the effect of which was inexplicable to those who listened to his limited and unmusical voice,— or by the rich anecdotes or shrewd comments of his table-talk; and, when released from this to him intolerable social thraldom, work off the nervous reäction, induced by so many hours of restraint, by throwing half-a-dozen summersets with the celerity and grace of a practised harlequin. He was, indeed, a compact embodiment of muscles and nerves; his agility and strength were such that his frame instantly obeyed his will, from the bound of a gladiator to the expressive restlessness of quivering fingers. His voice ranged through every note and cadence of power and sensibility; now by a whisper of tenderness bringing tears from callous men, and the next moment chilling their very hearts with the fierce tones of an imprecation. But these remarkable physical endowments would have merely subserved the narrow purposes of the athlete or the mimic, had they not been united to a mind of extraordinary sagacity and a face of unequalled expression; by virtue of these he rendered them the instruments of efficient art. The professors at Edinburgh were disappointed, after seeing him perform and hearing him converse, to find that he had no original theory of elocution to broach, and no striking principles of oratory to advocate. His touches were a composite and individual result, no more to be formally imparted than the glow of poetry or the zest of wit; they grew out of profound observation fused into a practical issue by the inspiration of genius.

Coleridge said that to see Kean act was like reading Shakspeare by lightning. The spell of his penetrating eyes and half-Jewish physiognomy was not more individual than his style of personation; and the attempt to transfer some of his points to another has almost invariably produced an incongruous effect. His excitable temperament was another secret of his magnetism and his foibles. While it enabled him wonderfully to engage the sympathies of an audience, it rendered him liable to be overcome by the least moral or physical excitement, and made him the slave of impulse. Regularly, in New York, every afternoon, he seized the copy of an evening journal inimical to him, with the tongs, rang for a waiter, and sent it away in this manner; while, at the same time, he scrupulously laid aside a guinea a week, during the whole of his sojourn, to reward the faithful services of a poor servant. Often drawn by his kind guardian from a haunt of debauchery, just in time to appear on the stage, he would, at others, attire himself like a finished gentleman, mix in the most refined society, and manifest a noble scorn of money, and an absolute reverence for mental superiority, that excited involuntary respect. Kean, the dissolute man, the inebriated boon companion, quoting Latin, the generous and loyal friend, the funny mimic, and the great impersonator of Shakspeare, seemed like so many different beings, with something identical in the eyes, voice, and stature. And as marvellous a disparity marked his fortunes; it being scarcely credible that the same man, whose appearance brought a solitary sixpence to the Dumfries theatre, is he who, glittering with the ornaments of Garrick, filled Drury Lane to suffocation for entire seasons; or that the luxurious apartments, crowded with men of note, are tenanted by him whose wife for years kept vigils of penury. It is creditable to Kean's magnanimity, under these bewildering transitions, that he never played the tyrant; that he was uniformly kind to poor and inferior actors, and manifested a spirit above envy. After seeing old Garcia perform Othello in New York, he sent him a costly gift in token of his admiration; he candidly acknowledged the superiority of Talma, and labored, with genuine zeal, to commemorate the histrionic fame of Cooke.

It is common to speak of great acting or vocalism as indescribable; and, to a certain extent, this is doubtless true; but distinctness of style is characteristic of genius in all things, and an intellectual observer can adequately report even the evanescent charms of dramatic personation when harmoniously conceived and efficiently embodied. Accordingly, we derive, from the criticisms and reminiscences of Kean's intelligent admirers, a very clear idea of his general merits. It is obvious that these consisted of simplicity and earnestness; that, endowed with fiery passions and a sagacious intellect, he boldly undertook to represent Shakspeare, not according to any prescriptive model or rules of art, but through his individual reflection and sympathy. Like the great master of the written drama, he followed closely the intimations of nature; cast, as it were, self-consciousness away, and assimilated the actual elements of human life with his own action and expression. Hence, the truth of his violent contrasts — the light and shade of art. Hence, the frequency and effect of his brief, suggestive, and thrilling exclamations, that made a single word or interjection reveal infinite woe, joy, surprise, or madness. It is for the same reason that, upon refined minds and earnest hearts, his acting unfolded ever new beauty and truth, as described by Dana, upon reading whose criticism Kean exclaimed, "This man understands me." By this firm, and, if we may so say, subtle yet instinctive adherence to nature, a certain grandeur and effect, only yielded her genuine votaries, seemed to invest and glorify the actor, so that his most incidental attitudes and by-play wore a reality undiscoverable in the most elaborate efforts of inferior performers. To the same principle we ascribe his versatility. Each character was a distinct study. Where his consciousness was at fault in suggesting the most authentic manner, tone, or expression, he had recourse to observation; he reflected deeply, and appeared to identify himself, by the process, with the being he was to enact, until his very soul became imbued with the melancholy of Hamlet, the insanity of Lear, and the mental agony of Othello.

THE YOUTHFUL HERO.

THEODORE KÖRNER.

On the high road near the village of Wobbelin there stands, beneath an oak, the Iron Monument of Theodore Körner. The material of which it is constructed, the simplicity of its design, the tree which overshadows it, and its isolated yet accessible position, would naturally induce an observant traveller to examine and a contemplative one to muse beside it; but how infinitely is the casual interest, thus awakened, enhanced when we recall the brief but thrilling history of him in whose remembrance it was erected, and realize how entirely the lineaments of his character accord with the solemn beauty of his grave! There is often as much room for conjecture in regard to the absolute endowments of the hero as of the poet; the fame of both is only settled by time; posterity not unfrequently reverses the original decree; and the frank soldier and candid bard sometimes dispel the charming illusions they have originated, by admitting certain facts of consciousness. Thus courage and inspiration are as fallacious, when judged by mere appearance, as more superficial qualities; accident, luck, animal excitement, vanity, and desperation, may be the only claim of the so-called hero to the title; and imitation, art, and tact, form the sole attributes of him whom the world of to-day denominates a poet. It is rare, indeed, for these noblest of human distinctions to be thoroughly vindicated by the same individual during his life; for genuine poetic gifts to be illustrated by their sensible effects upon the popular mind, and genuine heroism to be indicated clearly in the expressed purpose, the thoughtful resolve, and then realized by entire self-devotion and voluntary martyrdom. Such a course seems to include all the elements of the heroic character, and leave not the faint shadow of a doubt of a grand moral reality.

There is a courage of temperament which man shares with the inferior animals; that which leads the stag to stand at bay, the steed to rush into battle, and the mastiff and game-cock to lose the sense of safety in the vindictiveness of a contest. There is a courage of the imagination born of visions of glory, the zest of adventure, and the love of excitement; and there is a courage of the will, the calm resolve of valor inspired by patriotism or duty, and thoughtfully adopted after mature reflection. In proportion to the danger incurred, the personal advantage relinquished, and the consistency of its aim, is this latter species of courage to be estimated. It is this which essentially constitutes the hero; it is an element of character, not an impulse of feeling; it is the product of the soul, not of mere physical superiority; and exalts humanity by intensifying her active powers with the concentration of intelligent moral purpose.

Theodore Körner thus more completely realized this ideal of the youthful hero than any character of modern times; or rather left behind him the most authentic evidence and beautiful memorials of its reality. For, without reference to the mere facts of his life, we have the two most impressive revelations of his nature — the written thought and the noble achievement; the sentiment calmly yet earnestly expressed, and its practical embodiment; the motive and the deed to attest the hero; feeling shaping itself into deliberate action. We have successively the man, the poet, the soldier, and the martyr; and it is this unity of development that renders Körner's career almost unique. That the views he adopted were not the offspring of a heated imagination; that the sentiments he professed arose from a deeper source than the hot blood of youth; that he was perfectly conscious of all he risked, and quite aware of the sacrifice he offered, is apparent from his literary productions, his conversations, letters, and consistent behavior. His education was singularly adapted to develop, at once, mental energy and the gentlest affections; it encouraged physical strength and aptitude, and the highest moral aspiration; and hence he was capable of estimating for himself both the claims of duty and the charms of pleasure. The very atmosphere of his childhood was intellectual; his father, although ostensibly devoted to jurisprudence, was a man of the warmest literary sympathies and the highest culture: while his mother was the daughter of an artist. Schiller and Goëthe were their intimate friends. The former wrote Don Carlos in the elder Körner's house; and not the least pleasing chapters in the lives of both authors are those which record anecdotes of this early intercourse, and the correspondence to which it led.

Young Körner's first recollections are associated with the cottage in a vineyard, endeared to the three illustrious friends. His infancy was feeble, and he was, therefore, encouraged to practise manly exercises, in which he soon became an adept, having few equals among his companions in fencing and swimming. He was a most graceful equestrian and dancer, and excelled in gymnastic feats. To this admirable physical training, so essential to the martial hero, were added the accomplishments of musician and draughtsman. This early instruction was derived altogether from private tuition. Habitual exposure to the open air, and the influence of nature as well as the highest social intercourse, combined to invigorate and refine the capabilities of his soul. But judicious and comprehensive as was his education, it only accounts in part for the noble bias of his character. He very soon manifested the most decided tastes and aims, and the instinctive, far more than the acquired, moulded his destiny. Strength of mind and firmness of purpose, tenderness of heart and loyal attachments, soon gave promise of a characteristic life; while an appreciation of science and a facility of versification were equally obvious mental distinctions — the one giving vent to his enthusiasm and sentiment, and the other discipline and scope to his intellect.

Doubtless this need of an active life on the one hand, and mental exercise on the other, induced his first choice of a profession, which was that of mining; and his mineralogical and chemical studies were followed under Werner, at Freyburg, where Humboldt first entered upon his illustrious career. At home the companionship of his sister and her friends called out his gentle sympathies and delicate tastes, while that of his father's literary coteries elicited his noblest intelligence; summer excursions made him familiar with the most beautiful scenery of his country; and thus we have, as it were, a complete, though informal system of life, amply fitted to educate a poet and hero. It is remarkable that singular vivacity of temperament and facility of adaptation alternated, under these influences, with a solemn earnestness of character. In his boyhood and first youth Körner was lively, but never frivolous; he engaged with similar alacrity in the most sportive and most severe occupations; soon became a social favorite, and yet retained the nature of a contemplative enthusiast. His dislike of the French, the profound melancholy induced by the loss of an intimate friend, who was drowned, and a quick sense of honor, are traits vividly remembered by his earliest associates.

His first religious pieces seem to have been inspired during a foot excursion amid the scenery of Silesia. At the Berlin academy, whither he was sent after some years of varied teaching at home, Körner was engaged in a duel; and the impetuosity of his nature, combined with the strongest poetical tendencies, led his father to assent to his removing to Vienna, where he was cordially received by William Humboldt and Schlegel. His rashness of spirit having become subdued by a protracted fever, and his domestic sympathies revived by a pleasant sojourn with his family at Carlsbad, he exchanged college for metropolitan life, in a state of mind peculiarly fitted to render it both useful and happy. His cheerful temper, fine personal appearance, poetical reputation, and good birth, gave him every advantage at the outset of his brief yet brilliant career at the capital; but these only served him as the initiative steps of fame; and, after supporting himself for some months by means of his scientific attainments, he began to write for the stage. He was not less fortunate in the kind of discipline to which his boyhood was subjected. This was voluntary. He was never thwarted; his reason, his honor, and his tastes, were appealed to, and his will thus conciliated. To the absence of fear in youth we ascribe the manly freedom of his nature. The only authority claimed over him was that of love. His parents were companions not less than guides; they respected his idiosyncrasies, and only sought to keep him in true relations with nature, humanity, and God. Hence his faults were always those of excess, never of calculation; he was sometimes rash, but knew not a mean instinct; and the freshness and energy of his soul were preserved intact. Education only ripened and called out original endowments.

The spirit of enjoyment is more active at Vienna than in any city of Germany. If its libraries, museums, and galleries of art, give it intellectual character, its Prater, thronged with recreating groups, including every class, from the emperor to the humblest citizen, and boasting the richest *corso* in Europe, the prevalence of music as a pastime, the number of theatres, and the social taste of the people, render Vienna the centre of genial and varied life; while the devotees of art or letters often pursue their respective objects at Leipsic or Frankfort with isolated enthusiasm and earnest individuality, the tendency of the social atmosphere and prosperous activity at Vienna is to make the artist or man of letters an efficient and sympathetic intelligence, inspired by and giving impulse to the circles of fashion, taste, and conviviality. There lived Haydn, Mozart, and Beethoven; and, if their deeper revelations were born in the solitude of their own consciousness and the intensity of thoughtful emotion, doubtless the zest of life and the human interest around them yielded some of the mystic threads which link their harmonies to the universal heart. Into this enjoyable sphere Körner brought not only his own rare endowments of mind and character, but the *prestige* of good conversation and attractive manners. To feel the high and pleasurable excitement of writing successfully for the stage at this period, and in such a metropolis as Vienna, we must remember that the theatre was the central point of interest to all classes, the theme of enlightened criticism, the object of tasteful appreciation. Those who illustrated its power, in any department, with real genius, were sure, not only of professional rewards, but of social estimation. The theatre was peculiarly a national institution, and a fashionable and literary nucleus endeared by habit, association, and sympathy, to the most cultivated and respected, as well as the pleasure-loving citizens. The seeds of thought and sentiment in the mind of young Körner seemed to flower, all at once, in the encouraging sphere, and amid the inviting intercourse here opened to him.

His first efforts were light two-act pieces written in Alexandrines, of which the "Bride" and the "Green Domino" had such success that he began soon to meditate a more elaborate and finished production. At this era his time passed in a delightful alternation of study and society; idolized in the latter, he brought to the former all the ardent and noble feeling and facility of expression which characterized his nature; and while the one elicited his sportive and companionable graces, the other gave impulse to the more intense and thoughtful moods of his soul. An immediate and intelligent appreciation, like that which awaits the successful dramatic author in Germany, and the social privileges and sympathy awarded him in Vienna, naturally excited the enthusiasm of Körner, and, when he was appointed poet to the theatre, his fortune and position were truly eminent; but ambition was only a secondary inspiration, for two sentiments glowed in his heart, and gave the utmost eloquence to his expression. He was a genuine patriot and lover; and at this brilliant epoch, the companionship of his betrothed, the ardent devotion of his friends, and the new-born spirit of liberty that stirred the breasts of his countrymen, all united to quicken and evoke his genius. Time has proved that its most legitimate offspring was lyrical poetry. The directness, harmony, and spontaneous origin, of this kind of verse, accorded with the frank earnestness of his character, and more faithfully mirrored his inward life than the elaborate and studied drama. Yet one remarkable triumph in the latter style he soon achieved.

The tragedy of Zriny, whatever may be its imperfections as a work of art, is memorable as the composition of a youth, and as the deliberate record of his most profound sentiments. The period of this play is 1566, and the action is first at Belgrade, and then in and before the Hungarian fortress of Sigeth, which is heroically defended by Nicholas Von Irving, against Soliman. Lorenzo Juranitsch, the former's lieutenant, is the betrothed of his daughter, whose character, as well as that of her mother, are delineated with a grace and truth worthy of a poet's discriminating estimate of woman. The character of Lorenzo Juranitsch is doubtless Körner's own ideal; and the plot of the drama, in a striking manner, typifies his destiny. Indeed, the most emphatic passages of the tragedy are identical with the views, feelings, and purposes, he cherished, as uttered in familiar conversation and letters. In a literary point of view, the distinct characterization, the fine contrast between the oriental scenes and those in the Hungarian fortress, the powerful and consistent tone of self-devotion maintained by Zriny and his followers, the intense coëxistence of love and duty, are traits so happily manifest as to have seized at once on the popular feeling.

The play may be justly considered as an exposition of heroism, and what gives it a permanent interest is the fact that it embodies the habitual state of mind, foreshadows the sacrifice and glows with the very soul of the author. It also not inadequately represents the prevalent sentiment of Germany at the period. The flames of Moscow had kindled the dormant valor of northern Europe; deep indignation against her conqueror now found vent in action, and the love of country was thoroughly awakened; a spirit of self-consecration and a holy as well as martial zeal, such as the poet so well describes as nerving the Hungarian patriots of the tragedy, pervaded all hearts; so that "Zriny" may be regarded as vividly reflecting, not only the individual consciousness of the poet, but the public sentiment of his country. An impressive proof of the harmony between Körner's expressed and acted sentiments, between his character and writings, is the coincidence in tone and feeling of the letter he addressed his father after his valorous resolve, and some expressions that fall from the chief actors in "Zriny:"

"I would depart but as a hero should,
In the full splendor of my boldest love."

"What is there for us higher in this world
That 's left untasted in our hallowed wishes?
Can life afford a moment of more bliss?
Here happiness is transient as the day,
On high eternal as the love of God."

"For as with other slaves 't is nature's law,
The vital air is the demand of life,
So, maiden, is his honor to a man."

"For nothing is too precious for our country."

"Rash! nay, I am not so —
Yet am I venturous and bold for love,
And all enthusiast for my fatherland."

"That I devote myself to death were little —
My life I oft have ventured in the hazard;
But that I do so, 'mid such joy and pleasure,
'Mid happiness and highest earthly bliss,
This is the struggle, this deserves the prize —
My country may be proud of such an offering."

"I will clasp
The form of death with arms of youthful love,
And bravely press it to my youthful breast."

"For fate may shatter the heroic breast,
But it can awe not the heroic will;
The worm may creep, ignobly, to its rest, —
The noble mind must fight and triumph still."

"O, do not harshly chide with fate, my daughter,
But rather trust its kind paternal favor,
Which hath permitted us by this ordeal
To prove, like gold, our purity of heart."

"VIENNA, March 10, 1813.

"DEAREST FATHER:

"I write to you respecting an event which I feel assured will neither surprise nor shock you. I lately gave you a hint of my purpose, which has now arrived at maturity. Germany rises; the Prussian eagle, by the beating of her mighty wings, awakes in all true hearts the great hope of German freedom. My poetic art sympathizes for my country; let me prove myself her worthy son! Yes, dearest father, I will join the army, will cheerfully throw aside the happy, joyous life which I have here enjoyed, in order with my blood to assist in the deliverance of my country. Call it not impetuosity, levity, rashness. Two years since, it is true, I should have termed it thus myself; but now that I know what happiness can ripen for me in this life; now that the star of fortune sheds on me its most cheering influence; now is it, by

Heaven, a sacred feeling which inspires me, a conviction that no sacrifice can be too great to insure our country's freedom. Possibly your fond paternal heart may say, 'Theodore is meant for better things; in another field he might have accomplished objects more worthy and important; he owes as yet a weighty obligation to mankind.' But, father, my conviction is, that for the death-offering for the freedom and honor of our country no one is too good, though many are too base. If the Almighty have, indeed, inspired me with a more than common mind, which has been taught and formed by thy care and affection, where is the moment when I can better exert it than now? A great age requires great souls, and I feel that I may prove a rock amid this concussion of the nations. I must forth and oppose my daring breast to the waves of the storm.

"Shall I be content to celebrate in poetry the success of my brethren while they fight and conquer? Shall I write entertainments for the comic theatre, when I feel within me the courage and the strength to take part in the great and serious drama of life? I am aware that you will suffer much; my mother too will weep! May God be her comfort; I cannot spare you this trial. I have ever deemed myself the favorite of Fortune; she will not forsake me now. That I simply venture my life, is but of little import; but that I offer it, crowned as it is with all the flowery wreaths of love, of friendship, — that I cast away the sweet sensation which lived in the conviction that I should never cause you inquietude or sorrow,— this is, indeed, a sacrifice which can only be opposed to such a prize — our country's freedom. Either on Saturday or Monday I depart, probably accompanied by friends, or possibly H. may despatch me as a courier. At Breslau, my place of destination, I meet the free sons of Prussia, who have enthusiastically collected there, under the banner of their king. I have scarcely decided, as yet, whether I join the cavalry or infantry; this may depend upon the sum of money which may be at my disposal. As to my present appointment here, I know, as yet, nothing certain; possibly the prince will give me leave of absence; if not, there is no seniority in art, and should I return to Vienna, I have the assurance of Count Palfy that still greater advantages of a pecuniary nature await. Antonia has, on this occasion, proved the great, the noble character of her soul. She weeps, it is true, but the termination of the campaign will dry her tears. My mother must forgive me the tears I cause her; whoever loves me will not censure me; and you, father, will find me worthy of you.

"THY THEODORE."

At the very outset of their march, after joining his regiment, they bivouacked in a graveyard; one of the mounds was his pillow, and over another his horse stumbled, and it was regarded by the superstitious observers as ominous. When his sister, who was possessed of much artistic skill, and whose grief for his loss wore away her life, was painting his likeness, she suddenly wept, declaring that she saw his head bleeding. He wrote to a friend on the eve of his departure, "If I shall never again be in Meadows, perhaps I shall soon be on the green, and quite peaceful, quite still!" Indeed, even the most thoughtless of the students who, with all the ardor of youth, threw themselves into the impending struggle, were aware of the truth of Körner's declaration, "Every second man of us must die." With him this self-devotion was no sudden fit of martial enthusiasm, but the cherished purpose of years; many allusions in his letters and familiar talk afterwards became clear to his friends. He had felt deeply the misfortunes of his country, and pondered on the duty of a citizen, until it was his firm resolve to embrace the first occasion to fight, and, if needful, to die for his native land. The summons came when the goblet of life sparkled to the brim, when his mind and heart, his affections and his intellect, were thoroughly and genially absorbed; yet he hesitated not a moment, but enrolled himself in Lutzow's corps.

Few episodes in literary history, or rather in the biography of genius, have a more complete and harmonious moral beauty than the whole life of Theodore Körner. There is no wonderful precocity suddenly eclipsed by decay; no *finale* of insanity turning the sweetest melody into horrible discord; no sad compromise between the dreams of youth and the calculations of interest; all is sustained, noble, and consistent; — a childhood enriched with high acquisitions and refined by domestic love; —

a youth developed with freedom in an atmosphere of truth; genuine relations with nature and humanity; cheerfulness, intelligence, fortitude, and self-devotion; a unity of being that presents a remarkable contrast to the fragmentary, baffled, and too often incongruous experience of the gifted and the brave. It is affecting, and, at the same time, sublime to recall the happy life of the young poet at Vienna, environed by the delights of social and literary fame, the cordialities of hospitality, the consolations of friendship, the sweet communion of love, and then behold it suddenly yet calmly exchanged for hardship, peril, and death. Amid the pleasurable excitements of the gay capital, instead of being enervated, he was nerved.

It was his custom to retire to the neighboring village of Döblinger to write. "I always work in the garden," he says, "where I am now writing this letter. A thicket of chestnut trees spreads its cooling shade around me, and my guitar, which hangs behind me on the next tree, employs me in those moments when I cease to write." Antonia, his betrothed, appears to have united the most charming domestic feelings with that heroic spirit that endeared her to her lover. He used to visit her after his morning's labor, quit her presence to dine with Humboldt, or some other genial *savan*, pass the evening either at a party or the theatre, and return home to prosecute his literary task, his correspondence, or his studies. Love and art exclusively reigned in his soul. Yet, in accordance with that law by which the reäction of enthusiasm is inevitably melancholy, Körner often turned from the external sunshine of his lot to realize a gloom within. He had a distinct presentiment of early death, although with characteristic heroism it seldom found other than playful expression. When he was digging the foundation of a temporary hut, his comrades said to him, "You dig like a grave-digger;" and he replied, "We ought to practise the trade, for we shall doubtless have to render, each for the other, that labor of love."

These noble volunteers, comprising the flower of the German youth, were consecrated to the high office they had espoused, at the village church of Breslau; and the muse of their gallant comrade gave utterance to their religious zeal as well as to their patriotic sentiment. The popularity and influence of his martial songs had already endeared his name, not only to this chosen band, but to all his brave countrymen. At leisure intervals he wrote other lyrics suggested by the exigencies or feelings of the moment, and selected appropriate melodies that soon winged them, like seeds of valor, throughout the land. He made a final visit to his family at Dresden, before the regiment departed; and we next hear of him thus anticipating a premature death, after the battle of Darmeburg:

"FAREWELL TO LIFE.

WRITTEN IN THE NIGHT OF THE SEVENTEENTH AND EIGHTEENTH OF JUNE, AS I LAY SEVERELY WOUNDED AND HELPLESS IN A WOOD, EXPECTING TO DIE.

My deep wound burns — my pale lips quake in death —
I feel my fainting heart resign its strife,
And reaching now the limit of my life,
Lord, to thy will I yield my parting breath.

Yet many a dream hath charmed my youthful eye:
And must life's fairy visions all depart?
O, surely, no! for all that fired my heart
To rapture here shall live with me on high.

And that fair form that won my earliest vow,
That my young spirit prized all else above,
And now adored as freedom, now as love,
Stands in seraphic guise before me now;

And, as my fading senses fade away,
It beckons me, on high, to realms of endless day!"

Few heroic lyrics exhibit a more genuine spirit than the "Sword Song," and "Lützow's Wild Chase." The former was written on the eve of the engagement in which he fell. He was sending it to a friend, when the signal of attack was made, and it was found in his pocket-book after his death. The tirailleurs of the enemy fired from a dense grove; a ball, passing through the neck of his horse, entered Körner's spine, and he instantly expired. So immediate was the cessation of life, that the expression of his countenance remained unchanged when the body was carried off the field. One of his heart-stricken friends cried, "Let us follow Körner!" and they rushed upon the ambushed enemy with desperate valor. Adored by his companions in arms for his delightful social qualities, as well as for his transcendent gifts and peerless courage, with silent grief they dug his grave beneath a majestic oak by the road-side, and carved his name on its trunk. With this noble tree the memory of Körner is indissolubly associated; as indigenous to, and characteristic of, his country, it possessed for him a singular charm; and, in the luxuriance of its summer foliage, shaken off so bravely to meet the winter gale, it is an apt symbol of the young hero cheerfully throwing aside the prosperous crown that decked his brow, to war for liberty. One of his pieces derives a melancholy interest from the subject, that deepens its intrinsic pathos:

"THE OAKS.

'Tis evening — all is hushed and still;
  The sun sets bright in ruddy sheen;
As here I sit, to muse at will
  Beneath these oaks' unbrageous screen;
While wandering thoughts my fancy fill
  With dreams of life when fresh and green,
And visions of the olden time
Revive in all their pomp sublime.

While time hath called the brave away,
  And swept the lovely to the tomb;
As yonder bright but fading ray
  Is quenched amid the twilight gloom —
Yet ye are kept from all decay,
  For still unhurt and fresh ye bloom,
And seem to tell, in whispering breath,
That greatness still survives in death!

And ye survive! — 'mid change severe,
  Each aged stem but stronger grows,
And not a pilgrim passes here,
  But seeks beneath your shade repose.
And if your leaves, when dry and sere,
  Fall fast at autumn's wintry close,
Yet every falling leaf shall bring
Its vernal tribute to the spring.

Thou native oak, thou German tree,
  Fit emblem, too, of German worth!
Type of a nation brave and free,
  And worthy of their native earth!

Ah! what avails to think on thee,
  Or on the times when thou hadst birth?
Thou German race, the noblest aye of all,
Thine oaks still stand, while thou, alas! must fall!"

The mineralogical excursions and hardy exercises of Körner proved an admirable initiation to military service; and habits of activity and method soon made him thoroughly efficient in his new vocation. It is remarkable that his was the first blood shed after joining the corps; having been sent with a flag of truce, in violation of the armistice, he received a wound without drawing his sabre; and it is also worthy of notice, as illustrating the horrors of war, that he fell, as has been subsequently discovered, by the shot of one of his own countrymen in the enemy's ranks. How beautiful, in the retrospect, is the short, but illustrious career we have thus imperfectly traced; how truly deed responded to thought, and experience to sentiment, in Körner's life! Generous and devoted feelings exalted him above the bitterness of disappointment; his days were occupied with acts of high utility, and his nights in lofty contemplation.

He used to steal away from the bivouac to the forest, to think of those he loved; and, when overcome by the pleadings, tenderness, and the desire for sympathy, he sought refuge in heroic aspirations or pious thought. "If it has been denied me," he writes, "to kneel with my bride at the altar, a bride of steel has been intrusted to me, to whom I have sworn eternal truth." This calmness and resolution is the more striking when we picture Körner to our fancy, charming a select circle with his guitar, or his amateur performance of the Swedish Captain in "Wallenstein," and writing pieces for Humboldt's children; and realize his adaptation to the peaceful happiness of domestic and artist life. The total change in his pursuits and enjoyments is best revealed by his letters, varying in date but a few months. Thus at one time he writes from Vienna: "Would I could have seen you all in a box yesterday! The finest feeling is that of composition itself; next to this ranks the satisfaction of seeing one's work represented with affection and skill; the loftiest lies in the conviction that one has seized the souls of others." "I amuse myself here divinely; am always engaged a week beforehand; and, I may say, am quite the rage." And soon after, in this strain: "A great moment of my life is approaching. Be convinced you shall find me not unworthy of you when the trial comes." And again from the camp: "The corps already sing several of my songs, and I cannot describe to you how agreeable is the relation in which I live, as the most cultivated and select minds of all Germany are near me in rank and place."

The union of strength of moral purpose and sensibility of feeling in Körner's character was obvious in his appearance, and exhibits itself vividly in his poems. His dark hair shaded a brow open with truth and prominent with intelligence, but, in moments of determination, knit by a concentrated will; and his blue eye could wear a dauntless as well as a most gentle expression. Conscious of the apparent incongruity at times in his behavior, he thus naturally explains it in one of his letters: "If you, perchance, have occasionally conceived me to be deficient in warmth of heart, my external manner has deceived you. Too warm to be grave, and too proud to appear weak, I find I am often exposed to be mistaken, because it is not known why I am thus apparently severe and capricious; both of these moods being in fact only a relief to the overflow of my feelings."

Körner, fortunately, left us a faithful index of his nature in his poems. There we recognize both his heroism and his love in their elemental and spontaneous action; and two of them — one written on parting with his chosen bride, and the other embodying the religious sentiment that hallowed his patriotism — give us, as it were, a key to the apparent antagonism, but real and divine consistency, of his sentiments:

"Farewell, farewell! — with silent grief of heart
  I breathe adieu to follow duty now;
And if a silent tear unbidden start,
  It will not, love, disgrace a soldier's brow.
Where'er I roam, should joy my path illume,
Or death entwine the garland of the tomb,
Thy lovely form shall float my path above,
And guide my soul to rapture and to love!

O hail and bless, sweet spirit of my life,
  The ardent zeal that sets my soul on fire;
That bids me take a part in yonder strife,
  And for the sword a while forsake the lyre.

For, see, thy minstrel's dreams were not all vain,
Which he so oft hath hallowed in his strain;
O see the patriot-strife at length awake!
There let me fly and all its toils partake.

The victor's joyous wreath shall bloom more bright
That 's plucked amid the joys of love and song;
And my young spirit hails with pure delight
The hope fulfilled which it hath cherished long.
Let me but struggle for my country's good,
E'en though I shed for her my warm life-blood.
And now one kiss — e'en though the last it prove;
For there can be no death for our true love!"

"PRAYER DURING BATTLE.

Father, I invoke thee!
I am involvéd in clouds of vapor from the warring mouths of fire
The lightnings of those thunderbolts flash around me.
Ruler of battles, I invoke thee!
Father, lead me on.

Father, lead me on!
Conduct me to victory; conduct me to death!
Lord, I recognize thy will!
Lord, conduct me as thou wilt!
God, I acknowledge thee!

God, I acknowledge thee!
As in the autumnal whisper of the leaves,
So in the storm of the battle.
Thee, primeval fountain of grace, I recognize!
Father, O, bless me!

Father, O, bless me!
Into thy hands I commend my life!
Thou canst take it away, thou didst give it!
In living and in dying, bless me!
Father, I worship thee!

Father, I worship thee!
It is not a combat for the goods of this world;
The most sacred of things we defend with the sword;
Wherefore, falling or conquering, I worship thee!
God, to thee I resign myself!

God, to thee I resign myself!
If the thunders of death salute me,
If the blood flow from my opened veins,
To thee, my God, I resign myself!
Thee, Father, I invoke!"

Among the many epithets that may justly be given to our times, is that of the age of discrimination. Analysis is now universal; new definitions increase, and shades of meaning in character are observed and noted by the philosophic with no less care than the elements of matter by men of science; all subjects are tested either by the clever method of French nomenclature, the spiritual refinements of German thought, or the bold rhetoric and vigorous sense of the Anglo-Saxon mind. Perhaps no human trait has become so modified to common apprehension by this intellectual process as courage. It is now needful that something beyond bold adventure, impetuous warfare, or even patient endurance, should exist, in order to gain the renown of bravery. We hesitate at the action to search its motive; the temperament, intelligence, experience, and moral sensibility, of the individual are taken into account before we admit his claims to the title of hero.

Whoever has carefully read Foster's "Essay on Decision of Character," De Quincey's "Treatise on the Cæsars," and Carlyle's "Hero-Worship," — all books of the day and more or less popular,— cannot fail to discriminate somewhat between the indications of rashness and determination, ferocity and self-control, impulse and hardihood, in judging of those who occupy the foreground of history. Heroism is now regarded as a higher quality than instinct; as truly characteristic of Dante as Nelson, less questionable in Sir Thomas More than in Murat, and quite as obvious at Valley Forge as at Waterloo. With all the subtle distinctions, however, that modern enlightenment finds between real and apparent heroism, there are a few absolute principles that stamp the indisputable hero; and among these are a thorough consciousness of the hazard incurred, a voluntary self-renunciation, a deliberate purpose consistently followed, and an honest zeal based on individual sentiment. Thus intellect, will, and heart, combine to mould the hero, and inform his character with an ardor, a harmony, and a nobleness, equally removed from fanaticism on the one hand and mere hardihood on the other. Where the first development of this spirit is social and literary, and its subsequent phase action and martyrdom, the cycle of heroic life is adequately filled, its conditions realized, and its fame achieved.

Such was the case with Theodore Körner. The vivacity of his mind first exhibited itself in comic pieces, that amused the gay Viennese, and wafted the young author prosperously along the flattering tide of metropolitan success; his critics, however, attached to them little intrinsic value; but some of the minor poems scattered through the four volumes, published by his father after his death — most of them written before the age of twenty-two — are permanently enshrined in the literature of his country; they prove the sincerity of his after course; in them are manifest the fiery assailant and the poetical lover; while the more elaborate dramas of "Rosamund" and "Zriny" unfold at length the same innate vigor of the will and the affections — the one inducing fortitude, and the other tenderness. The spirit of chivalry and pathos, thus emanating from the poet, were actualized by the soldier; and this is Körner's beautiful distinction. His "Sword Song" became the Marseilles Hymn of Germany; and he bravely fought the battle of truth and liberty with the lyre and the sword — thenceforth and forever blended with his name.

THE MECHANICIAN.

ROBERT FULTON.

A CELEBRATED geographer speaks of the State of New York as an epitome or type of the whole country — representing the grand scale of its waters, the productiveness of its soil, and the picturesque beauty of its scenery. An analogous character may be recognized in the intellectual history of the state. Without the universal mental culture and the special literary development of New England, New York has given birth to men remarkable for comprehensive minds and social efficiency, such as Hamilton, Livingston, Jay, Morris, and Clinton; with whom originated liberal schemes of polity, and a great system of internal improvements. They proved wise and eloquent advocates of our national welfare; and justice refers us continually to their important services as the basis of much of our existent prosperity, freedom, and advancement. There was a scope, hospitality, and self-respect in their character, which betokened a noble race; and their names ever awaken sentiments of patriotic elation. It seems not less appropriate that a region of inland seas, with an ocean on one side and a vast extent of country on the other,— the state that links the eastern and western portions of the confederacy, and whose metropolis is the commercial port of the nation,— should have been the scene of triumph to the mechanician who first successfully applied steam to navigation, and thus supplied the grand desideratum to our physical resources and social unity. The interests of agriculture, commerce, and education, were intimately dependent on the experiment. Facility of intercourse between the island of Manhattan and the banks of her two rivers instantly enlarged her local power, while we are only now beginning to realize the political influence and new avenues of wealth incident to the same rapid and frequent communication with Europe and the Pacific. Both the results and the origin of Fulton's inventive energy are, therefore, naturally associated with New York; and the corporation of the city did but respond to a universal public sentiment when they gave his name to the thoroughfare extending through three sections of as many cities brought together by steam ferriage. The first steamboat voyage through Long Island Sound and up the Hudson, as well as the launch of the first steam-frigate, are among the memorable reminiscences upon which our elder citizens yet expatiate with enthusiasm, while the waters around now literally swarm with the improved and restless progeny of those comparatively recent achievements:

"See how yon flaming herald treads
The ridged and rolling waves,
As, clambering o'er their crested heads,
She bows her surly slaves!
With foam before, and fire behind,
She rends the clinging sea,
That flies before the roaring wind,
Beneath her hissing lee.

With dashing wheel and lifting keel,
And smoking torch on high,
When winds are loud and billows reel,
She thunders foaming by;
When seas are silent and serene,
With even beams she glides,
The sunshine glimmering through the green
That skirts her gleaming sides."

The Patent Office at Washington affords an extraordinary demonstration of the predominance of mechanical talent in the country; but it is in special and limited machines, in refinements upon old inventions, and in cleverness of detail, that this aptitude is chiefly indicated; there is more evidence of ingenuity than genius. Yet this characteristic of the American mind, which reached its acme in Franklin, is not without its higher types of development; men who unite to a taste for mechanics a compre hensive view of their utility and possible results; who have combined with a knowledge of material laws a rare sagacity in their application; and possessed both the faculty to invent and the enthusiasm and strength of moral purpose to advocate inventions of a kind essentially adapted to modify society, and advance the condition of the whole world. Such mechanicians are philosophers as well as artisans, and work in the spirit of a broad and philanthropic intelligence. They illustrate most effectively the true dignity of labor, by relieving humanity of its greatest burdens, and enlisting brain as well as muscle, and nature's mysterious agency not less than man's intelligence and hardihood.

Such a character was Robert Fulton, manifesting, through life, the ardor and pertinacity of a comprehensive enthusiast, united with the patient assiduity of a practical mechanic. Born in a secluded township in the interior of Pennsylvania, and indebted for his early instruction exclusively to a common school, it is natural that his sagacious and active mind should have embraced the sources of culture afforded by observation and thought with singular avidity. He studied in the woods, by the road-side, and in solitude, feeding his imagination by communion with nature, and his intellect with such waifs of knowledge as came in his way, and readily assimilated with his tastes; for, like all men of decided traits, Fulton seems to have been a nonconformist by instinct, and to have delighted in original ideas and individual opinion. The only means his isolated boyhood yielded for gratifying the artistic tendency of his mind was painting, into which he was initiated by a school-fellow, in a very crude and ineffective way, but sufficiently to give scope and incitement to his talent. With the facility thus acquired he removed, while a youth, to Philadelphia, and, in the course of four years, earned a sum adequate to the purchase of a farm in the interior of the state, upon which he established his widowed mother. On his return to the city, he visited some celebrated springs for his health, which had become seriously impaired by labor and exposure; and there met several intelligent gentlemen, who became so much interested in the promise and agreeable manners of the young artist, that they counselled him to hasten to London, and place himself under the teaching of his then renowned and prosperous countryman —

West. This advice he followed without delay, met with a cordial reception from the benign painter, and passed some years in his family. From London he went to Devonshire, and practised his art for a considerable period; but while there "a change came o'er the spirit of his dream." Never having greatly excelled in painting, and having a natural love of enterprise, his late social advantages had enlarged his views, and excited a deep and intelligent interest in plans of broad, practical utility. Before leaving home he had enjoyed the friendship of Franklin, who, indeed, first introduced him to West. With his mind thus quickened by the companionship of men of superior gifts and extensive ideas, while passing through the manufacturing towns of England he heard of the success of Arkwright's invention. His practical and at the same time imaginative mind took in, at a glance, the possible influence of manufactures upon human welfare, the new avenues to wealth incident to mechanical skill, and the extraordinary natural advantages of his own country as the arena of great improvements in political as well as social economy. An acquaintance formed at this period with the Earl of Stanhope and the Duke of Bridgewater — names honorably identified with recent improvements in inland navigation — tended still more to confirm Fulton's resolution to devote his energies to mechanical science. Accordingly, he began by experiments with the inclined plane as a means of canal transportation, invented a machine for sawing marble, one for spinning flax, one for making rope, another for scooping earth, and published a treatise, in 1796, on Canal Navigation. These, and other of Fulton's early labors in the new field he had chosen, were more or less recognized and honored. He obtained patents and medals, and, what was of equal importance to his future success, the confidence and sympathy of many persons of influence. It is to be regretted that the written memorials of this part of his life, when he was engaged in the study and observation upon which his subsequent career was based, were lost by shipwreck on their way to this country. In pursuance of the course he had now earnestly adopted, Fulton repaired to Paris, and there formed a life-long friendship with Joel Barlow, then our minister at the court of France, with whom he long resided. Here he was soon absorbed in experiments to perfect a scheme of submarine explosion, and sought the aid successively of the French, English, and Dutch governments, which appointed commissioners to examine the invention. In each case the report was adverse to its practical utility, yet Fulton continued to improve upon the original conception, invented a submarine boat to act in concert with the torpedo, and exhibited the greatest ingenuity and dauntless ardor in prosecuting this favorite scheme for a series of years, both at home and abroad. Already an accomplished draftsman, he made himself an efficient civil engineer while in Europe, studied physics, mathematics, and perspective, and returned to New York, in 1807, where he immediately began a series of attempts to perfect the application of steam to navigation, and to enlist the government in behalf of his plans of naval warfare. In the midst of his most active usefulness, after the triumph of his great invention, while contending for his right to a share of the vast emolument it already began to yield, and while enjoying the recognition and the domestic happiness which were the just reward of a life devoted to objects intimately connected with human welfare, in the prime of his usefulness, honor, and life, he died. It is said that this event called forth more public tokens of respect and sorrow than ever before attended the demise of a private citizen in the same city and state. If this was the case, it may be attributed, in a measure at least, to a consciousness of worth unappreciated, and character misunderstood; for, although Fulton had several friends whose devotion knew no bounds, it is undeniable that political and local prejudice, and a narrow view of his claims and purposes, rendered not a few of his countrymen insensible to his genuine value until death revealed to them the singular combination of moral energy, noble feeling, and inventive genius, which distinguished Robert Fulton. To realize this it is necessary to transcend the brief outline we have given, and survey his qualities together.

It is a very narrow view of Fulton's claims to grateful respect which estimates them solely according to the degree of originality he manifested in the application of steam to navigation. The idea is probably of older date than any of the records or traditions regarding it; for so favorable a project was it with men of science and experimental mechanics, that we read of attempts to realize it in various countries, and on the part of different individuals obviously unknown to each other. The great fact in the controversy remains indisputable, that the only inventor who persevered in giving a practical use to the knowledge already gained on the subject, and continued to try expedients until crowned with a success which introduced steam navigation to the world, was Robert Fulton. Never having claimed that the idea was original with him, and always having openly recognized the efforts of his predecessors, this acknowledgment is no disparagement to Hulls, whose treatise on the subject appeared in London, 1737; to De Garay, whose experiment in the harbor of Barcelona is alleged to have been made in 1543; to the Swiss clergyman, the French nobleman, the three Scotchmen, and the two other Americans, whose right to be considered inventors of the steamboat have been so strenuously advocated.

The same mutual dependence and slow advancement to a great end is exemplified in two inventions, which have, as it were, created manufactures. Arkwright, the inventor of the spinning-jenny, after experimenting, as an obscure watchmaker, in a provincial town, upon theories of perpetual motion, accidentally met with Kay, who had long tried in vain to perfect a spinning-machine; and when they coöperated, the result was achieved. Yet Arkwright, though he left an enormous fortune, the fruit of his inventive skill, was charged with unjustly appropriating the ideas of others. Kay, doubtless, originally conceived the notion of such a machine, but to the timely pecuniary means furnished the poor watchmaker by a gentleman of Liverpool, and the practical ingenuity he brought to the aid of his comrade's theory, is due the successful issue. Whitney proved beyond a doubt that, while on a visit to Georgia, he shut himself up in a room of the hospitable mansion of a friend, and toiled for months to contrive a machine for removing the seeds of the cotton-plant; yet, when his object was accomplished, his originality was denied, his model surreptitiously imitated, and his claims to a patent disputed. It was only after several lawsuits, and that tardy justice which time and patience bring, that his title to the invention of the cotton-gin was established.

It is a common error to attribute mechanical invention to a

happy chance; but no branch of human pursuit more directly originates in the calculating energy of the mind. It is the result of practical thinking; and the greatest inventors assure us that the intervals of their experimental toil are occupied with intense meditation upon the means and ends, the relation of matter and laws, or the process of overcoming a special difficulty. Whittemore, the inventor of the card-machine, one of the most ingenious and intricate of inventions, after having accomplished everything desired except bending the wires, was completely baffled; the subject haunted him day and night, and he declares that, while pondering upon it, he fell asleep, and the method came to him in a dream, which he instantly adopted on waking, and with entire success. Blanchard, the clever boy, who, at the age of thirteen, invented a machine for paring apples, based on observation of the graduating action of the thumb, when the process was done by hand; while riding in a wagon and musing on the obstacles to manufacturing gun-stocks by machinery, suddenly conceived the whole principle of turning irregular forms, and cried out, like Archimedes, at the idea, which he afterwards realized and patented. Watt's early practice as a mathematical instrument-maker, and his subsequent studies as an engineer, prepared him to improve so essentially the steam-engine. The naval architecture of Eckford, the Eddystone lighthouse,—that monument of Smeaton's scientific temerity, — the bridges of Edwards and Remington, the kitchen apparatus of Count Rumford, and the momentous discoveries of Faust, Jenner, and Daguerre, are not to be regarded as accidental triumphs of mere ingenuity, but as the results of patient study, numerous experiments, and intelligent resolution. It is the same with the mills of Evans, the water machinery of Slater, the clocks and globes of Ferguson, the steam-guns of Perkins, the safety-lamp of Davy, and almost every successful application of natural laws to mechanical aptitudes, whether by self-educated or professedly scientific men. We are apt to look only at the achievement, and disregard the process, which is often gradual, complicated, and only attained through earnest study and long experience. A certain natural shrewdness is doubtless characteristic of the mechanical inventor, and to the prevalence of this trait has been reasonably ascribed the facility and productiveness of the New Englanders in this branch of labor; but it is not less owing to their remarkable perseverance and energy. "It is through the collation of many abortive voyages to the polar regions," says De Quincey, "that a man gains his first chance of entering the polar basin, or of running ahead on the true line of approach to it."

Thus the history of mechanical inventions and the annals of the law of patents evince a gradual approximation to success, in almost every instance, and prove that a division of labor and a union of talent is the usual process of discovery, and essential to practical results. Accordingly, the litigation and rival claims to originality, which almost invariably follow the introduction of any new machine into use, are the inevitable result, not of plagiarism so much as simultaneous ideas, and the fact that the ostensible inventor is only an eclectic in mechanics, and skilfully brings together the scattered or fragmentary principles of a variety of minds. But this is generally accomplished through patient self-devotion, and by overcoming great and incessant difficulties; and therefore it is quite just, under ordinary circumstances, that the man who brings a great scientific idea, or mechanical project, to a wholly successful practical development, should reap the largest share of honor and emolument.

Genius may strike out novel and promising hints, but they are useless to mankind until embodied and applied by consistent and pertinacious thinkers; in this, as in other departments of social welfare, character must often appropriate and apply the fruits of talent; and the union of both in one individual is as rare as it is auspicious. Constructiveness is a distinct tendency and gift, but, in order to realize mechanical originality in its highest phase, the principles of science must be brought into action. It is on this account that the greatest inventions have sprung from the mutual labors of the scientific and the practical. A knowledge of the principle and aptitudes of the lever, wheel, inclined plane, screw, wedge, rope, and other natural forces, becomes infinitely more available when combined with equal intelligence in hydraulics, meteorology, and electro-magnetism. Through such an acquaintance with the laws of matter, human genius sways its energies, and makes it subservient to purposes of utility and enjoyment;

and these triumphs have reached such an extent as to signalize the age in which we live. The written scrolls that alone preserved the wisdom and poetry of antiquity, the old quarries of Sicily, the fragmentary arches on the Roman campagna, the beacon towers on the hills of Spain, and even the old crones that twirl the distaff in the sun around the Bay of Naples, yet remind us of the epoch when the art of printing, the railroad, Croton pipes, the electric telegraph, and the loom, were unknown. One of the "world's gray fathers" might be lost in admiration at the sight of the equipments and architectural beauty of a modern ship; but his sense of wonder would deepen into veneration when he beheld the self-impelling force in her hold, and the needle trembling to the pole in her compass, because of the wise advantage thus practically taken of two great natural laws; bringing a mechanical contrivance into the realm of science, and yoking the very elements into the service of man!

The career of the inventive mechanician exposes him to peculiar trials, not only of patience, but equanimity. The artist and author can privately test their works, before hazarding a public ordeal; but the public nature and great expense of the artisan's experiments render it often indispensable to submit himself to a kind of scientific jury, and sometimes to an ignorant and curious throng; the least failure, is, therefore, attended with singular mortification. Fulton experienced an unusual share of such discouragement; he prematurely exhibited his submarine apparatus to government commissioners, including such men as Sir Joseph Banks and Laplace; while his attempted negotiations with Pitt and the agents of Napoleon, as well as with his own government, were continually baffled. From individuals and societies he, however, obtained frequent sympathy and aid; and, while disappointed in the issue of many favorite projects, his incidental successes and the final triumph of his great design thoroughly vindicated his claims to the world.

For many years Fulton had thought, written, and acquired all possible information, with a view to the experiments which he assiduously tried on the Hudson, and one of his first conceptions seems to have been the use of paddle-wheels. The trial trip of the Clermont, so called from Mr. Livingston's domain near Hyde

Park, is yet memorable on the shores of the noble river now covered with elegant specimens of the same craft.* The British reviews were facetiously sarcastic when Colden's Life of Fulton appeared, chiefly on account of the enthusiastic view there taken of the effects of this invention upon the destinies of the world. Subsequent events, however, wholly justify the prophetic eulogy. The navigation of the Atlantic and Pacific oceans, and of the Mississippi river, by steam, is producing such changes in the course of empire and the welfare of society, that the imagination, as well as the reason, is baffled in contemplating ulterior results. It was a conviction of the extensive social benefits obtainable from mechanical science, that impelled and sustained Fulton in his career. This is evident from his written opinions, from the plans he advocated, and the arguments he invariably used, to advance his objects. His mind was comprehensive and philanthropic not less than ingenious; and it was by the inspiration of these sentiments that he achieved his triumphs. We have had countless fellow-countrymen of a mechanical turn, but no one who united

* The following letter, in reference to this event, was addressed by Fulton to Joel Barlow, Philadelphia:

"New York, August 2, 1807.

"My dear Friend: My steamboat voyage to Albany and back has turned out rather more favorable than I had calculated. The distance from New York to Albany is one hundred and fifty miles; I ran it up in thirty-two hours, and down in thirty. The latter is just five miles an hour. I had a light breeze against me the whole way going and coming, so that no use was made of my sails; and the whole voyage has been performed by the power of the engine. I overtook many sloops and schooners beating to windward, and passed them as if they had been at anchor.

"The power of propelling boats by steam is now fully proved. The morning I left New York, there were not, perhaps, thirty thousand people in the city who believed the boat would ever move a mile an hour, or be of the least utility. And while we were putting off from the wharf, which was crowded with spectators, I heard a number of sarcastic remarks. This is the way, you know, in which some people compliment what they call philosophers and projectors.

"Having employed much time, and money, and zeal, in accomplishing this work, it gives me, as it will give you, great pleasure to see it so fully answer my expectations. It will give a cheap and quick conveyance to merchandise on the Mississippi and Missouri rivers, which are now laying open their treasures to the enterprise of our countrymen. And although the prospect of personal emolument has been some inducement to me, yet I feel infinitely more pleasure in reflecting with you on the immense advantage that my country will derive from the invention."

with such a taste so genuine and earnest a public spirit. This was evinced everywhere and on all occasions. Thus, when in France, he corresponded with Carnot to persuade him to adopt the principles of free-trade; his leisure in Paris was devoted to the execution of the first panorama ever seen there, a branch of art since widely cultivated, and one to the scientific value of which Humboldt gives eloquent testimony. He wrote an urgent appeal to the citizens of Philadelphia to purchase West's pictures as the foundation of an American gallery; and, failing to enlist their aid, bought the two most characteristic of them himself, that his country might possess some evidence of her first artist's skill, and bequeathed them and his other works of art to the Académy of New York. He induced West to make designs for Barlow's ponderous epic, and had them engraved and the work published at his own expense. His avowed object in the torpedo invention, which he carried forward from one tried during the Revolution, was to annihilate war by rendering it absolutely instead of relatively destructive. His cable-cutter, plans for floating docks, and other incidental enterprises, show an indefatigable activity in the intervals of his more important scheme. He impaired his constitution by too long a fast while repairing his submarine boat, in France, after a storm; and his life was sacrificed to the imprudent zeal with which he travelled, at mid-winter, from Trenton, where his great law-suit was pending, and the exposure incurred in superintending the construction of his original steam-frigate.

Thus intent upon some great undertaking, the philosophy of which he eloquently expounded, while its practical details absorbed his active faculties, he pursued his way unbaffled by repeated failures, and undiscouraged by poverty and ridicule. He possessed the sublime patience of genius, maintained his cheerfulness under the failure of successive experiments, and manfully lived down the obstacles that crowded his path; now ardently reasoning for the freedom of the seas, like a statesman, and now sketching a grotesque figure by the road-side in Holland, like a vagrant artist; now trying his long-disused pencil upon the portrait of a friend, and, again, alarming a crowd by explaining the explosive power of a submarine battery; on the waters of the Seine, in the harbor of Rotterdam, about the quays of New York, his thin, active figure glided to and fro, as he directed some experiment, while his dark eye glowed, and his uncovered hair fluttered in the wind over his projecting brow, and some gazed on with frigid curiosity, others with a shrug of compassionate incredulity, and a few with intelligent admiration at the enthusiasm, simplicity, and confidence of genius. We are not surprised that when he received the first passage-money ever paid for a steamboat trip, in the little cabin of the Clermont, he shed tears at the tangible evidence of a public recognition of the success of his experiment, the crowning achievement of a life of study, disappointment, and irrepressible ardor. The latter quality is doubtless attributable to Fulton's Irish origin, as well as the instinctive and generous feeling which endeared him to his friends. He not only won but retained attachment, and was fortunate, even under the most adverse circumstances, in having the sympathy of men of character and talent. Franklin and West cheered his early life, and its maturity was sustained by the coöperation of Livingston, whose sister he married.

The charge made against Fulton's patriotism and honorable consistency, in regard to his offer of his submarine invention to different foreign governments, appears to have been quite gratuitous. It is evident from his writings, and the well authenticated history of his life in Europe, that his great object was to create a reputation, and perfect inventions there, with a view to return with them to his own country. At that period no aspirant, either in letters, science, or art, could fail to perceive how requisite for success in the New World was an endorsement from the Old; and the superior facilities there afforded in every branch of study, as well as the greater sympathy extended to the original inquirer and the gifted votary, were equally obvious. In each instance that Fulton contracted with a foreign power for aid in his torpedo experiments, and guaranteed, in case of success, the exclusive benefit of the invention, he made a special exception in favor of his native land. Thither he sent the written results of his studies; and it was with his own countrymen that he united himself in almost every useful project. Few Americans of that day were so alive to the extraordinary local aptitudes and unequalled natural advantages of this continent. It would seem as if a wise Providence raised up this energetic mechanical genius at the very moment that more rapid and frequent intercommunication became essential, not only to the prosperity, but to the nationality of a country destined to form a new, grand, and free arena for humanity. His keen and comprehensive glance took in the immense line of sea-coast, the vast and numerous inland lakes, and the mighty rivers of states embracing every variety of climate, soil, and natural resource; and he felt, and earnestly announced the conviction, that only by an intercourse at once easy, cheap, rapid, and constant, would it be possible to render produce available; to bring the inhabitants into sympathetic relations, and to stamp unity of expression and character upon the nation. The steam-engine and the electric telegraph have wrought this miracle; and illustrated signally in this country the truth of a statesman's assertion, that mechanical power is the vital principle of the age. This is not only evident in physical results; by creating leisure through economizing human labor, by rapidly transmitting intelligence, and multiplying the means of security, progress, and development, mechanical genius not only emancipates man from the tyranny of nature, but continually multiplies her beneficent agency in his behalf.

It is usual to consider imagination and reason in an antagonistic view; but the analysis of character and genius often reveals their mutual action and united result. To the inventive mind, in all departments of science and art, ideality is essential as the faculty which prefigures and anticipates what, if only realized by actual degrees, would scarcely sustain the courage and hope of the seeker. Hence the enthusiasm, the prophetic spirit, and the confidence of genius — founded on prescience, on the vision of the "mind's eye." Thus imagination gives enlargement and foresight, and is the source of inspiring presentiment. To wholly practical and unsympathetic men, however, those endowed by nature with this ardor, faith in the unachieved, and earnestness in its pursuit, are stigmatized as visionary until crowned with the garland of success, when the loudest scoffers are usually most extravagant in their laudation. All innovators upon the ordinary belief and practice of mankind pass through this ordeal. Columbus was but a dreamer in the estimation of his countrymen until he discovered a continent. Had Franklin announced his electrical theory before provided with evidence to uphold it, or Davy his nitrous oxide, or Morse his telegraphic chirography, they would have shared the same convenient title. Fulton endured an unusual share of indifference, not to say contempt, while prosecuting his mechanical researches. It is related that when he applied, in his native city, to a celebrated polemic for contributions toward steam-navigation experiments, that his eloquent argument in behalf of the cause was answered by the oracular theologian with the complacent statement that his own mind was absorbed in an inquiry of so much greater importance, namely, the discovery of all the facts relating to Shadrach, Meshach, and Abednego, that he could not attend to so idle a proposition. A few years have elapsed since the interview, and the polemic's thick octavo on the book of Daniel is already covered with the dust of oblivion; while the fruits of Fulton's constancy and genius are transforming the aspect of the earth, and giving wings to the progress of civilization. But it was his fate not only to contend with the scepticism of the learned, and the prejudices of the ignorant, who gave him the name of "crazy Fulton;" he also encountered, though with a dignified and urbane patience highly creditable to his manhood, the slights of the moneyed aristocracy. This incubus upon social progress in a republic is doubtless a necessary, but in all probability a temporary evil, incident to the early stage of national development in a free country devoted to commerce. There is, however, an essential opposition between the spirit of trade and the victories of intellect. In the former, attention to details and routine is the law of success; in the latter, superiority to immediate interests, and absorption in large and difficult undertakings of prospective utility, are equally requisite. Yet pecuniary means, which in this country are in the hands of the mercantile class, are often absolutely necessary to the cause of experimental science and art; and their votaries are, therefore, placed in a position of dependence which the very nature of the case renders galling to self-respect. The poverty of Fulton and his humble origin, as well as his utter indifference to the distinction of mere wealth, rendered him an inauspicious suitor to power based on money. He regarded mechanical science as an interest so vital to human welfare that it should be deemed a privilege and not a tax to promote it; and wealth, in his estimation, was only a means; its devotees, therefore, found little that was congenial in the noble mechanician, and amused themselves with what they considered his pretensions, instead of reaping honor by generous coöperation with him in his great designs. Among professional men, however, he was respected and beloved to an extent that amply consoled him under all social disparagement. The address of his friend, the celebrated Addis Emmett, in his argument for Fulton's rights as a patentee, when he urged him to call back his thoughts from inventive speculation and patriotic schemes, and remember what was due to his family, is one of the most affecting personal appeals on record; and is said to have been profoundly impressive in delivery. It eloquently assures us of the contemporary estimation in which Fulton was held by those capable of appreciating original merit. In Chancellor Livingston, also, he found, not only a consistent friend, but an efficient coädjutor; and, although his experience of the "law's delay" was sufficient to damp the ardor of a less mercurial temperament, and embarrassment and vexation continued to baffle him to the last, his serene firmness of purpose and genial animation of heart remained intact. He lived his own life, and was true to the reigning impulse of his nature. It was, therefore, by virtue of his character that he achieved his purposes, not less than through inventive talent. He persevered bravely in following truth to a practical issue, and thus bequeathed an incalculable benefit to mankind, and conferred permanent honor upon his country and his name.

THE LANDSCAPE PAINTER.

JOHN CONSTABLE.

THE quiet and isolated life of a genuine landscape painter has seldom been more consistently illustrated than in the memoirs of John Constable. His letters, collected and arranged by his friend Leslie, open to our view an existence ideal in spirit, and the more remarkable from the absolute contrast it affords to the frivolous, versatile, and bustling social atmosphere in which it was chiefly passed. Indeed, it may be said to embody the most natural and characteristic phase of English life — the rural sentiment, if we may so call it; for to Constable this was the inspiration and the central light of experience. He first rises to the imagination as "the handsome miller" of a highly-cultivated and picturesque district in Suffolk; and, since Tennyson's charming poem of the "Miller's Daughter," a romantic association easily attaches itself to that vocation. To the young artist, however, it was actually a better initiation to his future pursuit than might readily be supposed. Two phases of nature, or rather the aspects of two of her least appreciated phenomena, were richly unfolded to his observant eye — the wind and sky; and to his early and habitual study of these may be ascribed the singular truthfulness of his delineation, and the loyal manner in which he adhered, through life, to the facts of scenery.

It seems to us that the process by which he arrived at what may be called the original elements of his art is identical with that of Wordsworth in poetry; and his admiration of the bard arose not more from just perception than from the possession of a like idiosyncrasy. They resemble each other in discovering beauty and interest in the humblest and most familiar objects; and in an unswerving faith in the essential charm of nature under every guise. Thus the very names of Constable's best pictures evince a bold simplicity of taste akin to that which at first brought ridicule, and afterwards homage, to the venerated poet. A mill, with its usual natural accessories, continued a favorite subject with the painter to the last; and he sorely grieved when a fire destroyed the first specimen that his pencil immortalized. A harvest-field, a village church, a ford, a pier, a heath, a wain, — scenes exhibited to his eye in boyhood, and to the daily vision of farmers, sportsmen, and country gentlemen,—were those to which his sympathies habitually clung. No compliment seems ever to have delighted him more than the remark of a stranger in the Suffolk coach, "This is Constable's country." His custom was to pass weeks in the fields, and sketch clouds, trees, uplands — whatever object or scene could be rendered picturesque on canvas; to gather herbs, mosses, colored earth, feathers, and lichens, and imitate their hues exactly. So intent was he at times in sketching, that field-mice would creep unalarmed into his pockets. But, perhaps, the natural beauties that most strongly attracted him were evanescent; the sweep of a cloud, the gathering of a tempest, the effect of wind on corn-fields, woods, and streams, and, above all, the play of light and shade. So truly were these depicted, that Fuseli declared he often was disposed to call for his coat and umbrella before one of Constable's landscapes representing a transition state of the elements.

His fame gradually widened. The artists of Paris first appreciated his excellence; and it has been said that he "was as much the originator of modern French landscapes, as Scott was of French romance." When he came in after a day's sketching, he would sometimes say, "I have had a good skying." His clouds best attest the rarity of his skill, as well in the lucent depths as when completely effulgent.

If there be a single genuine poetic instinct in the English mind, it is that which allies them to country life. The poets of that nation have never been excelled either in rural description or in conveying the sentiment to which such tastes gave birth. What we recognize in Constable is the artistic development of this national trait. We perceive at a glance that he was "native here, and to the manner born." There is an utter absence of exaggeration, — at least in the still life of his pictures, — while no one can mistake the latitude of his atmospheres. They are not American, nor European, but thoroughly English. A great source of his aptitude was a remarkable local attachment. He not only saw distinctly the minute features of a limited scene, or a characteristic group of objects, but he loved them. He had the fondness for certain rural spots which Lamb confessed for particular metropolitan haunts; and, therefore, it was not necessary for him, in order to paint with feeling, to combine scattered beauties, as is the case with less individual limners, nor to borrow or invent accessories to set off his chosen subject; but only to elicit, by patient attention, such favorable moments and incidents as were best fitted to exhibit it to advantage.

In this way, few painters have done more to suggest the infinite natural resources of their art. Its poetry to him was two-fold, consisting of the associations and of the intrinsic beauty of the scene. There is often evident in genius a kind of sublime common sense — an intuitive intelligence, which careless observers mistake sometimes for obstinacy or waywardness. Constable displayed it in fidelity to his sphere, notwithstanding many temptations to wander from it. He felt that portrait and historical painting were not akin either to his taste or highest ability; and that the ambitious and elaborate in landscape would give no scope to his talent. In his view Art was not less a thing of feeling than of knowledge; and it was a certain indescribable sentiment in the skies of Claude, and the composition of Ruysdael, that endeared them to him more than mere fidelity to detail. Accordingly, he labored with zest only upon subjects voluntarily undertaken, and to which he felt drawn by a spontaneous attraction; and over these he rarely failed to throw the grace of a fresh and vivid conception. The word "handling" was his aversion, because he saw no evidence of it in nature, and looked upon her loving delineator as working, not in a mechanical, but in a sympathetic relation. "There is room enough," he says, "for a natural painter. The great vice of the present day is *bravura*—an attempt to do something beyond the truth." Harvest-men were to him more charming than peers; and the rustle of foliage sweeter than the hum of conversaziones.

In the foreground of a picture of a cathedral, described by Leslie, "he introduced a circumstance familiar to all who are in the habit of noticing cattle. With cows there is generally, if not always, one which is called, not very accurately, the master cow, and there is scarcely anything the rest of the herd will venture to do until the master has taken the lead. On the left of the picture this individual is drinking, and turns with surprise and jealousy to another cow approaching the canal lower down for the same purpose. They are of the Suffolk breed, without horns; and it is a curious mark of Constable's fondness for everything connected with his native county, that scarcely an instance can be found of a cow in any of his pictures, be the scene where it may, with horns." "Still life," says his friend Fisher, on the receipt of one of his pictures, "is always dull, as there are no associations with it; this is so *deliciously fresh*, that I could not resist it." These epithets reveal the secret of Constable's effects. What truly interests us, derives, from the very enthusiasm with which it is regarded, a vital charm, which gives relish and impressiveness even to description in words, and far more so in lines and colors. The "cool tint of English daylight" refreshes the eye in his best attempts; "bright, not gaudy, but deep and clear." It is curious that the term "healthy" has been applied to Constable's coloring — the very idea we instinctively associate with the real landscape of his country.

A newspaper, describing an exhibition of the Royal Academy, thus speaks of one of his pictures, and it gives, as far as words can, a just notion of his style of art: "A scene without any prominent features of the grand and beautiful, but with a rich, broken foreground sweetly pencilled, and a very pleasing and natural tone of color throughout the wild, green distance." The inimitable Jack Bannister said of another, that "from it he could feel the wind blowing on his face." Constable was delighted with the pertinacity of a little boy, who, in repeating his catechism, would not say otherwise than, "and walk in the *same fields* all the days of my life;" he declared, "Our ideas of happiness are the same." He also recorded his earnest assent to the remark of a friend, that "the whole object and difficulty of the art is to *unite imagination with nature.*" In one of his letters, he says: "I can hardly write for looking at the silvery clouds." Speaking of one of his own landscapes, he indulges in a remark, the complacency of which may be readily forgiven: "I have preserved God Almighty's daylight, which is enjoyed by all mankind, excepting only the lovers of old dirty canvas, perished pictures at a thousand guineas each, cart-grease, tar, and snuff of candle."

It is thus obvious that he pursued his art in a spirit of independence, and with a manly directness of purpose, which neither fashion nor interest for an instant modified. The sentiment which impelled him was the love of nature, and this, like the other love referred to by Shakspeare, "lends a precious seeing to the eye." It was not a vague emotion, but a definite attachment; and he possessed the rare moral courage to act it out. This the biography of artists convinces us is true wisdom. It would have been only the folly of a perverse ambition for Constable to have emulated the old Italian masters, and produced saints, madonnas, and martyrs. The scenery of his native country was not more familiar to his eye than endeared to his heart; and so attentively and fondly had he explored it that he used to declare he never saw an ugly thing, whose intrinsic homeliness was not relieved by some effect of light, shade, or perspective. His delight in nature was, indeed, inexhaustible. He has been quaintly said to have known the language of a windmill; and the most common forms of architecture, the most familiar toils of the husbandman, and the ordinary habits of animals, wore significance to his eye, because of the vast and intimate beauty amid which they are visible, and with which they are associated. Simplicity was his great characteristic, giving birth to that truth to himself which involves and secures truth to nature, both in art and in literature. His taste was permanently opposed to the factitious and the conventional, and never swerved in its allegiance to the primal and enduring.

Landscape painting, in its best significance, is a representation not only of the form and aspects, but of the sentiment of nature. If we regard it in its broad relations, it may be said to have a scientific and national value, as the authentic image of the features of the universe, modified by climate, vegetation, and history, eminently illustrative to the naturalist and the statesman. There are few departments of art more suggestive. The camel group and palm-tree of Eastern scenery, the snowy peaks of Alpine mountains, the luxuriant foliage of the tropics, and the ruined arch, shrine, and aloe, of southern Europe, each, in turn, convey to the mind of the spectator hints that imagination easily expands into entire countries. To the patriotic sympathies its appeal is inevitable; and the portfolios of travellers often contain the most satisfactory memorials of their pilgrimage. Few, except artists, however, realize the variety of meaning and the characteristic in scenery; and the number who recognize the minor and shifting language of the external world is still more limited. Yet even the insensible and unobservant, during a voyage, and when confined to a particular spot and isolated from society, will sometimes note attentively many successive sunsets, or the effect of the seasons upon a familiar prospect, and thus gradually awaken to that world of vision through which, when more preöccupied, they move almost unconscious of its ever-changing expression.

The eloquent work of Ruskin on the modern painters, whether its theories are accepted or not, ably unfolds the extent of interest derivable from this subject; but there is one common instinct to the gratification of which it ministers more than any branch of art — that of local association. A good picture of a birthplace, the scene of early life, of historical incident or poetical association, is invaluable; and this feeling has been greatly deepened by the transition of the art from graphic imitation to a picturesque reflection of the sentiment of a landscape. Herein lies its poetry. It is this soulful beauty that gives an undying charm to the sunsets of Claude, and has created an epoch in art by the glorious effects of Turner. Indeed, the ideality of the English mind has nowhere asserted itself more successfully than in her school of modern landscape. Morland and Gainsborough set an example of truth and feeling, which has been carried onward by such painters as Wilson and Constable. Genuine simplicity,— that manly Anglo-Saxon freedom from extravagance, and repose upon nature, — in such works is as clearly revealed as in the nobler literature and wholesome habits of the nation.

There is a beautiful harmony between the character and pursuit of Constable. His time was given only to art and domestic life, the routine of which knew no variation, except an occasional visit to Sir George Beaumont or Fisher. His capacity to inspire lasting attachment — a quality which seems to be the birthright of genius — is delightfully apparent in his correspondence with the latter friend. "Dear Constable," he writes, when the artist was in trouble, "you want a staff just now; *lean hard on me.*" The integrity of true affection is also manifest in his intercourse with the object of his early and latest love. The patience, self-respect, and gentleness, with which they endured the long and unreasonable opposition to their marriage, — the unfailing comfort imparted by their mutual regard, the blending of good sense, principle, and sentiment, in their relation to each other, from first to last, — are results only obtainable where generous, affectionate, and intelligent natures coalesce. The painter's love of children, humorous mention of his cat, constant kindness to a poor organist and unfortunate paint-grinder — his longings for home when absent — his delight there in the intervals of his toil — his charities, friendliness, and geniality, accord with the sweetness of his taste.

"Whenever I find a man," says Milton, "despising the false estimates of the vulgar, and daring to aspire in sentiment, language, and conduct, to what the highest wisdom in every age has taught us as most excellent, to him I unite myself by a sort of necessary attachment." By such a process Constable mainly rose in art, and kept the even tenor of his life. The appreciation of his artistic merits was very slow, as is obvious from the number of pictures in his studio at the time of his decease. Contemporary artists criticized oftener than they commended him. His ideas of his art, as expressed in conversation and in his lectures, were "caviare to the general." His election as an academician was a deserved honor, but somewhat grudgingly bestowed. His finances were often at the lowest ebb, his domestic cares unceasing; illness frequently weighed down his spirits, and bereavements caused his heart to bleed again and again, especially when his wife followed his parents to the land of shadows. But, through all, he lived in his affections and his art, with rare fidelity and singleness of heart; and his friends, and the beauty of his pictures, will long reflect his genial, serene, and consistent nature.

THE POET OF THE OLD RÉGIME.

CHATEAUBRIAND.

François-Auguste Vicomte de Chateaubriand associated his name with so many places and ideas, that almost every one, at some time or other, is drawn into an imaginative relation with him. The picture which first caught my eye, on entering the Louvre, was one representing an aged monk and a handsome youth about to commit the body of a lovely maiden to a grave, obviously hollowed by themselves, in the verdant depths of a forest. The pious tranquillity of the aged priest, the despairing grief of the young lover, and the exquisite loveliness of the corpse, instantly revealed that unity of effect which leaves an indelible impression On turning to the catalogue, I found the painting entitled "The Burial of Atala." With this souvenir of Chateaubriand, encountered within a week of landing in Europe, is linked the memory of the only Breton I ever knew. We stood together on the Campanile at Venice, and, while discussing that curious impulse which assails nervous organizations when looking down from a height, and induces an almost irresistible desire to leap, he calmly observed that it was his intention to gratify the propensity, in a few months, by springing from the precipitous cliff that bounded his family domain in Brittany. Many days of previous intercourse with this suicidal youth had revealed a thoughtful, self-possessed, and highly cultivated mind, that forbade my ascribing his remark to mere eccentricity; and his melancholy view of life and his fine endowments associate him in my recollection with his gifted countryman, who, at a similar age, "arrested the fowling-piece with a tear."

Chateaubriand owed his first literary fame to American subjects; through him our country assumed a poetical interest to European minds — although, it must be confessed, this result is to be ascribed rather to the fancy and enthusiasm than the authenticity of the writer. Lafayette had just returned to France, and awakened there a sentiment of glory in behalf of the new republic whose liberties he had assisted to rescue; and, while this feeling was yet prevalent, appeared the vivid descriptions of nature and the forest-life of the distant continent, from the glowing pen of Chateaubriand. The vicissitudes of his career, the tenacity of his opinions and sympathies, his extensive wanderings, and especially the remarkable identity of the man with his country and the age, render his memoirs of unusual interest. They exhibit the history of an eventful era, mirrored, as it were, upon a reflective and ardent soul; they illustrate how the spirit of reform wrestles with the mind of an intelligent conservative; and they afford the most impressive glimpses of nature, literature, revolutions, and society, as they appear to the consciousness of a man of sentiment and philosophy, thoroughly exposed to their agency, and yet capable of tranquil observation. Strongly attached to the ideas of the past,—religious, political, and domestic,—on account of his education and instincts, he was borne along the tide of those vital changes that mark the last century, at once their victim and expositor, — now inspired and now persecuted by the course of events, and yet always preserving intact the noble individuality of his character.

It is this which makes us the willing auditors of his story, and which, in spite of the constant egotism and occasional extravagance of his autobiography, wins our warmest attention and frequent sympathy. The hardihood with which he accepts the conditions of a destiny alternating between the greatest extremes of misfortune and prosperity; the zeal that sustains his pilgrimage in the trackless forests of the West and the arid desert of the East; over seas and mountains, through unknown crowds of his fellow-beings, and in the lonely struggles of bereaved affection, lend a warmth to every page of his narrative; and amid the varying panorama through which he conducts us, not for a moment are we unconscious of the Breton, the royalist, and the poet of the old *régime*. It is this combination of intense personal identity with the most changeful scenes and fortunes that gives its peculiar charm to the life of Chateaubriand. Other travellers have as well described America and the Holy Land, Napoleon and the Alhambra; we have pictures of the French Revolution more elaborate than his; the trials and the triumphs of the man of letters have been equally well chronicled, and the war of opinion as eloquently reported; but these, and the countless other phases of Chateaubriand's experience, are lighted up in his record by the fire of imagination, outlined, with wonderful distinctness, by strong feeling, and often exquisitely softened by the atmosphere of sentiment. Sketches which impress us with the intensely picturesque effect of Dante are interspersed with speculative gossip that would do credit to old Montaigne, and the author and lover seem to change parts with the adventurer and the statesman, as we find the experiences of each detailed with equal complacency; yet through and around them all the original man is apparent — his melancholy reveries, his poetic ecstasies, his profound sensibility to nature, his love of glory, his devotion to the past, his vast anticipations, his philosophic observation, keen sense of honor, patriotism, and independent yet loving spirit. Nothing can be more manly than his enterprises, his endurance, and his industry, and nothing more childlike than his account of them. We are often inclined to forget the offensiveness of vanity, as we read, in the fruits of its unconscious revelations; we cannot but perceive that it is the vividness of his own impressions and the importance he attaches to them that render Chateaubriand so effective an author; and intolerable as would be commonplace events thus unfolded, those of universal interest, which chiefly occupy his memoirs, derive from this cause an infinite attraction. Far more real appear the historic scenes reviewed, when thus linked with the thoughts and feelings of such a man, and the whole process of his authorship is ingeniously displayed by so minute a history of his life; indeed, the one is but the exponent of the other; his books are the genuine offspring of his experience, and his biography not the life of one man, but an episodical history of the times.

The most careful limning in this remarkable picture is that of the early scenes. Like all reminiscences, those of his childhood are the clearest, and the original elements of his character there defined give us the key to much of his subsequent history. Following him from St. Malo through the most exciting and dramatic incidents, and amid every variety of climate and condition, the image of the isolated, thoughtful, and baffled youth rises continually to our fancy, and explains every trait of the man. The sea, the turret, the woods, the paternal austerity, the sisters' love, the mother's piety, the suicidal purpose, the ideal attachment, the rude manners, and heart trembling with sensibility, — all this half-Crabbe-like and half-Shakspearian picture of a young provincial noble's existence in Brittany just before the Revolution, haunts the memory of the reader with its sad yet truthful lineaments. It also gives him the clue to Chateaubriand's solemnity of mind and loyalty of purpose. In the solitude and secret conflicts of his boyhood originated the strength of mind, the want of external adaptation, and the poetical habit of his nature. It drew him into intimacy with the outward universe and his own soul, and laid the foundation of the contemplative spirit that accompanied him in a career of almost incessant activity; thus inducing a kind of Hamlet or Jacques like idiosyncrasy, that, when deepened by exile, poverty, and baffled sentiment, gave the element of pathos which distinguishes the most effective of his writings, and is the key-note of his memoirs.

The life of Chateaubriand, thus minutely related, and made alive and dramatic by the fidelity and emotion with which it is portrayed, naturally arranges itself into scenes, each of which illustrates an entire act. Thus, from the chateau-life of his childhood, we follow him to college, and thence to Paris, and stand beside him at the window where his heart sickened as the heads of the first victims of the Revolution were borne along on pikes; then behold him seated by an Indian camp-fire, within hearing of the Falls of Niagara; a few months elapse, and he is discovered sauntering in Kensington Gardens, meditating a work of genius, or sharing his last crust with a brother exile in a London garret;

within a year the teacher of an English country maiden in a distant parish; shortly afterwards the secretary of Cardinal Fesch, at Rome; then a pilgrim to Jerusalem, animated by the old crusader spirit; previously a soldier in the French army besieging Thironville, or begging, wounded, at a fisherman's hut; again, in retirement at the *Vallée aux Loups*, planting or writing; now fraternizing with the Parisian *littérateurs* of a past generation, now braving Napoleon in an inaugural discourse before the French Institute, and now fêting the English nobility as ambassador to the Court of St. James; waging political battles in Paris, assisting at the Congress of Verona, or talking regretfully of the past, in his latter days, at Madame Recamier's *soirées*. The life of the province, the university, the capital — the voyageur, the soldier, the author, the *diplomat*, the journalist, the exile, the man of society, the man of state, and the man of sentiment — all were known to their full significance in his adventurous career. Stern as were the realities of his lot, a vein of absolute romance is visible throughout; continually an episode occurs which the writer of fiction would seize with avidity and elaborate with effect. Imagine the use to which might be thus adapted such incidents as the night he was an involuntary prisoner in Westminster Abbey, the circumstances of his emigration, and his departure from the army of the princes; his encounter with a French dancing-master among the Iroquois, his *mariage de convenance*, and his subsequent love-adventure in England; his brilliant *début* as an author, his shipwreck on returning from America, his vigil at the death-bed of Madame Beaumont, and his walk out of Brussels while listening to the cannons of Waterloo! The breath of every clime, the discipline of all vocations, the fiercest controversies, and the most abstract reveries, associations of the highest kind, and events of the most universal import; fame and obscurity, riches and poverty, devoted friendship and pitiable isolation, contact with the past through keen sympathy and intense imagination, identity with the present through indefatigable activity; made up the existence of Chateaubriand, which was the successive realization of all that constitutes the life of the mind, of the heart, and of the age itself.

His social experience was quite as varied, interesting, and historical, as the events of which he was a witness or an agent. Of the most illustrious of his acquaintance and intimate of his friends he has left excellent portraits, and highly characteristic personal anecdotes. Indeed, the manner in which descriptions of nature and adventurous incident are blended, in his memoirs, with those of renowned or attractive individuals, make them resemble a long picture-gallery, where the features of the great and loved beam from the wall amid beautiful or wild landscapes, domestic groups, and memorable scenes from history. Beginning with the members of his own family, he delineates the persons, traits of character, and manner, of Moreau and Mirabeau, Laharpe and his literary coterie, Napoleon and Washington, Canning, Neckar, Talleyrand, the Duchess de Berri, Charles X., Lafayette, the French emigrants in London, the aborigines in America, his Irish hostess, with her passion for cats, at Hempstead, Charlotte, his beloved English pupil, Madame Bacciocchi, Madame de Coulin, Madame Dudevant,— in a word, all his political, literary, and personal acquaintances. The distinct outline and graceful coloring of these portraits bespeak the artist; but we owe the effective style in which they are conceived to the relation in which the limner stood to the originals; the heat-lightning of his love or indignation often gives us veritable glimpses more impressive than a detailed but less vivid revelation could yield; thus his two interviews with Bonaparte and Washington, the manner in which Malesherbes infected him with that enthusiasm of discovery which sent him across the ocean in search of a north-west passage, and Madame de Stael's favorite appellation, "My dear Francis," bring each individual directly before us. Byron was a schoolboy at Harrow when Chateaubriand, the impoverished exile, caught sight of his curly head as he wandered by the seminary in his peregrinations round London; and De Tocqueville, the able expositor of our institutions, he knew as the intelligent child of a friend at whose country-house he visited. Compare the hunting party of Louis XIV., which he attended as a young noble of the realm, with the morning call upon Washington at Philadelphia, and we have the last glimmer of feudal royalty in the Old World, with the first dawn of republican simplicity in the New.

The business-like manner in which his marriage was contracted is in violent contrast with the romantic earnestness of his reminiscences of sentiment; and his veneration for the ties of family and rank strangely combined with a zest for the primitive in human nature. The instinct of glory led him to cherish enthusiasm for greatness, that of blood for races, and that of poetry for the original, the fresh, and the intrepid. Hence, he sympathized with genius, of whatever clime — with exiled princes and Indian chiefs; and, while wisdom, tenderness, and valor, so attached him that he dwells almost passionately upon those eras marked by satisfactory intercourse with others, ever and anon misfortune, pride, and a sense of the unattained, draw him back to self and the glow of companionship, and love fades into the "pale cast of thought." He survived the most renowned of his contemporaries and the most endeared of his friends. Yet few men have been more sincerely loved than Chateaubriand, and few have mingled intimately with the intellectual leaders of any epoch, and won a greater share of admiration with less compromise of self-respect; for he was quite as remarkable for the independence of his character as for the strength of his attachments.

One of his most pleasing traits was an ardent love of nature. To gratify this on a broad scale, he cheerfully undertook long and hazardous voyages, and delighted to expose his whole being to the influence of earth, sea, and firmament, with the *abandon* of the poet and the observant spirit of the philosopher. His sensibility in this regard is evident in the force and beauty of his impressions. His mind caught and reproduced the inspiration of the universe, and his affections linked themselves readily with objects hallowed by association. Thus he speaks of Madame de Beaumont's cypress, the poplar beside his window in the *rue de Mirousel*, the nightingales at the restaurant he frequented, and the doves whose brooding note accompanied his studies, with a degree of feeling rarely coëxistent with such rude experience of the world. "Je me sentais," he says, "vivre et végéter avec la nature dans une espèce de pantheisme." He possessed the genuine instinct of travel, and the migratory impulse of birds. It is remarkable that a disposition like this, characteristic of the naturalist and poet, should be so developed in a man whose name is identified with a long political career. The conventionalities of life, however, and "*tracasseries politiques*," were ungenial to him. He describes the two sides of his character very justly when he says: "Dans l'existence intérieure et théorique, je suis l'homme de tous les songes; dans l'existence extérieure et pratique l'homme des réalités. Aventureux et ordonné, passionné et méthodique." He was indeed a poetical cosmopolite — one of the most perfect examples of that style of character known to modern times. In his candid self-revelations, the primeval instincts of the natural, and the complex relations of the civilized human being are successively brought into view; for the rapture with which he first greets the virgin forest of the New World is soon followed by an instant resolution to join the army of his king, of whose flight he was informed by an old newspaper, accidentally picked up in the cabin of a backwoodsman; and if, as we accompany his musing steps along the banks of the Jordan, it seems as if one of the heroes of Tasso's epic had revived in the person of a French paladin, the associations of a later and less chivalric era are soon excited by the *procès verbal* that condemned his brother to the guillotine — printed in another page of his memoirs as a sad but authentic link in his family history. Listen to him as he thinks aloud in the Colosseum at moonlight, and you would infer that he was a bard unallied to the realities of the present — a dreamer whose life was in the past; but the idea is dispelled, almost when conceived, by an enthusiastic description that succeeds of one of those Parisian *réunions* or political climaxes in which he took so active a share.

His reminiscences of travel have a sweetness and vitality, like the dexterously preserved flowers of an herbal, as if he transmitted us the very hues and sensations of the regions he traversed with so keen a sympathy — the marine odor and crumbling architecture of Venice, the religious atmosphere of Rome, the fresh verdure and exuberant nature of the western hemisphere, the Petrarchan charms of southern France, the Moorish tints of Spain, the substantial glory of England, the grandeur of mountains relieved against the transparent and frosty air of Switzerland, the extremes of metropolitan and the simple graces of rural life — these, and all other sensitive and moral experiences of the traveller, Chateaubriand, as it were, imbibed as the aliment of his mind, and reproduced as memorials of his life. Like Byron, he became part of what he loved; and the intensity of his own consciousness rendered nature, art, and society, or rather their traits and essential spirit, his own. In the aboriginal wigwam and the Arabian tent; at Memphis, Carthage, and Jerusalem; at Golgotha and Hempstead, Granada and Rome; at the banquet of the monarch, on the sick-bed of the hospital, in the prison and the boudoir; when dragged triumphantly in his carriage by the applauding law-students from the Bibliotheque Genevieve to his domicile, and when left, propped against a wall, a wounded fugitive in Guernsey — he rose above the material and the temporary, caught the true significance, bravely met the exigency, and felt the ideal as well as the human interest of the scene and occasion.

It is this spirit of humanity, this poetical tone of mind — the lofty thought, the genuine feeling, in short, with which he encountered vicissitudes and contemplated beauty, and not the mere outward facts of his career — that gives a permanent and ineffable charm to his name. A halo of sentiment encircles his brow, not less evident when bowed in adversity than when crowned with honor. He demonstrates the truth of the brave old poet's creed, that the mind of man is his true kingdom. His self-respect never falters amid the most discouraging circumstances; he redeems misfortune of its worst anguish by the strength of his love or his religion. The scope of his view wins him from the limited and the personal; the ardor of his emotions compensates for the coldness of fortune; he is ever aware of the vast privilege of the rational being to look before and after; memories either glorious or tender, and visions of faith, shed a consoling light both upon the clouds of outward sorrow and inward melancholy; always a poet, a philosopher, a lover, and a Christian, Chateaubriand the man is "nobler than his mood," however sad, baffled, or absorbed, it may be. This dignity, this sense of the lofty, the comprehensive, and the beautiful, seldom deserts him. It gives tone, elevation, spirit, and interest, to each phase of his life, and makes its record poetic and suggestive.

The political career of Chateaubriand has been the subject of that diversity of opinion which seems inevitably to attend this portion of all illustrious lives. A rigid, narrow course in regard to party, it would be irrational to expect and illiberal to desire in a man of such broad insight and generous instincts. His imaginative tendency and chivalric tone also unfitted him to be either consistently subservient to a dogma or invariably true to a faction. The nobility and sentiment of the man, however, shed their light upon the politician. The character and spirit of his statesmanship, though at times too ideal in theory, were individual, and often indicative of the highest moral courage. He broke away from the life of a court, in his youth, with the intrepidity of the most zealous republican; when Mirabeau clapped him fondly on the shoulder, he thought his hand the claw of Satan; and while he sought, in voluntary exile, immunity from the horrors of the Revolution, he was loyal to his order when the time came to resist the fanaticism of the Jacobins — fought in its ranks, and shared the privations of emigration. It has been well said that he was "a monarchist from conviction, a Bourbonist from honor, and a republican by nature;" "le republicaine le plus dévoué à la monarchie;" and, incompatible as such principles may seem with each other, he suffered and toiled in behalf of all of them. He solicited a mission of discovery at the age of twenty to escape from the ungenial social and political atmosphere of France, as well as to gratify an adventurous taste. He dedicated his great work to the First Consul, and accepted from him the embassy to Rome, with a sincere faith in his patriotism; and bravely dared his anger, by instantly resigning another office the moment he heard of the Duke d'Enghien's execution. It was his boast that only after the "success of his ideas" was he dismissed from the political arena. In 1830 he stood alone among the peers, and urged them to protest in favor of the banished king; and yet, for the sake of tranquillity, acceded to the request of his opponents not to utter his intended speech against the new government. He also declined their offer of a portfolio, saying: "I only demand liberty of conscience, and the right to go and die wherever I can find freedom and repose." Thus, while Chateaubriand failed entirely to please both parties, he was yet eminently true to himself, and won respect from each. He declared of Bonaparte: "Il était animé contre moi de toute sa forfaiture, comme je l'étais contre lui de toute ma loyauté." The episode of the

Breton against the Corsican is one of the most characteristic in the history of both. It is conceded that he always sacrificed personal interest to his idea of public good; and if he sent a French army to crush liberty in Spain, he has, theoretically at least, vindicated his motives. His constant purpose was to give the people a system of graduated monarchy, in which he firmly believed their true welfare to consist, and, at the same time, to reässert the dignity of France. He was the invariable and eloquent advocate of the liberty of the press and of religion.

The most inveterate advocates of reform, if endowed with just moral perception and even an inkling of chivalric sentiment, can hardly fail to respect the devotion of Chateaubriand to that system which, despite its inhuman abuses, lends the highest dignity and value to the past. He clung with the almost absolute loyalty of the middle ages to those persons and usages amid which he was born, and in fidelity to which he thought consisted his honor. He sacrificed wealth, home, safety,— everything but character,— to principles outgrown by the world, but endeared to faith. Some one has said that independence is the essential test of a gentleman. Chateaubriand, thus judged, was not only a gentleman in the absolute sense of the term, but a knight according to the original standard. Loyalty was in him an immutable instinct, and one that redeems all the apparent perversities of opinion traceable in his career as a man of the state. He has been said to be the legitimate inheritor of that eclectic political feeling, attached at once to both past and future, to the people and the throne, of which Lafayette was the exemplar. From 1814 to 1825 he contended for the past; from then until 1830 he was the advocate of progress, and thenceforward strove to reconcile the interests of both. Such is the enlightened view taken by the liberal critic. During the Hundred Days he was one of the king's counsellors at Ghent. The anti-regicide doctrine of his first speech to the Institute forever disunited him from Napoleon, and he retired from public life on the accession of Louis Philippe. Deprived of a lucrative editorship, exiled, his property forfeited, he again and again evidenced his superiority to corruption, and sought refuge in nature and letters from the vicissitudes of public life. Ambassador at Berlin, Rome, and London,— minister, soldier, and journalist,— in the congress of nations, the cabinet, and the popular assembly,— however visionary, impulsive, and pertinacious, Chateaubriand nobly vindicated his title to the name of patriot. A citizen of the world by virtue of enlarged sympathies and intelligence, he was always a Frenchman at heart, and one of that school, now almost wholly traditional, about which lingers the venerable charm of a loyal, brave, courteous, and gallant race — touched, however, in him, to finer issues by an innate love of the grand, a natural ideality and depth of feeling, partly inherited, and somewhat owing to his Breton origin and remarkable experience. In a word, he was both a poet and a true scion of the old French aristocracy, which seems to have expired when the hearse containing his remains, followed by a single carriage, in which were his executor and valet, reached the shores of Brittany one summer day in 1849, and a veiled woman in deep mourning drew near and laid a bunch of flowers on the coffin, saying, tearfully, "This is all I have to offer."

The authorship, like the existence, of Chateaubriand, was chivalric, adventurous, and effective, usually originating in some want or impulse of the time, derived from his own experience or aimed at a positive and practical result; the man of action and of the age, the improvisator of the occasion, marks his labors in the field of letters. Thus, his first essay as a writer on a large scale was the Treatise on Revolutions, written in exile and for bread, and serving as a kind of initiative discipline to works of more instant and universal effect; yet even this, the most abstract and least spontaneous of his works, chiefly historical in its plan, being written at the epoch of the French Revolution, in which the author and his family so deeply suffered, had a vital and immediate significance. The subject thus chosen indicates his dominant taste for philosophy, history, and politics; in its execution, also, is evident his love of bringing ancient parallels to bear on contemporary events; the broad survey of governments it includes shows his comprehensive scope of mind, the instinctive grandeur of his conception; while some of the portraits and scenes betray that felicity of description which characterized his subsequent writings. However respectable as a literary undertaking, the *Essais sur les Revolutions* was rather a prophetic than realized test of his mission as a writer. The *Génie du Christianisme* is one of those works that, by meeting the conscious needs of an age and people, lift the author at once to the rank of public benefactor. When Europe recoiled from the barren and bitter fruits of anarchy and atheism, and humanity became conscious of her desolation, "without God in the world," this reässertion of the religious sentiment, of the incalculable benefits Christianity had bestowed upon the world, of its infinite superiority to all previous systems, of its accordance with nature and the heart of man, of its sacred relation to domestic life and to the human passions, seemed an echo of the latent hopes and recollections of every bereaved and aspiring soul amid the wrecks of social and civil life. With singular eloquence, Chateaubriand resummoned the saints, the angels, the myths, the ceremonial, and the sanctions of the Christian religion, from the eclipse they had undergone. He compared, as only a scholar, a philosopher, a poet, can do, Hell with Tartarus, Heaven with Elysium; Homer, Virgil, and Theocritus, with Dante, Milton, and Tasso; the Sibyls and the Evangelists, the Bible and the Iliad. He recounted the triumphs of Christian art, and described how the New Testament changed the genius of the painter: "Sans lui, rien ôter de sa sublimité, il lui donne plus de tendresse." He revealed its architectural signs — the dome and spire: "Les yeux du voyageur viennent d'abord s'attacher sur cette flèche religieuse dont l'aspect réveilee une foule de sentiments et de souvenirs; c'est la pyramide funèbre autour de la quelle dorment les aieux; c'est la monument de joie ou l'airain sacré annonce le vie du fidele; c'est là que l'epoux s'unisant; c'est là que les chrétiens se prosterent au pied des autels, le foible pour prier le Dieu deforce, le coupable pour implorer le Dieu de miséricorde, l'innocent pour chanter le Dieu de bonté." He pictures to the imagination the tangible evidences of his holy faith, Raphael's Madonnas and the Hotel Dieu, the Festival, the Cemetery, the Sisters of Charity, the Knight, the Missionary, the eloquence of Massillon, Bossuet, Pascal, and Fénélon. Thus, gathering up the trophies and opening the vistas of Christianity once more before the despairing eyes of multitudes, Chateaubriand was hailed by tearful praises. "Imagine," says one of his critics, "a vase of myrrh overturned on the steps of a blood-stained altar." To us and to-day the significance of his work is greatly modified and abated. In the light of a more advanced civilization, and a race of no less eloquent and deeper expositors, we look upon it, with Lamartine, rather as a reliquary than as a creative work. It is a panoramic view of the history of Christianity — a poem celebrating its dogmas and monuments, and "superstition's rod" seems to hang over the inspired defender of the Church. None the less beautiful, however, are many of its appeals to the past and to the human heart — none the less remarkable its success. He tells us it was undertaken not only from devout, but filial sentiment; his conversion having been induced by his mother's death, and grief for his scepticism. Over the book, therefore, hangs an atmosphere of poetical and adventurous interest, which lends it permanent attraction.

The *Etudes Historiques* were commenced and finished, as the author says, with a restoration; and he adds: "Le plus long et le dernier travail de ma vie, celui qui m'a coûté le plus de recherches, de soins et d'années, celui où j'ai peut-être remué le plus d'idées et de faits, paroît lorsqu'il ne peut trouver de lecteurs." This want of comparative success is easily accounted for by the absence of personal motive and interest in this elaborate, instructive, sometimes eloquent and characteristic work. The *Itinéraire, Voyage en Amérique*, and, in fact, all his books of travel, while they contain charming passages, are now more interesting as links in his career than for their facts and descriptions — there having been no department of recent literature more affluent in graces of style and attraction of details than that of voyages and travels. In the East and our own country, he is, therefore, in a great measure, superseded by later and standard writers. His literary and political miscellanies are often rich in thought and imagery. The opinions they embrace are, however, frequently inconsistent; but there is a harmony of tone, a vigor of argument, a keen critical appreciation, and a gift of expression, which indicate genius, amid much that is desultory, extravagant, and incomplete. The prejudices of the Roman Catholic, and the ignorance of the foreigner, sometimes rudely clash with the beautiful style of the rhetorician, and the lofty sentiment of the bard.

14

Amid the voluminous disquisition, the journals of travel, and the polemics of Chateaubriand, three gems of narrative — episodes and illustrations, in a truly poetic vein, of his arguments and descriptions — have served to wing his name abroad, and cause it to nestle in many hearts. These are *Atala*, *Rene*, and *Les Aventures du Dernier Abencerrage;* romantic in conception and most gracefully executed — prose poems, in short, and the flowers of his mind, terse, beautiful, and embalmed in sentiment, although to the unnatural passion described in the former work some critics attribute the exceptionable moral taste in modern French romance. In contrast with these is the most vigorous and the least charitable of his political essays, "Bonaparte and the Bourbons," which Lamartine well describes as "the bitter speech of the public executioner of humanity and liberty, written by the hand of the Furies against the great culprit of the age."

The passionate invective of this famous pamphlet would strike the reader differently could he imagine it addressed to the French people before the star of the conqueror began to wane; but it is associated with the image of Napoleon, not in the hour of his triumph, but as he sits at Fontainebleau, brooding in dishevelled garments, and with despair on his brow, over the defection of his household and the pitiless demands of the allies.

Wide, indeed, is the range of Chateaubriand's literary talent and achievement, and versatile as his fortunes: in politics singularly bold, almost ferocious; in history suggestive and ingenious; and in personal revelations often pathetic, picturesque, and sometimes vain, yet ever graphic. He knew the fever of mind incident to poetical conception — the long, patient vigil of the scholar, and the serene, contemplative mood of the philosopher. He experienced climaxes both of emotion and opinion, and vented both on paper. And with all the assiduity, the invention, and the glow, of these compositions, he had also the melo-dramatic, the exaggerated, and the artificial taste of a Frenchman. He loved effect, — he was carried away by the desire of glory, tenacious of individuality, and happy in a kind of wayward yet noble self-assertion. Such a writer is naturally open to critical assault, and fitted to excite admiration in equal degrees. Accordingly, his incongruities as a champion of religion have been often designated by writers of more chastened taste; the hardihood and inconsistencies of his partisan articles justly condemned, and the effects of a too sensitive mind easily detected. As an instance of his want of spontaneous expression, and the habitude of well-considered language, Lamartine relates, in his History of the Restoration, that when sent as a deputy to the Emperor Alexander to plead the Bourbon cause, Chateaubriand was silent because he could not, on the spur of the moment, as he afterwards declared, find language appropriate to the majesty of the occasion. He required time to utter himself in writing; and therefore, on this memorable occasion, allowed a younger and far less gifted member of the deputation to speak for him.

His style, too, has been censured for its *grandiose* tendency, and his authorship made the object of extreme laudation and scorn. What almost invariably claims our admiration, however, is the gallant and the comprehensive, the poetical and the sympathetic spirit in which he has written. Somewhat of the extravagance of his nation is indeed conspicuous; but we are impelled to view it leniently on account of the grace and bravery with which it is usually combined. He opened glorious vistas, and let fall seeds of eternal truth. The sound of the sea, the setting of the sun, the roaring of the wind amid the pines, the fall of the leaf, the associations of home and country, the solemnity of ruins, the griefs of humanity, the vicissitudes of life, the sanctions of religion, tenderness, heroism, reverence, faith, — all, in short, that hallows and sublimates this brief existence, and sheds a mystic glory over the path of empires, the scene of nature, and the lot of man, found eloquent recognition from his pen; and for such ministrations we give him love and honor, without losing sight of the vagueness, the prejudice, the artificiality, and the exaggeration, which occasionally mar such exuberant development. In him the conscious and personal sometimes dwarfs the essentially noble; but a kind of grandeur of feeling and thought often lifts him above the temporary. He cherished faith in his race: "Si l'homme," he says, "est ingrat, l'humanité est reconnaissante." "The masters of thought," he declares, "open horizons, invent words, have heirs and lineages." For a Gallic nature, his appreciation of Milton, Dante, Tasso — of the serious phase of greatness — was remarkable, although some of his criticisms on English literature excite a smile. In his influence as a man of letters, for half a century he was the successful antagonist of Voltaire and his school. Often he gave impetus and embodiment to public opinion; and if his portraits are sometimes fanciful and his judgments poetic, his literary achievements, on the whole, had a rare character of adventure and beauty; and the alternations from severe reasoning to imaginative glow are such as indicate a marvellous combination of intellectual power. For the complete revised edition of his works he received five hundred and fifty thousand francs; and perhaps no modern author boasts more remarkable trophies — such a blending of tinsel and truth — of the incongruous but efficient politician with the ardent, sensitive, heroic poet — incomplete and desultory in certain respects, fresh, courageous, true, eloquent, and original, in others; imprudent, but loyal; "worth an army to the Bourbons," yet enamored of American solitudes; as a journalist, said to unite "la hauteur de Bossuet et la profondeur de Montesquieu;" advising literary aspirants of his race and tongue not to try verse, and, if they have the poetical instinct, to eschew politics; carrying the war into Napoleon's retreating dominion, and, at the same time, hailed as the dove of the Deluge, whose mission it was "to renew the faith of the heart, and infuse the impoverished veins of the social body with generous sentiment." Enough of fame and of weakness we may, indeed, find in all this to crown a writer with admiration and pity. If his genius was somewhat too studied, it lent dignity to his times and country; if his youth was shackled by the pedantic coterie that ruled French letters, his maturity redeemed, by the independent advocacy of truth and nature, the casual vassalage; if he once over-estimated Ossian, he never lost sight of the need of clear expression, and repudiated, when engaged on practical subjects, the vague conceptions he admired.

Chateaubriand's genius thus responded to national subjects, and was modified by national imperfections—in his poetical sentiment reminding us of St. Pierre, Rousseau, and Lamartine; while many passages in the Martyrs, Natchez, the magazines, letters, romances, in the answers to his critics, and historical essays, challenge recognition for the philosopher; and yet, ever and anon, the manner in which he dwells upon his achievements, and the consideration he demands both from the reader and governments for his persecutions and his fame, cause us somewhat painfully to realize the weakness of the man. In this anti-Saxon and thoroughly Gallic egotism, sensitiveness, vanity, or by whatever name we designate a quality so obvious and characteristic, Chateaubriand was a genuine Frenchman. He describes this trait of his nation justly when accounting for the fruitfulness of its literature in memoirs and the comparative dearth of history: — "Le Francois a été tous les temps, même lorsqu'il étoit barbare, vain, léger et sociable. Il réfléchit peu sur l'ensemble des objets; mais il observe curieusement les détails, et son coup d'œil est prompt, sûr et délié; il faut toujours qu'il soit en scène. Il aime à dire; j'etois là, le roi me dit; J'appu du prince," etc.

From the casual frailties, however, and from the intrigues of the *salon*, the warfare of party, and the reverses of fortune—from all that is unworthy and mutable in this remarkable life, what is pure and effective in genius seems to rise and separate itself to the imagination, and we behold the true spirit of the man embodied and embalmed in the disinterested results of his thought and the spontaneous utterance of his sentiment; and therefore it is as a poet of the old *régime* that we finally regard Chateaubriand.

It has been acutely said that external life is an appendix to the heart; and the *Memoirs d'outre Tombe* signally evidence the truth. Dated, as they are, at long intervals of time, and in many different places, the immediate circumstances under which they are written are often brought into view simultaneously with a vivid retrospect, to which they form a singular contrast; and this gives an air of reality to the whole, such as is afforded by oral communication; we frequently seem to listen instead of reading. Chateaubriand first thought of composing the work where Gibbon conceived the idea of his great enterprise, in that haunt of eternal memories — Rome. It was commenced in his rural seclusion at La Vallée aux Loups, near Aulnay, in the autumn of 1811, and finally revised at Paris, in 1841. The intermediate period is strictly chronicled, and interspersed with details of the antecedent and the passing moment, together with countless portraits, criticisms, and scenes, both analytical and descriptive; but the deep vein of sentiment, which prompts the author's movements and arrays his experience and thoughts, continually reminds us that the life depicted is but the appendix to the heart that inspires. Thus his intimacy with Malesherbes, whose granddaughter his elder brother married, fostered that passion for exploration which made him a traveller; his repugnance to priestly shackles induced him to enroll his name in the regiment of Navarre; his adherence to his party made him a translator and master of languages in England; his fraternal love redeemed his boyhood from misanthropic despair, and his religious and poetic sentiment impelled him to the East. This oriental tendency — if we may so call it — is evident, as he suggests, in the whole race of modern genius, and seems to spring both from delicate organization, giving a peculiar charm to the atmosphere and life of that region, and from historical associations that win the imagination and the sympathies — romantically evident in Byron, and religiously in Chateaubriand and Lamartine. The former, despite the battles, conclaves, and literary affairs, that make up the substance of his memoirs, never loses his identity with sentiment, whether luxuriating in the scenery of the Grand Charteuse, invoking the departed at Holyrood or Venice, setting out the trees of every land he had visited on his domain, breaking away from his English love with the exclamation, "*Je suis mari!*" or recording his last interview with his sister Lucille and her obscure burial; claiming his chair at Corinne's fireside, or discovering auguries in the fierce tempest that broke over St. Malo the night he was born. The most utilitarian reader must confess, as he connects the practical efficiency and noble traits of Chateaubriand with his generous emotions, that sentiment is a grand conservative and productive element in human life, and to its inciting and elevated influence justly ascribe the usefulness, the renown, and the singular interest, that attaches to the man he may have seen a few years since threading the Boulevards of Paris with "irreproachable cravat and ebony cane;" recognizing in his gentle yet vigorous expression, in his broad forehead and projecting temples, the thick white hair around his bald crown, the inclination of the head, the long face and observant yet noble air, outward indications of his varied experience, rare gifts, and unique character.

THE REVIEWER.

FRANCIS JEFFREY.

ONE cool morning, during our last war with England, a group of Knickerbocker *savans* might have been seen on the Battery, eagerly watching the approach of a vessel. On her deck, at the same moment, the inspection of a passenger's baggage was going on, under the eye of a vigilant officer of the customs, whose herculean proportions and deliberate air were in amusing contrast with the brisk movements and diminutive figure of the indignant owner of the trunks and boxes thus overhauled and scrutinized. At last, swelling with indignation, the little man turned to his burly tormentor, with the question — à la Cæsar — "Sir! do you know who I am?"

"Yes," replied the officer, "you are the editor of a Scotch magazine;" and immediately continued his examination, as if determined to prove the querist a smuggler.

Quite different were the manners of the expectant group at the pier, when the irritated gentleman stepped upon shore. Their deferential greeting and urgent hospitality soon put him in better humor, without, however, diminishing the self-complacency of his bearing. The scene perfectly illustrated a singular characteristic of the times — the ascendency gained over public opinion by the press, and the newly-established power of criticism.

The gentleman, whose arrival in the United States was thus signalized, was Francis Jeffrey, who, having contracted an engagement of marriage with an American lady whom he met abroad, had come over, under the protection of a cartel specially granted for the purpose, in a government ship, to marry the woman of his choice. The practical independence and good sense of the scion of democracy who examined his baggage rebelled at a certain vague idea he had somewhere acquired, that the wise men of his native city pinned their faith upon a foreign periodical; and, sharing in the animosity then cherished against Great Britain, he was far from pleased at the demonstration of respect to the Scotch editor manifested in the vessel that brought and the reception that awaited him; while the learned coterie, who eagerly seized upon the stranger, beheld in him the incarnation of mental vigor, wit, knowledge, and pleasantry, which, under the name of the Edinburgh Review, had been their chief intellectual repast for several preceding years. There was nature and reason on both sides; a resistance to foreign domination, even in matters of taste and speculation, on the one hand, — for the custom-house officer had published a book or two in his day, — and a hearty recognition of mental obligation on the other. Looking upon the man through the expanding vista of succeeding triumphs in periodical criticism and enlarged literary culture, we can readily take that medium ground between the extremes of independence and admiration, where the truth doubtless lies.

At the period referred to, however, Jeffrey's position was a remarkable social phenomenon. The son of a Glasgow tradesman or mechanic, and educated for the bar, by means of a certain degree of taste, a winning style, polished irony, and clever argumentative ability, he vaulted to the throne of criticism — became a literary autocrat, the Napoleon of the world of letters; not without some claim to the distinction, indeed, but yet owing it chiefly to ingenuity, perseverance, and audacity. The reason of this success is obvious. He was the pioneer reviewer; the first who discovered the entire significance of the cabalistic "*we.*" With an acute, though not comprehensive, power of reflection, he united remarkable tact; and, by virtue of these two qualities, naturally succeeded in pleasing that large class of readers who are neither wholly superficial nor profound, but a little of both. He had a metaphysical turn, without rising to the title of a moral philosopher; and could speculate upon abstract questions with an ease and agreeableness that rendered them entertaining. Accordingly, he made abstruse subjects familiar, and delighted many, who had never been conscious of great insight, with the idea that they could appreciate the mysteries of knowledge. There is more, however, that is plausible and attractive, than original or suggestive, in the metaphysical dissertations of Jeffrey. The talent of the writer, rather than the novelty or consistency of his theories, is to be admired. The article, for instance, on Alison's Taste, is a charming specimen of this kind of writing; but it wants definite and satisfactory impressions. It gratifies a taste in composition rather than a passion for truth, which should guide and inspire such investigations.

Qualities attractive in themselves become obnoxious when incongruously united with others of an opposite moral nature. To an honest and loving spirit the coëxistence of beauty and falsehood is too painful for contemplation; and the most fascinating manners revolt when their hypocrisy is once discovered. Sterne prays for a reader who will surrender the reins of imagination to the author's hands. Now, it is a law of human nature that such a tribute is only spontaneously yielded to geniality; and the difficulty of a hearty concession, even of opinion, to Lord Jeffrey, is, that he is more peremptory and acute than sympathetic and respectful. An independent, and, especially, a reverent mind, naturally distrusts the dogmatical tone and plausible reasoning of his criticisms. He discusses a subject with charming vivacity, exhibits an ingenuity that is admirable, and displays a knowledge of outward relations and historical facts that commands respect; and, if the theme is purely objective, unassociated with sentiment of any description, and appealing to mere curiosity, there are few writers who are more delightful. But, when he approaches a subject dear to affection, or consecrated by hallowed memories, we often shrink as from the touch of a coarse and mechanical operator. He then seems to speak without authority; we instinctively question his right to teach, and feel that he is a ruthless intruder into sacred places.

The truth is, that Lord Jeffrey, by nature, education, and habits of thought, was a special pleader. He used words and ideas for an immediate purpose; his object, when most in earnest, is to gain a point; his liberality and depth of feeling were in reverse proportion to his cleverness and information. His great moral defect was want of modesty. He does not appear to have known, by experience, the feeling of self-distrust, but thought himself quite competent to dictate to the world, not only on legal, but on literary and social topics. This reliance upon his own reason gives force and point to those disquisitions the scope of which come within his legitimate range, but makes him offensive, with all his agreeability of style, the moment he transcends his proper sphere. He manifests, in an extraordinary degree, the Scotch idiosyncrasy which refers everything exclusively to the understanding. He was essentially literal.

The interest of Lord Jeffrey's memoirs centres in the fact that its subject was the prime agent of a literary revolution. The incidents of his life are the reverse of extraordinary; his professional career has been surpassed, in many instances, by his fellow-advocates; his habits were systematic and moral; and his outward experience was the usual alternation of business, society, journeys, and rural seclusion, which constitutes the routine of a prosperous and intelligent citizen. A native of Edinburgh, where he was chiefly educated, he passed a few uncomfortable months at Oxford; returned home and finished his preparatory studies, under excellent teachers; after much hesitation, adopted the law as a pursuit; in due time was admitted to the bar, rose to the office of Lord Advocate, took an active part in politics, was twice happily married. He visited London frequently, and there enjoyed the best intellectual society; made excursions to different parts of England, Wales, Ireland, and Scotland; engaged zealously in the debates and genial intercourse of one of the most brilliant clubs ever instituted; and died in his seventy-seventh year, deeply lamented by a large and gifted circle of Edinburgh society, as well as by a tenderly attached family, and a host of noble friends. In this career, so eminently respectable and fortunate, there is obviously little to impress the public. No dramatic scenes, curious adventures, tragic combats with fate, or touching mysteries of inward life; all is plain, sensible, prudent, and successful. With the exception of a rhetorical triumph, a good descriptive hint of scenery or character, and those interludes of sorrow incident to the lot of man, when the angel of death bears off the loved and honored, a singularly even tenor marks the experience of Jeffrey, as described in his correspondence.

Neither is there discoverable any surprising endowment, or fascinating gift, such as renders the very name of some men a spell to quicken fancy, and to draw tears. The order of his mind is within the sphere of the familiar; only in aptness, in constant exercise and skill, was it above the average. With the utilitarian instinct and thorough rationalism of his country, Jeffrey wisely cultivated and judiciously used his powers; above all, he never distrusted them, but, with the patience and the faith of a determined will, kept them at work to the best advantage, and probably reaped as large a harvest, in proportion both to the quality of the soil and the quantity of the seed, as Scotch shrewdness and thrift ever realized. Yet, to continue the similitude, it was more by successive crops, than by grand and lasting fruits, that his labor was rewarded. Some flowers of fancy and a goodly stock of palatable fodder grew in his little garden, but no stately evergreens, sacred night-bloom, or glowing passion-flowers, such as make lovely forever the haunts of original genius. To drop metaphor, Lord Jeffrey owes his reputation, and is indebted for the interest of his biography, to the éclat, influence, and fame, of the Edinburgh Review. The merit of taking the initiative in a more free and bold style of periodical literature, the advantages of the reform thus induced, and the intellectual pleasure derived from the open and spirited discussion, by adequate writers, of public questions, are benefits justly associated with his name, and altogether honorable to his memory. These services, however, are identified, in many minds, with an undue sense of his critical authority, and a submission to his dicta, occasioned by a graceful effrontery of tone, rather than absolute capacity.

Circumstances greatly favored his literary success. At the epoch of the commencement of his enterprise, the liberal party stood in need of an efficient organ. The existent periodicals were comparatively tame and old-fashioned. It was one of those moments in public affairs when a bold appeal was certain to meet with an emphatic response; and the party of friends, among whom originated the idea of a new and spirited journal, were not only fitted by the vigor of their age, the warmth of their feelings, and their respective talents, for the undertaking in view, but were urged by their position, sympathy, and hopes. The great secret of the immediate popularity of the work was undoubtedly its independence. The world instinctively rallies around self-reliance, not only in the exigencies of actual life, but in the domain of letters and politics. Accordingly, the freedom of discussion at once indulged, the moral courage and spirited tone of this fraternal band, won not less than it astonished. The example, so unexpectedly given, in a region distant from the centre of taste and action in the kingdom, of candid and firm assertion of the right of private judgment, the fearless attitude assumed, and the enlightened spirit displayed, carried with them a novel attraction and the highest promise.

The Edinburgh Review was the entering wedge in the old tree of conservatism which had long overshadowed the popular mind; it was like the trumpet-note of an intellectual reinforcement, the glimmering dawn of a more expansive cycle in the world of thought. The feverish speculations ushered in by the French Revolution had prepared the way for the reception of new views; the warfare of parties had settled down into a truce favorable to the rational examination of disputed questions. The wrongs of humanity were more candidly acknowledged; a new school of poetry and philosophy had commenced; and in Scotland, where Jeffrey declares there was a remarkable "intellectual activity and conceit of individual wisdom," a medium of opinion and criticism such as this was seasonable and welcome. Yet it is characteristic of his cool, uninspired mind, that he entered upon the experiment with little enthusiasm. He says, in his correspondence, that his "standard of human felicity is set at a very moderate pitch," and that he has persuaded himself that "men are considerably lower than angels;" his expectations were confessedly the reverse of sanguine; and he eagerly sought to establish his professional resources, and make literature subsidiary. His allies were finely endowed. The wit of Sydney Smith alone was a new feature in journalism; and the remarkable coterie of writers, of which the Review soon became the nucleus, gave it the prestige of more versatile talent than any similar work has ever boasted; so that the editor justly says: "I am a feudal monarch at best, and my throne is overshadowed by the presumptuous crests of my nobles."

A novelty in Lord Jeffrey's position was the social and even civic importance this species of literature acquired. The idea of a man of letters had been associated with refinement, meditation, and a life abstracted, in a great degree, from the active concerns of the world. There was, however, something quite adventurous, exciting, and eventful, in a vocation that so constantly provoked resentment and elicited admiration. Challenged by Moore, carrying Boswell drunk to bed in his boyhood, in correspondence with Byron, dining with Scott, living within constant range of Sydney Smith's artillery of *bon-mots*, the companion of Brougham, Mackenzie, Playfair, Erskine, Campbell, Hamilton, and other celebrated men of the day, his natural fluency derived point and emphasis from colloquial privileges; and doubtless somewhat of the antagonistic character of his writings was derived from the lively debates of the club, and excited by the attrition of such vigorous and individual minds. We are told of his "speculative playfulness," "graceful frankness," and "gay sincerity." These, and epithets of a similar kind, sufficiently indicate the causes of his success. It was through the very qualities that constitute agreeability in society that he pleased as a critic. More serious and intense writing would have repelled the majority. Lord Jeffrey made no grave demands on the thinking faculty; he did not appeal to high imagination, but confined himself to the level of a glib, polished, clever, and often very pleasant style. It was a species of man-of-the-world treatment of books, and therefore very congenial to mediocre philosophers and complacent men of taste.

But to recognize in such a critic the æsthetic principles which should illustrate works of genius, is to wantonly neglect those more earnest thinkers and reverent lovers of the noblest developments of humanity who have, through a kindred spirit, interpreted the mysteries of creative minds. There are passages in Coleridge, Ulrici, Schlegel, Mackintosh, Hazlitt, Wilson, Carlyle, Lamb, and Hunt, which seize upon the vital principle, give the magnetic clue, prolong the key-note of the authors they have known and loved, compared to which Jeffrey's most brilliant comments are as a pyrotechnic glare to the beams of the sun. The list of two hundred articles contributed by him to the Edinburgh displays such a variety of subjects as it is quite impossible for any one mind either thoroughly to master or sincerely relish. The part which he most ably performs, as a general rule, is what may be called the digest of the book; he gives a *catalogue raisonée*, in the broadest sense of the term, and this is excellent service. Biographies, travels, works of science and history, are thus introduced to the world under a signal advantage, when there is no motive to carp or exaggerate in the statements. Next to this class of writings, he deals skilfully with what, for the sake of distinction, may be called the rhetorical poets — those who give clear and bold expression to natural sentiment, without a predominance of the psychological and imaginative. The school of Pope, which appeals to the understanding, the fancy, and to universal feeling, he understands. Hayley, Crabbe, Campbell, Scott, and portions of Byron, he analyzes well, and often praises and blames with reason; to Miss Edgeworth, Irving, and Stewart, he is just. But the sentiment of Barry Cornwall, the suggestive imagery of Coleridge, the high philosophy of Wordsworth, and the luxuriant beauty of Keats, often elude the grasp of his prying intellect.

The lack of spiritual insight was another disqualification of Lord Jeffrey as a critic of the highest poetry. Trained to logical skill, and apt in rhetoric, he never seems to have felt a misgiving in regard to their sufficiency as means of interpretation of every species of mental product. The intuitive creations of genius, born of the soul and not ingenuously elaborated by study, the "imagination all compact" of the genuine bard, were approached by his vivacious mind with an irreverent alacrity. To place himself in sympathetic relation with an individual mind, the only method of reliable criticism, was a procedure he ignored; the play of his own fancy and knowledge, and the oracular announcement of his judgment, were the primary objects; the real significance of the author quite secondary. He reviewed objectively, and arraigned books at his tribunal without that jury of peers which true genius claims by virtue of essential right. A merely agreeable or indifferent subject thus treated may afford entertainment, exactly as a lively chat on the passing topics of the day amuses a vacant hour; but when the offspring of an earnest mind, and the overflowing of a nature touched to fine issues, are sportively discussed and despatched with gay authority, the impatience of more reverent minds is naturally excited.

There was a philosophical elevation in Burke that tempered his severest comments; a noble candor in Montaigne that often reconciles us to his worldliness. Carlyle betrays so deep a sympathy that it robs his sarcasm of bitterness, and Macaulay is so picturesque and glowing that the reader cheerfully allows an occasional want of discrimination to unity of effect. But to that mental superiority which consists in sprightliness of tone and ingenuity of thought we are less charitable; pertness of manner is not conciliating; and off-hand, nonchalant, and superficial decisions, in the case of authors who have excited real enthusiasm and spoken to our inmost consciousness, are not received without serious protest. It is for these reasons that Lord Jeffrey occupies but a temporary place. He did not seize upon those broad and eternal principles which render literary obligations permanent; he was an excellent pioneer, and cleared the way for more complete writers to follow; his independence was conducive to progress in criticism, and his agreeable style made it attractive; but a more profound and earnest feeling is now absolutely required in dealing with the emanations of genius. Too much of the merely clever and amusing manner of Horace Walpole, and too little enthusiasm for truth, characterize his remarks on the really gifted. In the discussion of current literature, the claims of which are those of information and style only, no reviewer can give a better compend, or sum up merits and defects with more brilliancy and tact.

It is natural to expect, in the posthumous biography of influential men, a key to the riddle of their success, a solution of the problem of character, and such a revelation of personal facts as will throw light upon what is anomalous in their career, or explain, in a measure, the process of their development. The lives of Dr. Johnson, of Sir Walter Scott, of Schiller, and, among recent instances, of Keats, Lamb, and Sterling, by the new information they convey in regard to the domestic situation, the original temperament, and the private circumstances of each, have greatly modified previous estimates, and awakened fresh sympathy and more liberal judgments. The life of Lord Jeffrey leaves upon the mind a better impression of the man than obtains among those who knew him only through the pages of the Edinburgh Review, while it confirms the idea which those writings suggest of the author. On the one hand is found a love of nature and a life of the affections which could not have been inferred, at least to their real extent, from the articles on which his literary fame rests; and, on the other, we perceive exactly the original habits of mind, course of study, and tendencies of opinion, to be anticipated from his intellectual career. Accordingly, the integrity, steady friendships, conjugal and parental devotion, and enjoyment of the picturesque, which are so conspicuous in the man, and so worthy of respect and sympathy, should not be allowed to interfere with our consideration of his merits as a writer and critic.

Jeffrey belongs essentially to the class of writers who are best designated as rhetoricians; that is, if closely analyzed, it will be seen that his force lies entirely in sagacity and language. Fluency, vitalized by a certain animation of mind, is his principal means of effect; words he knows well how to marshal in brilliant array; he points a sentence, rounds a paragraph, gives emphasis to an expression, with both grace and spirit. But the value of these elements of style is to be estimated, like the crayons and pigments of the artist, by the qualities they are made to unfold, the ideas they embody, the uses to which they are devoted. Jeffrey possessed them by virtue of an original quickness of intellect and patient industry.

The most striking fact of his early culture is the perseverance with which he practised the art of composition, not as an academic exercise, but as a means of personal improvement; he wrote elaborate papers on various subjects; and at the end recorded his opinion of them, usually the reverse of complacent; and this course he pursued for years, as is proved by the quantity and the dates of the manuscripts he left. No stronger evidence is required of the predominance of the technical over the inspired in his authorship, than this deliberate toil to master the art of expression, as a means of success and a professional acquisition. It now appears that he carried the experiment into verse, and imitated the manner of all the English poets, evidently hoping to obtain the same facility in poetry as in prose. His good sense, however, soon induced him to abandon the former attempt; but the knowledge of versification and the machinery of this highest department of letters, thus acquired, was the basis of his subsequent criticisms, and accounts for his familiarity with the letter, and ignorance of the inward spirit, of the Muse. It is, indeed, a perfectly Scotch process, to set about a course of study and practice in order to think correctly even on subjects so identified with natural sentiment as to repudiate analysis. The romance of literature, or rather its highest function, — that of appealing to human consciousness and unfolding the mysteries of the passions and the awakened sense of beauty, — is effectually destroyed by so cool and premeditated an application of causality to emotion. There is in it a literal mode of thought utterly destructive of illusion; the vague and inexplicable, the "terror and pity" which lift our nature above itself, and ally it with the infinite, are quite unrecognized; the oracles of humanity are rudely disrobed, the sanctities of art violated for the sake of conventional propriety; and what should be instinctively regarded as holy, precious, and apart from the familiar, is made to wear a commonplace aspect.

Jeffrey seems to have mistaken a zest for external charms for a sympathy with poetical experience. Even his essay on Beauty, in the Encyclopædia Britannica, is commended by his biographer for its graceful ingenuity, and not for sympathetic insight or profound analysis. His flippancy, however pleasant when expended on casual topics, is often intolerable as applied to men of genius. He sees that Joanna Baillie is a "nice old woman," but faintly realizes the positive grandeur of feeling which, like a solemn atmosphere, exhales from Basil and De Montfort. He designates faults in Southey's poems, and recognizes the looming of his gorgeous fancy, as one might point out an agreeable pattern of chintz. He is very charitably disposed towards "Tommy Campbell," wonders at the "rapidity and facility" of Burns, and thinks, with his own "present fortune and influence," he could have preserved him a long time. He is of opinion that Wordsworth, upon acquaintance, is "not the least lakish, or even in a degree poetical, but rather a hard and sensible worldly sort of a man;" and that Crabbe, "the wretch, has outrageous faults." He writes dunning letters to Horner, urging him to "do" Malthus or Sismondi, very much as a sea-captain might write to his mate to scrape a deck, or a farmer order his man to hoe a field of potatoes. He praises Dickens' "Notes" on this country, — as shallow a book of travels as ever appeared, — but does not relish the character of Micawber, one of the best creations of the author; and he indulges in reminiscences of the New York Park and Bloomingdale, without having taken the trouble, during some months' residence in that city, to go up the Hudson.

The most creditable of his literary tastes were his admiration of Sir James Mackintosh, and his sensibility to the pathos of such characters as Little Nell and Tom Pinch. Indeed, the "gentle sobs" he confesses, and the hearty appreciation he felt towards the humane novelist, seem to indicate that, with advancing life, his nature mellowed and his sensibilities deepened. A kindness for men of genius, which led him frequently to offer them judicious advice and pecuniary aid, is one of Jeffrey's most excellent traits; and a social enterprise, which made his house the centre of intellectual companionship in Edinburgh, and induced habits of genial intercourse among his contemporaries, men of state, letters, and science, is also to be regarded as a public benefit. Nor less frankly should be acknowledged his unsullied honor, refined hospitality, habits of patient industry, and free and often brilliant conversation. But these benign and useful qualities, while they challenge respect and gratitude, and endear the memory of Jeffrey, do not give authority to his principles of literary judgment, or sanction his claim to be the expositor of the highest literature and the deepest truth.

It is difficult to realize that the amiable character depicted in these volumes is the same individual whose critical severity once caused such a flutter in the dovecote of authors; whose opinion was expected with almost the trepidation of a judicial sentence, and whose praise and rebuke were deemed, by so large and respectable an audience, as final tests of literary rank. Lord

Cockburn assumes, what, indeed, facts seem greatly to confirm, that his award was usually conscientious, and that he had warmly at heart the best interests of literature as he understood them. Of malice or selfish views there is scarcely any evidence; and his personal feelings, towards the very writers he most stringently condemned, appear to have been kind. There is a striking contrast between the amenities of taste, good fellowship, domesticity, and rural enjoyment, amid which he lived, and the idea of a ferocious critic so generally identified with his name. It is another and a memorable instance of the want of correspondence, in essential traits, between authorship and character. To have inspired confidence, respect, and affection, to the extent visible in his memoirs, among the most gifted and the best men of his day, is ample proof of the merit claimed in his behalf by the friend who describes his career. Yet, even admitting the conclusion drawn from these premises, — that "he was the founder of a new system of criticism, and this a higher one than had ever existed," and that "as an editor and a writer he did as much to improve his country and the world as can almost ever be done by discussion, by a single man," — there is a progressive as well as a retrospective standard, an essential as well as a comparative test, and a degree not less than an extent of insight to which such a writer is amenable, and by which alone he can be philosophically estimated. It is doubtless a most useful and desirable object of criticism to elucidate the art and discover the moral influence of literature; the censor in both these spheres is a requisite minister to social welfare; but they do not cover the whole ground. Genius may transgress an acknowledged law of taste in obedience to a higher law of truth; and the so-called moral of a work may be, and often is, misinterpreted by conventional rules. Comprehensive sympathies, as well as quick perception, recognition of the original, as well as knowledge of the prescriptive, are needful qualities in the critic. Loyalty to intuitive sentiment, as well as to external standards, is demanded; and a catholic temper, which embraces with cordiality the idiosyncrasies that invariably distinguish original minds, is indispensable to their appreciation.

It is not what Lord Jeffrey "rather likes," or what "will never do" in his opinion, that disposes of those appeals to the human soul which the truly gifted utter, and to which mankind respond; and the courteous dogmatism and the jaunty grace with which this famous reviewer sometimes pronounces upon the calibre and the mission of the priests of nature, are, therefore, not only inadmissible, but frequently impertinent. One is occasionally reminded of Charles Lamb's impatience at the literal character of the Scotch mind, and his quaint anecdotes to illustrate it, in Jeffrey's positive rule-and-compass style when discussing the productions of genuine poets. How to enjoy these benefactions is as important a lesson as how to judge them; and it is no less an evidence of discrimination deeply to feel beauties, than readily to pick flaws.

The art of philosophizing attractively upon literary and political questions of immediate interest was, indeed, excellently illustrated by Jeffrey, in those instances which did not surpass his power of insight. Where the personal feelings were not engaged, it was also an agreeable pastime to follow his destructive feats; see him annihilate a poetaster, or insinuate away the pretensions of a book-wright. This he did in so cool a manner, and with such a gentlemanly sneer, and refinement of badinage, that it was like watching an elegant fencing-match, or capital shots in a pistol-gallery. The process and the principle, however, of this kind of reviewing were based upon that French philosophy which delights in ridicule, and ignores reverence. Accordingly, its spirit is essentially sceptical, fault-finding, narrow, and smart, and therefore quite inapplicable to the intuitive, the latent, delicate, and more lofty emanations of literature. Its office is to deal with talent, not genius; with attainments, not inspiration; with the form and *rationale*, not with the minute principles and divine mysteries of life. Where knowledge, tact, and wit, were available, Jeffrey shone. He possessed a remarkable degree of what may be called the eloquence of sense; but he lacked soul — the assimilating and revealing principle in man. His intellect needed humanizing. He looked upon an author objectively, with a scientific, not a sympathetic vision, and, therefore, as regards the highest, never came into a legitimate relation with them. He wanted that enthusiasm which, if it sometimes exaggerates merit, and is blind to defects, yet always warms the mind into an unity of perception, and an intensity of observation, which opens new vistas of truth. Jeffrey's analytical power is not denied; but one only demurs at the extent of authority as a critic which, by virtue of it, he claimed. There is a captious tone in his reviews of poets, an unimpassioned statement, a self-possessed balancing of the scales of justice, quite too mechanical to be endured with patience. He thrusts himself arrogantly into a sphere of thought or feeling sacred to thousands, and peers about with the bold curiosity of a successful attorney. He really appreciates only knowledge, reasoning power, and the external laws of taste; and whatever appealed to instincts which were deficient in him, he pronounced either false or absurd.

A man of any real modesty or respect for others would hesitate before utterly condemning a foreign work held in universal admiration in the country of its origin; and would ascribe the fact of its not impressing him to his own ignorance of the language, or insensibility to the sentiment. Jeffrey, on the contrary, flippantly ridicules, as puerile and meaningless, the favorite fiction of the Germans, while confessedly ignorant of their language, and obviously wanting that imagination to which it appeals. He rails against the errors of Alfieri, Swift, and Burns, with a scornful hardihood that shows how little their genius won his sympathies, or their misfortunes touched his heart.

With a practical gauge, regulated by the intellectual tone of an Edinburgh clique, and having for its highest standard only intelligence and the laws of outward morality, he discusses the lives of such men, without a capacity to enter into their motives, to appreciate the circumstances in which they were placed, or to estimate the trials and triumphs of their natures. He ascribes Franklin's self-education to the antagonism of an unfavorable situation rather than to his own perseverance and love of knowledge; and is chiefly struck in Cowper's poetry with the ballad on the loss of the Royal George. A novel of Miss Edgeworth, in which prudence and common sense are the ideal of human character, he can heartily praise; a well-written, authentic narrative, like Irving's Life of Columbus, or a faithful and graphic biography, like the Memoirs of Colonel Hutchinson, he gives a very intelligent account of. But, not content with such useful labors, he has the temerity to wander out of his course, and tell the world that the Excursion "will never do," and that the author of Genevieve and the Ancient Mariner is a foolish mystic. His want of enthusiasm, however, in certain instances, is advantageous to a fair judgment, where works of pure imagination or sentiment are not in question. Thus, having cherished no unreasonable anticipations in regard to Fox's Life of James I., he was not disappointed on its appearance, like the rest of the world, but did the author and his book critical justice; and he exhibited with great candor the brilliant ideas of Madame de Staël, while he repudiated her perfectionist theories. Indeed, one of the greatest merits of Jeffrey is his able synopsis of works of fact and reasoning. He sums up a book as he would a case, and makes a statement to the literary world with the ingenious brevity and emphasis that he would use to a jury. One great reason of the popularity of the Edinburgh Review was that he made it an intelligent and readable epitome of current literature.

Jeffrey claims a high and consistent morality for his long series of articles. It is true he always speaks disapprovingly of the errors of genius; but we fail to perceive in them that enlarged and tender spirit of humanity which softens judgment, and throws the mantle of charity over the shivering form exposed to the pitiless world. He failed in parliament, notwithstanding the shrill melody of his voice; it was too piercing to fascinate; and so we imagine his mind was too acute to embrace cordially the interests and mysteries of his race. Upon the former his attention was too exclusively fixed; for the latter he had not that sentiment of awe which gives a solemn meaning and a sublime pity to the contemplation of genius. Copious in information, vivacious in expression, dogmatical in tone, Jeffrey's talk, like his writing, was animated, witty, and fluent; he was often abstracted in manner, his conversation was interlarded with French epithets, and, in seclusion, he was often depressed. There was more tact and less seriousness of purpose and feeling about him than any of his brilliant contemporaries; and, therefore, his writings have not the same standard value. He sacrificed to the immediate, and was a representative of the times.

There was, with all his apparent readiness and candor, no little prudence in his character. He was a kind of sublimated Yankee, and the ideal of a clever literary Scotchman. The poets he really did appreciate are Campbell and Crabbe — the one by his direct rhetoric and high finish, and the other by his detail and Flemish tone, rendered themselves intelligible to Jeffrey; this was partially the case, also, with Byron, Moore, and Keats; but, where they trench upon the highly imaginative, or earnestly sentimental, he is obviously nonplussed. It is on account of the want of completeness in Jeffrey's views and sympathies that one is disposed to regard him as an able reviewer, instead of a great critic. The evidence of this may be found in the very small quantity of his voluminous writings that now possesses any vital interest and permanent beauty. So many of his speculations want originality and a solid basis, and so many of his judgments have been superseded, that only here and there the lightsome aptness of a remark, the grace of a description, or the analytical justice of a comment, detain us; while the sensible tone and pleasing style vividly realize the cause of the sway once enjoyed by this autocrat of literature.

THE TOLERANT COLONIST.

ROGER WILLIAMS.

PERHAPS the best definition of true greatness is loyalty to a principle; it is certainly the secret of eminent success, and the pledge of true fame. Fidelity to a grand and worthy aim is the highest inspiration; and it is because the subject of this memoir looked steadily beyond the pale of sect, and the motives of self-interest, and strove earnestly for an invaluable, progressive, and essential truth, that his memory is hallowed and his influence permanent.

It is somewhat remarkable that so few incidents have been recorded of a man who first introduced a knowledge of the Indian languages into England, who first established a colony in the New World upon the recognized basis of toleration, and who anticipated Locke and Bayle in maintaining the excellence of that principle in its unlimited significance. The absence of the usual details in his biography may, perhaps, be accounted for by the prejudice which his individuality excited among his cotemporaries, and the influence of sectional jealousy. It was at once the glory and the misfortune of Roger Williams to vindicate a great practical truth, and to experience the transitions of opinion to which every independent mind is liable; hence, while he is endeared to all generous thinkers, he is the absolute exponent of no sect; and it is only within a few years that justice has been awarded his name by the historian. Educated at Oxford, he entered the Church of England, but soon left her priesthood for the more simple faith of the Puritans, came to America, and, by questioning the justice of the king's colonial patents, and the right of legal interference with religious faith and observance, drew upon himself reproach and persecution, before which he fled to the wilderness, and founded a colony in a more liberal spirit, embraced some of the doctrines of the Anabaptists, and, for a while, was a settled preacher of their denomination, but, finally, renounced their main tenet, and went through various phases of religious conviction, often to the detriment of his popularity and worldly success. He was repeatedly chosen to preside over the colony, twice sent on embassies to England in its behalf, and, throughout his life, successfully defended its interests. He was on terms of high confidence with all the New England governors, and exerted a rare influence over the neighboring aboriginal tribes. He was born in Wales, in 1624, and died at Providence, R. I., in April, 1683.

The only memorials of this remarkable man, previous to Elton's Life, except incidental notices, are his life by Professor Knowles, an elaborate poem by Judge Durfee, and a biographical introduction to a modern edition of one of his controversial tracts. Mr. Elton's book has the advantage of being a consecutive narrative, with no more documents than are absolutely requisite to render it authentic. Many new facts, principally the result of inquiries in England, are also now made public for the first time; and thus the volume is a valuable contribution to American biography, as well as a most interesting memorial of colonization and the progress of religious freedom. The subject deserves, and will ultimately attain recognition as one of those rare combinations of the saint and hero which redeem the annals of our race.

Roger Williams implicitly believed in a Providence, and has identified himself with this faith by giving that name to the settlement he founded; and it must be acknowledged that the facts of his career justify the sentiment he cherished. It would be difficult, in the annals of the period, to imagine a combination of events more adapted to educate a pioneer of toleration than those which attended his life. Of inherited endowments it is sufficient to note the remarkable identity of his genealogy with that of Cromwell. Moral courage and independent opinion were thus native to his blood. The next individual with whom his name is associated was Sir Edward Coke. From his birthplace, amid the beautiful scenery of Wales, we trace him to the Star Chamber in London, where his remarkable skill as a reporter gained him the favorable notice of this first lawyer of the age. Coke sent him to school and college; and, subsequently, for a brief space, instructed him in his own profession. The insight thus obtained, as to the principles of jurisprudence, was of great practical benefit to the future colonial legislator; but a higher advantage resulted from this early contact with a mind seldom equalled for acuteness, and a man who, notwithstanding his pitiless arrogance of temper, clearly understood the grounds of English liberty, and first stated them with precision and legal effect. It was certainly a propitious accident that rendered the author of the Bill of Rights, and the defender of the Commons, a benefactor of the youth destined to become the advocate of free principles in the New World. Williams early chose theology as a vocation; and, when admitted to orders in the Church of England, became the companion of Hooker, and the most eminent divines of the times. If he did not have a parish in Lincolnshire, it was his place of residence; and there, as is well known, the bishop of the diocese tacitly encouraged the Nonconformists, so that Williams had the best opportunity to realize his latent convictions; and, when the persecution of Laud became intolerable, followed the example of his fellow-dissenters, and emigrated.

The manner in which the arrival of the young clergyman at Boston, on the 5th of February, 1631, is mentioned, evinces the reputation he had already gained as a man of vigorous understanding and individuality of character. He was first settled at Salem, and soon rose in the respect and attachment of the inhabitants; but, having openly asserted that the magistrates had no authority to punish a breach of the Sabbath, the civil power interfered, and thus began the series of intolerant acts which finally drove him to the complete assertion and practical development of religious liberty. The question ostensibly at issue, however, between the municipal authorities and the clergymen, was not the real ground of alienation. His offence actually consisted in a refusal to recognize a society that professed allegiance to the

English Church. The force of public opinion drove him from Salem; and he became the minister of Plymouth, subsequently returning to his first residence. His known views on the subject of Church and State, and the emphasis with which he claimed the right of private judgment and free action in religion, neutralized the personal influence which a blameless life and signal abilities created. Governor Winthrop, always his friend, advised him to remove to a region where he could enjoy and advocate his sentiments without molestation; and suggested, as the nearest place, the country then designated as Narraganset Bay. He first went to Seekonk; but Winslow, the Governor of Plymouth, warned him, even after he had built and planted there, that he was still within the jurisdiction of their state; and, accordingly, loäth, as he says, "to displease the Bay," he transferred his settlement across the water.

The circumstances of his departure from his old associates, and of his selection of a locality for the new colony, have an additional pathos and beauty that might inspire a poet. Having battled in vain against the narrow prejudices of his townsmen, he was sentenced to banishment; but the season of the year, and the claims of a family, induced him to postpone his departure. The acquiescence of the magistrates in this delay did not, however, prevent Williams from giving utterance to his opinions in conversation, and the attachment he had inspired gained him many willing auditors. This casual success irritated his enemies, and information was privately conveyed to their victim that a plan had been arranged to send him to England by a vessel about to sail. His only resource was flight; and, on a winter's night, with a hatchet, compass, tinder-box, some provisions, and the Bible, he left his fireside and tearful wife and children, and plunged into the forest, trusting rather to savage hospitality than the mercy of his own race; and, like Lear, in his keen sense of human cruelty, ready to brave the fury of the elements. The sufferings incident to such an expedition it is easy to imagine; they form another episode in the drama of his life, infusing a spirit of endurance and the sanction of martyrdom into the heroic purpose of his soul. Less stern and wearisome was the subsequent exploration of the river upon which his little band floated in search of a new asylum.

It was a beautiful summer day. Their leader had already enjoyed an interval of comparative ease; his life had been miraculously preserved, and his confidence renewed. It was decided to select a location in accordance with the greeting of the Indians; and thrice *What-cheer?* welcomed the fugitives to the site of Providence.

When Roger Williams entered this wild territory an exile, he determined to make it his abode: he selected his burial-place; forty-seven years elapsed; his thin and baffled settlement had become a flourishing colony; the principle of spiritual freedom, so dear to his heart, was practically realized — when, full of years and honor, his remains were laid away in this chosen sepulture.

The Baptists claim Roger Williams as one of the founders of their church in America; but this claim is but partially substantiated, and his true fame is that of the stanch advocate of toleration in New England. He introduced a redeeming principle into the conflict of sects; and, amid a people narrowed and hardened with bigotry, set an invaluable example of forbearance on the one hand, and bold self-assertion on the other. His name became a watchword of defence, and his settlement a home for the persecuted. There the civil and ecclesiastical powers were unmixed; every citizen was at liberty to enjoy and peaceably inculcate his peculiar doctrine; and the rights of all were respected. How greatly such a refuge and champion were needed is obvious from a glance at the condition of society in the earlier settlements. The clergy exercised a personal influence that overshadowed the community; they were jealous of power, and sternly reprobated any variance from their standard of faith; public opinion was tyrannical, individual aspirations quelled, and private thought awed. The opponents of agencies like those, however honest and gentle, were immediately ostracized; and fortunate was it that a safe retreat for such victims of fanatical resentment existed in Rhode Island. Thither fled the poor Quakers to escape whipping and the gallows, and there Anne Hutchinson and her disciples found sympathy and protection. Like the miniature republic of San Marino, and the constitutional monarchy of Sardinia to-day, was Rhode Island in the early colonial times. Without those mountainous features which render part of the scenery of Vermont so grand, or that fertile reach of meadow through which winds the Connecticut, this little state has attractive features which may well endear it as a home of freedom. The sea breathes its most tempered air upon its shores; a sky as clearly azure as that of Rome, and sunsets as glowing as those that warm the Apennine peaks, characterize the region. A bracing, yet, for New England, singularly mild climate, belongs to that portion of the state which borders on the Atlantic. These advantages drew to this section of the country many intelligent settlers, and afterwards attached to it not a few illustrious men, whose names are now associated with its local charms and noble annals, such as Bishop Berkeley, Allston, and Malbone, the artists; Stiles and Channing, the divines; Perry, and a score of other naval heroes.

While procuring the charter in England, Roger Williams was greatly assisted by Sir Henry Vane, another glorious spirit, and subsequently a martyr to the principles which his compatriot established in America. Acting as his medium with the commissioners, Vane procured all the desired articles of the charter; and Williams dedicated to Lady Vane his first work, which was published about this time. An incident of peculiar interest, brought to light by a letter of Roger Williams in this volume, is his intimacy, when thus occupied in London, with Milton. It appears they both were then engaged in the instruction of youth; and while the poet enlightened the reformer on some of the niceties of Hebrew and Latin, the latter gave the secretary of Cromwell lessons in the Indian tongues. Thus Williams enjoyed the sympathy and counsel of the two noblest men of his age, Milton and Vane, and was doubtless inspired by their confidence to maintain the rights of conscience in his settlement. On turning thither, after his successful embassy, he was greeted at Seekonk by a fleet of canoes, and, under their escort, arrived at home, where the new charter was read in public, amid grateful acclamations. His second visit to England, to procure a renewal of these privileges, the revocation of Coddington's charter, and other benefits for the colony, was equally fortunate; the occasion also enabled him to publish other works, and to enjoy the society of many brave and wise men who approved his noble purposes.

The daughter of Sir Edward Coke, his first kind friend and patron, treated his advances, however, with disdain, on account of their diverse religious views; and the correspondence between them, now first published in Elton's volume,* exhibits, on her part, a lamentable narrowness of soul and harsh bigotry, and, on his, a gentleness and forbearance worthy of his character.

The hostility of the elder colony towards the first legislator for liberty of conscience, did not remit when he had passed beyond its limits. He was obliged to go to New York to embark for England, not being able to obtain the consent of the Boston authorities to pass through their province. They even denied him the compliment of a vote of thanks for his eminent services during the Pequot war; and when the states of New England formed a defensive league against their common and savage enemy, Rhode Island was not permitted to join. The policy of that infant state at this period was, indeed, a constant reproach to her less tolerant but more prosperous neighbor, of which the contrast of their respective behavior to the Quakers is a striking illustration.

Lamartine has given a highly dramatic picture of Napoleon's solitary advance towards the regiment of Grenoble after his flight from Elba; not less courageous was the appeal to savage magnanimity of Roger Williams, when he ventured alone into the midst of an exasperated tribe collected for battle, and, by the force of his calm and kindly resolution, subdued their vindictive purpose. Indeed, one of the most interesting features of his career is his relation with the Indians. By the magnetism of consistent kindness and fearless bearing, he won the confidence and respect of those children of the forest. Canonicus signed a deed of the land he purchased, and caused his nephew to attest it; thenceforth a most friendly intercourse subsisted between the two chiefs and their pale guest. The magnanimity of Roger Williams is shown in his effective mediation with these savage allies, when a formidable conspiracy threatened the colony which had so ignominiously expelled him. In 1663 he writes to Winthrop: "I discerned cause of bestirring myself, and staid the longer; and, at last, through the mercy of the Most High, I not only sweetened his spirit, but possessed him that the plague and other sicknesses

* Life of Roger Williams, by Romeo Elton, D.D., F. R. P. S.

were alone in the hand of God." He is speaking of Canonicus, and his delusion that the English brought a pestilence among the aborigines, and deserved, therefore, to be cut off. When the venerable sachem expired, Williams compares the feeling manifested by his tribe and that of the Bay colonists at the funeral of their excellent governor: "He so lived and died, and in the same most honorable manner and solemnity (in their way) as you laid to sleep your prudent peacemaker, Mr. Winthrop, did they honor their prudent and peaceable prince." The romance which has been associated with the Indian race of this continent is fast vanishing. Well-informed writers, intent rather upon the scientific than poetical view, have demonstrated that, with much that is curious, there is little of promise or beauty in the nature of the red man; and nowhere did the Indian present a more hopeless character than in the region colonized by Williams. It is a remarkable evidence of their drunken propensity, that a special vote of the Town Council was requisite even for so judicious a citizen as Williams to supply them with alcoholic medicine. In the state record, it is noted that "leave was granted to Roger Williams to sell a little wine or strong water to some natives in case of sickness." It was not by direct expostulation only that he warded off impending danger from the other settlements. Through his Narraganset friends, in repeated instances, he obtained seasonable notice of the vindictive plans of other tribes, and gave due warning; thus, in the Pequot war, he prevented an Indian league, and saved the colony from destruction. He was also a mediator between the Indians themselves, and carried their petition, "that they might not be forced from their religion," to the English king. These offices gave him a strong hold upon their sympathies; and we find in his correspondence that the influence thus acquired was constantly invoked by those who had most wantonly persecuted this brave messenger of peace. To his knowledge of Hebrew, Greek, and Latin, Williams had now added the Indian tongue, of which he prepared a key during his first voyage to England. It was published in London. Few of the new settlers were able to maintain such direct intercourse with the natives; and he endeared himself to them by publicly advocating strict payment and definite boundaries for all lands occupied by the whites, notwithstanding the charter, by virtue of which they were held. The domain, ceded to him in 1638 by Canonicus, was given in consideration of "many kindnesses." "Thousands nor tens of thousands of money," he says, "could not have bought of him an English entrance into this bay; but I was the procurer of that purchase by the language, acquaintance, and favor of the natives, which it pleased God to give me." This spirit of justice, however, was not relished by many of his countrymen, and increased the unpopularity incident to some of his opinions. The most heretical of these, it would appear from the charges preferred at his trial at Boston, in July, 1635, were the following: "That the magistrate ought not to punish the breach of the first table (or law of the Sabbath) otherwise than in such cases as did disturb the civil peace; that he ought not to tender an oath to an unregenerate or irreligious man; that a man ought not to pray with such, however near and dear; and that a man ought not to give thanks after sacrament, nor after meat." The authorities "professedly declared" that he ought to be banished from the colony for maintaining the doctrine "that the civil magistrate might not intermeddle even to stop a church from heresy or apostasy;" and, in order to annoy him, they refused a civil right demanded by the people of Salem, because it came through their obnoxious pastor. The cruel decree was indignantly opposed by the minority, for, says the historian, "he was esteemed an honest, disinterested man, and of popular talents in the pulpit."

Of his mental powers we have no means of judging, except the respect and interest he awakened in those with whom he dwelt, and the writings he left. These are chiefly of a controversial nature, and on questions which have, in a great measure, lost their significance. The style, too, is involved, quaint, and often pedantic. The views, however, advocated even in his polemic discussions, are often in advance of his time, and the sentiments he professes are noble and progressive. Thus, "The Bloody Tenent" is an earnest plea with the clergy for toleration; and "A Hireling Ministry" presents bold and just arguments in support of free churches, and against an arbitrary system of tithes. In the Redwood Library, at Newport, is a copy of "George Fox digged out of his Burrows," a characteristic specimen of the theological hardihood of Williams, as exhibited in his controversy with the Quakers. But it is from his original force of character, and his loyalty to a great principle, that Roger Williams derives his claim to our admiration. His shades of opinion are comparatively unimportant; but the spirit in which he worked, suffered, and triumphed, enrols his name among the moral heroes and benefactors of the world. His correspondence, not less than his life, evinces the highest domestic virtue, scrupulous fiscal integrity, a truly forgiving temper, rare tenacity of purpose, and a speculative turn of mind. Whatever changes of opinion he exhibits, his sentiments are always consistent, and genuine piety elevates a heart nerved by true courage, and expanded with generous emotions.

When from the empyrean of contemplation we survey the map of history, it is sometimes possible to trace the converging lines of opinion along the current of events until they unite to reveal and actualize truth. Accordingly, if the history of Toleration was written by a philosophic annalist, it would appear that a remarkable coincidence, both of speculation and action, at widely separate points, occurred to elucidate the great problem. In such a discussion, the life of Roger Williams would form a significant chapter; and it would be noted as a singular combination, that while Coke made clear and authoritative the political rights of the people, Vane broached philosophical arguments for republicanism, and Milton nobly pleaded for the freedom of the press in England, Roger Williams, their friend and ally, vindicated religious toleration in America; each of these achievements being elements of the same great cause.

THE LITERARY ADVENTURER.

RICHARD SAVAGE.

THE distinction of civilized society is, that human life is systematic, and the natural effect of those circumstances which, in any degree, except an individual from its usual routine and responsibilities, is to induce the impulsive action and precarious expedients that belong to wild races. In the world of opinion and habit we occasionally see those who, goaded by misfortune, or inspired by an adventurous temper, break away from the restraint which custom ordains, and, by hardihood in action, or extravagance of sentiment, practically isolate themselves from nearly all the social obligations acknowledged by mankind. Indeed, every human pursuit may be said to have its respectable and its vagabond followers. In trade, these extremes are obvious in the merchant and the pedler; in the church, we have the bishop and the field-preacher; and in literature, the author, who devotes the leisure that intervenes between the care of his estates and the engagements of fashionable society to a review, a poem, or a history, and the man about town, who lives by his wits, and whose dinner is contingent upon a happy epigram, or a successful farce. Even when fortune and rank obtain, natures imbued with a vagrant or adventurous spirit will cut loose from social bondage through mere waywardness or courage, as if there were gypsy blood in their veins, or the instinct of heroism or discovery in their hearts.

The enthusiasm of misanthropy made Byron a pilgrim, that of

reform drove Shelley into exile, and that of sentiment won Rousseau to a picturesque hermitage. How much of human conduct depends upon the source whence is derived the inspiration or the sanction of existence! Family pride leads to a constant reference to the standard of external honor; the desire of wealth, to a keen adaptation of all occasions to interest; while the consciousness of having nothing beyond personal resources to look to for advancement or happiness, breeds in earnest minds an independence of mood almost defiant. To this we attribute, in no small degree, the recklessness of Savage. Every circumstance of his life tended to encourage self-will. He found neither in his birth, his fortunes, nor the incidents of his daily experience, any vantage-ground for confidence. Fate seemed to ordain between him and society a perpetual enmity. Hence his dauntless egotism. Driven from the outworks of life, he fortified the citadel. Sure of no palladium but his genius, he held it up as a shield against the arrows of scorn, or thrust it forth as an authentic emblem of his right to demand from others the satisfaction of his wants. Perhaps there is no instance, if we except Benvenuto Cellini, of more ferocious self-reliance, or rather pertinacity in levying tribute. In his career we realize that the essential traits of civilized and barbarian life may assimilate; that refined mental aptitude may coëxist with extreme personal degradation; and that the support of existence is often as precarious, and the habits of life as vagrant, in a Christian metropolis, as among the Indian tribes of America, or the wild hordes of the East.

The genuine literary adventurer is, indeed, a kind of social Ishmaelite, pitching the tent of his convenience as necessity or whim suggests. It is his peculiar destiny to "take no note of time;" for he falls into any incidental scheme of festivity at morning, noon, or night, joins any band of roysterers he may encounter, takes part in the street-corner discussions of any casual knot of politicians, and is always ready to go to the theatre, the club, a private domicile, or a coffee-house, with the first chance-acquaintance he meets. He hangs loose upon the skirts of society. If the immediate is agreeable, he scorns change, and hence will prolong his social visits to the infinite annoyance of those who keep regular hours. Where he breakfasts, dines, or sleeps, is problematical in the morning. As the itinerant musician goes forth to win entertainment by his dulcet notes, the vagabond man of genius trusts to his fund of clever stories, his aptitude as a diner-out, his facility at pen-craft, or his literary reputation, to win upon the sympathies of some humane auditor, or chain the attention of the inquisitive, and thus provide for the claims of physical necessity.

His appeal is three-fold — to the benevolent, the curious, and the vain; and, in a large city, with the *entrée* of a few circles and places of resort, it will be, indeed, a strange hazard that deprives him wholly of these long-tried expedients. His agreeability makes him friends, whom his indiscretions at length weary: but, as he generally prefers to do all the talking himself, he gradually ceases to be fastidious, and, when he cannot fraternize with a scholar or a gentleman, contents himself with inferior society. The consciousness of superior gifts and singular misfortunes soon blunts that delicacy which shrinks from obligation. He receives a favor with the air of a man to whom consideration is a birthright. He is, as Landor says of woman, more sensitive than grateful; borrows money and books without a thought of returning them; and, although the most dependent of beings, instantly resents the slightest approach to dictation as a personal insult. He is emphatically what Shakspeare denominates a "landless resolute;" considers prudence too mean a virtue for him to adopt, and industry a habit unworthy of his spirit. His wits are his capital, which he invests day by day; now and then, perhaps, embarking them in a more deliberate venture, by way of polishing his tarnished escutcheon. Equally exempt from the laws of sentiment and those of economy, he makes unconscionable drafts upon the approbativeness and the malignity of others, by inditing panegyrics and lampoons.

A subscription, a dedication, or a satire, by awakening the generosity, the pride, or the fear of the world, alternately supply the exigencies of the moment; while the utter loss of self-respect is prevented by some occasional effort in a nobler vein, or complacent memories of past renown. Custom renders him at home everywhere; address repudiates individual rights; and a kind of happy boldness annihilates, by a stroke of humor or a phrase of geniality, the barriers of artificial reserve. He is the modern knight-errant; prompt to challenge recognition, and, with gallant bearing, win the guerdon to which he aspires, whether it be the smile of beauty, the companionship of rank, or the privileges that wealth dispenses.

Experience in shifts, and a sanguine temper united to capacity for reflection, render him withal a philosopher; so that, although keenly alive to present enjoyment, he can suffer with fortitude, and heroically sport with deprivation. He is vividly conscious of what Madame de Staël declares is one great secret of delight —its fragility. His existence is singularly detached from routine, and, like a bird or a butterfly, he soars or alights, as caprice suggests — a chartered adventurer, to whom has been presented the freedom of nature. Leisure gives scope to his observation; need quickens his perception; and the very uncertainty of subsistence adds infinitely to the relish of each gratification. A voluntary outlaw, he claims ransom from those his talents have made captive; regarding himself as a public benefactor, he deems society under obligations to take care of him; prodigal in his mental riches, he despises those who are parsimonious either of their time or their hospitality; and sincere in his admiration, and perhaps in his advocacy, of all that is magnanimous and beautiful, he learns to regard material advantage as his just inheritance, which directly to seek would obscure the heraldry bestowed by his genius, and sanctioned by misfortune.

To him might be literally applied Valentine's argument in Fletcher's comedy of "Wit without Money:"

"Means—
Why, all good men 's my means; my wit 's my plough,
The town 's my stock, tavern 's my standing-house
(And all the world knows there 's no want); all gentlemen
That love society love me; all purses
That wit and pleasure open are my tenants;
Every man's clothes fit me; the next fair lodging
Is but my next remove; and, when I please
To be more eminent, and take the air,
A piece is levied, and a coach prepared,
And I go I care not whither."

"What 's my knowledge, uncle?
Is 't not worth money? What 's my understanding?
Travel! reading! wit! all these digested! My daily
Making men, some to speak, that too much phlegm
Had frozen up; some, that spoke too much, to hold
Their peace, and put their tongues to pensions.
Besides these ways to teach
The way of nature, a manly love, community
To all that are deservers, not examining
How much or what 's done for them; it is wicked."

It is peculiar to this class of men to be unconscious of the diverse attractions of talents and character. Their egotism prevents an habitual recognition of the important fact that the entertainment afforded by conversational abilities and personal sympathy are two very distinct things. Because their talk is listened to with avidity, their wit productive of laughter, and their reputation of deference, they deduce the erroneous conclusion that individually and for themselves an interest is awakened; whereas, in most cases, the charm is purely objective. By men of the world genius of a literary kind is regarded in the same light as dramatic, artistic and juggling cleverness; the result is not associated with the person; it is the pastime, not the man, that wins. A conviction so wounding to self-love is not easily adopted; and, as a natural consequence, the deluded victims of social applause continue, in spite of mortifying experience, to look for a degree of consideration, and demand a sympathy, which it is absurd to expect from any but the very liberal and the naturally kind, who confessedly form the exception, not the rule, in general society. Yet, in actors, authors, and artists, who possess great self-esteem, this error is the rock upon which the bark of hope invariably splits. There seems to be a kind of inevitable blindness in this regard. Slowly and by long degrees comes home the feeling that it is what the man of genius does, not what he is, that excites admiration. When the pageant of an hour fades, what care the narrow-minded and the selfish for those who have ministered to their pleasure? Only enthusiasm lingers and pays tribute; only gratitude is sensible of an obligation incurred; reverence alone dreams of any return, and conscientiousness is the sole monitor that pays the debt.

The incidents of his life rather than the creations of his genius have preserved the fame of Savage. His poems are his only writings now recognized, and we find them regularly included in editions of the British anthology. It is, however, but here and there, scattered through a long array of heroics, that we can detect either originality or raciness. Like his life, these effusions are crude and unsustained; they lack finish, completeness, and unity. Deformed by coarseness, and sometimes by obscurity, they often repel taste; and their frequent want of clear and uniform design induces weariness. Their most genuine interest is personal; we naturally associate them with the misfortunes of the author, and the special references are not without a pathetic zest. The "Progress of a Divine" and "The Bastard," although redeemed by wit and cleverness, are too grossly indelicate for general perusal. The bitterness of the one, and the confident hilarity with which the other begins, are very characteristic of Savage. It is evident that he possessed, in an uncommon degree, what the phrenologists call the organ of wonder, and metaphysical writers a sense of the sublime. In his descriptions of nature and life, we perceive the inspiration of a reflective ideality. His couplets occasionally glow with vital animation, and his choice of epithets is often felicitous. Vigor, fluency, and expressiveness, at times, indicate that there was an original vein in his nature, though too carelessly worked to produce a great and consistent result. "The Wanderer" is the poem upon which he evidently bestowed the greatest care. It may be regarded as his own epitaph, written by himself, and embodying the dark phases of his career, the most vivid of his sensations, and the beauty of his moral sentiments, combined with the want of system, the self-esteem, recklessness, and courage, which alternated in his feelings and conduct.

The following passages evidently allude to actual experience:

"Is chance a guilt? that my disastrous heart,
For mischief never meant, should ever smart?
Can self-defence be sin? Ah, plead no more!
What though no purposed malice stain thee o'er?
Had Heaven befriended thy unhappy side,
Thou hadst not been provoked, or thou hadst died."

* * * *

——— "No mother's care
Shielded my infant innocence with prayer;

> No father's guardian hand my youth maintained,
> Called forth my virtues, or from vice restrained."

He learned the process of glass manufacturing, by sleeping during winter nights, when a vagrant, near the furnaces:

> "Yon limeless sands, loose driving with the wind,
> In future cauldrons useful textures find,
> Till, on the furnace thrown, the glowing mass
> Brightens, and brightening hardens into glass."

The homeliness of such lines is like Crabbe, yet his capacity for more polished versification is shown in his allusion to Pope, as polished and emphatic as that of the master rhymer himself:

> "Though gay as mirth, as curious though sedate,
> As elegance polite, as power elate,
> Profound as reason, and as justice clear,
> Soft as compassion, and as truth severe;
> As bounty copious, as persuasion sweet,
> Like nature various, and like art complete,
> So firm her morals, so sublime her views,
> His life is almost equalled by his muse."

In metaphor, also, Savage is effective. Thus he compares the "steamy currents" at morning twilight to "veins blue winding on a fair one's arm;" and, of a river hidden in umbrage, observes:

> "Yet, at one point, winds out in silver state,
> *Like virtue from a labyrinth of fate.*"

He calls shells "tinctured rivals of the showery bow;" and, describing a vast prospect, says:

> "The herds seem insects in the distant glades,
> And men diminished as, at noon, their shades."

His adjectives are sometimes very graphic, however inelegant; he speaks of warming himself at "*chippy* fires," and, detailing a repast, informs us,

> "That o'er a homely board a napkin 's spread,
> Crowned with a *heapy* canister of bread."

The gleams of high sentiment that, like flashes of heat-lightning from a dense cloud, emanate from Savage, are refreshing, and justify his biographer's tribute to his better nature. Self-indulgent as he was, he declares that

"Reason's glory is to quell desire."

Although he obviously is in his element when

"In gay converse glides the festive hour,"

he yet recognizes a providence in affliction:

"Why should I then of private loss complain,
Of loss that proves, perchance, a brother's gain?
The wind that binds one bark within the bay,
May waft a richer freight its wished-for way.
Man's bliss is like his knowledge, but surmised,
One ignorance, the other pain disguised.
When seeking joy, we seldom sorrow miss,
And often misery points the path to bliss.
Know, then, if ills oblige thee to retire,
Those ills solemnity of thought inspire."

The following random extracts betray a vivid consciousness of his own fate and tendencies:

"False pride! what vices on our conduct steal
From the world's eye one frailty to conceal!
Ye cruel mothers! soft! those words command!
So near shall cruelty and mother stand?
Can the dove's bosom snaky venom draw?
Can her foot sharpen like the vulture's claw?"

* * * *

"Loosed to the world's wide range, enjoined no aim,
Prescribed no duty, and assigned no name,
Nature's unbounded son, he stands alone,
His heart unbiased, and his mind his own."

* * * *

"From ties maternal, moral, and divine,
Discharged my gasping soul; pushed me from shore,
And launched me into life without an oar."

* * * *

"Born to himself, by no profession led,
In freedom fostered, and by fortune fed,
Nor guides, nor rules, his sovereign choice control,
His body independent as his soul."

* * * *

"Inly secure, *though conscious soon of ill,*
Nor taught by wisdom how to balance will,
Rashly deceived, I saw no pits to shun,
But thought to purpose and to act were one."

That we have not exaggerated the prominent claim of Savage to represent the literary adventurer, a glance at the account of him by Johnson — the most remarkable and original of his "Lives of the Poets" — will, at once, evidence. We are there told that, when a guest, he "could neither be persuaded to go to bed at night, or rise by day;" that "he considered himself discharged, by the first quarrel, from all ties of honor and gratitude;" that "when he loved a man, he suppressed all his faults, and, when he had been offended by him, suppressed all his virtues;" "always asked favors without the least submission or apparent consciousness of dependence;" "purchased the luxury of a night by the anguish of cold and hunger for a week;" "though he scarcely ever found a stranger whom he did not often leave a friend, he had not often a friend long, without obliging him to become a stranger;" and that "the reigning error of his life was that he mistook the *love* for the *practice* of virtue."

We could easily multiply well authenticated instances of the foibles and the inconsiderateness, the casual triumphs and low expedients, that doomed him to vibrate "between beggary and extravagance." To indicate the relative value he attached to his inware resources and his outward obligations, a few anecdotes will suffice. While an inmate of Lord Tyrconnel's family, he sold several books which his host had presented him, with his lordship's arms stamped upon them; and, at the same time, betrayed the most fastidious and even "superstitious regard to the correction of his proof-sheets." While on the most intimate and friendly terms with Dennis, he wrote an epigram against him; and when his friends, their patience quite exhausted, contributed to secure him a permanent retreat in the country, he indulged in the most illusive dreams of rural felicity, and before he was half-way on the road to Wales, sent back to London for new supplies, which he soon expended among pleasant companions in Bristol, whose keen appreciation of his social qualities induced a versified comparison of their merits with those of his London protectors, by no means to the advantage of the latter, notwithstanding his recent obligations. The reverse of Dominie Sampson, he was very scornful at the idea of new habiliments being furnished him without the intervention of his own taste and authority. The mortification of illegitimacy was solaced by that of noble blood and the advantages he traced to "the lusty stealth of nature." Scenes of profligacy, social ostracism, and a criminal trial, utterly failed in undermining a "steady confidence in his own capacity;" while he only regarded poverty as an evil from the contempt it is apt to engender; and he always thought himself justified in resenting neglect "without attempting to force himself into regard." Such a combination of traits, developed under extraordinary vicissitudes, completely illustrates the spirit of literary adventure, and the perversity of unregulated talent.

Yet this dark biographical picture, gloomy as one of Spagnoletto's martyrdoms, is not without mellow tints, nor its hard outlines unrelieved by touches of humanity. Upon his first discovery of a mother's name and existence, revealed to him by several documents found among the effects of his deceased nurse, the heart of Savage awakened to all the latent tenderness inspired by a new-born affection. It was his habit, long after the determined repulse of his unnatural parent had quenched the hope of recognition, to walk to and fro before her house, in the twilight, amply compensated if, through his tears, he could obtain but a glimpse of her robe as she passed near the window, or see the gleam of a candle in her chamber. At the period of his greatest want and highest mental activity, he composed while perambulating a verdant square, or retired mall, and then entered a shop, asked for a scrap of paper, and noted down his conceptions. In this manner he is said to have written an entire tragedy; and certainly few instances of resolute authorship in the grasp of poverty can equal its touching fortitude.

His speech to the court, when arraigned for sentence after being convicted of homicide, is said to have been manly and eloquent, and certainly won for him great sympathy and respect. There must have been something in his character that inspired esteem, as well as in his fortunes to kindle compassion, from the interest so frequently excited and patiently manifested in his behalf by individuals widely separated in position and opinions. In some instances, too, the independence of his nature exhibited itself in a noble manner. The spirited letter which he addressed to a friend from the prison at Bristol, where he was incarcerated for debt, and so drearily terminated his eventful career, is a fine example of self-respect and elevation of sentiment. Hunt justly remarks, in his notice of the once celebrated Mrs. Oldfield, that her annuity to Savage gave posterity a liking for her; and Dr. Johnson assures us that the subject of his remarkable memoir, when banished from London, parted from him with tears in his eyes.

Indeed, the phases of character and the actual experiences of Savage, if analyzed and dramatically unfolded by a thoroughly sympathetic delineator, would afford a most fruitful theme. Imagine it handled by Dickens, in his best vein: we should have night-wanderings as forlorn as those of little Nell and her grandfather, a trial scene more effective than that of Barnaby Rudge, jollities eclipsing those of Dick Swiveller, and reveries more grandly pathetic than the death-bed musings of Paul Dombey. For accessories his acknowledged relation to the nobility and his intimate association with the men of talent of the day would furnish ample scope; for so notorious was his story at the time, that Macaulay, in his "History of England," says that Earl Rivers is remembered chiefly on account of his illegitimate son; and the Countess of Macclesfield, brazen as was her temper, was obliged to fly from Bath to escape the observation of fashionable crowds induced by the satirical poem of Savage, called "The Bastard."

Prompted by that love of excitement which becomes the ruling impulse of the improvident and forlorn, Savage went forth one night from his obscure lodgings in search of profitable meditation, a boon companion, or a lucky adventure. There was in his elongated and rough face a sad expression that indicated habitual melancholy; not the resigned air of meek endurance, nor the gravity of stern fortitude, but that dark, brooding pensiveness which accompanies undisciplined passions and a desolate existence. There was, however, a redeeming dignity in his measured gait, and an unsteady accent in his voice as he soliloquized, that would have "challenged pity" in a sensitive observer.

He entered a tavern — an accustomed haunt, where conviviality had often beguiled him of "the thing he was." The sight of one or two familiar faces, and the anticipation of a jolly evening, changed, at once, the mood of the homeless wit. That coarse exterior suddenly wore a milder aspect; that solemn air gave way to *abandon ;* and, all at once, he looked like a man ready to "flit the time lightly," and "rouse the night-owl with a catch." It was thoughtfulness eclipsed by good fellowship — Hamlet transformed into Sir Toby Belch. The carousal brought on the hour of feverish reäction, and the party at length sallied out to breathe the fresh air, and vent their superfluous merriment. Attracted by a light that gleamed from another house of entertainment, they entered, and unceremoniously disturbed a group already in possession. High words arose, swords were unsheathed, and when the morning dawned, Savage found himself a prisoner awaiting trial for murder. At this crisis of his fate, with the ban of the law impending, amid the solitude of captivity, how must the events of his life have passed in gloomy succession before his mind, and what desperate emotion must the retrospect have engendered !

We can scarcely imagine a more contradictory and pathetic story invented by fiction. The illegitimate offspring of a countess and an earl, brought up by a hireling, taken from St. Albans grammar-school in boyhood to be apprenticed to a shoemaker; cut off by an infamous falsehood from the inheritance assigned him by his father; accidentally discovering his birth only to become the object of relentless maternal persecution; with the loss of his nurse, cast adrift upon the world and forced into authorship to escape starvation, and now only with the prospect of an ignominious death incurred in a tavern brawl; what incentives his memory could furnish to remorse and despair! His whole experience was anomalous. Of noble origin, yet the frequent associate of felons and paupers; with a mother for his most bitter enemy, and the slayer of one who never offended him; long accustomed to luxury, yet finding his best comfort in a jail; conscious of superior abilities, yet habituated to degrading expedients; his written life touching the hearts of thousands, while his actual condition annoyed more often than it interested; the guest of a wealthy lord, the confidant of men of genius, the intimate of Wilkes and Steele, and the cynosure of many select circles in London and Bristol, he sometimes famished for want of nourishment, and "slept on bulks in summer and in glass-houses in the winter." From the king he received a pardon, after being condemned to the gallows, and from a fashionable actress a pension; the queen's volunteer-laureate, he died in a prison-cell, and was buried at the expense of the jailer. The records of human vicissitude have few more painful episodes; the plots of few tragedies boast more pathetic material; and the legacies of genius, to those who explore them to analyze character and trace the influence of experience upon mental development, rarely offer the adventurous and melancholy interest that is associated with the name of Richard Savage. He is the type of reckless talent, the ideal of a literary vagabond, the synonym for an unfortunate wit. In his history the adventures of hack-writers reach their acme; and his consciousness embraced the vital elements of dramatic experience, the internal light of fancy and reflection, and the external shade of appalling fact.

THE NATIONAL ECONOMIST.

DE WITT CLINTON.

The leaders of opinion and men of executive genius, in all nations and eras, sustain an inevitable relation to their age; and it is a curious study to investigate how circumstances of time and place modify their activity. The memories of Westminster have enshrined the oratorical triumphs of Fox, Pitt, and Burke, and their agency on public sentiment is woven into the very texture of England's political annals; while the monuments and galleries of Florence bear witness to the dominant taste for art which was fostered by Lorenzo de Medici. In a young republic whose material progress is without example, the evidence of patriotic self-devotion is continually obliterated by the advancing tide of civilization, radical improvements are superseded by new inventions, and it is often a difficult task to recall to grateful recognition the labors and triumphs of national benefactors. The insatiable present renders men oblivious of the past; the inviting future precludes retrospection. Yet, to those alive to local history and the origin of great practical ideas, daily observation keeps fresh the memory of Clinton in his native state. As a stranger enters her unrivalled bay, he sees in the fortified Narrows a proof of his patriotic forethought; in an afternoon excursion the Bloomingdale Asylum and Sailor's Snug Harbor, whose endowment he secured, bear witness to his benevolent enterprise; while the grand systems of public instruction, of mutual insurance, of internal navigation, of savings-banks, reform of the criminal law, and agricultural improvement, however modified by the progress of science, constantly attest the liberal and wise polity which under his guidance gave them birth.

Born on the second of March, 1769, and dying on the eleventh of February, 1828, De Witt Clinton entered upon life when the contest between the two original parties under the Federal government was at its height, and closed his existence at the epoch of their virtual dissolution. By inheritance and sympathy he ardently espoused one class of opinions, and experienced the modifications of political sentiment incident to the course of events and the development of the nation. He became one of the gladiators in the civic arena, when state rights, foreign influence, and a thousand exciting questions, agitated the land. It is not our purpose to review his political career, to recall the misrepresentation, ingratitude, and insult, of which he was the victim, or to trace the tortuous current of alternate proscription and idolatry that bore him over the changeful sea of party strife. The same battle, in divers forms, is continually fought, and its chief incidents belong to the history of contemporary opinion. Like all aspirants, he was baffled; like all chiefs, envied; like all loyal men, persecuted. In an impartial estimate of his character, it is sufficient proof of his integrity that it was never successfully assailed; of his patriotism, that it was ultimately recognized; of his republicanism, that his faith in the people never faltered; of his magnanimity, that he forgave injury; and of his statesmanship, that it was victorious. Doubtless, a want of flexibility, a temper too dictatorial, a power of invective sometimes unchastened, and an extreme tenacity of personal conviction, led him into errors. But now that the storm has passed away, his traits are reflected in noble relief upon the calm horizon, visible to the eyes of posterity. The test of time has proved the sterling qualities of the man, and we impatiently scatter the web of intrigue and the mist of prejudice, to contemplate only those characteristic services that planted his star forever in the galaxy of our country's firmament.

The domestic antecedents of De Witt Clinton were favorable to the inheritance both of energetic character and of public spirit. His name is of Norman origin, and is often cited by the old

18

French chroniclers of knightly achievements. Among his immediate ancestors was a Royalist cadet, one of the Continental refugees after the civil war, who, on the restoration of the house of Stuart, experienced its faithless ingratitude. The son of this progenitor vainly sought to regain the estates forfeited by the loyalty of his exiled father, who died in Ireland; nor were the family misfortunes retrieved by the next generation, for Charles Clinton, in the prime of his life, resolved to emigrate to America. With a view to pastoral advantages, he made choice of that fertile district of Orange County, in the State of New York, whose grassy acres still supply the best products of the dairy. Here his superior intelligence gave him the lead in social life among the isolated band that formed the infant colony; and on the frontier and fortified farm, sixty miles from the city, the father of De Witt Clinton was born. Thus, by a sad experience of king-craft and the discipline of primitive colonial life, was our young statesman nurtured in patriotic self-reliance, while his ancestral qualities were enriched by the old Dutch blood of his mother's race. Sprung from educated and loyal, adventurous and brave progenitors, he entered upon life early enough to witness the sacrifices which acquired freedom for his country; and first beheld the city whose glory he was destined to promote, when the inhabitants were giving expression to their joy on the departure of the British troops. Already the name of Clinton was honorably identified with military and civic life in America, officers of his family having served in the French and Revolutionary wars, and associated their names with the capture of Fort Frontenac, with the Indian battles in the valley of the Mohawk, with the surrender of Cornwallis, and subsequently with the government of the state. Public duty, courage, and self-sacrifice, were household words in the settlement where his childhood was passed; historical events were his nursery tales; and when, having exhausted the educational privileges of his native county and passed some months at the College of New Jersey, he sought for academic culture in the metropolis of his own state, the application was the signal for recombining the apparatus of learning dispersed by war, and baptizing anew the University of New York with the title of an emancipated country. With the advent of

De Witt Clinton as a pupil, the fortunes of King's, now Columbia, College revived; and it might seem prophetic of his future relation to the cause of learning and civil advancement, that he was the first graduate of that institution after it became American both in name and in principles.

It has been suggested that the germs of political science were planted in Clinton's mind by the lectures of Dr. Kemp, his college preceptor; but they were developed by the exigencies and opportunities of his subsequent career. He had scarcely completed his law studies, when the accidental death of his brother, who was private secretary to Governor Clinton, led to his acceptance of the office. Thus early was he initiated as a political student. To promote his uncle's reëlection, he became a writer for the journals of the day, and soon acquired rare power and readiness in that capacity. He reported the debates of the convention that discussed the new constitution; and while a mere youth, by the demands upon his recognized ability and the promise of his character, he became the chief of a volunteer military corps, and a harbor commissioner. When his kinsman was defeated at the polls, and the Federal party triumphed, there was a pause in his official life, during which his love of the natural sciences found scope; but no sooner did his own party predominate, than he was elected successively state representative and senator, United States senator, mayor of the city and governor of the state of New York — posts whose functions were then more important and responsible than at present. The mere outline of his official honors gives no idea of what he made the career of a public servant. In each station he exhibited a vigor of action, a wise polity, and a social influence, quite original and of rare efficiency; in each he illustrated the prerogatives of statesmanship, — in congressional debate winning from his noble rival, Gouverneur Morris, an honest admiration that rose above the virulence of partisan dislike; in municipal rule, by memorable judicial decisions and the courageous exercise of his magistracy, eliciting the ardent praise of the most eminent jurists, and the spontaneous trust of his fellow-citizens. Diplomatic skill, philosophical insight, heroic purpose, generous aims, and legal acumen, were so manifest in his administration of every office, however limited or temporary its character, as to demonstrate that, under free institutions, it is not the rank but the use of office which makes it illustrious. In support of this view we might cite his new inspection of wheat, that soon raised its market value, his speech against war with Spain, his negotiations with the French and English men-of-war in the waters of New York to preserve neutrality, his condemnation of the turbulent and highly connected students tried before him, his repeal of the acts intolerant to Catholics, the charters he secured for the Fur Company, the Academy of Arts, and the Manumission Society, his moral courage in repudiating an act intended to mar the freedom of debate, his personal devotion to the establishment of the first free school, and his exertions in rescuing from unhallowed neglect the bones of the prison-ship martyrs.

It is one of the penalties exacted by official life that its votary is obliged to expend the highest gifts of his nature upon objects which, however important as parts of a series, leave few permanent memorials. The artist or the author bequeaths a picture, statue, or book, in which are embodied his aspirations and the spirit he was of; but the active intelligence of the statesman is usually so exclusively devoted to administrative duties, as to leave no time for the finished record of his genius. The life that occupied so large a space in the public eye, the name that was on every lip, seems to pass away with the funeral pageant and the tearful eulogy. In the archives of an historical society the curious explorer finds in a fragmentary shape the writings which, a few years before, were the charts of opinion over which fiery partisans wrangled and ardent champions exulted. The documentary history of De Witt Clinton's life bears ample evidence of his varied learning, his large discourse of reason, his broad views, and his unwearied activity. It comprises orations before philosophical and benevolent societies, speeches, reports, letters, journals, and messages to the legislature. It attests facility as a writer, versatile knowledge, and earnestness of purpose, embracing discussions of questions of policy, data for the naturalist and historian, and systematic digests of studies in almost every department of scientific, literary, and political inquiry. Much of the significance of these papers is, however, lost, through the progress of events and the diffusion of knowledge. Orators have multiplied since his day, and many able legislators have won reputation in the same fields; yet these incidental writings are valuable for reference, and interesting as the literary exposition of a noble character. The Address before the Philosophical Society, the Discourse on the Iroquois, and the Letters of Hibernicus, are valuable illustrations of the habits of research, the intellectual tastes, the powers of observation, and the impressive style, of a man whose life was mainly occupied with executive duties, and whose fame is eminently that of a practical statesman. It is delightful to cite, after the lapse of fifty years, his eloquent defence of literature and science as elements of a wise policy,— to hear him glory in the memories of Hunter and Burnett, the educated provincial governors of his native state, advocate the need of a knowledge of the past in order to reap the fruits of the present, and designate the advantages, both natural and civil, offered in this country to the votary of science and letters. It is equally pleasing to follow his ethnological investigations of the savage tribe that once possessed the fair domain around him, and to share the patriotic zest with which he examines its soil, forests, and waters, to fix the nomenclature of their varied products. He anticipated, by hints of projects such as De Foe's famous essay bequeathed to posterity, many of the subsequent victories of practical science, when he declared that "here the hand of art will change the face of the universe, and the prejudices of country will vanish before the talisman of merit;" that "it will not be debated whether hills shall be perforated, but whether the Alps and the Andes shall be levelled; not whether sterile fields shall be fertilized, but whether the deserts of Africa shall feel the power of cultivation; not whether rivers shall be joined, but whether the Caspian shall see the Mediterranean, and the waves of the Pacific shall lave the Atlantic shores."

The account of his exploration of Western New York, which originally appeared in one of the journals of the day, offers a wonderful contrast to our familiar experience. Then, to use his own language, "the stage-driver was a leading beau, and the keeper of a turnpike-gate a man of consequence." Our three hours' trip from New York to Albany was a voyage, occupying ten times that period. At Albany stores were laid in, and each member of the commission provided himself with a blanket, as caravans, in our time, are equipped at St. Louis for an expedition to the Rocky Mountains. Here they breakfast at a toll-keeper's, there they dine on cold ham at an isolated farm-house; now they mount a baggage-wagon, and now take to a boat too small to admit of sleeping accommodations, which leads them constantly to regret their "unfortunate neglect to provide marquees and camp-stools;" and more than six weeks are occupied in a journey which now does not consume as many days. Yet the charm of patient observation, the enjoyment of nature, and the gleanings of knowledge, caused what, in our locomotive era, would seem a tedious pilgrimage, to be fraught with a pleasure and advantage of which our flying tourists over modern railways never dream. We perceive by the comparison that what has been gained in speed is often lost in rational entertainment. The traveller who leaves New York in the morning, to sleep at night under the roar of Niagara, has gathered nothing in the magical transit but dust, fatigue, and the risk of destruction; while, in that deliberate progress of the canal enthusiast, not a phase of the landscape, not an historical association, not a fruit, mineral, or flower, was lost to his view. He recognizes the benign provision of Nature for sugar, so far from the tropics, by the sap of the maple; and for salt, at such a distance from the ocean, by the lakes that hold it in solution near Syracuse. At Geddesburg he recalls the valor of the Iroquois, and the pious zeal of the Jesuits; at Seneca Lake he watches a bald-eagle chasing an osprey, who lets his captive drop to be grasped in the talons of the king of birds; the fields near Aurora cheer him with the harvests of the "finest wheat country in the world." At one place he is regaled with salmon, at another with fruit, peculiar in flavor to each locality; at one moment he pauses to shoot a bittern, and at another to examine an old fortification. The capers and poppies in a garden, the mandrakes and thistles in a brake, the blue-jays and woodpeckers of the grove, the bullet-marks in the rafters of Fort Niagara, tokens of the siege under Sir William Johnson, the boneset of the swamp, a certain remedy for the local fever, a Yankee exploring the country for lands, the croaking of the bull-frog and the gleam of the fire-fly, Indian men spearing for fish, and girls making wampum, — these, and innumerable other scenes and objects, lure him into the romantic vistas of tradition or the beautiful domain of natural science; and everywhere he is inspired by the patriotic survey to announce the as yet unrecorded promise of the soil, and to exult in the limitless destiny of its people. If there is a striking diversity between the population and facilities of travel in this region as known to us and as described by him, there is in other points a not less remarkable identity. Rochester is now famed as the source of one of the most prolific superstitions of the age; and forty years ago there resided at Crooked Lake Jemima Wilkinson, whose followers believed her the Saviour incarnate. Clinton describes her equipage,— "a plain coach with leather curtains, the back inscribed with her initials and a star." The orchards, poultry, corn-fields, grist-mills, noted by him, still characterize the region, and are indefinitely multiplied. The ornithologist, however, would miss whole species of birds, and the richly-veined woods must be sought in less civilized districts. The prosperous future, which the various products of this district foretold, has been more than realized; with each successive improvement in the means of communication, villages have swelled to cities; barges and freight-cars with lumber and flour have crowded the streams and rails leading to the metropolis; and, in the midst of its rural beauty and gemmed with peerless lakes, the whole region has, according to his prescient conviction, annually increased in commerce, population, and refinement.

A more noble domain, indeed, wherein to exercise such administrative genius, can scarcely be imagined than the State of New York. In its diversities of surface, water, scenery, and climate, it may be regarded more than any other member of the confederacy as typical of the whole Union. The artist, the topographer, the man of science, and the agriculturist, can find within its limits all that is most characteristic of the entire country. In historical incident, variety of immigrant races, and rapid development, it is equally a representative state. There spreads the luxuriant Mohawk valley, whose verdant slopes, even when covered with frost, the experienced eye of Washington selected for purchase as the best of agricultural tracts. There were the famed hunting-grounds of the Six Nations, the colonial outposts of the fur-trade, the vicinity of Frontenac's sway, and the Canada wars, the scenes of André's capture, and Burgoyne's surrender. There the very names of forts embalm the fame of heroes. There lived the largest manorial proprietors, and not a few of the most eminent Revolutionary statesmen. There Fulton's great invention was realized; there flows the most beautiful of our rivers, towers the grandest mountain-range, and expand the most picturesque lakes; there thunders the sublimest cataract on earth, and gush the most salubrious spas; while on the seaboard is the emporium of the Western world.

A poet has apostrophized North America, with no less truth than beauty, as "land of the many waters;" and a glance at the map of New York will indicate their felicitous distribution within her limits. This element is the natural and primitive means of intercommunication. For centuries it had borne the aborigines in their frail canoes, and afterwards the trader, the soldier, the missionary, and the emigrant, in their batteaux; and, when arrived at a terminus, they carried these light transports over leagues of portage, again to launch them on lake and river. Fourteen years of Clinton's life were assiduously devoted to his favorite project of uniting these bodies of water. He was the advocate, the memorialist, the topographer, and financier, of the vast enterprise, and accomplished it, by his wisdom and intrepidity, without the slightest pecuniary advantage, and in the face of innumerable obstacles. Its consummation was one of the greatest festivals sacred to a triumph of the arts of peace ever celebrated on this continent. The impulse it gave to commercial and agricultural prosperity continues to this hour. It was the foundation of all that makes the city and state of New York preëminent; and, when recently a thousand American citizens sailed up the Mississippi, to commemorate its alliance with the Atlantic, the ease and rapidity of the transit, and the spectacle of virgin civilization thus created, were but a new act in the grand drama of national development, whose opening scene occurred twenty-seven years before, when the waters of Lake Erie blended with those of the Hudson.

The immense bodies of inland water, and the remarkable fact that the Hudson river, unlike other Atlantic streams south of it, flows unimpeded, early impressed Clinton with the natural means of intercourse destined to connect the seaboard of New York with the vast agricultural districts of the interior. He saw her peerless river enter the Highlands only to meet, a hundred and sixty miles beyond, another stream, which flowed within a comparatively short distance from the great chain of lakes. The very existence of these inland seas, and the obvious possibility of uniting them with the ocean, suggested to his comprehensive mind a new idea of the destiny of the whole country. Within a few years an ingenious geographer has pointed out, with singular acumen, the relation of his science to history, and has demonstrated, by a theory not less philosophical than poetic, that the disposition of land and water in various parts of the globe predetermines the human development of each region. The copious civilization of Europe is thus traceable to the numerous facilities of approach that distinguish it from Africa, which still remains but partially explored. The lakes in America prophesied to the far-reaching vision of Clinton her future progress. He perceived, more clearly than any of his contemporaries, that her development depended upon facilities of intercourse and communication. He beheld, with intuitive wisdom, the extraordinary provision for this end, in the succession of lake and river, extending, like a broad silver tissue, from the ocean far through the land, thus bringing the products of foreign climes within reach of the lone emigrant in the heart of the continent, and the staples of those midland valleys to freight the ships of her seaports. He felt that the state of all others to practically demonstrate this great fact was that with whose interests he was intrusted. It was not as a theorist, but as a utilitarian, in the best sense, that he advocated the union by canal of the waters of Lake Erie with those of the Hudson. The patriotic scheme was fraught with issues of which even he never dreamed. It was applying, on a limited scale, in the sight of a people whose enterprise is boundless in every direction clearly proved to be availing, a principle which may be truly declared the vital element of our civic growth. It was giving tangible evidence of the creative power incident to locomotion. It was yielding the absolute evidence then required to convince the less far-sighted multitude that access was the grand seeret of increased value, that exchange of products was the touchstone of wealth, and that the iron, wood, grain, fruit, and other abundant resources of the interior, could acquire their real value only through facilities of transportation. Simple as these truths appear now, they were widely ignored then; and not a few opponents of Clinton predicted that, even if he did succeed in having flour conveyed from what was then called the "Far West" to the metropolis, at a small expense of time and money, the grass would grow in the streets of New York. The political economists of his day were thus converted into enemies of a system which, from that hour, has continued to guide to prosperous issues every latent source of wealth throughout the country. The battle with ignorance and prejudice, which Clinton and his friends waged, resulted in more than a local triumph and individual renown. It established a great precedent, offered a prolific example, and gave permanent impulse and direction to the public spirit of the community. The canal is now, in a great measure, superseded by the railway; the traveller sometimes finds them side by side, and, as he glances from the sluggish stream and creeping barge to the whirling cars, and thence to the telegraph-wire, he witnesses only the more perfect development of that great scheme by which Clinton, according to the limited means, and against the inveterate prejudices, of his day, sought to bring the distant near, and to render homogeneous and mutually helpful the activity of a single state, and, by that successful experiment, indicated the process whereby the whole confederacy should be rendered one in interest, in enterprise, and in sentiment.

Before the canal policy was realized, we are told by its great advocate that "the expense of conveying a barrel of flour by land to Albany, from the country above Cayuga Lake, was more than twice as much as the cost of transportation from New York to Liverpool;" and the correctness of his financial anticipations was verified by the first year's experiment, even before the completion of the enterprise, when in his message to the legislature he announced that "the income of the canal fund, when added to the tolls, exceeded the interest on the cost of the canal by nearly four hundred thousand dollars." Few, however, of the restless excursionists that now crowd our cars and steamboats, would respond to his praise of this means of transportation when used for travel. His notion of a journey, we have seen, differed essentially from that now in vogue, which seems to aim chiefly at the annihilation of space. To a philosophic mind, notwithstanding, his views will not appear irrational, when he declares that fifty miles a day, "without a jolt," is his ideal of a tour, — the time to be divided between observing, and, when there is no interest in the scenery, reading and conversation. "I believe," he adds, "that cheaper or more commodious travelling cannot be found."

The tendency of public life, in this country, is to merge statesmanship in politics. The broad views and high aims of the fathers of the republic have but occasionally inspired modern leaders of party. Sagacity, oftener than comprehensiveness, adroitness in the use of temporary expedients, rather than appreciation of general principles, has secured to them casual success; but they could have bequeathed hallowed memories only through identity with grand and progressive ideas. At the head of the second generation of great public men stands De Witt Clinton. His conception of the duty and the privilege of office had in it somewhat of the enlarged and disinterested spirit which endears the names of Washington, Franklin, and Hamilton, and the rest of that noble brotherhood, whose reach of thought and tone of action were on a scale commensurate with the national life, of whose genius they were the legitimate guardians. Not only in the extent and wisdom of his projects, and the intelligent zeal of his administration, was Clinton the worthy successor of that extraordinary race of patriots. His endowments, tastes, and habits, were those of a republican statesman. Instead of giving his energies to organizing cliques, and political machinery, he meditated extensive plans for the advancement of the state, and with dauntless industry sought their realization. The authentic lore of history and philosophy, and not the ephemeral chart of a newspaper, disciplined his mind. By virtue of heroic self-reliance, not through the artifices of cunning, he pursued his objects; his claims were based on self-respect; the force of intelligence, and not the blandishments of the courtier, gave eloquence to his appeals; and moral energy was his method of achievement.

Like Scott and Webster, he began to labor at dawn; like Gouverneur Morris, he preferred the intellectual refreshment of conversation to the idle pastime of a game of hazard. In diction, in manner, and in association, there was obviously the innate dignity of a man conscious of lofty purposes and official responsibility. His foible was pride, not vanity; the sense of beauty was less cultivated than acuteness of wit; and imagination was secondary to good sense. He furnished his mind for the wise treatment of affairs by assiduous and universal reading, by earnest thought, and keen observation. Thus the whole nature of the man was trained for practical efficiency; and he habitually looked above and beyond the limits of incidental questions, to the essential welfare of the state. His confidence in himself and his measures, accordingly, was justified by more enduring testimony than the caprices of popular favor. He saw before and after. His private tastes had the same character. He was a naturalist, but no connoisseur; preferred satire to poetry, fact to fiction, law to speculation. His journeys were inspired, not by the zest of adventure, but by the love of knowledge; his studies were directed, not to the gratification of a vague curiosity, but to the acquirement of valuable truth. His talent was executive; his ambition, to open new avenues of prosperity, to found expansive institutions, to develop natural resources, to bring out the latent powers of mind and matter, of nature and society, and to give a wise and effective direction to the elements of national prosperity. Like all benefactors whose memories survive, he worked by the light of philosophy; like all artists whose ideas find permanent shape, he never lost sight of general effect while absorbed in details.

He thus combined the qualities which illustrate public and official duty in accordance with the genius of our institutions. Examined as a whole, his character is of a kind which signally meets the wants and honors the suffrages of the people. How often, during the few years that have elapsed since his decease, has the country suffered from the lack of integrity, firmness, devotion, and intelligence, like his, in her national and municipal affairs! The method of his statesmanship was thoroughly American,—instinct with republican courage and directness, above considerations of gain, mainly cognizant of prospective good, and undisturbed by the dictum of faction. His nature was cast in a Roman, not a Jesuitical, mould. As became a priest of freedom, he was inspired by the practical sense of a Franklin and the dauntless will of a Loyola, and not by the calculating shrewdness of a Talleyrand or the visionary expedients of a Necker. The original idea of the canal policy has been ascribed to others; and, as in every similar instance of invention and of enterprise, many honored names are identified with the conception and the progress of the undertaking — capitalists, engineers, rhetoricians, and patriots. But history shows that the great requisite for such achievements is the indomitable perseverance of men endowed with the genius or vested with the authority to insure success. It was this that crowned Fulton's weary years of experiment with triumph in the application of steam to navigation, and enabled Morse to prove his theory, at last, by the construction of an electric telegraph from the Capitol where an appropriation was so long withheld. In form, discourse, and feature, Clinton bore the impress of his intrinsic character, noble, fearless, and determined. His stature and brow instantly conveyed the idea of moral dignity; his expression wore the severity of a man of thought, yet, in more genial moods, expanded with benign recognition or mirthful humor; in his dark eye beamed a keen intelligence, and in his smile a winning grace. In social life he was upright and faithful; in his home, kind and attractive; and his faculties were unimpaired and active within a few moments of his death. The austerity of reflection in his hours of respite from labor was tempered by the amenities of love and taste; and he thus represented, in manners and person, the union of strong volition, generous sentiment, and vivid intelligence.

The slow appreciation of Clinton's character is a striking evidence of the narrow views of mere politicians. That a legislator should preside over a philosophical society, correspond with foreign *savans*, describe new species of fish, birds, and grain, and leave the routine of public affairs to explore the resources of nature, was an incongruity they could neither understand nor tolerate. The distinction of an empty civic title they estimated, but the celebrity arising from the discovery of a wild farinaceous product in New York, before thought indigenous only on the banks of the Caspian, was beyond their comprehension. That philosophy and letters constituted an essential part of the culture of a statesman, was a truth they ignored; and that it was possible to execute the behests of the people, and maintain, at the same time, the individuality and self-respect of an accomplished and honest citizen, was a theory which the radicals of both parties hesitated to accept. It is for this very reason, however, that the example of Clinton was invaluable as a precedent. He raised the standard of public life, and enlarged the boundaries of official utility. He illustrated, with peculiar emphasis, the value of liberal education, mental discipline, and dignity of character, in the sphere of republican office; and left imposing landmarks in the path of ambition, which survive the suffrage of his own and the criticism of the adverse party.

He was, indeed, one of that rare and invaluable class of men who cherish a disinterested love of knowledge for its own sake, and keep habitual vigil at its shrine. An indefatigable purveyor, he sought the facts of nature as the only reliable basis for human well-being. The universe was to him a treasury of *arcana*, in which laws of vast practical utility, and resources of unimagined worth, await the earnest inquirer. To bring these latent means into relation with the needs and capacities of mankind was in his view the great problem of life. The scope of his enterprise included nature, government, and society; and no inference was too broad or detail too insignificant for the grasp of his mind. Thus, at one time, we find him announcing the discovery of a new kind of wheat, and, at another, bringing a Dutch scholar from an obscure village to translate the early archives of his native state; now watching a mullein-stalk to verify the deposit of young bees in its seed-vessels, and now broaching a plan for the defence of the city when threatened with invasion; noting the minerals and trees of the interior, the history of the Iroquois, and the "melancholy notes of the loon," advocating a vast project for inland navigation, and describing the various species of wood indigenous to the soil. From a charitable institution to a fossil, and from a man of genius to the plumage of a kingfisher, all that could increase the sum of recorded knowledge, or give scope to human ability, he earnestly recognized. It is this singular union of the naturalist and statesman which gives to his character a stamp of distinctive beauty. It was not as associated with the tactics of party, but as the almoner of a higher economy, that he regarded the functions of a ruler. To discover and promote all that ministers to the welfare of the state was, in his regard, the genius of administration. He sought to build up a noble commonwealth, rather than the power of faction. The elements of knowledge and philanthropy he considered as vital, and accordingly originated and sustained, as primary objects, educational, economical and benevolent institutions, which still bear gracious witness to his memory. His mind was, however, of too contemplative a tone to be on the alert for occasions to conciliate opponents; his manly integrity precluded resort to the arts of the demagogue. He thought too much to be minutely vigilant of the wayward current of popularity, and was too much absorbed in great undertakings to "catch the nearest way" to the favor of the multitude. The soundness of his intellectual growth and moral energy may be inferred from the rectitude and industry of his college life, wherein the youth prefigured the man. His acquisitions were gradual, but thorough; and, while an undergraduate, he drew up a masterly address to the regents, in behalf of his fellow-students. He was remarkably superior to selfish considerations, invariably devoting his official revenue to promoting the influence of whatever station he filled, and contributing largely from his private purse to science, hospitality, and charity. He was indifferent to emolument, but zealous for usefulness and honor. More adroit tacticians and political courtiers superseded him in office; but their very names are now forgotten, except when recalled as associated with his; while the measures they ridiculed, and the achievements they deemed chimerical, are indissolubly wrought into the local features and the civic life of the country.

It would be now an ungracious task to review the forms of political animosity, which, like a swarm of venomous insects, hung around the career of this brave citizen. When we compare the incidental annoyance with the ultimate triumph, the struggle with the victory, we are tempted to exclaim, with the hero of that lake whose tide he married to the sea, "There is glory enough," and, in a like generous spirit, to pass unrecorded the mean arts of faction and the outrages of party hatred. The history of Clinton's great achievement is like that of every undertaking that is in advance of the time. It is fortunate that in men of true genius the will is usually as strong as the aim is original, and that perseverance goes hand in hand with invention. It is remarkable that even Jefferson thought the governor of New York a century beyond his age in the design he cherished. To the scepticism of intelligent friends was united the bitter opposition of partisan foes. Indignities, gross slanders, violent newspaper attacks, personal disrespect, and all the base weapons of sectional jealousy, were employed in vain. The thunders of Tammany Hall proved innocuous; satirical pamphlets only excited equally caustic replies; his failure as a presidential candidate, and his unjust removal from the office of canal commissioner, only drew more strongly towards him the few who appreciated his abilities and shared his projects. He was offered the secretaryship of state by a chief magistrate who subsequently, at the festive board of the opposition, proposed the health of Clinton as a public benefactor. He retreated from official toil to his library, and knew how to soothe the wounds inflicted by reckless ignorance with the balm of literature and science. A man who can forget personal grievances over the pages of Linnæus or Bacon is above the need of sympathy. His courtesy was never laid aside, even when the poisoned shafts of detraction were flying thickly around him, nor his dignity invaded while the insolent shout of revengeful triumph filled the air. He was conscious of a mission above the spoils of office. The social consideration he enjoyed more than atoned for the casual loss of political distinction; foreigners of renown sought his dwelling; men of science were his favorite companions, books his most reliable consolation; and the great scheme he so long advocated, with the labor incident to its progress and consummation, gave genial employment to all his faculties. Now that the watchwords of party are forgotten, and the ravings of faction have died away, his noble presence stands forth in bold relief, on the historical canvas of that era, as the pioneer of the genius of communication, whose magic touch has already filled with civilized life the boundless valleys of the West, then an untracked forest; as the Columbus of national improvement, and the man who most effectually anticipated the spirit of the age, and gave it executive illustration.

19*

THE VOCALIST.

JENNY LIND.

THE Life of the North is to us a fresh revelation; and, by a striking coincidence, one after another of its phases have come upon our transatlantic vision in rapid succession. Previously, Swedenborg, Charles XII., and Linnæus, were the names most gratefully associated with that region. To many Americans, Thorwaldsen was the only name associated with art, but a few years since; and to those who have visited Rome, the benign and venerable man is a vivid and pleasing reminiscence, appropriate to the idea of his grand apostolic figures, and the affectionate honor in which his native Denmark holds the memory of its noble sculptor. But with a Norwegian violinist fairly commenced our popular knowledge of the genius of Northern Europe. The play of the wind through her forest pines, the glint of her frozen streams, the tenderness of her households, and the solemnity of her faith, seemed to breathe in the wizard tones of his instrument. Then the spirit of her literature began slowly to win its gentle but impressive way to the American heart. Longfellow's translation of Bishop Tegner's "Children of the Lord's Supper," with the graphic introduction descriptive of rural life in Sweden, touched the same chord in New England breasts that had vibrated to the religious pathos of Bryant, Dana, and Hawthorne; while not a few readers became simultaneously aware of a brave Danish poet, recently followed to the tomb by the people of Copenhagen, with every token of national grief. The dramas of

Œhlenschläger, from their union of familiar expression with the deepest feeling, though but partially known in this country, awakened both curiosity and interest. Then, too, came to us the domestic novels of Miss Bremer, portraying so heartily the life of home in Sweden, and appealing to the most universal sympathies of our people. Finally, Hans Andersen's delicious story-books, veiling such fine imaginative powers under the guise of the utmost simplicity, raised up for him scores of juvenile admirers, while children of a larger growth enjoyed the originality of his fictions with equal zest, as the offspring of rare human sympathy and original invention. The pictures wafted to our shores by the late revolutionary exigencies of the Continent have often yielded glimpses of northern scenery. Norwegian forests, skies, and mountains, attracted the eye at the Dusseldorf gallery; and thus, through both art and literature, the simple, earnest, and poetic features of life in the North were brought within the range of our consciousness. It developed unimagined affinities with our own; and, as it were, to complete and consecrate the revelation, we heard the vocal genius of Northern Europe — the Swedish nightingale, Jenny Lind.

Stockholm is justly regarded as the most elegant city of Northern Europe. It is situated at the junction of the lake Mälar with an inlet of the Baltic. Although usually described as founded on seven isles, it is, in point of fact, mainly situated on three; the smallest and most central having been the original site, and still constituting the most populous and active section. The irregularity of its form, and the blending of land and water, render the appearance of the city remarkably picturesque. From the elevated points, besides the various buildings, craft of all kinds in motion and at anchor, numerous bridges and a fine background of mountains are discernible, and combine to form a beautiful panorama. The royal palace is exceeded in magnificence only by that of Versailles.

From an unpretending edifice in one of the by-streets of the city of Stockholm, in Sweden, a quarter of a century ago, a troop of children might have been seen to emerge, at noon, and break the silence that at other hours invested the place, with the lively chat and quick laughter natural to emancipated scholars. In a few moments they dispersed to their several homes, and early the next day were again visible, one by one, disappearing, with a more subdued bearing, within the portal of the humble domicile.

Towards the seminary, on a pleasant day, there moved rapidly the carriage of one of those useful, though unrecognized beings, who seem born to appreciate the gifts which God so liberally dispenses, but which the insensibility and selfishness of mankind, in general, permit to languish in obscurity until a fortunate circumstance brings them to light. Some time previous, the good lady, in passing the school, had been struck with the beauty of a child's voice that rose blithely from the dwelling. She was induced to alight and enter; and her astonishment was only increased upon discovering that this cheerful song came from a diminutive girl, busied in arranging the schoolroom, during a temporary recess. She learned that this maiden was the daughter of the schoolmistress; and the somewhat restricted air of homely comfort visible in the establishment, and the tinge of severity in the manners of the mother, contrasted forcibly in the lady's imagination with the apparently instinctive soaring of the child's spirit into the atmosphere of song, from her dim and formal surroundings, as the skylark lifts itself from a lowly nest among the dark weeds up to the crystal heavens. It was a sweet illustration of the law of compensation.

The air the child was singing, as she busied herself about the room, was a simple native strain, quite familiar, and by no means difficult of execution; it was the quality of the voice, the natural flow of the notes, the apparent ease, grace, and earnest sweetness of the little songstress, that gained the visitor's ear and heart. And now she had come to urge upon the parents the duty of affording every encouragement to develop a gift so rare and beautiful; she expressed her conviction that the child was born for a musical artist, and destined not only to redeem her parents from want, but to do honor to her country. This impression was deepened when she learned that this musical tendency manifested itself as early as the age of three, and that the little girl had long awakened the wonder of the family by repeating accurately even intricate airs, after having heard them but once; that she had thus sung habitually, spontaneously, and seemed to find of her own volition a peculiar consolation in the act for the dry routine of her life, though from without not a single circumstance gave any impulse or direction to this vocal endowment.

She exhibited also to the just perception of Madame Lundberg, herself a celebrated Swedish actress, as well as a benevolent woman, the usual conditions of genius, in backward physical growth, precocious mental vigor, and mature sensibilities. The latter, indeed, were so active, that her mother, and even her kind adviser, doubted if she possessed sufficient energy of character for so trying a profession as that of an artist; and this consideration, added to the prejudice of the parents against a public, and especially a theatrical career, for a time chilled the hopes of the enthusiastic patroness. At length, however, their consent was obtained that the experiment should be tried, and the diffident little girl, only accustomed to domestic privacy, but with a new and strange hope wildly fluttering in her bosom, was taken to Croelius, a veteran music-master of Stockholm, who was so delighted with her rare promise that one day he led her to the house of Count Pucke, then director of the court theatre. Her reception, however, did not correspond with the old man's desires; for the nobleman coldly inquired what he was expected to do with such a child. It must be confessed that the absence of beauty and size did not, at the first glance, create any high anticipations in behalf of the demure maiden. Croelius, though disappointed, was quite undismayed; he entreated the director to hear her sing, and declared his purpose to teach her gratuitously, if he could in no other way secure the cultivation of her voice and talents. This earnestness induced the count to listen with attention and candor; and the instant she had finished, he exclaimed, "She shall have all the advantages of the Stockholm Academy!" Such was Jenny Lind's initiation into the life of an artist.

She now began regularly to appear on the stage, and was soon an adept in juvenile parts. She proved widely attractive in vaudevilles, which were written expressly for her; and it is remarkable that the charm did not lie so much in the precocious intelligence, as in the singular geniality, of the little actress. Nature thus early asserted her dominion. There was an indefinable human interest, a certain original vein, that universally surprised and fascinated, while it took from the child the *eclât* of a mere infant phenomenon, by bringing her from the domain of vulgar wonder into the range of that refined sympathy, one touch of which "makes the whole world kin." In a year Croelius reluctantly gave up his pupil to Berg, who to kindred zeal united far more energy; and by him she was inducted thoroughly into the elements of her art.

Probation is quite as essential to the true development of art as encouragement. The eager, impassioned, excitable temperament needs to be chastened, the recklessness of self-confidence awed, and that sublime patience induced through which reliable and tranquil energy takes the place of casual and unsustained activity. By nature Jenny Lind was thoughtful and earnest, disposed to silence, and instinctively reserved; while the influence of her early home was to subdue far more than to exhilarate. The change in her mode of life and prospects was so unexpected, her success as a juvenile prodigy so brilliant, and the universal social favor she enjoyed, on account of the winsome amiability of her character, so fitted to elate a youthful heart, that we cannot but regard it as one of the many providential events of her career, that just at the critical moment when the child was losing herself in the maiden, and nature and education were ultimately shaping her artistic powers, an unexpected impediment was allowed to check her already too rapid advancement; and a pause, sad enough at the time, but fraught with enduring benefit, gave her occasion to discipline and elevate her soul, renew her overtasked energies, and plume her wings for flights more sustained and lofty.

Yet, while thus aware of the utility of her trial, we can easily imagine its bitterness. The loss of a gift of nature through which a human being has learned to find both the solace and the inspiration of existence, upon which the dearest hopes were founded, and by which the most glorious triumphs were achieved, is one of those griefs few can realize. Raphael's gentle heart bled when feebleness unnerved the hand that guided the pencil to such lovely issues, and big tears rolled down Scott's manly cheek when he strove in vain to go on with his latest composition. How desolate then must that young aspirant for the honor and the delights of the vocal art have felt when suddenly deprived of her voice! The dream of her youth was broken in a moment. The charm of her being faded like a mist; and the star of hope, that had thus far beamed serenely on her path, grew dim in the cold twilight of disappointment, keen, entire, and apparently irremediable. This painful condition was aggravated by the fact that her age now rendered it out of the question to perform childish parts, while it did not authorize those of a mature character.

The circumstances, too, of her failure were singularly trying. She was announced to appear as Agatha in Weber's "Frieschutz," a character she had long regarded as that in which her ability would be genially tested. To it her young ambition had long pointed, and with it her artistic sympathies were familiarly identified. The hour came, and that wonderful and delicate instrument, which as a child she had governed so adroitly that it seemed the echo of her mind; that subtle medium, through which her feelings had been wont to find such ready and full vent, refused to obey her will, yielded not to the pleadings of love or ambition, was hushed as by some cruel magic — and Jenny Lind was mute, with anguish in her bosom; her friends looking on in tearful regret, and her maestro chagrined beyond description! Where had those silvery tones fled? What catastrophe had all at once loosened those invisible harp-strings? The splendid vision of fame, of bounteous pleasure, of world-excited sympathy, and of triumphant art, disappeared like the gorgeous cities seen by the traveller, from the Straits of Messina, painted in tinted vapor on the horizon.

Jenny Lind ceased to sing, but her love of art was deepened, her trust in nature unshaken, her simplicity and kindliness as real as before. Four long years she lived without the rich promise that had invested her childhood; but, with undiminished force of purpose, she studied the art for which she felt herself born, with patient, acute, earnest assiduity, and then another and blissful episode rewarded her quiet heroism. The fourth act of "Robert le Diable" had been announced for a special occasion, and it so happened that in consequence of the insignificant *rôle* of Alice, consisting of a single solo, no one of the regular singers was disposed to adopt the character. In this emergency, Berg was reminded of his unfortunate pupil. She meekly consented to appear, pleased with an opportunity to be useful, and oblige her kind maestro.

While practising this solo, to the delight and astonishment of both teacher and pupil, the long-lost voice suddenly reäppeared. It seemed as if Nature had only withdrawn the gift for a season, that her child might gather strength and wisdom to use it efficiently, and in an unselfish spirit; and then restored it as a deserved recompense for the resignation and truth with which the deprivation had been borne. We can fancy the rapturous emotions of the gentle votary that night, when she retired from the scene of her new and unanticipated triumph. The occasion has been aptly compared to the memorable third act of the "Merchant of Venice" on the evening of Kean's *début* at Drury Lane. Jenny Lind immediately reverted to her cherished ideal part — that of Agatha. She was now sixteen years of age; her character rendered firm by discipline, her love of music deepened by more comprehensive views and a better insight, and her whole nature warmed and softened by the realization of the fondest and earliest hopes, long baffled, yet consistently cherished. The most experienced actors were struck with wonder at the facility and perfection of her dramatic style. In this, as in her vocalism, was, at once, recognized that peculiar truth to nature which constitutes the perfection of art — that unconsciousness of self and circumstance, and that fresh idea of character, at once so uncommon and so delightful. She drew the orchestra after her by her bold yet true execution; and seemed possessed with the genius of the composer as well as with the idiosyncrasies of the character she sung, so complete and individual was the result.

Already the idol of her native city, and the hope of the Swedish stage, her own ideas of art and aims as an artist remained unchanged. Her first desire was to seek the instruction of Garcia, with a view to perfect her method and subdue some vocal difficulties. She gracefully acknowledged the social homage and theatrical distinction awarded her; but these were but incidental to a great purpose. She had a nobler ambition to satisfy, a higher ideal to realize, and pressed on her still obstructed way, unallured by the pleasures of the moment, and undismayed by the distance of the goal. In order to obtain the requisite means for a sojourn at Paris, she made excursions through Norway and Sweden, with her father, during the vacations of the theatre, to give concerts; and when sufficient had thus been acquired, she obtained leave of absence from the Stockholm director, and left home for Paris, notwithstanding the dissuasion of her parents. They confided, however, as before, in her own sense of right; and she hastened to place herself under the instruction of Garcia.

Here another keen disappointment subdued her reviving hopes. At the first trial, her new teacher said: "My child, you have no voice; do not sing a note for three months, and then come and resume again." Once more she wrapped herself in the mantle of patience, went into studious retirement, and, at the prescribed time, again returned to Garcia, whose cheering words now were, "My child, you can begin your lessons immediately." Simple words, indeed, but more welcome to that ardent child of song, intent on progress in the art she loved, than the wildest plaudits. She returned with an elastic step, and entered with joyful enthusiasm upon her artistic career. Meyerbeer immediately offered her an engagement at Berlin. The consummate skill of her teacher, and her own enlarged experience and high resolves, made her advancement rapid and genuine. Thenceforth a series of musical triumphs, unexcelled in the history of the lyrical drama, attended the life of Jenny Lind. We might repeat countless anecdotes of the universal admiration and profound sympathy she excited at Berlin, Vienna, Dresden, Bremen, Munich, Aix la Chapelle, and, indeed, wherever her voice was heard on the stage and at concerts. The testimonies of the highest private regard, and public appreciation, were lavished upon her in the shape of costly gifts, wreaths of silver, poetic tributes, philosophical criticisms, the breathless silence or overwhelming applause of entranced multitudes, and all the signs of enthusiastic delight at the advent of a true child of nature and of song. To us the record of her two visits to England is yet vivid, and it is needless to reiterate the extraordinary demonstrations which there attested her singular merits and unequalled attractiveness.

The population of Berlin and Vienna assembled at midnight

to bid her adieu; and when she last left her native city, every ship in the harbor was manned and every quay crowded to see her embark in the presence of the queen. Nor are these spontaneous tributes to be exclusively ascribed to the love of novelty and the excitement of renown. Heroes and heroines the world cannot do without, unless it lapses into frigid and selfish materialism; admiration for talent and sympathy with genius are but human instincts. It is seldom, however, that these sentiments are upheld and sanctioned by reverence for worth. Therefore is it beautiful to witness the voluntary oblations which attend the great artist whose expression, however eloquent, is the true manifestation of a pure, noble, and disinterested spirit. It is not Jenny Lind in her personality, but as a priestess of art, an interpreter of humanity, a gifted and loyal expositor of feelings that lend grace to life and elevation to the soul, that draws the common heart toward her with such frank and ardent gratulation. Her well-known and unostentatious charities, her simplicity of life, her sympathy with her fellow-creatures, and unaffected manners, so accord with the glorious art she so rarely illustrates, as to justify to reflection the impulsive admiration she excites.

It is not in sublimity that Jenny Lind excels; and whatever excellence her Norma may possess, it is not of that characteristic species which renders her impersonations of "La Figlia del Regimento," of Alice, of Lucia, and of Amina, so memorable. In the former character she makes innocence play, through the rude habits acquired in the camp, in a way so exquisite as to enchant as by the spell of reality. In the "Bride of Lammermoor" there is a melancholy beauty which haunts the listener. It is her greatest tragic part. The pathos of the third act seems reproduced from the very genius which created the romance. Her Amina is Bellini's; and this is saying all that praise can utter. We may realize her versatility by comparing the comic jealousy so archly displayed in the "Noces de Figaro" with the tenderness of the sleep-walking scene in "La Somnambula." It has been well observed of her that, in the former opera, "she adheres to the genius of Mozart with a modest appreciation of the genius of that master"— a commendation as high as it is rare. One of the most remarkable traits of her artistic skill is its exquisite and wonderful discrimination — a quality no description can make obvious.

The peculiar charm of Jenny Lind, as an artist, is her unconsciousness. We are disposed to regard this as one of the most reliable tests of superior gifts. It at least proves the absorption of self in what is dearer — a condition essential to all true greatness. The most acute observers of this beautiful vocalist fail to detect the slightest reference either to her audience or herself while engaged in a part. For the time being her very existence seems identified with the character she represents. It is the afterthought, not the impression of the moment, that brings us to the artist. Infected by the complete realization of the scene, we think of it alone; and only when it has passed away do we become aware that the genius of another has, as it were, incarnated a story or a sentiment before us, through will, sympathy, and talent. The process is quite as unthought of as that by which a masterpiece of painting or sculpture has been executed, when we stand before it rapt in that harmonious spell that permits no analysis and suggests no task-work, any more than the landscape of summer, or the effulgence of a star. We feel only the presence of the beautiful, the advent of a new creation, the irresistible appeal to the highest instincts of the soul.

Carlyle says "the unconscious is the alone complete" — an aphorism which Jenny Lind robs of all mystery; for her superiority consists in the wholeness and unity of her effects, and this is produced by a kind of self-surrender, such as we rarely see except in two of the most genuine phases of humanity — genius and childhood; in this tendency they coalesce; and hence the freshness that lingers around the richly-endowed nature, and the universal faith which it inspires. The secret is that such characters have never wandered far from nature; they have kept within sight of that "immortal sea that brought us hither;" they constitute an aristocracy spontaneously recognized by all; and they triumph as poets, artists, and influential social beings, not through the exercise of any rare and wonderful gift, but from obedience to the simple laws of truth — to the primal sympathies, and to a kind of innate and glorious confidence which lifts them above ignoble fear and selfish tricks. The true hero, poet, artist, the true man or woman, who seem to the multitude to be peculiarly endowed, differ from those who do them voluntary homage chiefly in this unconsciousness of self; this capacity to be ever "nobler than their moods;" this sympathetic breadth of life that enables them to go forth with a kind of elemental power and enter into other forms of being; the principle of their existence is faith, not dexterity; sentiment, not calculation.

It will be seen that we recognize a moral basis as the source of Jenny Lind's fascination; and, if we were obliged to define this in a single word, perhaps the lexicon would furnish none so expressive as the homely one — *truth*. But we use it as significant of far more than the absence of falsehood; we mean by it candor, trust, spontaneity, directness. We believe, that Jenny Lind inspires sympathy in spite of her petite figure, not altogether because she warbles enchantingly, and has amiable manners, but also on account of the faith she at once excites. We perceive that love of approbation is not her ruling impulse, although her profession might excuse it; but that she has an ideal of her own, an artistic conscience, a love of art, a musical ministry to satisfy and accomplish, and that these considerations induce a nobler ambition than coëxists with mere vanity. It has been said that the remarkable novel of "Consuelo," by George Sand, is founded on the character and history of Jenny Lind; and, although this is not the case, the theory of the tale, the guileless devotion to art, as such, which stamps the heroine with such exalted grace, finds a parallel in this famed vocalist of the North; the same singleness of purpose and intact clearness of soul, the same firm will and gentle heart, are evident. Much, too, of her success is attributable to the philosophy of Consuelo's *maestro* — that, to reach the highest excellence in art, the affections, as well as the mind, must be yielded at her shrine. There is a subtle and deep relation between feeling and expression; and the biographies of those who have achieved renown in the latter, under any of its artistic forms, indicate that it has embodied that within them that found no adequate response in actual life.

The highest efforts of the poet and musician are confessedly the result of baffled or overflowing emotion; disguised, perhaps, as to the form, but clearly evident in the tone of their productions. Mozart and Raphael, Byron and Paganini, have illustrated this most emphatically. Jenny Lind seems to have kept her better feelings alive by the habitual exercise of benevolence, and a diffusive friendliness, while her concentrated and earnest activity finds utterance in her art. Hence the sway she has gained over countless hearts, each absorbed in its own dream, or shadowed by its own regrets, that glow again in the kindling atmosphere of song, which gushes from a soul over which no overmastering passion has yet cast a gloom, and whose transparent waters no agitation of conflicting desires has ever made turbid and restless. Jenny Lind has been a priestess at the shrine of art, and therefore interprets its oracles "as one having authority."

In this country the idea of fashion, and the mere relish of amusement, have blended so exclusively with the support of the opera, that we seldom realize its artistic relations and influence. The taste for the Italian Opera seems to have extended in the ratio of civilization; and, although it is, after all, an exotic among the Anglo-Saxons, — a pleasure born in the "sweet South," and, in its very richness of combination, suggestive of the impassioned feeling and habitual luxury of those climes, — yet, on the other hand, it is typical of the complex life, wants, and tendencies, of modern society. The old English tragic drama, robust, fierce-hearted, and unadorned, has faded before it; the theatre, as a reünion of wits, and an arena for marvellous histrionic effects, as a subject of elegant criticism, and a nucleus for universal sympathy, may be said not to exist; while the opera has become the scene of display, elegance, and pleasure, and of the highest triumphs.

The sentiment of the age has written itself in music. Its wild intelligence, its keen analysis, its revolutionary spirit, its restlessness, and its humanity, may be traced in the rich and brilliant combinations of Rossini, in the grand symphonies of Beethoven, in the pleading tenderness of Bellini, and in the mingled war-notes and sentiment of Verdi. The demand for undisguised and free expression, characteristic of the times, finds also its requisite scope in the lyrical drama. Recitation is too tame, pantomime too silent, scenic art too illusive, costume too familiar, music too unpicturesque; but all these combined are, at once, as romantic, exciting, impressive, and melodramatic, as the various aptitudes, the exacting taste, and the broad, experimental genius of the age. The gifts of nature, the resources of art, the gratification of the senses, the exigencies of fashion and taste, and the wants of the heart and imagination, find in the opera a most convenient luxury. The lyrical drama has thus gradually usurped the place of tournament and theatre; it is a social as well as an artistic exponent of the day; and those who have best illustrated it are justly regarded as public benefactors. Few, however, have ministered in this temple with the artless grace, the pure enthusiasm, the glory, of Jenny Lind. The daughters of the South, ardent and susceptible, but capricious and extravagant, have heretofore won its chief honors; their triumphs have been great but spasmodic, gained by impulse rather than nature, by glorious gifts of person rather than rare graces of soul.

Jenny Lind, with her fair hair and blue eyes, her unqueenly form, and childlike simplicity, has achieved almost unparalleled success, by means quite diverse. Her one natural gift is a voice of singular depth, compass, flexibility, and tone. This has been, if we may be allowed the expression, mesmerized by a soul earnest, pure, and sincere; and thus, with the clear perception and dauntless will of the North, has she interpreted the familiar musical dramas in a new, vivid, and original manner. One would imagine she had come with one bound from tending her flock on the hill-side, to warble behind the foot-lights; for, so directly from the heart of nature springs her melody, and so beyond the reach of art is the simple grace of her air and manners, that we associate her with the opera only through the consummate skill — the result of scientific training — manifested in her vocalism. The term warbling is thus adapted peculiarly to express the character of her style; its ease, fluency, spontaneous gush, and the total absence of everything meretricious and exaggerated in the action and bearing that accompany it. It is like the song of a bird, only more human. Nature in her seems to have taken Art to her bosom, and assimilated it, through love, with herself, until the identity of each is lost in the other.

Her career in the United States was signalized by the same enthusiasm, judicious and liberal benefactions, and independence of character. She was repelled by the "self-idolatry," as she termed it, of the Americans, and forced into an antagonistic social attitude by the encroachment of the lionizing mania; but, with those she respected and loved, her manners were full of sweetness. The blind, the aged, the poor, followed her triumphant progress with benedictions. She remitted one hundred thousand dollars of her American earnings to establish free schools in Sweden. Her marriage took place in Boston; and one of the leading journals thus truly chronicled the results of her visit:

"The Swedish Nightingale has folded her wings and hushed her song for a time, and betakes herself to the enjoyment of a little rest, after her year's great and incessant labors. It is very nearly twelve months since she arrived on our shores, and, up to this moment, she has been almost constantly before the public. She has given one hundred and twenty-three concerts, and has travelled more than sixteen thousand miles, in various parts of the United States, and in Cuba. How enthusiastically her wondrous song has been greeted by the tens of thousands who have flocked to listen to it, the press has faithfully and minutely chronicled, as her brilliant progress has extended itself over the land. Never was there a more powerful impression made by any artist who has ever been among us, and never a richer fund of private respect and regard accumulated by any stranger visiting our shores. Her personal virtues have won as much upon our countrymen's and countrywomen's love, as her wonderful music has upon their admiration and delight."

The union of such musical science, such thoroughly disciplined art, with such artlessness and simplicity, is, perhaps, the crowning mystery of her genius. To know and to love are the conditions of triumph in all the exalted spheres of human labor; and, in the musical drama, they have never been so admirably united. Her command of expression seems not so much the result of study as of inspiration; and there is about her a certain gentle elevation which stamps her to every eye as one who is consecrated to a high service.

Her ingenuous countenance, always enlivened by an active intelligence, might convey, at first, chiefly the idea of good-nature and cleverness in the English sense; but her carriage, voice, movements, and expression, in the more affecting moments of a drama, give sympathetic assurance of what we must be excused for calling a crystal soul. In all her characters she transports us, at once, away from the commonplace and the artificial—if not always into the domain of lofty idealism, into the more human and blissful domain of primal nature; and unhappy is the being who finds not the unconscious delight of childhood, or the dream of love, momentarily renewed in that serene and unclouded air.

In accordance with this view of Jenny Lind's characteristics, the enthusiasm she excited in England is alluded to by the leading critics as singularly honest. No musical artist, indeed, was ever so fitted to win Anglo-Saxon sympathies. She has the *morale* of the North; and does not awaken the prejudice so common in Great Britain, and so truly described in "Corinne," against the passionate temperament and tendency to extravagance that mark the children of the South. No candidate for public favor was ever so devoid of the ordinary means of attaining it. There is something absurd in making such a creature the mere nucleus of fashionable vanity, or the object of that namby-pamby criticism that busies itself with details of personal appearance and French terms of compliment. Jenny Lind is not beautiful; she does not take her audiences by storm; she exercises no intoxicating physical magnetism over their sensitive natures. She is not classic either in form of feature, or manner, or style of singing. Her loveliness as a woman, her power as an artist, her grace as a character, lies in expression; and that expression owes its variety and its enchantment to unaffected truth to nature, sentiment, and the principles of art.

"A melody with Southern passion fraught
  I hear thee warble: 't is as if a bird
By intuition human strains had caught,
  But whose pure breast no kindred feeling stirred.
Thy native song the hushed arena fills,
  So wildly plaintive, that I seem to stand

Alone, and see, from off the circling hills,
  The bright horizon of the North expand !
High art is thus intact ; and matchless skill
  Born of intelligence and self-control, —
The graduated tone and perfect trill
  Prove a restrained, but not a frigid soul ;
Thine finds expression in such generous deeds,
That music from thy lips for human sorrows pleads ! "

THE CHRISTIAN PHILOSOPHER.

GEORGE BERKELEY.

THE relation of this country to Europe, as it is rendered more intimate by the facilities of modern intercourse and the increase of emigration, assumes a greater historical interest. When a long, tedious, and comparatively perilous voyage divided us from the Old World, the advent of a band of exiles or adventurers, or the sojourn of a distinguished foreigner, was a memorable incident. The primitive reverence and attachment which bound the early colonists to their fatherland, their dependence for intellectual resources upon an older civilization, and the nucleus afforded by a vast and unappropriated country for the establishment and growth of political and religious minorities transplanted from ancient states and hierarchies, combined to render the arrival of a refugee, an experimentalist, a member of a proscribed sect, or the advocate of an original scheme or doctrine, an event fraught with incalculable results and singular attraction. The motives, career, and influence, of the gifted, the unfortunate, and the philanthropic men, who have thus sought an asylum and an arena in America, would form a chapter in our history second to none in importance and romance. It would include the agency of puritan and cavalier, of missionary and gold-seeker, of the thrifty Dutchman, the mercurial Gaul, the Spanish soldier, of priest, statesman, and trader, in moulding the original elements of national life; and from these general types it would descend to the more temporary but not less illustrious examples of the chosen few who came hither to report the unrecorded wonders of a fresh continent, to examine its natural features, direct its policy, assert the claims of discovery and supremacy, minister to its wants, and do battle for its liberties. To the eye of the philosopher and the hero of Europe, this has ever been the land of infinite possibilities; here scope was yielded to enterprise and thought, to courage and ambition, to usefulness and faith, when their development elsewhere was checked by tyranny, overgrown population, conventionalism, exhausted means, and despotic prejudice. The obstacles thus impending on the one side of the ocean, and the free range open on the other, gave extraordinary impulse, not only to the latent forces of society, but to those of individual character. Hence the new phases of life, and the salient evolutions of opinion and effort, discoverable in the memoirs of the first transatlantic visitors. Their history contains some of the noblest and the most despicable exhibitions of human nature; all that is generous and base in character, — chivalry and selfishness, the high-minded and the rapacious, the benefactor and the foe of mankind, — alternate in the chronicle; science and bigotry, philanthropy and avarice, the saint and the ruffian, stand out upon the virgin page of our primitive annals, the more distinctly and impressively because of the solitary back-ground of an unsettled country, and the limitless perspective of its subsequent growth.

The annalist finds, in each company of Europeans who originally explored the forests and navigated the streams of America, a representative man around whom the colony or roving band is grouped on the uncrowded canvas of our early history; and the difference of nation, aim, and faith, is indicated at a glance by their very names. What varied associations and opposite elements of character are suggested by the figures thus delineated, of De Soto and Penn, Lord Baltimore and Hendrick Hudson, Roger Williams and Father Marquette! When the zeal for gain and the enthusiasm of adventure and religion had somewhat declined, liberal curiosity and humane sympathies influenced another class of men to seek our shores. The noble volunteers from abroad who rallied under the standard of Washington occupy the most honored place on this magnanimous roll, — Lafayette, Steuben, Pulaski, and their brave compeers; and when peace regained her empire consecrated by freedom, the champions of science and truth began to turn their aspirations in the same direction,—some urged by persecution, and others by the ardor of discovery and beneficence. Priestley, after the destruction of his laboratory by a Birmingham mob, brought hither the fearless spirit of inquiry and experiment that inspired his ingenious mind; Volney turned his sceptical gaze from the decaying monuments of the Elder World, to primeval nature in the New; Whitefield breathed here the eloquent appeals that had previously kindled the English dissenters; Humboldt came to take the altitude of our mountains; Michaux, to wander with delight through our glorious woodlands; Cobbet, to publish without restraint his political and economical maxims; Wilson, to give names to the feathered tribe; and Chateaubriand, to make the pilgrimage of a poet to the Falls of Niagara; Copley came to set up his easel in Boston, and delineate our colonial aristocracy in their velvet coats, lace ruffles, huge wigs, and brocade robes; Talleyrand, Moreau, and Louis Philippe, found a temporary shelter from persecution among us, and a primitive simplicity of manners and government which contrasted strangely with the *old régime* of their native courts and armies; Genet vainly attempted to graft a radical disaffection on the yet tender institutions of our republic; Emmet brought the forensic eloquence of the Irish bar and the patriot regrets of an exile; Joseph Bonaparte, the philosophic content of a kindly heart, weary of the "smooth barbarity" of regal care; and Francis Jeffrey was drawn hither by the tender passion, and made New York dining-rooms familiar with the complacent sprightliness of an Edinburgh critic. Then succeeded the swarm of cockney travellers, whose egotistical comments proved so annoying to the sensitive pride of embryo nationality; and after them the ephemeral race of lions, — authors and actors, — who often proved so recreant to the memory of a public appreciation too frank and hospitable for their merits, — itinerant lecturers, pretentious strangers, fastidious pilgrims, whose casual triumph was followed by enduring contempt; and interspersed with these, men of higher faculty and less selfish aims, worthy ministers at the altar of knowledge, who observed the phenomena of our development with the insight of philosophy and the sentiment of humanity, — such as the lamented Spurzheim, the candid Lyell, and the analytical De Tocqueville. It is, indeed, a curious study and an amusing experiment, thus to compare the impressions of the illustrious visitors to America, from Charlevoix's quaint travels to Tom Moore's lampoons and "Lake of the Dismal Swamp," and from Kossuth's speeches to Thackeray's table-talk.

Among the traces yet discoverable of the American sojourn of celebrated individuals during the youth of the country, none are more pleasing, or more worthy of commemoration, than those which yet keep fresh the memory of George Berkeley. He is known to the multitude chiefly by the frequent quotation of his prophetic stanza, and by one of those terse compliments with which the heroics of Pope abound. It is, therefore, a grateful task to recall the details of his life and the prominent traits of his character, associated as they are with a public spirit and generous projects, of which, for many years, this land was the chosen scene.

When Shaftesbury, in phrases of studied elegance, was advocating a modified Platonic system, and Bishop Sherlock represented the eloquence of the church; when Swift's pungent satire ruled in politics, and Pope's finished couplets were the exemplars of poetry; when Sir Robert Walpole's ministry and Queen Caroline's levees were the civic and social features of the day, there moved, in the circles of literature, of state, and of religious fellowship, one of those men to whom, by virtue of their guileless spirit and ingenious minds, their sweet repose of character, gentle manners, and speculative tendency, we instinctively give the name of philosopher. Amid the partisan bitterness and critical rivalry of that era, a contemplative habit and kindly heart offer a refreshing contrast to the more aspiring and malevolent elements in society. A rare dignity and a potent charm invest the memory of the peaceful and disinterested enthusiast. He purifies the turbid stream of intellectual life, and hallows the pursuit of fame. Of this class of men was George Berkeley, who was born at Kilcrinin, Ireland, March 12th, 1684. The period embraced in his life was one of great political activity and scientific achievement. He occupied at the school on the Ormond foundation at Kilkenny, the form where, shortly before, Swift had studied.

Locke, Leibnitz, Bayle, and Sir Isaac Newton, died between his childhood and his mature fame.

His countenance was remarkably expressive of intellect and benevolence. His strength of limbs was unusual; his constitution was naturally robust, though gradually impaired by the inactivity of a student's life; and an ardent temperament animated his frame and manner, and enhanced the effect of his candid disposition and attractive intellect. To these obvious charms were united the confidence inspired by his integrity and his liberal sympathies, and the respect cherished for his learning and piety. His life was comparatively uneventful; its interest is derived almost wholly from his character and opinions; yet his lot was cast at a period and among influences singularly favorable to the gratification of his tastes and the exercise of his powers. To a childhood passed in Ireland we ascribe, at least, a degree of the frank warmth of feeling and the imaginative zest which endeared him to contemporaries. The suspicion of Jacobite opinions, the unfavorable effect of which upon Lord Galway was diverted by Molyneux, a former pupil, seems first to have directed public attention to his merits. After becoming a fellow of Trinity College, Dublin, he enjoyed the benefit of foreign travel, as companion to a son of the Bishop of Clogher; and soon afterwards received the appointment of chaplain to the Duke of Grafton, lord-lieutenant of Ireland. Through Sir Richard Steele he became known to the Earl of Peterborough, who took him to Italy as chaplain. On his promotion to the deanery of Derry, in 1724, he resigned his fellowship. He subsequently visited America on his self-imposed mission, returned to become Bishop of Cloyne, and died at Oxford, whither he had repaired to superintend the education of his sons, in 1753. To learning and benevolence his whole existence was devoted. He illustrated the sentiments of Christianity more by his example as a man than by his functions as a priest; and, throughout his career, he was a vigilant observer of nature, a patient student of books, a minister to the wants of his race, an earnest seeker for psychological truth, and a delightful specimen of the genuine Christian philosopher.

Berkeley's metaphysical opinions are known under the generic title of the "Ideal Theory," according to which "the belief in an exterior material world is false and inconsistent with itself; those things which are called sensible, material objects are not external, but exist in the mind by the immediate act of God, according to certain rules, termed laws of nature, from which he never deviates; and that the steady adherence of the Supreme Spirit to these rules is what constitutes the reality of things to his creatures; and so effectually distinguishes the ideas perceived by sense from such as are the work of the mind itself, or of dreams, and there is no more danger of confounding them together on this hypothesis than that of the existence of matter." "It is an opinion," he observes, in "The Principles of Human Knowledge," "strongly prevailing among men, that houses, mountains, rivers, and, in a word, all sensible objects, have an existence natural, real, distinct from their being perceived by the understanding. What are the forementioned objects but the things we perceive by sense, and what do we perceive beside our own ideas and sensations? All those bodies which compose the mighty frame of the world have not any subsistence without a mind." The germ of this philosophy appears in Berkeley's "Theory of Vision," which has been aptly described as illustrating "the immediate presence and providence of the Deity," and as "a practical apprehension of idealism." Stewart assimilates it with the theories of Hindoo philosophers, who, according to Sir William Jones, thought "the whole creation was rather an *energy* than a *work*, by which the Infinite Mind, who is present at all times and in all places, exhibits to his creatures a set of perceptions like a wonderful picture, or a piece of music, always varied, yet always uniform." The practical effect of such views, in the opinion of some of Berkeley's opponents, is in the highest degree baneful; and Bishop Hoadley thought they "corrupted the nature and simplicity of religion by blending it with the subtlety and obscurity of metaphysics." The singular purity of Berkeley's faith, and the integrity of his character, in the opinion of some of his religious friends, could alone have furnished an antidote for the bane of his philosophical doctrines.

Berkeley is recognized by standard psychological writers as having contributed a positive and brilliant truth to their science in his "Theory of Vision." The doctrine is thus briefly stated in an article attributed to J. Stewart Mill:

"Of the information which we appear to receive, and which we really do, in the maturity of our faculties, receive, through the eye, a part only is originally and instinctively furnished by that sense; the remainder is the result of experience. The sense of sight informs of nothing originally except light and colors, and a certain arrangement of colored lines and points. This arrangement constitutes what are called by opticians and astronomers apparent figure, apparent position, and apparent magnitude; of real figure, position, and magnitude, the eye teaches us nothing; these are facts revealed exclusively by the sense of touch. We judge an object to be more distant from us by the diminution of its apparent magnitude, that is, by linear perspective, or by that dimness or faintness of color which generally increases with distance, or, in other words, by aërial perspective. Berkeley alleges that, to a person born blind and suddenly made to see, all objects would seem to be in his eye, or rather in his mind. It would be more correct to say such a person would, at first, have no conception of *in* or *out*, and would only be conscious of colors, and not of objects."*

By this work Berkeley met a great problem of human nature, and, it appears to us, in a way which, so far from tending to materialism and scepticism, involves, in the last analysis, a profound recognition of the spiritual being and destiny of man. Hume may have drawn from it arguments which, at the first glance, seem to favor his disbelief in the foundations of religious faith; but it is evident that the reverse was the case with Berkeley, who was one of the most ardent and skilful opponents of the infidelity of his day. Much of the discussion which his metaphysical views excited was devoted to words rather than to ideas. All our external experience is, in point of fact, but a series of *impressions;* the question is, how they are produced; and the chief peculiarity of Berkeley was, that he ascribed a larger share of this process to the mind, and less to the senses, than his predecessors. His error, perhaps, consisted not in false premises, but in conclusions broader

* Westminster Review, vol. xxxviii., p. 318.

than his premises would warrant. The idea which lies at the root of his philosophy, so clearly developed in the "Theory of Vision," has been accepted by the best thinkers; but the elaboration of this idea into a complete system of immaterialism in the "Principles of Human Knowledge" finds comparatively few adherents. It is in this extreme application that truth becomes vague, and the philosopher gives place to the dreamer. None the less, however, on this account, should we acknowledge our obligations to Berkeley as a pioneer in the most difficult theme of human inquiry. That was but a dogmatical argument of Dr. Johnson, who, in reference to this doctrine of the non-existence of matter, said, as he kicked a stone, "I refute it thus;" for Berkeley never called in question the fact of sensation, but contended that the sensation and its causes existed only in the mind. Bayle, speaking of his "Theory of Vision," declares that, of all Berkeley's writings, it is that, "qui fait le plus honneur à sa sagacité et le premier où l'on ait entrepris de distinguer les operations immédiates de sens, des inductions que nous tirons habituellement de nos sensations."* "The doctrine of this Theory of Vision," says the reviewer already quoted, "has remained one of the least disputed doctrines in the most disputed and most disputable of all sciences — the science of man."

It would far exceed the scope of our present object, however, to analyze the argument and cite the illustrations by which Berkeley endeavors to prove his bold formula. Those interested in the subject will find in the volumes devoted to it an exposition remarkable for beautiful simplicity of style, clearness of statement, and ingenious reasoning; and, if unimpressed with its logic, they cannot fail to be charmed with its tone, and won by many a glimpse of the mysterious analogies which link our spiritual consciousness with outward experience. Sir James Mackintosh thus estimates Berkeley as a mental philosopher: "His immaterialism is chiefly valuable as a touchstone of metaphysical sagacity, showing them to be altogether without it, who, like Johnson and Beattie, believe that his speculations were sceptical, that they implied any dishonesty, or that they had the

* Biographie Universelle.

smallest tendency to disturb reasoning or to alter conduct." Of his style, Sir James remarks: "It is the finest model of the philosophical since Cicero;" and elsewhere, alluding to his last tract, he says: "His immaterialism, indeed, modestly appears, but only to purify and elevate our thoughts, and to fix them on mind — the paramount and primeval principle of all things."

The origin of works that betray strong individuality is always an interesting subject of inquiry. The varied learning and the charitable instincts of Berkeley might have found ample scope in the exercise of his profession; and the tendency of his mind was towards the natural and exact sciences, as is evident from the objects which attracted him in travel, and the books and companions he sought. He adventured in the field of metaphysics in consequence of the excitement his young imagination derived from works of fiction, and the subsequent reäction of his judgment and taste from the prescribed text-books in mental philosophy at the University; and he was still further inspired by the enthusiasm for such investigations awakened by the writings of Locke and Malebranche. These causes fixed his thoughts on the study of our mysterious nature; and the ideas he evolved were enhanced in value by the ardor of his disposition, and were the more strongly advocated because vehemently opposed. The form of dialogues imitated from Plato, in which some of his principal treatises are cast, gives them an obsolete air; and the main problem he undertook to solve, viewed apart from his acute arguments, is one of those broad generalizations which it is far easier for less noble minds to ridicule than to appreciate.

It is remarkable that Berkeley's mind, though so visionary in speculation, was keenly observant and exact. When the "Minute Philosopher" was republished in this country, it excited unusual attention, and was esteemed an excellent argument against irreligion, though somewhat too elaborate and dry for prolonged popularity. A marked resemblance has been traced between parts of this work and Butler's Analogy. Besides his metaphysical writings, a mathematical treatise in Latin, a number of controversial tracts, occasional sermons, and a few of his letters, admit us still further into a knowledge of his opinions and disposition. In every instance these casual efforts are inspired by an enthusiasm for truth, which, he quaintly says, "is the cry of all, but the game of few," or by a desire to enlighten and benefit others. The titles of these writings indicate their purpose: — "A Discourse to an Infidel Mathematician;" another to "Magistrates on Irreligious Living;" "A Word to the Wise," wherein he successfully sought to pacify the Catholic clergy of Ireland and promote more liberal feelings towards them; "The Querist," in which many useful and benevolent suggestions are offered for the public welfare, and several original hints are given worthy of a political economist, before the science had attained its present consideration; "A Proposal for better supplying Churches in our Foreign Plantations." Every one has read the pensive description of the old South-sea house in London, in which Lamb reveals in mellow tints its monitory decay. When the distress incident to the failure of that splendid scheme was rife, Berkeley improved the occasion to offer suggestions both of warning and counsel worthy of his sagacious mind and benevolent heart. As a writer he was thus of great immediate utility, especially as the affectionate esteem in which he was held gave sanction to his counsels. When we examine his literary remains, however, with the more concise and varied forms of didactic writing brought into vogue during the last half-century fresh in our minds, there appears a want of life and brilliancy in his most sensible remarks. His style, however deserving of eulogy as a medium for abstract discussion, is somewhat monotonous and diffuse, more that of a scholarly sermonizer than of a modern essayist. And yet it is impossible to recur to his candid and ingenious writings, in which an intrepid love of truth and a liberal grace of character seem to breathe from the unexaggerated, clear, and tranquil diction, without feeling a certain admiration of the author, springing from love for the man, more than from sympathy with the philosopher. His extensive knowledge and catholic tastes are apparent even in the advocacy of his special opinions, and the genial light of a humane, bold, and comprehensive mind, gives a charm to ideas that often have no present importance, and to objects for some of which it is no longer needful to plead.

It was a sagacious remark of Madame de Staël, that when we are much attached to our ideas we endeavor to connect everything with them; and seldom has this trait of the intellectual enthusiast been more emphatically illustrated than in the case of Berkeley. Whenever his feelings were enlisted in behalf of a theory or an enterprise, he derived an argument or a charm from the most distant associations. One of the last of his favorite ideas was a faith in the curative qualities of tar-water, which had proved useful in a malady under which he suffered. His treatise on the subject deserves no mean rank among the curiosities of literature. The research, ingenuity, and scholarship, elicited by his ardent plea for this specific, evince a patient and elaborate contemplation seldom manifest in the discussion of the most comprehensive questions. He analyzes the different balsams, from the balm of Gilead to amber; he quotes Leo Africanus to describe the process of making tar on Mount Atlas, and compares it with that used in New England; he cites Herodotus and Pliny, Theophrastus and Plato, Boerhaave and Evelyn; he surveys the whole domain of vegetable physiology, points out the relation of volatile salts to the economy of the blood, and discusses natural history, the science of medicine, chemistry, and the laws of life, space, light, and the soul itself,— all with ostensible reference to the virtues of tar-water. He enumerates every conceivable disease as a legitimate subject of its efficacy; and, while thus prolix and irrelevant, fuses the whole with good sense, fine rhetoric, and graceful zeal.

His early travels form a pleasing episode in his life. Though somewhat restricted by professional duties, he improved every opportunity to observe and record his impressions. The few letters from Italy published in his memoirs convey the zest and intelligence with which he enjoyed his tour, and his affectionate remembrance of home. He was repelled by the "cold, trivial conceits" of the modern Italian poets, and hailed their newly awakened interest in English authors, as manifested in the translation of Milton that had just appeared. He was present at a disputation at the Sorbonne when in Paris, and, at the English college there, saw the body of the last king James. He was carried over part of the Alps during winter in a chair. From the fact that all volcanoes are near the sea, he inferred a vacuum caused in the bowels of the earth by a vast body of inflammable matter taking fire, the water rushing in and being converted into steam, which gives rise to the eruption. In one of his epistles is a minute and eloquent description of the island of Ischia, which he calls "an epitome of the whole earth;" in another he gives an account of the people of Naples, which shows that they lived a century and a half ago exactly as at present.

"Would you know," he asks, "how we pass the time at Naples? Our chief entertainment is the devotion of our neighbors. Besides the gayety of their churches (where folks go to see what they call *una bella devozione*, that is, a sort of religious opera), they make fireworks almost every week, out of devotion; the streets are often hung with arras, out of devotion; and, what is still more strange, the ladies invite gentlemen to their houses, and treat them with music and sweetmeats, out of devotion; in a word, were it not for this devotion of its inhabitants, Naples would have little else to recommend it, except the air and situation."

The following passages of one of his letters to Pope are characteristic:

"LEGHORN, May 1, 1714.

"As I take ingratitude to be a greater crime than impertinence, I choose rather to run the risk of being thought guilty of the latter than not to return you my thanks for a very agreeable entertainment you just now gave me. I have accidently met with your Rape of the Lock here, having never seen it before. Style, painting, judgment, spirit, I had already admired in other of your writings; but in this I am charmed with the magic of your invention, with all those images, allusions, and inexplicable beauties, which you raise so surprisingly, and at the same time so naturally, out of a trifle. And yet I cannot say that I was more pleased with the reading of it than I am with the pretext it gives me to renew in your thoughts the remembrance of one who values no happiness beyond the friendship of men of wit, learning, and good-nature.

"I remember to have heard you mention some half-formed design of coming to Italy. What might we not expect from a muse that sings so well in the bleak climate of England, if she felt the warm sun, and breathed the same air with Virgil and Horace?"

* * * * * * *

"Green fields and groves, flowery meadows and purling streams, are nowhere in such perfection as in England; but if you would know lightsome days, warm suns, and blue skies, you must come to Italy; and to enable a man to describe rocks and precipices, it is absolutely necessary that he pass the Alps."

As chaplain to the Earl of Peterborough, Berkeley preached regularly at the English factories in Leghorn, and used to relate with much humor a visit he there received from a troop of priests, who walked around his chamber, sprinkling holy water, and muttering Latin prayers. He imagined the ceremony to be an exorcism of heresy, but discovered that it was only the observance of the day enjoined by the Roman calendar for blessing the house and clearing it of vermin. Another and more grave adventure befell him at Paris, where a warm and protracted argument he held with Malebranche, who, in a dressing-gown, and over a pipkin on the coals, was nursing himself for an inflammation of the lungs, so aggravated the disorder as to cause the metaphysician's death a few days after. While at Lyons he wrote an ingenious tract, "De Motu," and sent it to the Royal Academy of Sciences. It is deeply to be regretted that his copious and studiously gathered notes for a Natural History of Sicily — the fruit of his zealous observation there — were lost, with his journals, at Naples.

The social and friendly relations of Berkeley well illustrate both his character and his position. He was a favorite of Queen Caroline, at whose *soirées* spirited discussions of his theory occurred between himself, Clark, Hoadley, and Sherlock. She was in the habit of sending for him to talk over the American project; and when her generous intentions were thwarted, by some considerations of etiquette, that prevented his obtaining a deanery in Ireland, she declared that "if he could not be a dean he should be a bishop," and appointed him to Cloyne. Steele and Swift introduced him to their coteries of wits and to men of influence. He was a contributor to the Guardian, and, to his great surprise, among the principal heirs of Esther Vanhomorigh (Vanessa). No prominent man of that day enjoyed so many permanent and eligible friendships. Satire, then so much in vogue, was melted into kindness, and criticism softened to eulogy, when his name occurred in verse, letter, or conversation. Swift could not sympathize with his dreams, yet he earnestly advocated his cause. Addison laid aside his constitutional reserve to promote Berkeley's wishes. Pope made an exception in his favor, and suffered encomium to remain on his musical page unbalanced by censure. "I take you," says one of his letters, inviting the dean to Twickenham, "to be almost the only friend I have that is above the little vanities of the town." Atterbury declared, after an interview with him: "So much understanding, so much innocence, and such humility, I did not think had been the portion of any but angels, until I saw this gentleman." It is related by Lord Bathurst, that, on one occasion, when several members of the Scriblerius Club met at his house to dine, it was agreed to rally Berkeley, who was also invited, upon his American scheme. The latter heard the merry banter with the utmost good-nature, and then asked permission to reply; and, as his noble host afterwards declared, "displayed his plan with such an astonishing and animating fiery eloquence and enthusiasm, that they were struck dumb, and, after some pause, rose all up together, with earnestness, exclaiming, 'Let us set out immediately!'" When he determined to make Oxford his abode, he tendered the resignation of the bishopric of Cloyne; but the king refused to accept it, declaring that he "should live where he pleased and die a bishop." "He is," writes Warburton, "a great man, and the only visionary I ever knew that was."

Beloved and respected as he was, however, and not without eminent disciples as the advocate of a metaphysical theory, Berkeley seems to have been regarded by many of the prominent men of his day as an amiable dreamer. "Poor philosopher Berkeley," alluding to his illness, writes Swift, "has now the *idea* of health, which it was very hard to produce in him, for he had an *idea* of a strange fever, so strong that it was very hard to destroy it by introducing a contrary one." "I have not seen Dean Berkeley," writes Gay to Swift, "but I have read his book

(The Minute Philosopher), and like many parts of it; but in general think, with you, that it is too speculative." When one of his converts, after a sharp argument during an evening visit, rose to depart, "Pray, sir," said Dr. Johnson, "don't leave us, for we may perhaps forget to think of you, and then you will cease to exist." Similar witticisms are of frequent occurrence in the anecdotes preserved of his illustrious friends; and even when they urged those in power to aid the realization of his benevolent enterprise, the plea is often modified by some compassionate allusion to that romance of character to which his ardent projects were ascribed. It is, however, a law of disinterested action, that, when baffled in its specific aim, incidental good is sure to result; and, in order justly to estimate the personal influence of Berkeley in the world of opinion and the cause of humanity, we must take into view the indirect agency of his doctrine, the casual services he fulfilled, and the efficiency of the spirit he was of. Thus considered, it will be seen that the example and writings of few church dignitaries have proved more beneficent and attractive.

When he returned home, after the failure of his college scheme in America, he instantly paid back all the contributions he had received in aid of that object. When he became the legatee of Swift's indignant mistress, he honorably burned all her love-letters.* His last act at Cloyne, where his residence had been fraught with blessings to the people, was to sign a lease of the demesne lands there, to be renewed yearly, at a rent of two hundred pounds, for distribution to the poor of the neighborhood.

He enjoyed true philosophic content. "We behold these vicissitudes," says one of his letters, "with an equal eye from this serene corner of Cloyne;" and, speaking of the gout, from which he occasionally suffered, he observes, "It throws off a sharp excrement from the blood to the limbs and extremities of the body, and is no less useful than painful." The following passage from

* It was said, indeed, that Vanessa made it a condition of her legacy, that her correspondence with Swift should be published, and Berkeley has been reproached for its non-fulfilment. Sir Walter Scott, in his Life of Swift, explains the whole affair. There was no such condition in the will, and, although Berkeley destroyed the letters, his co-heritor retained copies, and from these extracts subsequently found their way into print.

another letter gives us a charming idea of the same spirit when age began to subdue his vivacity:

"For my own part," he writes, under date of April 6, 1752, "I submit to years and infirmities. My views in this world are mean and narrow; it is a thing in which I have a small share, and which ought to give me small concern. I abhor business, and especially to have to do with great persons and great affairs. The evening of life I choose to pass in a quiet retreat. Ambitious projects, intrigues and quarrels of statesmen, are things I have formerly been amused with, but they now seem to me a vain and fugitive dream. We have not the transports of your castle-hunters, but our lives are calm and serene."

The love of retirement, native to the scholar, was confirmed in Berkeley by domestic affections. His wife had some skill in painting, and music was cultivated in the family, for it was their custom to assemble early in the morning to receive instruction in that art from an Italian professor. The day the bishop passed in his study, and gave the evening to his family and social intercourse. Beautiful, even in its sadness, was the death of this benignant and gifted man, and singularly appropriate to the close of such a life. One Sabbath afternoon, in the winter of 1753, as he lay on a couch, in the full possession of those noble faculties he had borne so meekly, listening to one of Sherlock's sermons, his wife beside and his children around him, the gentle and exalted spirit of Berkeley took its flight, without a struggle, and so quietly that it was not until his daughter, approaching him to offer refreshment, found his hand cold, that they knew he was no more.

Such was the character and such the career of the man who, a century and a quarter ago, turned manfully from the allurements of clerical distinction and literary society, from the pleasures of wealth and fame, to bring religious truth and intellectual culture to the aborigines of this continent; who anticipated its marvellous destinies, and hailed it as a new field for the triumphs of humanity. There are more imposing monuments in the venerable precincts of Oxford, recalling the genius which hallows our ancestral literature, but at the tomb of Berkeley we linger with affectionate reverence, as we associate the gifts of his mind and the graces of his spirit with that disinterested and memorable visit to our country.

In 1725, Berkeley published his proposals in explanation of this long-cherished purpose; at the same time he offered to resign his livings, and to consecrate the remainder of his days to this Christian undertaking. So magnetic were his appeal and example, that three of his brother fellows at Oxford decided to unite with him in the expedition. Many eminent and wealthy persons were induced to contribute their influence and money to the cause. But he did not trust wholly to such means. Having ascertained the worth of a portion of the St. Christopher's lands ceded by France to Great Britain by the treaty of Utrecht, and about to be disposed of for public advantage, he undertook to realize from them larger proceeds than had been anticipated, and suggested that a certain amount of these funds should be devoted to his college. Availing himself of the friendly intervention of a Venetian gentleman whom he had known in Italy, he submitted the plan to George I., who directed Sir Robert Walpole to carry it through parliament. He obtained a charter for "erecting a college, by name St. Paul's, in Bermuda, with a president and nine fellows, to maintain and educate Indian scholars, at the rate of ten pounds a year, George Berkeley to be the first president, and his companions from Trinity College the fellows." His commission was voted May 11, 1726. To the promised amount of twenty thousand pounds, to be derived from the land sale, many sums were added from individual donation. The letters of Berkeley to his friends, at this period, are filled with the discussion of his scheme; it absorbed his time, taxed his ingenuity, filled his heart, and drew forth the warm sympathy and earnest coöperation of his many admirers, though regret at the prospect of losing his society constantly finds expression. Swift, in a note to the lord lieutenant of Ireland, says: "I do humbly entreat your excellency either to use such persuasions as will keep one of the first men of the kingdom for learning and genius at home, or assist him by your credit to compass his romantic design." "I have obtained reports," says one of his own letters, "from the Bishop of London, the board of trade and plantations, and the attorney and solicitor-general;" "yesterday the charter passed the privy seal;" "the lord chancellor is not a busier man than myself;" and elsewhere, "I have had more opposition from the governors and traders to America than from any one else; but, God be praised, there is an end of all their narrow and mercantile views and endeavors, as well as of the jealousies and suspicions of others, some of whom were very great men, who apprehended this college may produce an independency in America, or at least lessen her dependency on England."

Freneau's ballad of the "Indian Boy," who ran back to the woods from the halls of learning, was written subsequently, or it might have discouraged Berkeley in his idea of the capacity of the American savages for education; but more positive obstacles thwarted his generous aims. The king died before affixing his seal to the charter, which delayed the whole proceedings. Walpole, efficient as he was as a financier and a servant of the house of Brunswick, was a thorough utilitarian, and too practical and worldly-wise to share in the disinterested enthusiasm of Berkeley. In his answer to Bishop Gibson, whose diocese included the West Indies, when he applied for the funds so long withheld, he says: "If you put the question to me as a minister, I must assure you that the money shall most undoubtedly be paid as soon as suits with public convenience; but if you ask me as a friend whether Dean Berkeley should continue in America, expecting the payment of twenty thousand pounds, I advise him by all means to return to Europe." To the project, thus rendered unattainable, Berkeley had devoted seven years of his life, and the greater part of his fortune. The amount realized by the sale of confiscated lands was about ninety thousand pounds, of which eighty thousand were devoted to the marriage portion of the Princess Royal, about to espouse the Prince of Orange; and the remainder, through the influence of Oglethorpe, was secured to pay for the transportation of emigrants to his Georgia colony. Berkeley's scheme was more deliberate and well-considered than is commonly believed. Horace Walpole calls it "uncertain and amusing;" but a writer of deeper sympathies declares it "too grand and pure for the powers that were." His nature craved the united opportunities of usefulness and of self-culture; he felt the obligation to devote himself to benevolent enterprise, and at the same time earnestly desired both the leisure and the retirement needful for the pursuit of abstract studies. The project he contemplated promised to realize all these objects. He possessed a heart to feel the infinite wants, intellectual and religious, of the new continent, and had the imagination to conceive the grand destinies awaiting its growth. Those who fancy that his views were limited to the plan of a doubtful missionary experiment do great injustice to the broad and elevated hopes he cherished; he knew that a recognized seat of learning open to the poor and uncivilized, and the varied moral exigencies of a new country, would insure ample scope for the exercise of all his erudition and his talents; he felt that his mind would be a kingdom wherever his lot was cast; and he was inspired by a noble interest in the progress of America, and a faith in the new field there open for the advancement of truth, as is evident from the celebrated verses in which these feelings found expression:

"The Muse, disgusted at an age and clime
   Barren of every glorious theme,
In distant lands now waits a better time,
   Producing subjects worthy fame.

In happy climes, when from the genial sun
   And virgin earth such scenes ensue,
The force of art by nature seems outdone,
   And fancied beauties by the true;

In happy climes, the seat of innocence,
   Where nature guides and virtue rules,
Where men shall not impose for truth and sense
   The pedantry of schools;

Then shall we see again the golden age,
   The rise of empire and of arts,
The good and great inspiring epic rage,
   The wisest heads and noblest hearts;

Not such as Europe breeds in her decay;
   Such as she bred when fresh and young,
When heavenly flame did animate her clay,
   By future poets shall be sung.

Westward the course of empire takes its way;
   The four first acts already past,
A fifth shall end the drama with the day;
   Time's noblest offspring is the last."

In August, 1728, Berkeley married a daughter of the Honorable John Foster, speaker of the Irish House of Commons, and, soon after, embarked for America. His companions were, his wife and her friend, Miss Hancock; two gentlemen of fortune, James and Dalton; and Smibert the painter. In a picture by the latter, now in the Trumbull gallery at New Haven, are preserved the portraits of this group, with that of the dean's infant son, Henry, in his mother's arms. It was painted for a gentleman of Boston, of whom it was purchased, in 1808, by Isaac Lothrop, Esq., and presented to Yale College. This visit of Smibert associates Berkeley's name with the dawn of art in America. They had travelled together in Italy, and the dean induced him to join the expedition partly from friendship, and also to enlist his services as instructor in drawing and architecture, in the proposed college. Smibert was born in Edinburgh, about the year 1684, and served an apprenticeship there to a house-painter. He went to London, and, from painting coaches, rose to copying old pictures for the dealers. He then gave three years to the study of his art in Italy.

"Smibert," says Horace Walpole, "was a silent and modest man, who abhorred the *finesse* of some of his profession, and was enchanted with a plan that he thought promised tranquillity and an honest subsistence in a healthy and elysian climate, and in spite of remonstrances engaged with the dean, whose zeal had ranged the favor of the court on his side. The king's death dispelled the vision. One may conceive how a man so devoted to his art must have been animated when the dean's enthusiasm and eloquence painted to his imagination a new theatre of prospects, rich, warm, and glowing with scenery which no pencil had yet made common." *

Smibert was the first educated artist who visited our shores, and the picture referred to, the first of more than a single figure executed in the country. To his pencil New England is indebted for portraits of many of her early statesmen and clergy. Among others, he painted for a Scotch gentleman the only authentic likeness of Jonathan Edwards. He married a lady of fortune in Boston, and left her a widow with two children, in

* Anecdotes of Painting, vol. iii.

1751. A high eulogium on his abilities and character appeared in the London Courant. From two letters addressed to him by Berkeley, when residing at Cloyne, published in the Gentleman's Magazine, it would appear that his friendship for the artist continued after their separation, as the bishop urges the painter to recross the sea and establish himself in his neighborhood.

A considerable sum of money, and a large and choice collection of books, designed as a foundation for the library of St. Paul's College, were the most important items of the dean's outfit. In these days of rapid transit across the Atlantic, it is not easy to realize the discomforts and perils of such a voyage. Brave and philanthropic, indeed, must have been the heart of an English church dignitary, to whom the road of preferment was open, who was a favorite companion of the genial Steele, the classic Addison, and the brilliant Pope, who basked in the smile of royalty, was beloved of the church, revered by the poor, the idol of society, and the peer of scholars; yet could shake off the allurements of such a position to endure a tedious voyage, a long exile, and the deprivations attendant on a crude state of society and a new civilization, in order to achieve an object which, however excellent and generous in itself, was of doubtful issue, and beset with obstacles. Confiding in the pledges of those in authority, that the parliamentary grant would be paid when the lands had been selected, and full of the most sanguine anticipations, the noble pioneer of religion and letters approached the shores of the New World.

It seems doubtful to some of his biographers whether Berkeley designed to make a preliminary visit to Rhode Island, in order to purchase lands there, the income of which would sustain his Bermuda institution. The vicinity of that part of the New England coast to the West Indies may have induced such a course; but it is declared by more than one that his arrival at Newport was quite accidental. This conjecture, however, is erroneous, as in one of his letters, dated September 5, 1728, he says: "To-morrow, with God's blessing, I set sail for Rhode Island." The captain of the ship which conveyed him from England, it is said, was unable to discover the island of Bermuda, and at length abandoned the attempt, and steered in a northerly direction.

They made land which they could not identify, and supposed it inhabited only by Indians; it proved, however, to be Block Island, and two fishermen came off and informed them of the vicinity of Newport harbor. Under the pilotage of these men, the vessel, in consequence of an unfavorable wind, entered what is called the West passage, and anchored. The fishermen were sent ashore with a letter from the dean to Rev. James Honyman. They landed at Canonicut Island, and sought the dwellings of two parishioners of that gentleman, who immediately conveyed the letter to their pastor. For nearly half a century this faithful clergyman had labored in that region. He first established himself at Newport, in 1704. Besides the care of his own church, he made frequent visits to the neighboring towns on the main land. In a letter to the secretary of the Episcopal mission in America, in 1709, he says, "You can neither believe, nor I express, what excellent services for the cause of religion a bishop would do in these parts; these infant settlements would become beautiful nurseries, which now seem to languish for want of a father to oversee and bless them;" and in a memorial to Governor Nicholson on the religious condition of Rhode Island, in 1714, he observes: "The people are divided among Quakers, Anabaptists, Independents, Gortonians, and Infidels, with a remnant of true Churchmen." * It is characteristic of the times and region, that with a broad circuit and isolated churches as the sphere of his labors, the vicinity of Indians, and the variety of sects, he was employed for two months, in 1723, in daily attending a large number of pirates who had been captured, and were subsequently executed; one of the murderous bands which then infested the coast, whose extraordinary career has been illustrated by Cooper, in one of his popular nautical romances.

When Berkeley's missive reached this worthy pastor, he was in his pulpit, it being a holiday. He immediately read the letter to his congregation, and dismissed them. Nearly all accompanied him to the ferry wharf, which they reached but a few moments

* Hawkins' Historical Notices of the Missions of the Church of England in the North American Colonies, p. 173.

before the arrival of the dean and his fellow-voyagers. A letter from Newport, dated January 24th, 1729, that appeared in the New England Journal, published at Boston, thus notices the event: "Yesterday arrived here Dean Berkeley, of Londonderry, in a pretty large ship. He is a gentleman of middle stature, and of an agreeable, pleasant, and erect aspect. He was ushered into the town by a great number of gentlemen, to whom he behaved himself after a very complaisant manner. 'T is said he purposes to tarry here about three months."

We can easily imagine the delightful surprise which Berkeley acknowledges at first view of that lovely bay and the adjacent country. The water tinted, in the clear autumn air, like the Mediterranean; the fields adorned with symmetrical haystacks and golden maize, and bounded by a lucid horizon, against which rose picturesque windmills and the clustered dwellings of the town, and the noble trees which then covered the island; the bracing yet tempered atmosphere, all greeted the senses of those weary voyagers, and kindled the grateful admiration of their romantic leader. He soon resolved upon a longer sojourn, and purchased a farm of a hundred acres at the foot of the hill whereon stood the dwelling of Honyman, and which still bears his name.*

There he erected a modest homestead, with philosophic taste choosing the valley, in order to enjoy the fine view from the summit occasionally, rather than lose its charm by familiarity. At a sufficient distance from the town to insure immunity from idle visitors; within a few minutes' walk of the sea, and girdled by a fertile vale, the student, dreamer, and missionary, pitched his humble tent where nature offered her boundless refreshment, and seclusion her contemplative peace. His first vivid impressions of the situation, and of the difficulties and consolations of his position, are described in the few letters, dated at Newport, which his biographer cites. At this distance of time, and in view of the subsequent changes of that region, it is both curious and interesting to revert to these incidental data of Berkeley's visit.

* The conveyance from Joseph Whipple and wife to Berkeley, of the land in Newport, is dated Feb. 18, 1729.

"NEWPORT, IN RHODE ISLAND, April 24, 1729.

"I can by this time say something to you, from my own experience, of this place and its people. The inhabitants are of a mixed kind, consisting of many sects and subdivisions of sects. Here are four sorts of Anabaptists, besides Presbyterians, Quakers, Independents, and many of no profession at all. Notwithstanding so many differences, here are fewer quarrels about religion than elsewhere, the people living peacefully with their neighbors of whatever persuasion. They all agree in one point, — that the Church of England is the second best. The climate is like that of Italy, and not at all colder in the winter than I have known everywhere north of Rome. The spring is late, but, to make amends, they assure me the autumns are the finest and the longest in the world; and the summers are much pleasanter than those of Italy by all accounts, forasmuch as the grass continues green, which it does not there. This island is pleasantly laid out in hills and vales and rising ground, hath plenty of excellent springs and fine rivulets, and many delightful rocks, and promontories, and adjacent lands. The provisions are very good; so are the fruits, which are quite neglected, though vines sprout of themselves of an extraordinary size, and seem as natural to this soil as any I ever saw. The town of Newport contains about six thousand souls, and is the most thriving place in all America for its bigness. I was never more agreeably surprised than at the first sight of the town and its harbor."

"June 12, 1729. — I find it hath been reported in Ireland that we intend settling here; I must desire you to discountenance any such report. The truth is, if the king's bounty were paid in, and the charter could be removed hither, I should like it better than Bermuda. But if this were questioned before the payment of said money, it might perhaps hinder it and defeat all our designs. I snatch this moment to write, and have time only to add that I have got a son, who, I thank God, is likely to live."

"May 7. — This week I received a package from you *via* Philadelphia, the postage of which amounted to above four pounds sterling of this country money. I am worried to death by creditors, and am at an end of patience, and almost out of my wits.

Our little son is a great joy to us: we are such fools as to think him the most perfect thing of the kind we ever saw."

To the poet, scenery of picturesque beauty and grandeur is desirable, but to the philosopher general effects are more congenial. High mountains, forests, and waterfalls, appeal more emphatically to the former, and luxuries of climate and atmosphere to the latter. Accordingly the soft marine air and the beautiful skies of summer and autumn, in the region of Berkeley's American home, with the vicinity of the sea-coast, became to him a perpetual delight. He alludes, with grateful sensibility, to the "pleasant fields," and "walks on the beach," to "the expanse of ocean studded with fishing-boats and lighters," and the "plane-trees," that daily cheered his sight, as awakening "that sort of joyful instinct which a rural scene and fine weather inspire." He calls Newport "the Montpelier of America," and appears to have communed with nature and inhaled the salubrious breeze, while pursuing his meditations, with all the zest of a healthy organization and a susceptible and observant mind. A few ravines, finely wooded and with fresh streams purling over rocky beds, vary the alternate uplands; from elevated points a charming distribution of water enlivens the prospect; and the shore is indented with high cliffs or rounded into graceful curves. The sunsets are remarkable for a display of gorgeous and radiant clouds; the wide sweep of pasture is only broken by low ranges of stone wall, clumps of sycamores, orchards, hay-stacks, and mill-towers; and over luxuriant clover-beds, tasselled maize, or fallow acres, plays, for two thirds of the year, a south-western breeze, chastened and moistened by the Gulf Stream.

Intercourse with Boston was then the chief means on the island of acquiring political and domestic news. A brisk trade was carried on between the town and the West Indies, France, England, and the Low Countries, curious memorials of which are still visible, in some of the old mansions, in the shape of china and glass ware, of obsolete patterns, and faded specimens of rich brocade. A sturdy breed of Narraganset ponies carried fair equestrians from one to another of the many hospitable dwellings scattered over the fields, on which browsed sheep and cackled geese, still famous in epicurean reminiscence; while tropical fruits were constantly imported, and an abundance and variety of fish and fowl rewarded the most careless sportsman. Thus blessed by nature, the accidental home of the philosophic dean soon won his affection. Intelligent members of all denominations united in admiration of his society and attendance upon his preaching. With one neighbor he dined every Sunday, to the child of another he became god-father, and with a third took counsel for the establishment of the literary club, which founded the Redwood Library. It was usual then to see the broad brim of the Quakers in the aisles of Trinity Church; and, as an instance of his emphatic yet tolerant style, it is related that he once observed in a sermon, "Give the devil his due: John Calvin was a great man." * We find him, at one time, writing a letter of encouragement to a Huguenot preacher of Providence, and, at another, visiting Narraganset with Smibert to examine the aboriginal inhabitants. His own opinion of the race was given in the discourse on "The Propagation of the Gospel in Foreign Parts," delivered in London on his return. To the ethnologist it may be interesting, in reference to this subject, to revert to the anecdote of the portrait-painter cited by Dr. Barton. He had been employed by the Grand Duke of Tuscany to paint two or three Siberian Tartars presented to that prince by the Czar of Russia; and, on first landing in Narraganset with Berkeley, he instantly recognized the Indians there as the same race as the Siberian Tartars; an opinion confirmed by Wolff, the celebrated Eastern traveller.

During his residence at Newport, Berkeley became acquainted with the Rev. Jared Elliot, one of the trustees of Yale College, and with the Rev. Samuel Johnson, an Episcopal minister of Stratford, Connecticut, who informed him of the condition, prospects, and wants, of that institution. He afterwards opened a correspondence on the subject with Rector Williams, and was thus led, after the failure of his own college scheme, to make his generous donations to a seminary already established. He had previously presented the college with a copy of his writings. In

* Updike's History of the Narraganset Church.

1732, he sent from England a deed of his farm in Rhode Island, and, the conditions and descriptions not being satisfactory, he sent the ensuing year another deed, by which it was provided that the rents of his lands should be devoted to the education of three young men, the best classical scholars; the candidates to be examined annually, on the sixth of May; in case of disagreement among the examiners, the competitors to decide by lot; and all surplus funds to be used for the purchase of classical books. Berkeley also gave to the library a thousand volumes, which cost over four hundred pounds,—the most valuable collection of books then brought together in America. They were chiefly his own purchase, but in part contributed by his friends. One of the graduates of Yale, educated under the Berkeley scholarship, was Dr. Buckminster, of Portsmouth, N.H. Unfortunately the income of the property at Newport is rendered much less than it might be by the terms of a long lease. This liberality of the Bishop of Cloyne was enhanced by the absence of sectarian prejudice in his choice for the stewardship of his bounty of a collegiate institution where different tenets are inculcated from those he professed. That he was personally desirous of increasing his own denomination in America, is sufficiently evinced by the letter in which he directs the Secretary of the Episcopal Mission there to appropriate a balance originally contributed to the Bermuda scheme. This sum had remained at his banker's for many years unclaimed, and he suggests that part of it should be devoted to a gift of books for Harvard University, "as a proper means to inform their judgment, and dispose them to think better of our church." His interest in classical education on this side of the water is also manifested in a letter advocating the preëminence of those studies in Columbia College.*

It is a remarkable coincidence that Berkeley should have taken up his abode in Rhode Island, and thus completed the representative character of the most tolerant religious community in New

* "I am glad to find a spirit towards learning prevails in these parts, particularly in New York, where, you say, a college is projected, which has my best wishes. Let the Greek and Latin classics be well taught; be this the first care as to learning."—*Berkeley's Letter to Johnson. Moore's Sketch of Columbia College. New York*, 1846.

England, by the presence of an eminent Episcopal dignitary. A principal reason of the variety, the freedom, and the peace of religious opinion there, to which he alludes, is the fact that, through the liberal wisdom and foresight of Roger Williams, that state has become an asylum for the persecuted of all denominations from the neighboring provinces; but another cause may be found in the prevalence of the Quakers, whose amiable tenets and gentle spirit subdued the rancor and bigotry of fanaticism. Several hundred Jews, still commemorated by their cemetery and synagogue, allured by the prosperous trade and the tolerant genius of the place, added still another feature to the varied population. The lenity of Penn towards the aborigines, and the fame of Fox, had given dignity to the denomination of Friends, and their domestic culture was refined as well as morally superior. Enterprise in the men who, in a neighboring state, originated the whale-fishery, and beauty among the women of that sect, are traditional in Rhode Island. We were reminded of Berkeley's observations, in regard to the natural productions of the country, during a recent visit to the old farm-house where he resided. An enormous wild grape-vine had completely veiled what formed the original entrance to the humble dwelling, and several ancient apple-trees in the orchard, with boughs mossy with time, and gnarled by the ocean gales, showed, in their sparse fruit and matted twigs, the utter absence of the pruning-knife. The dwelling itself is built, after the manner common to farm-houses a century ago, entirely of wood, with low ceilings, broad fire-place, and red cornice. The only traces of the old country were a few remaining tiles, with obsolete designs, around the chimney-piece. But the deep and crystal azure of the sea gleamed beyond corn-field and sloping pasture; sheep grazed in the meadows, hoary rocks bounded the prospect, and the mellow crimson of sunset lay warm on grass slope and paddock, as when the kindly philosopher mused by the shore with Plato in hand, or noted a metaphysical dialogue in the quiet and ungarnished room which overlooks the rude garden. Though, as he declares, "for every private reason," he preferred "Derry to New England," pleasant was the abode, and grateful is the memory of Berkeley, in this rural seclusion. A succession of green breastworks along the brow of the hill beneath which his domicile nestles, by reminding the visitor of the retreat of the American forces under General Sullivan, brings vividly to his mind the Revolution and its incalculable influence upon the destinies of a land which so early won the intelligent sympathy of Berkeley; while the name of Whitehall, which he gave to this peaceful domain, commemorates that other revolution in his own country, wherein the loyalty of his grandfather drove his family into exile. But historical soon yield to personal recollections, when we consider the memorials of his sojourn. We associate this landscape with his studies and his benevolence; and, when the scene was no longer blessed with his presence, his gifts remained to consecrate his memory. In old Trinity, the organ he bestowed peals over the grave of his first-born in the adjoining burial-ground. A town in Massachusetts bears his name. Not long since a presentation copy of his "Minute Philosopher" was kept on the table of an old lady of Newport, with reverential care. In one family his gift of a richly wrought silver coffee-pot, and in another that of a diamond ring, are cherished heirlooms. His rare and costly books were distributed, at his departure, among the resident clergy. His scholarship at New Haven annually furnishes recruits to our church, bar, or medical faculty. In an adjacent parish the sacramental cup was his donative. His legacy of ingenious thoughts and benign sentiment is associated with hanging rocks that are the seaward boundary of his farm; his Christian ministry with the ancient church, and his verse with the progress of America.

THE SCEPTICAL GENIUS.

GIACOMO LEOPARDI.

PROVINCIAL life in Italy can scarcely be realized by an American except through observation. However remote from cities, or sequestered in location, a town may be in this country, if not connected with the great world by railroad and telegraph, the newspaper, the political representative, and an identity of feeling and action in some remote enterprise or interest, keep alive mutual sympathy and intelligence. But a moral and social as well as physical isolation belongs to the minor towns of the Italian peninsula. The quaint old stone houses enclose beings whose existence is essentially monastic, whose knowledge is far behind the times, and whose feelings are rigidly confined within the limits of family and neighborhood. A more complete picture of still life in the nineteenth century it is difficult to imagine, than many of these secluded towns present. The dilapidated air of the palaces, the sudden gloom of the narrow streets, as one turns into them from the square, where a group of idlers in tattered cloaks are ever engaged in a game or a gossip, the electrical effect of a travelling carriage, or a troop of soldiers invading the quiet scene, at once inform even the casual visitor of the distance he is at from the spirit of the age. With the decayed air of the private houses, their worn brick floors and primitive furniture, contrast impressively the extensive and beautiful view usually obtainable from the highest windows, and the architectural magnificence of the church. We are constantly reminded that modern amelioration has not yet invaded the region; while the petty objects to which even the better class are devoted, the importance attached to the most frivolous details of life, the confined views and microscopic jealousies or dilettante tastes that prevail, assure us that liberal curiosity and enlarged sympathy find but little scope in these haunts of a nation devoid of civil life, and thrust upon the past for mental nourishment.

It is, however, comparatively easy to imagine the influence of such an environment upon a superior intelligence. Recoiling from the attempt to find satisfaction in the external, thus repressed and deadened, the scholar would there naturally turn to written lore with a singular intensity of purpose; the aspirant would find little to tempt him from long and sustained flights into the ideal world; and the thinker would cling to abstract truth with an energy more fond and concentrated from the very absence of all motive and scope for action and utterance. It is thus that we account, in part, for the remarkable individuality and lonely career of Giacomo Leopardi, one of the greatest scholars and men of genius modern Italy has produced. He has left a glimpse of this monotonous and ungenial life in one of his poems—*La Vita Solitaria:*

> "La mattutina pioggia, allor che l'al
> Battendo esulta nella chiusa stanza
> Le gallinella ed al balcon s'affaccia
> L'abitator de'campi, e il Sol che nasce
> I suoi tremuli rai fra le cadenti
> Stille saetta, alla capanna mia
> Dolcemente picchiando, mi risveglia;
> E sorgo, e i lievi nugoletti, e il primo
> Degli augelli susurro, e l' aura fresca,
> E le ridenti piagge benedico;
> Poichè voi, cittadine infauste mura,
> Vidi e conobbi assai, là dove segue
> Odio al dolor compagno; e doloroso
> Lo vivo, e tal morrò, deh tosto! Alcuna
> Benche scarsa pietà pur mi dimostra
> Natura in questi lochi, un giorno oh quanto
> Verso me piu cortese."

Leopardi was the son of a count, whose estates are situated at Recanti, in the March of Ancona; and here his early youth was passed chiefly in his father's library, which consisted wholly of theological and classical books. After being taught Latin and the elements of philosophy by two priests, he seems to have been left to pursue his own course; and, at ten years old, he describes himself as having commenced a wild and desperate life of study, the result of which was a mastery of ancient classic and church literature, not only displayed in positive knowledge, but reproduced habitually in the form of translations and commentaries. Greek is little cultivated in Italy, and in this, as well as other branches of learning, he was quite isolated. In seven years his health was completely ruined by unremitted mental application. Niebuhr and Angelo Mai soon recognized him as a philologist of remarkable acumen and attainment; and laudatory articles in the French, German, and Holland journals, as well as complimentary letters from distinguished men, found their way to his secluded home. He duped scholars by tricks like those of Macpherson and Chatterton, in the pretended translation of an Hellenic fragment; he engaged in a literary correspondence with Monti and Gioberti; wrote able commentaries on the rhetoricians of the first and second centuries, annotations on the chronicle of Eusebius; invented new narratives of martyrdoms that passed for genuine; translated parts of the Odyssey, Epictetus, and Socrates; and, in fact, performed Herculean labors of research and criticism.

But the most remarkable feature of his life is the contrast between its profound scholarship and its domestic environment. During this period Leopardi was treated like a child, kept at home by poverty, utterly destitute of companionship, except what he found in an occasional disputation with the Jews of Ancona; wretched in appearance, consumed by melancholy, struggling with his father against the project to dedicate him to the church; without sympathy from his kind, or faith in his Creator, or joy in his youth, or hope in his destiny. He only found temporary solace when consciousness was absorbed in his studious vigils, in the solitary library of a forlorn palace in that secluded town. Such is an epitome of Leopardi's youth. Of his works thus produced there are but few and imperfect copies, many being still unedited; and his peculiar genius would be faintly revealed to us, had it not found more direct and personal expression in a few sincere and highly finished original writings, which shadow forth and embody, with singular eloquence, the life and the nature of the man.

Leopardi was born at Recanti, on the twenty-ninth of June, 1798, and died at Naples, on the fourteenth of June, 1837. The restraint under which he lived, partly that of circumstances, and partly of authority, both exerted upon a morbidly sensitive and lonely being, kept him in his provincial birthplace until the age of twenty-four. After this period he sought a precarious subsistence in Rome, Florence, Bologna, and Naples. Of the conscious aim he proposed to himself as a scholar, we may judge by his own early declaration: "Mediocrity frightens me; my wish is to love, and become great by genius and study." In regard to the first desire, he seems, either from an unfortunate personal appearance, or from having been in contact with the insincere and the vain, to have experienced a bitter disappointment; for the craving for sympathy, and the praise of love, continually find expression in his writings, while he says of women, "L'ambizione, l'interesso, la perfidia, l'insensibilità delle donne che io definisco un animale senza cuore, sono cose che mi spaventano." He translated, with great zest, the satire of Simonides on women. Elsewhere, however, there is evinced a remarkable sensibility to female attractions, and indications appear of gratified, though interrupted, affinities. Indeed, we cannot but perceive that Leopardi belongs to that rare class of men whose great sense of beauty and "necessity of loving" is united with an equal passion for truth. It was not, therefore, because his taste was too refined, or his standard too ideal, that his affections were baffled, but on account of the extreme rarity of that sacred union of loveliness and loyalty, of grace and candor, of the beautiful and the true, which, to the thinker and the man of heart, alone justifies the earnestness of love.

Nature vindicated herself, as she ever will, even in his courageous attempt to merge all youthful impulse in the pursuit of knowledge, and twine around abstract truth the clinging sensibilities that covet a human object. He became, indeed, a master of lore, he lived a scholar, he kept apart from the multitude, and enacted the stoical thinker; but the ungratified portion of his soul bewailed her bereavement; from his harvest-fields of learning went up the cry of famine; a melancholy tone blended with his most triumphant expositions; and an irony that ill conceals moral need underlies his most vivacious utterance.

In his actual life Leopardi confesses himself to have been greatly influenced by prudential motives. There was a reserve in his family intercourse, which doubtless tended to excite his thoughts and feelings to a greater private scope; and he accordingly sought in fancy and reflection a more bold expansion. His scepticism has been greatly lamented as the chief source of his hopelessness; and the Jesuits even ventured to assert his final conversion, so important did they regard the accession of such a gifted name to the roll of the church; but his friend, Ranieri, in whose arms he died, only tells us that he "resigned his exalted spirit with a smile." He presents another instance of the futility of attempting to graft religious belief externally, and by prescriptive means, upon a free, inquiring, and enthusiastic mind. Christianity, as practically made known to Leopardi, failed to enlist his sympathies, from the erroneous form in which it was revealed, while, speculatively, its authority seemed to have no higher sanction than the antique philosophy and fables with which he was conversant. Had he learned to consider religion as a sentiment, inevitable and divine; had he realized it in the same way as he did love — as an experience, a feeling, a principle of the soul, and not a technical system, it would have yielded him both comfort and inspiration.

Deformed, with the seeds of decay in his very frame, familiar with the history, the philosophy, the languages, of the earth, reflective and susceptible, loving and lonely, erudite, but without a faith, young in years, but venerable in mental life, he found nothing, in the age of transition in which he lived, to fix and harmonize his nature. His parent was incapable of comprehending the mind he sought to control. Sympathy with Greece and Rome, compassion for Italy, and despair of himself, were the bitter fruits of knowledge unillumined by supernal trust. He says the *inesplicabile mistero dell 'universo* weighed upon his soul. He longed to solve the problem of life, and tried to believe, with Byron, that "everything is naught"— *tutto é nulla;* and wrote, *la calamità é la sola cosa che vi convenga essendo virtuoso. Nostra vita*, he asks, *che val? solo a spregiarla.* He thought too much to be happy without a centre of light about which his meditations could hopefully revolve; he felt too much to be tranquil without some reliable and endeared object to which he might confidently turn for solace and recognition. The facts of his existence are meagre; the circle of his experience limited, and his achievements as a scholar give us no clue to his inward life; but the two concise volumes of prose and verse are a genuine legacy; a reflection of himself amply illustrative to the discriminating reader.

As regards the diction of Leopardi, it partakes of the superiority of his mind and the individuality of his character. Versed, as he was, both in the vocabulary and the philosophy of ancient and modern languages, he cherished the highest appreciation of his native tongue, of which he said it was *sempre infinita.* He wrote slowly, and with great care. In poetry, his first conception was noted, at once, and born in an access of fervor; but he was employed, at intervals, for weeks, in giving the finishing touches to the shortest piece. It is, indeed, evident that Leopardi gave to his deliberate compositions the essence, as it were, of his life. No one would imagine his poems, except from their lofty and artistic style, to be the effusions of a great scholar, so simple, true, and apparently unavoidable, are the feelings they embody. It is this union of severe discipline and great erudition with the glow, the directness, and the natural sentiment, of a young poet, that constitutes the distinction of Leopardi. The reflective power, and the predominance of the thoughtful element in his writings, assimilate him rather with German and English than modern Italian literature. There is nothing desultory and superficial; vigor of thought, breadth and accuracy of knowledge, and the most serious feeling, characterize his works.

His taste was manly, and formed altogether on the higher models. In terse energy he often resembles Dante; in tender and pensive sentiment, Petrarch; in philosophical tone he manifested the Anglo-Saxon spirit of inquiry and psychological tendency of Bacon and Coleridge; thus singularly combining the poetic and the erudite, grave research and fanciful speculation, deep wisdom and exuberant love. Of late Italian writers, perhaps no one more truly revives the romantic associations of her literature; for Leopardi "learned in suffering what he taught in song," as exclusively as the "grim Tuscan" who described the world of spirits. His life was shadowed by a melancholy not less pervading than that of Tasso; and, since Laura's bard, no poet of the race has sung of love with a more earnest beauty. He has been well said to have passed a "life of thought with sorrow beside him." The efflorescence of that life is concentrated in his verse, comparatively limited in quantity, but proportionally intense in expression; and the views, impressions, fancies, and ideas, generated by his studies and experience, we may gather from his prose, equally concise in form and individual in spirit. From these authentic sources we will now endeavor to infer the characteristics of his genius.

His faith, or rather his want of faith, in life and human destiny, is clearly betrayed in his legend or allegory, called *Storia del Genere Umano.* According to this fable, Jove created the world infinitely less perfect than it now exists, with obvious limits, undiversified by water and mountains; and over it man roved without impediment, childlike, truthful, and living wholly in the immediate. Upon emerging from this adolescent condition, however, the race, wearied by the monotony and obvious bounds to their power and enjoyment, grew dissatisfied. Satiety took the place of contentment, and many grew desperate, loathing the existence in which they originally rejoiced. This insensibility to the gifts of the gods was remedied by introducing the elements of diversity and suggestiveness into the face of nature and the significance of life. The night was made brilliant by stars; mountains and valleys alternated in the landscape; the atmosphere, from a fixed aspect, became nebulous and crystalline by turns. Nature, instead of ministering only to vitality and instinctive enjoyment, was so arranged and developed as constantly to excite imagination and act upon sympathy. Echo was born, at this time, to startle with mysterious responses; and dreams first invaded the domain of sleep, to prolong the illusive agencies thus instituted to render human life more tolerable.

By these means Jove awakened to consciousness the soul, and increased the charities and the grace of existence through a sense of the grand and beautiful. This epoch was of longer duration than that which preceded it; and the weary and hackneyed spirits once more realized enjoyment in experiencing the same vivid impressions and zest of being which had marked the primitive era. But, at length, this warfare between the real and ideal, this successive interchange of charming delusion and stern fact that made up existence, wore upon the moral energies, and so fatigued the spirits of men, that it gave rise to the custom, once prevalent among our progenitors, of celebrating as a festival the death of friends. Impiety was the final result of this period in the history of the race. Life became perverted, and human nature shorn of its original beauty. This fallen condition the gods punished by the flood of Deucalion. Admonished to repair the solitude of the earth, he and Pyrrha, though disdainful of life, obeyed the command, and threw stones behind them to restore the species. Jove, admonished by the past of the essential nature of man, that it is impossible for him, like other animals, to live happily in a state of freedom from evil, always desiring the impossible, considered by what new arts it was practicable to keep alive the unhappy race. These he decided were first to mingle in his life real evils, and then to engage him in a thousand avocations and labors, in order to divert him as much as possible from communing with his own nature, or, at least, with the desire of the unattained. He, therefore, sent abroad many diseases and misfortunes, wishing, by the vicissitudes of mortal life, to obviate satiety, and increase, by the presence of evil, the relish of good; to soften the ferocity of man, to reduce his power, and lead him to succumb to necessity, and to temper the ardor of his desires.

Besides such benefits, he knew that, when there is room for hope, the unhappy are less inclined to do violence to themselves, and that the gloom of disaster thus illumined is endurable. Accordingly, he created tempests, armed them with thunder and lightning, gave Neptune his trident, whirled comets into space, and ordained eclipses. By these and other terrible phases of the elements, he desired to excite a wholesome awe, knowing that the presence of danger will reconcile to life, for a time at least, not only the unhappy, but those who most abominate it. To exclude the previous satiety, he induced in mankind appetites for new gratifications, not to be obtained without toil; and whereas, before the flood, water, herbs, and fruit, sufficed for nourishment, now food and drink of great variety and elaborate preparation became a necessity. Until then, the equality of temperature rendered clothing useless; the inclemency of the weather now made it indispensable.

He ordered Mercury to found the first city, and divide the race into nations, tongues, and people, sowing discord among them. Thus laws were originated and civil life instituted. He then sent among men certain sentiments, or superhuman phantasms of most excellent semblance, such as Justice, Virtue, Glory, and Patriotism, to mould, quicken, and elevate society. The fruit of this revolution was admirable. Notwithstanding the fatigues, alarms, and griefs, previously unknown to our race, it excelled, in sweetness and convenience, its state before the deluge; and this effect was owing mainly to the phantasms or ideas before alluded to, which inspired poets and artists to the highest efforts, and to which many cheerfully sacrificed their lives. This greatly pleased Jove, who justly thought that men would value life in proportion as they were disposed to yield it in a noble cause. Indeed, this order of things, even when superseded after many centuries, retained its supremacy so well that, up to a time not very distant from the present, the maxims founded upon it were in vogue.

Again, the insatiable desires of man alienated him from the will of the gods. Unsatisfied with the scope given to imaginative enjoyment, he now pleaded for Truth. This unreasonable exaction angered Jupiter, who, however, determined to punish importunity by granting the demand. To the remonstrances of the other deities he replied by describing the consequences of the gift. It will, he assured them, destroy many of the attractive illusions of life, disenchant perception, and forever chasten the fervor of desire; for Truth is not to mortals what she is to divinities. She makes clear the beatitude of the one, but the misery of the other, by revealing the conditions of their fate, the precarious nature of their enjoyments, and the deceptive character of human pursuits. The long-sought blessings thus proved to the multitude a bane; for, in this new order of things, the semblance of the infinite no longer yielded satisfaction, but aggravated the soul, created weariness, longing, and aspiration. Under the dominion of Truth, universality supervened among men, landmarks lost their distinctness, nations intermingled, and the motives to earnest love or hate became few and tame. Life thus gradually lost its original interest and significance to human consciousness, and its essential value was so greatly diminished as to awaken the pity of the gods at the forlorn destiny of the race.

Jove heard their intercession benignly, and consented to the prayer of Love that she might descend to the earth. The gentle daughter of the celestial Venus thus preserved the only vestige of the ancient nobility of man. Often before had men imagined that she dwelt among them; but it was only her counterfeit. Not until humanity came under the dominion of Truth, did Love actually vouchsafe her genuine presence, and then only for a time, for she could not be long spared from heaven. So unworthy had mankind become, that few hearts were found fit to receive the angelic guest, and these she filled with such noble and sweet emotions, such high and consistent moral energy, as to revive in them the life of the beatific era. This state, when realized, so nearly approached the divine, that Jove permitted it to but few, and at long intervals. By this means, however, the grand primeval sentiments were kept in relation with man, the original sacred fire remained unextinguished, and the glorious imaginings and tender charms of humanity yet lingered to nourish a sublime faith and infinite hope. The majority, however, continued insensible to this redeeming element, and profaned and ignorantly repudiated it; yet it ceased not to hallow, exalt, and refine, the weary, sated, and baffled soul of man.

Such is a meagre outline of the allegory which shadows forth Leopardi's views of life. It would appear that he recognized no sign of promise in the firmament of existence, radiant as it was to his vision with the starry light of knowledge, but the rainbow of Love, upon which angels seemed to ascend and descend — the one glowing link between earth and the sky, the bridge spanning the gulf of time, the arc made up of the tears of earth and the light of heaven.

In a note to this fable, he protests against having had any design to run a philosophical tilt against either the Mosaic tradition or the evangelists; but it is evident that he did aim to utter the convictions which his own meditations and personal experience had engendered. Nor is the view thus given of the significance and far-reaching associations of human love, when consecrated by sentiment and intensified by intelligence, so peculiar as might appear from his manner of presenting it. In Plato, Dante, and Petrarch, in all the higher orders of poets and philosophers, we find a divine and enduring principle recognized under the same guise. The language in which Leopardi expresses his faith on the subject is not less emphatic than graceful: "Qualora viene in sulla terra, sceglie i cuori piu teneri e piu gentili delle persone piu generose e magnanime; e quivi siede per alcun breve spazio; diffondendovi sì pellegrina e mirabile soavità, ed empiendoli di affetti sì nobili, e di tanta virtù e fortezza, che eglino allora provano, cosa al tutto nuova nel genere umano, pinttosto verità che rassomiglianza di beatitudine."

The satire of Leopardi is pensive rather than bitter; it is aimed at general, not special error, and seems inspired far more by the sad conviction of a serious mind than the ascerbity of a disappointed one. In the dialogue between Fashion and Death, the former argues a near relationship and almost identity of purpose with the latter; and the folly and unwholesome effects of subservience to custom are finely satirized, in naïvely showing how the habits she induces tend to shorten life and multiply the victims of disease. So in the proposal of premiums by an imaginary academy, the mechanical spirit of the age is wittily rebuked by the offer of prizes to the inventor of a machine to enact the office of a friend, without the alloy of selfishness and disloyalty which usually mars the perfection of that character in its human form. Another prize is offered for a machine that will enact magnanimity, and another for one that will produce women of unperverted conjugal instincts. The imaginary conversation between a sprite and a gnome is an excellent rebuke to self-love; and that between Malambruno and Farfarello emphatically indicates the impossibility of obtaining happiness through will, or the agency even of superior intelligence. Leopardi's hopelessness is clearly shown in the dialogue of Nature and a Soul, wherein the latter refuses the great endowments offered because of the inevitable attendant suffering. In the Earth and Moon's interview, we have an ingenious satire upon that shallow philosophy which derives all the data of truth from individual consciousness and personal experience.

One of the most quaint and instructive of these colloquies is that between Federico Ruysch and his mummies, in which the popular notion of the pain of dying is refuted by the alleged proof of experience. The mummies, in their midnight song, declare the condition of death to be *lieta no, ma sicura.* Physiologically considered, all pleasure is declared to be attended with a certain languor. Burke suggests the same idea in reference to the magnetical effects of beauty on the nervous system; and this agreeable state is referred to by the mummies to give their inquisitive owner an idea of the sensation of dying. The philosophy of this subject, the vague and superstitious fears respecting it, have recently engaged the attention of popular medical writers; but the essential points are clearly unfolded in this little dialogue of Leopardi.

In his essay entitled *Detti Memorabili di Filippo Ottonieri,* we have apparently an epitome of his own creed; at least, the affinity between the maxims and habits here described and those which, in other instances, he acknowledges as personal, is quite obvious. Ottonieri is portrayed as a man isolated in mind and sympathies, though dwelling among his kind. He thought that the degree in which individuality of life and opinion in man was regarded as eccentric might be deemed a just standard of civilization; as, the more enlightened and refined the state of society, the more such originality was respected and regarded as natural. He is described as ironical; but the reason for this was that he was deformed and unattractive in person, like Socrates, yet created to love; and, not being able to win this highest gratification, so conversed as to inspire both fear and esteem. He cultivated wisdom, and tried to console himself with friendship; moreover, his irony was not *sdegnosa ed acerba, ma riposata e dolce.*

He was of opinion that the greatest delights of existence are illusions, and that children find everything in nothing, and adults nothing in everything. He compared pleasure to odors, which usually promised a satisfaction unrealized by taste; and said, of some nectar-drinking bees, that they were blest in not understanding their own happiness. He remarked that want of consideration occasioned far more suffering than positive and intentional cruelty, and that one who lived a gregarious life would utter himself aloud when alone, if a fly bit him; but one accustomed to solitude and inward life would often be silent in company, though threatened with a stroke of apoplexy. He divided mankind into two classes — those whose characters and instincts are overlaid and moulded by conformity and conventionalism,. and those whose natures are so rich or so strong as to assert themselves intact and habitually. He declared that. in this age, it was impossible for any one to love without a rival; for the egotist usually combined with and struggled for supremacy against the lover in each individual. He considered delusion a requisite of all human enjoyment, and thought man, like the child who from a sweet-rimmed chalice imbibed the medicine, according to Tasso's simile, *e dal' inganno sus vita riceve.* In these, and many other ideas attributed to Ottonieri, we recognize the tone of feeling and the experience of Leopardi; and the epitaph with which it concludes breathes of the same melancholy, but intelligent and aspiring nature: "*Nato alle opere virtuose e alla gloria, vissuto ozioso e disutile, e morto sensa fama non ignaro della natura nè della fortuna sua.*"

The *Wager of Prometheus* is a satire upon civilization, in which a cannibal feast, a Hindoo widow's sacrifice, and a suicide in London, are brought into vivid and graphic contrast. To exhibit the fallacy which estimates life, merely as such, a blessing, and to show that it consists in sensitive and moral experience rather than in duration, as color is derived from light, and not from the objects of which it is but a quality, he gives us an animated and discriminating argument between a metaphysician and a materialist; and, in illustration of the absolute mental nature of happiness when closely analyzed, he takes us to the cell of Tasso, where a most characteristic and suggestive discussion takes place between him and his familiar genius. The tyranny of Nature, her universal and inevitable laws, unredeemed, to Leopardi's view, by any compensatory spiritual principle, is displayed in an interview between her and one of her discontented subjects, wherein she declares man's felicity an object of entire indifference; her arrangements having for their end only the preservation of the universe by a constant succession of destruction and renovation.

His literary creed is emphatically recorded in the little treatise on *Parini o vero della Gloria;* and it exhibits him as a true nobleman in letters, although the characteristic sadness of his mind is evident in his severe estimate of the obstacles which interfere with the recognition of an original and earnest writer; for to this result, rather than fame, his argument is directed. As a vocation, he considers authorship unsatisfactory, on account of its usual effect, when sedulously pursued, upon the animal economy. He justly deems the capacity to understand and sympathize with a great writer extremely rare; the preöccupation of society in the immediate and the personal, the inundation of books in modern times, the influence of prejudice, ignorance, and narrowness of mind, the lack of generous souls, mental satiety, frivolous tastes, decadence of enthusiasm and vigor in age, and impatient expectancy in youth, are among the many and constant obstacles against which the individual who appeals to his race, through books, has to contend. He also dwells upon the extraordinary influence of prescriptive opinion, wedded to a few antique examples, upon the literary taste of the age. He considers the secret power of genius, in literature, to exist in an indefinable charm of style almost as rarely appreciated as it is exercised; and he thinks great writing only an inevitable substitute for great action, the development of the heroic, the beautiful, and the true in language, opinion, and sentiment, which under propitious circumstances would have been embodied, with yet greater zeal, in deeds. He thus views the art in which he excelled, in its most disinterested and noblest relations.

There is great naturalness, and a philosophic tone, in the

interview between Columbus and one of his companions, as they approach the New World. In the *Eulogy on Birds*, it is touching to perceive the keen appreciation Leopardi had of the joyous side of life, his complete recognition of it as a phase of nature, and his apparent unconsciousness of it as a state of feeling. The blithe habits of the feathered creation, their vivacity, motive power, and jocund strains, elicit as loving a commentary as Audubon or Wilson ever penned; but they are described only to be contrasted with the hollow and evanescent smiles of his own species; and the brief illusions they enjoy are pronounced more desirable than those of such singers as Dante and Tasso, to whom imagination was a *funestissima dote, e principio di sollecitudini, e angosce gravissime e perpetue.* With the tokens of his rare intelligence and sensibility before us, it is affecting to read his wish to be converted into a bird, in order to experience a while their contentment and joy.

The form of these writings is peculiar. We know of no English prose work at all similar, except the Imaginary Conversations of Landor, and a few inferior attempts of a like character. But there is one striking distinction between Leopardi and his classic English prototype; the former's aim is always to reproduce the opinions and modes of expression of his characters, while the latter chiefly gives utterance to his own. This disguise was adopted, we imagine, in a degree, from prudential motives. Conscious of sentiments at variance with the accepted creed, both in religion and philosophy, the young Italian recluse summoned historical personages, whose memories were hallowed to the imagination, or allegorical characters, whose names were associated with the past, and, through their imaginary dialogues, revealed his own fancies, meditations, and emotions. In fact, a want of sympathy with the age is one of the prominent traits of his mind. He was sceptical in regard to the alleged progress of the race, had little faith in the wisdom of newspapers, and doubted the love of truth for her own sake, as the master principle of modern science and literature. Everywhere he lauds the negative. Ignorance is always bliss, and sleep, that "knits up the ravelled sleeve of care," the most desirable blessing enjoyed by mortals. He scorns compromise with evil, and feels it is "nobler in the mind to suffer" than to reconcile itself to error and pain through cowardice, illusion, or stupidity. He writes to solace himself by expression; and he writes in a satirical and humorous vein, because it is less annoying to others, and more manly in itself, than wailing or despair. Thus, Leopardi's misanthropy differs from that of Rousseau and Byron in being more intellectual; it springs not so much from exasperated feeling as from the habitual contemplation of painful truth. Philosophy is rather an available medicament to him than an ultimate good.

Patriotism, learning, despair, and love, are expressed in Leopardi's verse with emphatic beauty. There is an antique grandeur, a solemn wail, in his allusions to his country, which stirs, and, at the same time, melts the heart. This sad yet noble melody is quite untranslatable; and we must content ourselves with an earnest reference to some of these eloquent and finished lyrical strains. How grand, simple, and pathetic, is the opening of the first, *Al' Italia!*

"O patria mia, vedo le mura e gli archi
E le colonne e i simulacri e l'erme
Torri degli avi nostri,
Ma la gloria non vedo,
Non vedo il lauro e il ferro ond'éran carchi
I nostri padri antichi. Or fatta inerme
Nuda la fronte e nudo il petto mostri.
Oimè quante ferite,
Che lividor, che sangue! oh qual ti veggio,
Formosisiima donna! Io chiedo al cielo
E al mondo: dite, dite,
Chi la ridusse a tale? E questo é peggio,
Che di catene ha carche ambe le braccia,
Sì che sparte le chiome e senza velo
Siede in terra negletta e sconsalata,
Nascondendo la faccia
Tra le ginocchia, e piange."

In the same spirit are the lines on the *Monument to Dante*, to whom he says:

"Beato te che il fato
A viver non danno fra tanto orrore;
Che non vedesti in braccio
L'itala moglie a barbaro soldato.
* * * * *

> Non si conviene a sì corrotta usanza
> Questa d 'animi eccelsi altrice a scola:
> Se di codardi é stanza,
> Meglio l'è rimaner vedova e sola."

The poem to Angelo Mai, on his discovery of the Republic of Cicero, is of kindred tone — the scholar's triumph blending with the patriot's grief. An identical vein of feeling, also, we recognize, under another form, in the poem written for his sister's nuptials. Bitterly he depicts the fate of woman in a country where

> "Virtù viva sprezziam, lodiamo estinta;"

and declares —

> "O miseri o codardi
> Figluioli avrai. Miseri eleggi. Immenso
> Tra fortuna e valor dissidio pose
> Il corrotto costume. Ahi troppo tardi,
> E nella sera dell 'umane cose,
> Acquista oggi chi nasce il moto e il senso."

Bruto Minore is vigorous in conception, and exquisitely modulated. In the hymn to the patriarchs, *La Primavera*, *Il Sabato del Vilaggio*, *Alla Luna*, *Il Passaro Solitaria*, *Il Canto notturno d' un Pastore errante in Asia*, and other poems, Leopardi not only gives true descriptive hints, with tact and fidelity, but reproduces the sentiment of the hour, or the scene he celebrates, breathing into his verse the latent music they awaken in the depths of thought and sensibility; the rhythm, the words, the imagery, all combine to produce this result, in a way analogous to that by which great composers harmonize sound, or the masters of landscape blend colors, giving birth to the magical effect which, under the name of tone, constitutes the vital principles of such emanations of genius.

But not only in exalted patriotic sentiment, and graphic portraiture, nor even in artistic skill, resides all the individuality of Leopardi as a poet. His tenderness is as sincere as it is manly. There is an indescribable sadness native to his soul, quite removed from acrid gloom, or weak sensibility. We have already traced it in his opinions and in his life; but its most affecting and impressive expression is revealed in his poetry.

Il Primo Amore, La Sera del Dì di Festa, Il Risorgimento, and other effusions, in a similar vein, are instinct with this deep yet attractive melancholy, the offspring of profound thought and emotion. "*Uscir di pena*," he sadly declares, "*é diletto fra noi ; non brillin gli ochi se non di pianto ; due cose belle ha il mondo : amore e morto.*" In that most characteristic poem, *Amore e Morte*, he speaks of the maiden who *la gentilezza del morir comprende :*

"Quando novellamente
Nasce nel cor profondo
Un amoroso affetto,
Languido e stanco insiem con esso in petto
Un desiderio di morir si sente :
Come, non so : ma tale
D' amor vero e possente é il primo effetto ;
Forse gli occhi spaura
Allor questo deserto : a se la terra
Forse il mortale inabitabil fatta
Vede omai senza quella
Nova, sola, infinita
Felicità che il suo pensier figura ;
Ma per cagion di lui grave procella
Presentendo il suo cor, brama quiete,
Brama raccorsi in porto
Dinanzi al fier disio,
Che già, rugghiando, intorno, intorno oscura."

THE WRITER FOR THE PEOPLE.

DANIEL DE FOE.

FEW of the crowd that throng the old avenues of Cripplegate, at the present day, revert to the prophet and thinker born and bred there, whose romance has been the household story of two great nations, and has been domesticated, as a model narrative, in every country of Europe for more than a century. Yet there is no name which should be more gratefully honored by a London citizen than that of Daniel De Foe. His genius and efficiency vindicate the claims even of "a nation of shopkeepers," and turn that satire into eulogy. His book has survived the more finished writings of the courtly authors who ridiculed him. In literature and politics he was essentially a representative man; in life he stood in the front rank of the people, and their universal recognition has long since crowned his memory with enduring fame.

In the great national problem worked out and permanently solved by the course of events and the war of opinion, between the birth of Puritanism in England and the realization of constitutional liberty under William of Orange, many illustrious names appear identified with the progress of civil and religious freedom. In the field, the council, the church, the courts, in society and in literature, these noble advocates taught, struggled, endured, and often died, in behalf of truths and privileges sacred to humanity. Among those who promoted the great end in the noblest way, — that is, by appeals to reason, and by assiduous endeavors to enlighten the masses, — no one deserves higher credit than Daniel

De Foe. And yet, by one of those caprices of fame, which so often astonish us in the history of gifted men, this voluminous writer and stanch advocate of human freedom and a progressive civic life is chiefly, and, so far as the many are concerned, exclusively, known as the author of the most popular story in the English language. The fierce polemical works upon which the vigor of his years was expended, the strange vicissitudes, the public services, and the private virtues, of the man De Foe, have been lost sight of in the renown of the author of Robinson Crusoe. Indeed, that familiar book, in the popular imagination, is rather esteemed as a lucky hit of inventive genius, than as the flowering of a mind rendered earnest and fruitful through a life of anxious mental toil and relentless persecution. To one thoroughly acquainted with De Foe's career, and aware of his fortunes and achievements, the remarkable fiction which embalms his memory has a new and pathetic significance. It was his first attempt to enlist his extraordinary powers in a work of pure literary art. To write it, he stood aloof from the party strife in which, for thirty years, his thoughts had been engaged. Like a brave soldier who had returned home from a long but successful campaign, with victory achieved, yet no spoils acquired, he seems to have laid aside the armor of political and religious warfare, cheered only by a sense of duty bravely performed, and then, in the autumn of life, the lull of the storm, the pensive twilight of honest age, yielded himself to a work prompted by his own idiosyncrasies, unmarred by faction, and thoroughly adapted to the popular heart. The intrinsic charm of the narrative, therefore, is infinitely expanded when thus viewed with reference to De Foe's circumstances and aims.

Could the life of this extraordinary man be represented in a dramatic form, we should behold him in the utmost extremes of social position, each explicable by his course as an author. He might be seen the familiar and admired *habitué* of a Puritan coffee-house, ardently discussing the latest news from the seat of war, or the local question of the hour; alternating between his hosier's shop in Cornhill and the Dissenters' chapel at Surrey; in arms for the Duke of Monmouth; one of the handsomely-mounted escort of volunteers who attended William and Mary from Whitehall to the Mansion House; a bankrupt refugee, talking with Selkirk at the Red Lion Tavern in Bristol; the confidential visitor ensconced in the cabinet of William of Orange; the occupant of a cell in Newgate; an honored guest at Edinburgh, promoting the Union; a secret ambassador to the Continent; the delegate of the people, handing to Harley a mammoth petition; the cynosure of a hundred sympathetic and respectful eyes as he stands in the pillory; in comfortable retirement at Newington; and at last a victim of filial ingratitude, his health wasted in noble intellectual toil, dying at the age of seventy. Such are a few of the strong contrasts which the mere external drama of De Foe's life presents.

To appreciate his course we must vividly recall the events of his time and the spirit of his age. As if ordained by Providence for a legitimate representative of the English mind, he derived his descent from the better class of yeomen; his birthplace was the heart of London; and his home was chiefly there at a period when its citizenship was a high distinction and privilege, when municipal glory had not faded before the splendor of fashion, now dominant in a region which, in De Foe's time, was suburban, and when locomotive facilities had not almost identified town and country. One of the people by birth and association, he became more intimately related to them through his public spirit, his political ideas, and his religious sentiments. These were all essentially democratic. The wants of the ignorant many, the thirst for social reform, the popular basis of the constitution, and the right of free judgment and action in religion, appear to have been original instincts rather than mere opinions in the mind of De Foe. They were confirmed by the family discipline, the non-conformist rites, the simple habits, and the manly self-reliance, incident to the household of a dissenting London trader of that day.

Although so obviously endowed for the vocation of an author, De Foe began life as a tradesman. Cut off by his religious associations from any share in a university education, he studied the higher academic branches with a preceptor of his own faith, of acknowledged scholarship; and at first designed to adopt the clerical profession. In his commercial speculations he was unsuccessful, as might have been anticipated; for his mind was too speculative to engage prosperously in business, for which, however, he was not deficient in talent, as his appointment as secretary, first to a glass and then to a brick manufacturing company, sufficiently proves. His friends also arranged a mercantile enterprise for him at Cadiz; but he yielded to a strong innate conviction that his appropriate sphere was England, and his first duty that of a writer. Trade, however, while it proved unfortunate as a pursuit, elicited character, and yielded valuable lessons. He, with rare integrity, paid the balance of his debts, when subsequently enriched, although legally acquitted by a compromise; and his knowledge of the wants, usages, and condition, of the "English Tradesman," enabled him to write the useful and suggestive treatise which bears that title. It gave him also a fund of experience; and we trace in his books a familiarity with human nature and London life, that could in few other ways have been so authentically gained. While Swift was noting the banquets he attended for the diversion of Stella, Steele dodging bailiffs in his luxurious establishment, Addison, in elegant trim, paying his court to the Countess of Warwick, and Bolingbroke embodying his heartless philosophy in artificial rhetoric, De Foe was wrestling for truth in Cripplegate. A man of the people, a writer of plain, vigorous, unembellished English, there he stood, manfully claiming the right of private judgment; battling to the death against the prejudices which interfered with a liberal government; explaining, with intelligent emphasis, the popular basis of the constitution; initiating that philosophy of trade, of social economy, of charitable institutions, and of literature, then a bold and radical innovation, now, in its varied forms, recognized as the evidence of human progress, and the pledge of a glorious future. Taste, wit, and refined sensualism, were the dominant traits of the acknowledged men of genius in society around him; privation, slander, imprisonment, and ridicule, were the reward of his manly self-consecration. His contemporary authors are known to us through elaborate and loving memoirs; their portraits adorn noble galleries; scholars still emulate their works, and glorify them in reviews; while their monumental effigies are clustered in imposing beauty in the venerable Abbey. Our knowledge of

De Foe's appearance is chiefly derived from an advertisement describing him as a fugitive.* His birth and name have been subjects of dispute. Of his domestic correspondence we have only a letter describing the unfilial improvidence of his son.† It is impossible to identify all his works. He is mentioned by the writers of his day only in the bitter terms of party hatred; and his mortal remains are blended with the martyred dust of Bunhill Fields.

The political writings of De Foe emphatically define his career as an English citizen; and, although many of them have lost their chief interest from the temporary nature of the subjects discussed, yet they are all impressive landmarks to indicate the consistent, fearless, and rational spirit, the indomitable industry, and loyalty of purpose, which distinguished his life. With every

* "Whereas Daniel De Foe, alias De Fooe, is charged with writing a scandalous and seditious pamphlet, entitled 'The Shortest Way with the Dissenters;' he is a middle-sized, spare man, about forty years old, of a brown complexion, and dark brown-colored hair, but wears a wig; a hooked nose, a sharp chin, gray eyes, and a large mole near his mouth; was born in London, and for many years was a hose-factor, in Freeman's yard, in Cornhill, and now is owner of the brick and pantile works near Tilbury Fort, in Essex. Whoever shall discover the said Daniel De Foe to one of her majesty's principal secretaries of state, or any of her majesty's justices of the peace, so as he may be apprehended, shall have a reward of fifty pounds, which her majesty has ordered immediately to be paid on such discovery." — *London Gazette, Jan.* 10, 1702–3.

† "But it has been the injustice, unkindness, and, I must say, inhuman dealing of my own son, which has both ruined my family, and, in a word, has broken my heart; and, as I am at this time under a very heavy weight of illness, which I think will be a fever, I take this occasion to vent my grief in the breasts who I know will make a prudent use of it, and tell you, nothing but this has conquered or could conquer me. *Et tu, Brute!* I depended upon him, I trusted him, I gave up my two dear, unprovided children into his hands; but he has no compassion, and suffers them and their poor dying mother to beg their bread at his door, and to crave, as if it were an alms, what he is bound, under hand and seal, and by the most sacred promises, to supply them with — himself at the same time living in a profusion of plenty. It is too much for me. Excuse my infirmity; I can say no more; my heart is too full. I only ask one thing of you as a dying request. Stand by them when I am gone, and let them not be wronged while he is able to do them right. Stand by them as a brother; and if you have anything within you owing to my memory, who have bestowed on you the best gift I had to give, let them not be injured and trampled on by false pretences and unnatural reflections. I hope they will want no help but that of comfort and counsel; but that they will indeed want, being too easy to be managed by words and promises."—*Letter of De Foe to his son-in-law, Mr. Baker, the celebrated naturalist.*

successive phase of history, every important act of the government, or significant demonstration by the people, an essay, a satire, or an appeal, from his ready and earnest pen, gives token of vigilance and enthusiasm. His pamphlets, like alert guerilla parties, keep up a running and sometimes isolated, yet none the less effective fire, along the line of political combatants. Always ranged on the side of popular right and religious liberty, his pleas, by their simplicity and good sense, invariably won the attention of the masses, and irritated the tory faction. Usually published anonymously, and often under the disguise of irony or quaint allegory, they betrayed a cleverness which even the fashionable wits could not deny. Thus, by seasonable invective and keen satire, De Foe scattered the elements of great political truths among the heated minds of his fellow-countrymen, anticipated the progress of popular enlightenment, and furnished the ignorant and the oppressed with arguments that sanctioned their endeavors.

It was opposition to the plans of James in regard to the succession, and not affinity with the character of Monmouth, that enlisted him in the romantic and vain enterprise of the latter. To Queen Anne's natural goodness of heart and Harley's secret political bias he owed his enfranchisement. His ironical tirade against the Hanoverian cause was so utterly misunderstood, that, for a while, he suffered persecution as its enemy. But his relation to William of Orange was intimate and genuine. The character of that monarch was akin to his own. There was between them a sympathy of mind; courage, liberal views, and moral energy, were alike the characteristics of the author and the king. De Foe effectively advanced the measures of his royal patron, and was devoted to his cause and his memory.

If we examine critically his miscellaneous writings, and refer to the dates of important civil and social reforms, his direct agency in their achievement will impressively appear. With the foresight attained only by a lover of truth, he anticipated the great improvements of the last and the present century, and often gave the first hint of their necessity, or the primal argument for their adoption. The superior brilliancy of later writers has kept his precedence out of view. Yet there is scarcely a remarkable social or literary phenomenon, resulting from the progress of ideas, which we cannot trace directly or indirectly to De Foe. He was a pioneer in the great cause of human advancement, and his name should be identified with many of the popular topics and enterprises of our own day. The universal political theme of this moment is what is called "the Eastern Question."* The first pamphlet of De Foe, written before the age of manhood, was devoted to a kindred subject, in which he argued that it was "better that the Popish house of Austria should ruin the Protestants in Hungary, than that the infidel house of Ottoman should ruin both Protestants and Papists." The reality of spiritual communications is now a fertile text for tongue and press. De Foe's essay on "Apparitions" may not only be read with advantage by the credulous and the sceptical, but is a striking evidence of the identity of feeling on that subject then and now. "Between our ancestors' laying too much stress upon them," he says, "and the present age endeavoring wholly to explode and despise them, the world seems hardly ever to have come to a right understanding." And again: "Spirit is certainly something we do not fully understand in our present confined circumstances; and, as we do not fully understand the thing, so neither can we distinguish its operation. Yet, notwithstanding all this, it converses here, is with us and among us, corresponds, though unembodied, with our spirits, and this conversing is not only by an invisible, but to us an inconceivable way," etc. To these speculations he brought no ordinary learning and philosophy, and while he recognizes the spiritual element in life, he considers it with logic, with good sense, and in the light of truth. Constitutional freedom has been the favorite idea of English and American statesmen; but De Foe's treatise on the "Original Power of the Collective Body of the People of England" was one of the first and most daring popular expositions of a doctrine that lies at the foundation of all free governments. Political economy is generally considered a new science; De Foe's commercial writings, his tract entitled "Giving Alms no Charity," and the financial suggestions thrown out in his "Essay on Projects," anticipate many of the axioms of later philosophers in this department. It is to the papers in the Spectator that the first appreciation of Milton's

* Written in 1854.

poetry is ascribed; yet seven years before Addison designated the sublimities of Paradise Lost, De Foe set forth its author's transcendent claims. The institution of marriage has been freely examined in our day; De Foe, in his bold reproach of its abuse and his eloquent exposition of its religious character, was in advance of his times. He was the first effectually to set forth the public duty of instituting asylums for the insane and the idiotic, of establishing commissioners of bankruptcy, and pensions for the indigent. Sydney Smith's humorous appeal is thought by many the earliest popular argument for a higher grade of female culture; but at a time when the chivalric element was all but extinguished, and women were treated either as toys, slaves, or idols, De Foe became an eloquent and able advocate for the education of women. "A woman of sense and manners," he wrote, "is the finest and most delicate part of God's creation; and it is the sordidest piece of folly and ingratitude to withhold from the sex the lustre which the advantage of education gives to the natural beauty of their minds." One of the most successful of modern *ruses* is the famous "Moon Hoax;" De Foe, in a political satire, developed lunar language, and narrated incidents of lunar adventure. He recommended the establishment of a society for "encouraging polite learning and improving the English language," prior to Swift's celebrated letter to Lord Oxford. The most interesting fact, however, of his influence as a thinker, at least to our American sympathies, is, that it was the perusal of De Foe that aroused the dormant sentiments and quickened the mental enterprise of Franklin. "I found, besides," he says in his Autobiography, "a work of De Foe's, entitled an 'Essay on Projects,' from which, perhaps, I derived impressions that have since influenced some of the principal events of my life." His zest for new truth, and his recognition of liberal principles, were thus confirmed and enlarged, in early youth, by the author of Robinson Crusoe. De Foe anticipated the colonial revolt and the triumph of freedom in America. He was the predecessor of Rousseau as a social reformer. He ably vindicated the right of authors to a permanent share in the income of their works. His geographical speculations were confirmed by the subsequent discoveries of Denham and Lander. He was the father of periodical literature; for his "Review," first planned in Newgate, was the harbinger of those popular miscellanies that delighted and improved the readers of Queen Anne's day. Nor is this the world's only obligation to him in literature. His unprecedented and instantly successful fiction originated the English novel, and the celebrated authors who have since enchanted us and made themselves renowned in this field, all trace back the spells they evoke to Daniel De Foe.

It is a singular coincidence, that the most classical poet and the most successful romancer of that period, in England, were the sons of butchers. Akenside, born ten years before De Foe's death, carried to his grave a memorial of the paternal vocation, in regard to which he was morbidly sensitive, in the form of a wound that caused him always to limp, received from one of his father's cleavers, which was accidentally dropped on the embryo poet's foot. Gifford made cruel use of the plebeian occupation of the elder Keats, in his attempt to mortify the sensitive author of Hyperion. De Foe, if we may judge by the spirit of his writings and the tenor of his life, cheerfully accepted the rank in which his lot was cast. He knew the true dignity of human nature, and understood that all genuine power and fame originate with, or must be sanctioned by, popular sentiment. It was an axiom of his to defy the critics, if he could but have the people with him. It may seem to involve no great heroism or perspicacity so to think and act; but we must remember that De Foe thus reasoned at a time when the London Gazette, with its meagre semi-weekly announcement of court news, constituted journalism; when Baxter's voice was hushed in prison, and when our brave author himself had barely escaped the fangs of Jeffreys, to endure the long torture of inveterate proscription.

With the virtues De Foe combined the prejudices of the nonconformists. He expresses an unreasonable contempt for May-poles and the theatre; but we must not forget that it was against the profligate levity ushered in by the Restoration, of which these and similar pastimes were emblems, rather than against amusement as such, that his indignation was levelled. De Foe and his colleagues deeply felt their responsibleness to the noble cause in which they were engaged. A battle was to be waged, a great national reform wrought; politics and religion, freedom and civil progress, were to them, in a great measure, identical; the social exigencies of the times impressed them too keenly to admit of convivial enjoyment. In a word, they were in earnest, and such is not the mood in which mere pleasure-seeking can be tolerated. Yet De Foe wonderfully preserved his candor and self-respect in the heat of controversy; and boasts with reason, that, while engaged in satirizing his opponents, he never used their personal misfortunes or infirmities to make "the galled jade wince." He early acquired the lessons of self-discipline, and bore himself with prowess, but in a calm and self-reliant manner. "In the school of affliction," he says, "I have learned more than at the academy, and more divinity than from the pulpit."

De Foe's career as an author was quite as remarkable for its versatility as for its extent. Besides the hundred and thirty-three political works identified as his, during the reigns of Anne and George, we have numerous speculative and narrative writings, and, finally, his series of fictions. He turned his pen to any subject, and cast his thoughts into any form which circumstances made desirable, with an extraordinary facility. Now we find him recording the casualties of a remarkable storm, now hard at work upon a "Seasonable Caution;" one day engaged on a versified eulogy of Scotland, — while on a visit there, — published under the title of "Caledonia," and another, deep in a "History of the Union," which he had been an effective agent in promoting. To-day it is a commercial essay; to-morrow, a book of travels. He prepares an impressive story of Mrs. Veal's ghost, which, attached to a heavy book on "Death," gives it life at once. He is no sooner out of the pillory, than he indites a philosophical hymn to the infamous machine. Shut up in Newgate, he starts a journal on a new and better plan than any before known. He welcomes Marlborough home with stanzas to Victory; and, when the war is over, chants the glory of Peace. Opposed to the existing school of speculation, he groups in ironical verse the poets, sceptics, and metaphysicians, of his day. He translates Du Fresnoy's Art of Painting; and tilts, in pungent rhymes, against the divine right of kings. As might have been anticipated, such rapid and varied composition admitted of no finish or revision. De Foe's cleverness and industry are more remarkable than his taste and care. His object usually was to produce an immediate impression on the world of opinion, or to supply his own wants by his pen-craft. Hence the temporary interest and merely incidental value of many of his writings. No small part of them, however, are not only of practical use, but of historical importance. De Foe has been declared by a good critic Locke's equal in reasoning. Of his "Essay on Projects" it has been said, that it is more rich in thought than any book since Bacon, and that it embodies the French Revolution without its follies. His great mental quality was vigorous sense. He was deficient in the love of the beautiful, and seems to have had an inadequate perception of art. He was not poetical by nature. His metrical essays owe their effect wholly to the epigrammatic hits and the sound argument they contain; the melodious versification of his contemporaries never taught him rhythm; not only are his verses destitute of refined sentiment, but they are singularly harsh and unmusical. He belongs to the same school of rhymers with Butler, Swift, and Crabbe; not imagination and grace, but graphic touches and wit, redeem his lines. As a literary artist his merit lies almost exclusively in prose narrative. Here he exhibited all the individuality of his genius, and achieved his permanent renown. The secret of his effective style of narration lies in simple force of diction, homely and expressive words, and an elaborate and precise statement of details. Together, these traits form a whole that affects the mind with all the distinctness of reality. Dr. Johnson thought that the "Adventures of Captain Singleton," De Foe's second work of fiction, was a record of facts; Lord Chatham quoted his "Memoirs of a Cavalier" as a genuine piece of biography; and Dr. Wood, the account of the Plague in London as the result of personal observation; while the credence that the mass of readers bestowed upon the story of Mrs. Veal's apparition is evident from the large sale it at once secured for Drelincourt's unpopular essay.

It is curious to trace the progress of the modern novel from Ionia to Italy, and thence to England; its rudimental and imaginative style in the East, its pedantic and sentimental development in Arcadian romances, and its simple, direct, matter-of-fact, and human interest as exhibited by De Foe, destined to be rendered more and more complex and artistic with the increased refinements and divisions of society, as painted by Bulwer and Thackeray. The element of probability, the artistic use of natural incidents in their legitimate order and specialties, so admirably illustrated by De Foe, is, however, as indispensable to the successful novelist to-day as when Robinson Crusoe appeared. We can easily perceive its recognition by the masters of romance. It is obvious in the minute local and personal descriptions of Scott, in Godwin's details of consciousness, and even in the grotesque pictures of still-life by Dickens. Verisimilitude is the great merit of De Foe as a novelist. The seeming authenticity of his stories is also greatly enhanced by the autobiographic form in which they are cast. He is a model narrator; passages of his fictions read like the testimony elicited in a court of justice; and incidental and apparently trifling circumstances are so naturally interwoven, as to give a singular air of truth to the whole. Now the plots of the novelist are more intricate, his characters more finely shaded and elaborately wrought, and his style of composition raised to a much higher standard. Yet the profound actuality and stern truth of De Foe give him a tenacious hold on the common sympathy; he excites deeper faith, and inherits household fame. He had been a close student of human life and human nature, in their most inartificial and significant phases. Born of a sect that disdained the trappings and acknowledged the spiritual meaning of existence, he was wedded to reality from his cradle. His conflict with fortune was hand to hand and unintermitted. He used to seek communion with soldiers, sailors, and other adventurous offspring of his own transition era. He was well acquainted with Dampier, the navigator; he saw much of foreign countries, took counsel with kings, studied economics in the experience of trade, authorship, and office, witnessed the most remarkable political vicissitudes, explored the mysteries of crime while an inmate of the Old Bailey, knew intimately the care and the solace of domestic ties, the viper sting of filial ingratitude, and the inexpressible worth of woman; he was ever a worker, and no butterfly, — always observing, reflecting, noting facts, musing on the past, scanning the future, and keenly watching the present. Thus disciplined and enriched, De Foe's mind was tempered in the furnace of affliction, and hence it is that he writes of men and things with such truthful power and practical sense. As a child, he listened to incidents of the civil war from survivors; as a youth, he fraternized with the returned soldiers of Marlborough, and the maritime heroes who explored unknown seas. The coffee-house, the docks, the shop, the palace, the jail, the fireside, the strife of party, and the sanctions of a proscribed religion, inspired and moulded his Anglo-Saxon intelligence, his lion spirit, and humane sentiments, and enabled him to invent from experience with unequalled tact and an enduring charm.

There is no contrast in English literature more entire than that between De Foe and the fashionable writers of his day. They indeed ushered in a more graceful epoch, and are identified with the amenities of literary and social life; but their humor, tact, skill, and beauty, and even the reform in manners and in taste they achieved, languish before the robust and practical truths advanced by De Foe. His writings, though comparatively neglected at present, from the actual triumph of the ideas they embody, were distinguished then by a quality in which his more brilliant contemporaries were sadly deficient, — earnestness; his object was moral, theirs artistic; he sought to modify opinion and build up institutions, they to refine style and gratify taste; their sphere was sentiment, his action; they strove with art to refine, he with argument to invigorate and make self-reliant the elements of national life and individual character; he dealt conscientiously with principles, they daintily with forms.

When De Foe abandoned controversy for fiction, he had already achieved a long career of authorship, and had suffered enough to damp the energy of a less vigorous mind. But he entered this new and promising field with characteristic spirit and industry. Encouraged by the extraordinary success of "Robinson Crusoe," he published a series of tales similar in design, though much inferior in novelty and effect. It is to be regretted that the majority of these narratives are devoted to low life, and as De Foe's *forte* was adventure, and not characterization, the coarseness of some of his graphic histories is only redeemed by the matter-of-fact, self-possessed, and authentic style with which he "forges the handwriting of Nature." No writer ever drew more clearly the lines that divide vice from virtue. There is nothing insidious in his pictures of human frailty. "Roxana," "Colonel Jack," "Moll Flanders," and other narratives of unprincipled vagabondage, while they repel the discriminating reader of the present day, are yet historically worthy of attention, as being the genuine precursors of the modern English novel. To ignore the early specimens of any class of writings, would be as unjust to literature historically regarded, as for the painter, in his admiration of Leonardo da Vinci and Raphael, to forget Giotto and Perugino. "Captain Carleton" and "Memoirs of a Cavalier" are the germs of the historical romance of our day; even as the "Essay on Projects" may be regarded as the rough chart whence modern philanthropy and social science have derived much of their original impulse. Yet De Foe, with the usual perversity of authors, seems to have valued his metrical treatise, called *Jure Divino*, now quite neglected, above his influential pamphlets and his unrivalled story. He wrote in the spirit of Franklin and Cobbett; his very lack of ideality, his self-reliance, and his practical mind, fitted him to become an exemplar in that literature which deals with common things in the universal heart. When Kean returned from his great experiment at Drury Lane, his anxious wife inquired what Lord Essex thought of the performance. The answer of the triumphant actor was, "The pit rose to me." It was this popular recognition that De Foe sought and won; and of this the permanent fame of Robinson Crusoe is the best illustration.

No charge of plagiarism was ever more irrational than that which his enemies strove to affix to the author of this world-wide favorite. That the narrative was founded on reality appears from the well-known fact that Selkirk's Adventures were published in 1712, seven years before Robinson Crusoe. This work, and the paper by Steele on the subject, when compared with the story of De Foe, will be found to bear a relation to it as inadequate to explain the conception, as one of the Italian tales, upon the dramatized version of which Shakspeare founded his immortal plays, to those priceless dramas. Selkirk was cast on a desert island, kindled a fire by rubbing bits of wood together, diverted himself by dancing with the goats he tamed, made a bed of their skins, built two huts, wrought a needle out of a nail and a knife-blade from a piece of iron hoop, fell from a precipice, and learned to run swiftly and to hunt animals. Such were the material hints thus furnished. In regard to the metaphysical, Steele remarks of Selkirk, that "it was a matter of great curiosity to hear him give an account of the different revolutions of his own mind in that long solitude." With our knowledge of De Foe's antecedents, of his narrative powers, and his graphic, plain, and lucid diction, it is easy to imagine how such meagre suggestions would become expanded under his pen into an elaborate, detailed, and consistent story, alive with the truths of nature and consciousness. His habit of composition, his facility in the use of the vernacular tongue, his long political warfare, which deepened thought and quickened perception, his social isolation, and his very deficiency in scholarship and ideality, were but so many preparatives. The alternation of the seasons, the notches on the calendar-post, the visions of fever, the explorations, the domestic economy of bower and cave, inventions suggested by necessity, periods of religious self-communion, and keeping a journal of reflections, are the facts which, given out in Flemish detail, and in a style of familiar and homely directness, make up Robinson Crusoe's twenty-eight years of solitude. It has been remarked that the only essentially poetical scene is the discovery of the footprint. The original of Friday was, according to D'Israeli, a Mosquito Indian described by Dampier. What a striking proof of the universal charm of truth to nature is indicated by the popularity of such a work! Minds as diverse and as highly endowed as those of Rousseau, Dr. Johnson, Lamb, Scott, and our own Webster, acknowledged for it a life-long partiality. Cervantes and Bunyan are De Foe's only peers in the common heart. He has been justly called the Murillo of the novelists. Boccaccio's warm and musical style is not more national than De Foe's stern outline and colloquial plainness. His poetry was that of the Bible, which Hazlitt well describes as that of solitude. All of grandeur that he develops is that of simplicity and self-reliance; and, paradoxical as it seems, the great charm of his fiction is its truth. His convictions were grave, his observation minute, and his experience of life singularly painful, but conscience and intelligence were profoundly active; and to these causes we can easily trace both the individuality and the attraction of his genius.

Robinson Crusoe is a thoroughly English romance. It has none of the southern glow of the Italian *novelle.* Sentiment is in abeyance to sense in its hero. The interest is derived chiefly from external adventure, and not from impassioned scenes; and the amusing and melodramatic elements, so conspicuous in French stories, are entirely ignored. It has the severity, the strong individuality, of the Anglo-Saxon mind. The chapter descriptive of domestic life in the household of a pious citizen of the middle class, is a most characteristic introduction; the passion for sea-life is a national trait; the religious feeling that struggles in the wanderer's breast, at the outset, with his own perverse desires, is also, both in its form and expression, singularly true to the character of the English dissenters. The inventive talent which Robinson exhibits is a source of peculiar interest to a thrifty and commercial race; his self-dependent, methodical, and industrious spirit was but a type of his nation; his recognition of conscience and providence, the absence of imagination, and the multiplicity of facts, are phases of the story in strict accordance with the English mind. The very problem of the book — that of a human being thrown entirely upon his own resources — is one remarkably adapted to the genius of an Englishman, and it is worked out with equal significance. Solitude has been made the basis of novels and memoirs in many notable instances; but how diverse the treatment from that of De Foe! The biography of Trenck, the "Prisons" of Pellico, and the "Picciola" of De Saintine, borrow their moral interest from the isolation of their heroes; but it is affection and fancy that lend a charm to such narratives. Poets, the most eloquent of modern times, have sung the praises of solitude; Byron, Foscolo, and Chateaubriand, have set it forth as the sphere of imaginative pleasure; Zimmerman has argued its claims; St. Pierre and Humboldt have indicated how much it enhances the enjoyment of nature. But in these and similar instances, the idiosyncrasy of the writers, and not human nature in general, is alive to the experiment. De Foe gives a practical solution to the idea. He describes the physical resources available to a patient and active hermit. He brings man into direct contact with Nature, and shows how he, by his single arm, thought, and will, can subdue her to his use. He places a human soul alone with God and the universe, and records its solitary struggles, its remorse, its yearning for companionship, its thirst for truth, and its resignation to its Creator. Robinson is no poet, mystic, or man of science, but an Englishman of average mind and ordinary education; and on his desert island he never loses his nationality. Fertile in expedients, prone to domesticity, fond of a long ramble, mindful of the Sabbath, provident, sustained by his Bible and his gun, a philosopher by nature, a utilitarian by instinct, accustomed to introspection, serious in his views, — against the vast blank of solitude, his figure clad in goat-skins stands in bold relief, — the moral ideal and exemplar of his nation and class.

Writings that thus survive a miscellaneous group will be found to contain a vital element of the author's nature or experience. They triumph over the oblivious influence of change and time, because created "in the lusty stealth of nature;" and are more vigorous by virtue of this spontaneous origin. De Foe's life was a moral solitude. If he knew not the discipline of an uninhabited island, he was familiar with that deeper isolation which the tyranny of opinion creates. He was separated from his kind, not indeed by leagues of ocean, but by the equally inexorable sea of faction. Prejudice, in an uncharitable age, divided him as effectually from society as a barrier of nature. Nor in his case did the sympathy of those for whom he thought and suffered relieve the grim features of solitude. He was too independent, and too much in advance of his time, not to be essentially apart from those who were ostensibly near and around him. He was driven into the intrenchments of consciousness. Like all bold and individual thinkers, he was often alone. From his earliest years his lot was cast and his choice made with a despised minority; and not until his head was bleached did the party and the class with which he acted hold the balance of power. As Bunyan was the spiritual prophet of the people, De Foe was their practical expositor. He espoused their cause before philanthropic organizations and public opinion had won respect for it. Oberlin had then regenerated no poor village; Penny Magazines were undreamed of; Burns had not set to undying music the cottager's life; the vulgar were divided by an immense gulf from the educated. Heroic then was it to brood over the dark problems of civilization. Literature was the privilege and the ornament of the few. Pope translated the Iliad, and celebrated the graces of Belinda; Swift did a courtier's taskwork; Addison, with scholarly zest, described his Italian journey; but De Foe pleaded for the rights of Dissenters, expounded the principles of trade, and wrote manuals for the religious, political, and domestic guidance of the masses. He was an intellectual pioneer, the herald of utility in letters, the advocate of practical truth. Instead of social distinction and the pleasures of taste, he aimed at reform. Ignored by the elegant, despised by the gay, persecuted by those in authority, he sternly rebuked corruption, boldly announced principles, and incessantly advocated humanity.

The brutal injustice of party spirit in England is signally illustrated in the life of her most characteristic author. The ferocity of her baronial era seems transferred to her literary and political annals. The same inhuman and relentless cruelty, insensate prejudice, and dogmatic will, reign in the world of opinion, as in the scenes of the ring, the duel, the criminal law, the domestic tyranny, and other barbarisms that deform her social history. Genius enjoys no immunity from this instinctive exercise of arbitrary power. The robbers of Italy spared Ariosto when they discovered that their captive was the author of the Orlando; the French mob that besieged the Tuileries and decapitated the king, protected from mutilation the beautiful statues that adorned the palace-garden; but no sentiment checks the rabid pen or melts the bigoted judge that sought, in De Foe's age and country, to awe or vanquish obnoxious writers. The terms in which they are assailed are those of execration or contempt; all sense of justice, honor, truth, and humanity, is repudiated; and the victim is coolly neglected, or heartlessly crushed, without an emotion of pity or a scruple of remorse. Even the comparatively liberal criticism of a later day is tinctured with this savage arrogance. The impertinent sarcasm with which the fashionable reviews treated Keats and Wordsworth, the faint praise with which Reynolds kept the merits of Gainsborough in the shade, the fanatical calumnies heaped upon Shelley, the coarse ridicule that drove Byron into satire, and the imprisonment of Hunt and Montgomery, attest an identical tyranny of opinion. Happily De Foe vindicated and endeared his own memory by the legacy he bequeathed in his unrivalled fiction. But it serves not only to make him remembered with gratitude; it is a nucleus for the indignation and sympathy of subsequent generations. Think of that inventive mind, that heart overflowing with manly emotion, that reason ever exercised for the honor of his country and the advancement of his race, tortured, darkened, and baffled, throughout a long and heroic life, by the falsehood, the scorn, and the cruelty, of mankind. Swift denied him learning; Oldmixon declared that his vocation was espionage; Prior pronounced his pen venal; Pope put him into the Dunciad; the courts of London doomed him to the pillory and a felon's cell; one writer charged him with prefixing a De to his name to escape the reputation of an English origin; another insinuated that he appropriated Selkirk's papers, and stole the materials of his famous story; one day he is advertised as an absconding debtor, the next published as the author of a vile tract that he never saw; now the stupidity of his own party misinterprets the satirical intent of a pamphlet, which is essentially promoting their cause; and now the Bill of Rights is openly violated by the ministers of justice, in order to wreak upon him their vindictive fiat. And all this time De Foe was the most thorough Englishman and writer of his day, a model of integrity, and as consistent, sincere, and brave, as he was gifted.

THE ORNITHOLOGIST.

JOHN JAMES AUDUBON.

A PECULIAR charm invests the lives of naturalists. The path of the military conqueror is blood-stained, that of the statesman involved and tortuous, while the pale legions of avarice usually beset the goal of maritime discovery, and associate the names of its heroes with scenes of anarchy and oppression; but the lover of Nature, who goes forth to examine her wonders, or copy her graces, is impelled by a noble enthusiasm, and works in the spirit both of love and wisdom. We cannot read of the brave wanderings of Michaux in search of his sylvan idols; of Hugh Miller, while at his mason's work, reverently deducing the grandest theories of creation from a fossil of the "old red sandstone;" or of Wilson, made an ornithologist, in feeling at least, by the sight of a red-headed woodpecker which greeted his eyes on landing in America, without a warm sympathy with the simple, pure, and earnest natures of men thus drawn into a life-devotion to Nature, by admiration of her laws, and sensibility to her beauty. If we thoughtfully follow the steps and analyze the characters of such men, we usually find them a most attractive combination of the child, the hero, and the poet, with, too often, a shade of the martyr. An inkling of the naturalist is, indeed, characteristic of poets. Cowper loved hares; Gray, gold-fish; Alfieri, horses; and Sir Walter Scott, dogs; but, when pursued as a special vocation, ornithology seems the most interesting department of natural history.

Audubon's career began and was prosecuted with an artistic rather than a scientific enthusiasm. His father appears to have been an intelligent lover of nature, and took pleasure in walking abroad with his son to observe her wonders. These colloquies and promenades made a lasting impression upon his plastic mind. It is evident that the habits and appearance of animated nature at once enlisted his sympathies; the accidental view of a book of illustrations in natural history excited the desire of imitation, and he began in a rude way to delineate the forms, colors, attitudes, and, as far as possible, the expression of the creatures he so admired. Chagrined, but never wholly discouraged, at the ill-success of his early attempts, he annually executed and destroyed hundreds of pictures and drawings, until long practice had given him the extraordinary skill which renders his mature efforts unequalled, both for authenticity and beauty. He artlessly confesses that, finding it impossible to possess or to live with the birds and animals which inspired his youthful love, he became ardently desirous to make perfect representations of them; and in this feeling we trace the germ of his subsequent greatness. Thus the origin of Audubon's world-renowned achievements was disinterested. His love of nature was not philosophic, like that of Wordsworth, nor scientific, like that of Humboldt, nor adventurous, like that of Boone; but special and artistic, — circumstances, rather than native idiosyncrasy, made him a naturalist; and his knowledge was by no means so extensive in this regard as that of others less known to fame. But few men have indulged so genuine a love of nature for her own sake, and found such enjoyment in delineating one of the most poetical and least explored departments of her boundless kingdom. To the last his special ability, as an artistic naturalist, was unapproached; and, while one of his sons drew the outline, and another painted the landscape, or the foreground, it was his faithful hand that, with a steel-pen, made the hairy coat of the deer, or, with a fine pencil, added the exquisite plumage to the sea-fowl's breast. For years he fondly explored woods, prairies, and the Atlantic shores, and drew and colored birds and beasts, without an idea of any benefit other than the immediate gratification thus derived. It was not until his interview with Lucien Bonaparte in 1824, and the latter's unexpected offer to purchase his drawings, that he conceived the project of giving the results of his explorations to the world. Although, in pursuance of this intention, he embarked soon after for Europe with characteristic promptitude and eager hopes, the loneliness of his position, and the want of means and influence, depressed him on landing; but the instant and cordial recognition he met with from the active literary and scientific men abroad soon confirmed his original resolution. Roscoe, Wilson, Jeffrey, Brewster, Herschel, and Humboldt, successfully advocated his claims, and cheered him with their personal friendship; and, under such favorable auspices, his first contributions to ornithology appeared in Edinburgh. Indeed, notwithstanding the privations and difficulties he encountered, an unusual amount of sympathy and encouragement fell to the lot of Audubon. Compared with other votaries of a special object purely tasteful and scientific in its nature, he had little reason to complain. Of the one hundred and seventy subscribers of a thousand dollars each to his great work, eighty were his own countrymen; and his declining years were passed in independence and comfort in the midst of an affectionate and thriving family, the participants of his taste. His elasticity of temperament, also, was not less a distinction than a blessing; it supported his wearisome and lonely wanderings both in search of birds in the forest and of encouragement among men; and, when the labor of years was destroyed, after a brief interval of mental anguish, it nerved him to renewed labor, so that in three years his portfolio was again filled.

Born the same year that independence was declared by the Americans, his father an admiral in the French navy, and his birthplace Louisiana, he was early sent to France for his education, where he received lessons in drawing from David, but pined the while for the free life and the wild forests of his own country. On his return, his father gave him a beautiful plantation on the banks of the Schuylkill, and he married. But neither agricultural interests nor domestic ties could quell the love of nature in his breast; and for months he wandered in search of objects for his pencil, unsustained by any human being except his wife, who seems to have realized from the first the tendency and promise of his mind. At length, in order to enjoy the opportunities he craved, and at the same time have the society of his family, Audubon determined to emigrate, and selected the village of Henderson, in Kentucky, for his new home. In the autumn of 1810 he floated down the Ohio, in an open skiff, with his wife, child, and two negroes, his mattress, viands, and rifle, happy in the prospect of nearer and more undisturbed intercourse with nature, and intensely enjoying the pomp of the autumnal woods, the haze of the Indian summer, and the wildness and solitude around him. The locality chosen proved adequate to his aims; day after day, with his dog, gun, and box of pencils and colors, he made excursions, now shooting down a fresh subject, now delineating its hues and form; one moment peering into a nest, and at another scaling a cliff, for hours watching the conduct of a pair of birds, as, unconscious that their doings were to be set in a note-book, they constructed a graceful nest, fed their young, or trilled a spontaneous melody. Over streams, through tangled brushwood, amid swamps, and in stony ravines, beneath tempest, sunshine, and starlight, the indefatigable wanderer thus lived; the wild beast, the treacherous Indian, the gentle moon, and the lowly wild-flower, sole witnesses of his curious labors.

Audubon returned from Europe to prosecute his ornithological researches with fresh zest and assiduity; and his first expedition was to the coast of Florida, where he made rich additions to his portfolio among the sea-fowl of that region. He afterwards successfully explored Maine, the British Provinces, and the ice-clad and desolate shores of Labrador. The most remarkable and happiest era of his life was, doubtless, that employed in collecting the materials, executing the pictures, and obtaining the subscribers to his "Birds of America." His wanderings previously have the interest of adventure, and the charm derived from the indulgence of a passionate love of nature; and his subsequent excursions, and artistic labors, in behalf of the work on the "Quadrupeds of America," begun in 1842, afford pleasing evidence of his enduring taste and noble perseverance. But the period included by his ornithological enterprise is more characteristic and satisfactory. He had a great end in view, and the wildest forest and most unfrequented shores, the highest and most cultivated sphere of society, and the most patient and delicate limning, were the means of its realization; and it is when contemplating him in this threefold relation that we learn to appreciate the mingled hardihood, enthusiasm, firmness, and dignity, so remarkably united in his character. In the woods, a genial companion, a single-hearted, kind, and generous friend, as well as a childlike enthusiast and manly sportsman; he stood before the council of an institution with his first delineation,— the bald-headed eagle,— or opened his portfolio to the inspection of an English nobleman in his lordly castle, with quiet self-possession, an independent air, and without exhibiting the least solicitude either for patronage or approbation. Arriving at a frontier village, after a tramp of months in the wilderness, his long beard, tattered leather dress, and keen eye, made him an object of idle wonder or impertinent gossip; but none imagined that this grotesque hunter-artist enjoyed the honors of all the learned societies of Europe. His exultation at the discovery of a new species, and his satisfaction at the correct finish and elegant verisimilitude of a specimen, amply recompensed him for days of exposure or ill success. On his journey from the South, he kept pace with the migration of the birds; and he proclaimed the Washington sea-eagle to his country and the scientific world with the pride and delight of a conqueror.

His passion for rambling caused Audubon to fail in several business enterprises he undertook; and at one period he applied to Sully for instruction in portrait-painting, but soon abandoned the idea. So faulty did Dawson, the engraver originally employed by the Prince of Musignano to illustrate his ornithology, consider the early specimens of Audubon's skill as a draftsman, that he refused to execute them, and appeared to consider the pigments invented by the woodland artist as the most remarkable feature they presented. Although thus discouraged on every hand, we can readily believe his declaration, that he left America with profound regret, although his career abroad affords yet another striking evidence of that memorable and holy saying, "that a prophet is not without honor save in his own country." It is natural that a man who succeeded by virtue of toil and fortitude should repudiate the commonly received faith in mere genius; and we are not surprised that his settled view of the philosophy of life was patient self-reliance, and meditation on facts derived from personal observation, with unremitted habits of labor. To these resources he owed his own renown and achievements; and his high-arched brow, dark-gray eye, and vivacious temperament, marked him as fitted by nature to excel in action as well as thought — a destiny which his pursuits singularly realized. There was something bird-like in the very physiognomy of Audubon, in the shape and keenness of his eye, the aquiline form of the nose, and a certain piercing and vivid expression when animated. He was thoroughly himself only amid the freedom and exuberance of nature; the breath of the woods exhilarated and inspired him; he was more at ease under a canopy of boughs than beneath gilded cornices, and felt a necessity to be within sight either of the horizon or the sea. Indeed, so prevailing was this appetite for nature, if we may so call it, that from the moment the idea of his last-projected expedition was abandoned,— in accordance with the urgent remonstrances of his family, mindful of his advanced age,— he began to droop, and the force and concentration of his intellect visibly declined. Both his success and his misfortunes, therefore, proved the wisdom of Richter's advice, to steadfastly and confidently follow the permanent instincts of character, however they may seem opposed to immediate interest.

The style of Audubon reflects his character with unusual emphasis and truth. He was one of that class of men who united intellectual and physical activity in their natures so equally, that while their very temperament forbids them to be exclusively students, their intelligence demands a constant accession of new ideas. Professor Wilson and Baron Humboldt belong to the same species. No one can glance over Audubon's Biography of Birds without being struck with the unusual animation and reality of the style. He writes with an ease and enthusiasm that makes portions of his work quite as entertaining and far more suggestive than a felicitous novel. Instead of a formal nomenclature or pedantic description, he digresses continually from the technical details which are requisite to the scientific value of his treatise, to charming episodes of personal adventure, sketches of local scenery and habits, and curious anecdotes illustrative of natural history or human character. The titles of these incidental chapters adequately suggest their aim and interest, such as "Hospitality in the Woods," "Force of the Waters," "The Squatters of Labrador," "Wreckers of Florida," "A Maple Sugar Camp," "A Ball in Newfoundland," "Breaking Up of the Sea," "Pitting of Wolves," "Long Calm at Sea," "A Kentucky Barbecue," etc. We are thus genially admitted to the knowledge of much that is characteristic and interesting, by spirited and graceful narratives. His artist's eye and his sportsman's zest give liveliness and a picturesque grace to the best of these interludes; they relieve the monotony of mere description, and also impart an individuality to the entire work, by associating the positive information it conveys with the fortunes and feelings of the author. His habit of naming newly-discovered birds after his friends is another pleasing feature. Thus genially is our view of nature enlarged, the attractiveness of romance given to a department of natural history, and one part of the world made perfectly acquainted with the feathered tribes of another. We need not enlarge upon the amenities resulting from pursuits of this kind, and their encouragement by individuals of taste and wealth, — of the innocent and available gratification thus extensively yielded, or of the more liberal and pleasing views resulting therefrom. In a literary point of view, the style of Audubon, notwithstanding an almost unavoidable vein of egotism, in its clearness, colloquial facility, and infectious enthusiasm, proves how much more effectively intimacy with nature develops even the power of expression than conformity to rules; and vindicates completeness of life, animal and mental, as essential to true manhood even in literature.

This, in our view, is one of the most important lessons derived from such a career as that of Audubon philosophically considered. There is a cant of spiritualism, at the present day, which repudiates the vital relation of genius to material laws. In the view of this shallow philosophy, to trace intellectual results in any degree to physical causes is derogating from the essential beauty of mind. The class of persons who affect this extreme devotion to ethereal systems, aim to sever body and soul while mutually alive, contemn physiology in their analysis of character, and recognize only the abstract in mental phenomena. This mode of reasoning is founded not less in irreverence than error. The most truly beautiful and significant phases of intellect, fancy, moral sentiment, and all that is deemed spiritual in man, is born of its combination with the human. Indeed, the grand characteristic of life, considered in a metaphysical light, is that it is a condition which brings together and gives scope for the action and reäction of material influences on spiritual genius. The end is development, growth, and modification. As the rarest fruit owes its flavor and hues to qualities imbibed from earth and air, from rain and sunshine, so what is called the soul is the product of the thinking and sensitive principle in our nature, warmed, enriched, and quickened by the agency of an animal organism, — the channel of nature, — by sensation, physical development, appetites and sensations, as well as ideas.

An author differs from other men only by the gift and habit of expression. This faculty (to which, for the ordinary purpose of convenience and pleasure, speech is only requisite) through genial cultivation redoubles its force, meaning, and beauty, and is capable of affording a kind of permanent utterance to what is most dear and important to man. It is obvious, therefore, that the more thoroughly an author's nature embraces the traits peculiar to manhood, the more efficiently and satisfactorily will his vocation be fulfilled. Hence the universal recognition of Shakspeare's supremacy in authorship: it is because his range of expression included more of what is within and around life — more, in a word, of humanity — than any other single expositor. In general, authorship is partial, temporary, and its force lies in a special form. Writers devoted to abstract truth, like Kant and Jonathan Edwards, are not to be included in the proposition, as their appeal is not to the sympathies, but to the pure intelligence of the race. But the authors who really affect the mass, and represent vividly the spirit of their age, are not less eminent for genuine human qualities, for prevailing traits of temperament, appetite, and sensibility, than for superior reflective and imaginative gifts. It is, indeed, essential that they should possess the former in a high degree in order effectively to exhibit the latter. This is constantly illustrated in literature and art. With a fancy which scarcely approached the idealism of Shelley, Burns thrilled the heart of his kind by virtue of an organization that humanized his genius. Landor is equipped with the lore of antiquity, and all the graces of classical diction, to advocate his liberal opinions; yet, while his elegant volumes adorn the libraries of scholars and men of taste, Dickens, by virtue of what may be called a more genial instinct, pleads for the oppressed in a million hearts. Jenny Lind sings many cavatinas with more precision and artistic power than Grisi; but her voice, uncharged with the sensuous life, whose vibration is inevitably sympathetic, does not so seize upon the nerves or quicken the blood. The element of sensation, as related to sound, form, and ideas, is essential to popular literature. It is the peculiar characteristic of this department of art that it depends upon sympathy, which can only be awakened in large circles by addressing the whole nature, by winning the senses as well as the mind, stirring the heart not less than eliciting the judgment, and, in a word, making itself felt in that universal human consciousness which, to distinguish it alike from mere intellect or mere feeling, we call the soul.

The author who expects reception there must write not only with his intelligence, his imagination, and his will, but with his temperament and his sensitive organism; he must, in a degree, fuse perception and sensation, nervous energy and moral feeling, physical emotion and aërial fancy; and then, at some point, he will be sure to touch the sympathy of others; not the scholar only, but the peasant. Accordingly, we always find in the habits and idiosyncrasies of popular authors a clue to their success. There is an analogy between their constitution and their writing. The tone of the latter is born of the man, and forms his personal distinction as an author. Reasoning, rhetoric, and descriptive limning, considered as processes, do not differ according to the writer, — they only vary in a certain spirit, manner, or, more properly, tone; and when we analyze this, we shall find it given out by the individual character, by the particular union of moral and physical qualities that make up the identity of the author, and not originating in a pure abstract and spiritual emanation. Far from diminishing, this but enhances the interest of authorship; it renders it a great social fact, and a legitimate branch of human economy. It teaches us to regard authors as we regard men, by the light of character; and from their human to deduce their literary peculiarities instead of the reverse, which is the method of superficial criticism.

The popular basis of Audubon's renown, as well as the individuality of his taste as a naturalist, rests upon artistic merit. We have alluded to the instinctive desire he so early manifested not only to observe, but to possess the beautiful denizens of the forest and the meadow; and he candidly acknowledges that he was induced to take their portraits to console himself for not possessing the originals. Rude as were his first attempts to delineate birds, few portrait-painters work in a more disinterested spirit. The motive was neither gain, nor hope of distinction, nor even scientific enthusiasm; for when Wilson called at his place of business, these primitive sketches were produced as the results of leisure, and the work of an unskilled amateur. It is evident, therefore, that a genuine love of the occupation, and a desire to have authentic memorials of these objects of his enthusiastic admiration, was the original cause of his labors with crayon and pigments; circumstances, an ardent temperament, and an earnest will, gradually developed this spontaneous tendency into a masterly artistic faculty; he sketched, painted, and destroyed, copied, retouched, and improved, until he succeeded in representing perfectly the forms, colors, attitudes, and expression, of the feathered tribe. The life-size of these delineations, their wonderful accuracy, the beauty of their hues, and the animation of their aspect, instantly secured for the backwoodsman-artist universal praise; but a minute inspection revealed yet higher claims; each plate, in fact, is an epitome of the natural history of the species depicted; male and female, young and adult, are grouped together, their plumage at different seasons, the vegetation they prefer, the soil, the food, sometimes the habits, and often the prey, of each bird, are thus indicated; and we take in at a glance not only the figure, but the peculiarities of the genus. This completeness of illustration, the result of vast study, united as it is with grace and brilliancy of execution, led the great naturalist of France to declare that America had achieved a work unequalled in Europe. No lover of nature, whether poet or *savan*, can contemplate these exquisite and vivid pictures in a foreign country, without delight and gratitude; for, without any exertion on his part, they introduce him to an intimate acquaintance with the varied and numerous birds which haunt the woods, sky, and waters, between Labrador and Florida, in hue, outline, and action, as vivid and true as those of nature; and their intrinsic value as memorials is enhanced by the consideration that a rapid disappearance of whole species of birds has been observed to attend the progress of civilization on this continent.

THE SENTIMENTALIST.

LAURENCE STERNE.

THERE is a peculiar incongruity in the associations which the name of Laurence Sterne excites. He represents several very distinct and inharmonious phases of character. There are the Prebendary of York, and the Vicar of Sutton in the Forest and of Stillington — most respectable designations; there is mirthful, plaintive, quaint Yorick, with his fancy and humor, his amorous trifling, his rollicking table-talk, and his vagrant sentimentalism; then the affectionate father of Lydia Sterne, a character worthy of esteem and love; again he appears as a fashionable preacher, a standard author, and a "loose fellow about town," whom it is somewhat disreputable to praise, and even about whose literary merits modesty is often instinctively silent; publishing alternately a volume of Tristram Shandy and a volume of sermons — the man of the world and the priest making a simultaneous appeal to the reading public. Yet, withal, those of us who, in some old sunny, rural home, early became familiar with that long array of little volumes, in obsolete type, and found them here and there exhaling the mellow breath of a gentle, pensive mood, embodied in most apt and graceful phraseology, must confess a kindliness for the author, however we may condemn his freedom of speech, and resent his abuse of the canons of taste and the integrity of feeling.

Inclined as English writers are to literary biography, and constant as has been the revival of memorials and critiques of their standard authors, since the establishment of the leading reviews, Sterne has proved an exception. That he was born at Clonmel, in Ireland, November 24, 1713, and died in London, March 18, 1768; that he preached, dined out, visited the continent, published books, left debts, one daughter, and the fame of rare gifts and doubtful conduct, is the sum of what we know of the man, except from his writings. Time has added little to the sparse details recorded in his own sketch; and the scattered and meagre notices of his career have not been gathered and arranged with the reverential and loving care bestowed on whatever throws light upon such intellectual benefactors as Milton and Goldsmith. The feeling which prompts such tributary labor has been chilled, in this instance, by a consciousness that Sterne so violated the proprieties of life and the harmonies of character, as to afford a subject too perverse for hearty eulogium, and too imperfect for entire sympathy. The parish register of Sutton contains data, in his handwriting, from which we learn such unimportant items, as that at one time he planted an orchard, and at another the parsonage was destroyed by fire. In a work entitled the *Memoires d'un Voyageur qui se repose*, by M. Dutens (a refugee Abbé, one of Sydney Smith's visitors during his first sojourn in London), that appeared in London in 1806, occurs the following anecdote, which affords a vivid idea of his social peculiarities:

"Nous étions au temps de l'anniversaire du Roi d'Angleterre. Milord Tavistock invita la peu d'Anglois qui étoient à Paris à dîner avec lui, pour le celébrér. Je fus de la partie, où je ne trouvai de ma connoissance que ceux avec que j'étois venu à Paris. Je fus assis entre Milord Berkeley et le fameux Sterne, auteur de Tristram Shandy, regardé comme la Rabelais de l'Angleterre. On fut fort gai pendant le dîner et l'on but à l'Anglaise et selon le jour. La conversation vint à tomber sur Turin, où plusieurs de la compagnie alloient; sur quoi M. Sterne m'addressant la parole, demande si j'y connoissois Monsieur Dutens; je lui dis qu'oui et même fort intimement. Tout la compagnie se prit à rire; et Sterne, qui ne me croyoit si prês de lui, s'imagina ce Monsieur D. devoit être un homme assez bizarre, puisque son nom seul faisoit rire ceux qui l'entendoient. 'N'est ce pas un homme singulier?' ajouta il tout de suite; 'Oui,' repris-je, 'un original.'"

Upon this hint, Sterne drew an imaginary, and by no means flattering, portrait of his neighbor, and related many amusing stories about him, unconscious, the while, that these inventions were heard by their good-natured subject. He did not discover the identity of his auditor with M. Dutens until the company separated, when he made ample apologies, which were graciously accepted. All wits have a mode of their own. Addison, we are told by Swift, would flatter the opinions of a man of extreme views on any subject, until he betrayed him into absurdity; Lamb had a way of startling literal people by humorous sallies; Hook was a genius in practical jokes; and Sterne, it appears, used to draw fancy portraits of real characters, to divert his boon companions. Had his accidental victim, in the instance related, been other than an urbane Frenchman, who could make allowance for a *spirituelle* invention, even though it somewhat compromised his own dignity, the "Rabelais d'Angleterre" might have been forced to protect himself from a duel under the very cloth whose immunities he so little deserved. A similar instance is recorded by Dr. Hill, who says that at a dinner-party the professional talk of a pedantic physician wearied the company and annoyed the host, when "good-humored Yorick fell into the cant and jargon of physic, as if he had been one of Radcliffe's travellers," and told such a ridiculous story of curing himself of an adhesion of the lungs by leaping fences, as restored the guests to mirthfulness.

The alleged insensibility of Sterne, the man, may be ascribed, in part, to his extreme frankness. He calls discretion "an understrapping virtue," and seems to have been singularly deficient in caution and reserve. He gave expression to the alternations of his mood and feelings with a reckless disregard to the effect of such inconsistency. At the University, we are told, he "amused himself by puzzling the tutors," and "left Cambridge with the character of an odd man, who had no harm in him, and had parts if he would use them." Thence he went to "the lap of the Church in a small village in Yorkshire," and, "as he advanced in literary fame, left his livings to the care of his curates," and preferred "luxurious living with the great." The following charitable epitaph well describes such a man:

> "Wit, humor, genius, hadst thou, all agree;
> One grain of wisdom had been worth the three."

His patient courtship shows that he was truly in love with his wife. Their marriage, in the face of inauspicious circumstances, proves that they were both in earnest; and his frank acknowledgment, a year after, that he was tired of his conjugal partner, argues no uncommon experience, but a rare and unjustifiable candor. His letters to Mrs. Draper, however wrong in the social code, and unprincipled in a married divine, were undoubtedly sincere. His first efficient stroke as a lay writer consisted of a satire to oust the monopolist of a situation which one of his friends desired, and so successful was it that the incumbent offered to resign if the publication was suppressed. His parental affection has never been questioned; no one can doubt that his heart was devoted to, and engrossed with, his daughter Lydia. Inconstancy is one thing, insincerity quite another. The critics of Sterne invariably confound the two; and, because he was so unreliable in his attachments, and not proof against a succession of objects, they endeavor to discredit his pathos as artificial. As well might we seek to invalidate Bacon's philosophy because it failed to elevate him above sycophancy, or Scott's romantic genius in view of his material ambition, or Byron's love of nature on account of his dissipation.

Science, of late years, has thrown new light on the apparent contradictions of human nature, by investigating the laws of temperament, and the relation of the nervous system to intellectual development. A whole category of phenomena has been recognized by acute observation directed to susceptible organizations; and whoever is thus prepared will find no difficulty in explaining the incongruities so obvious between Sterne the man and Sterne the author. His will and intelligence were continually modified by physical causes. He lacked hardihood, and was peculiarly alive to magnetic agencies. Hence his vagaries, his tender moods reäcting to selfish calculation, and the theory of life which he was so fond of elaborating from sensation and fancy. "Sweet pliability of man's spirit," he exclaims, "that can at once surrender itself to illusions which cheat expectation and sorrow of their weary moments!" "I can safely say, that, for myself, I was never able to conquer one single bad sensation in my heart so decisively, as by beating up, as fast as I could, for some kindly and gentle sensation to fight it upon its own ground." "A man who has not a sort of affection for the whole sex is incapable of ever loving a single one as he ought." "I know not how it is, but *I am never so perfectly conscious of a soul within me*, as when I am entangled in them." Again, in the sermon on the Pharisee, he says: "In benevolent natures the impulse to pity is so sudden, that, like instruments of music which obey the touch, the objects which are fitted to excite such impressions *work so instantaneously that you would think the will was scarce concerned.*" Now, if we admit such confessions to be what Sterne claims for them,— "loose touches of an honest heart,"—they explain, by the want of balance, the incompleteness of the man, his overplus of sensibility and deficiency of will and moral harmony, and show that it is quite possible for genuine feeling to coëxist with "infirmity of purpose," and emotional sympathy with an absence of disinterestedness. Hence, Thackeray's censure is indiscriminate, when he sums up the character of this author with the statement that he "had artistical sensibility," and "exercised the lucrative gift of weeping," and that he is represented entirely by "tears and fine feelings, and a white pocket handkerchief, a procession of mutes, and a hearse with a dead donkey inside." This is satire, not criticism. Somewhat more real must Sterne's writings have contained to have survived the fluctuations of taste, and proved more or less models for subsequent and popular authors. Affectation and indecency are so alien to Anglo-Saxon instincts in literature, that only a large admixture of wit or grace could have preserved writings thus meretricious.

This temperament, so undesirable for moral efficiency, was favorable to authorship. Its almost reckless impulse gave a certain sociability to pen-craft. It led, indeed, to the expression of much that offends refined taste and elevated sentiment, but, at the same time, what he wrote was all the more human for being unreserved. As a good table companion, while he entertains, often in the same proportion forfeits respect, so a writer of this species attracts, by virtue of an *abandon* which is full of peril as a trait of character, and yet induces a thousand felicities of invention and style. Allied to genius, it is a great element of success. Without it Byron would never have imparted the sensation of his own experience, which is the source of his intensity. So largely does it enter into the old English drama, that we are continually startled and thrilled by a boldness of language which, unchastened as it is, takes hold at once upon the emotional in our nature. One secret, therefore, of the charm whereby Sterne maintains so definite a rank in English literature, is the freedom of his tone, involving, with much that is gross, a frank challenge to our sympathies as human beings,— a companionable appeal, which the reader, with even an inkling of geniality, cannot resist. He professes to write for the benefit of those who, "when cooped up betwixt a natural and positive law, know not, for their souls, which way in the world to turn themselves." He thus establishes a relation with his reader, personal, direct, and genuine — the first condition of success in authorship. This relation is never long forgotten. He addresses both sexes, in a colloquial, friendly, trustful manner, and seems to identify himself with each by the magnetism of a determined recognition, which it is as unpleasant to evade as it is to repel the courteous and benign advances of an urbane stranger whom we accidentally encounter. He is so confidential, communicative, at his ease, and agreeable, that we instinctively yield.

Contemporary records give us quite a lively idea of Sterne's *début* in the world of letters. The same prestige has attended many an author before and since, who found in London a market for his books and an arena for social consideration; and the real significance of such prandial honors as attend success in that metropolis is now estimated at its true value. Unless the popular author boasts more legitimate credentials than his fame as a writer, the "dinners fourteen deep" suggest only a casual position. Walpole, in his usual satirical way, treats the "run" which the early volumes of Tristram Shandy enjoyed as one of the absurdities of fashion. Johnson sneered at the author's countless invitations; even the amiable Goldsmith called him a dull fellow. Warburton repudiated his intimacy, in despair of the reform he attempted; and Gray, the poet, declared it made one nervous to hear him preach, because his discourse continually verged on the laughable. Meanwhile Sterne encountered these and other better-founded objections with an insensibility which in a nobler cause would have been heroic, but in his case argues little else than recklessness.

Sterne came honestly both by his improvident spirit and his clerical title. His great-grandfather was Archbishop of York, and his father was killed in a duel which originated in high words about a goose. His boyhood was passed in the vagabondage of the camp, his young imagination kindled by the stories of Marlborough's veterans; his prime degraded by intimacy with an obscene writer, whose library was a unique collection of works especially adapted to pervert his taste; literary success introduced him suddenly to the pleasures of the town, and to the most perilous of all situations for a man of quick intellect and keen passions — that of a favorite diner-out and convivial buffoon; the prestige of an unscrupulous wit awaited him at the French capital; and to all his moral exposures he brought a mind unbraced by any clear force of purpose, a nature, both physical and moral, far more sensitive than vigorous, with morbid constitutional tendencies, and enslaved to pleasurable sensations. Thus born and bred, the creature of the immediate, only by a rare and felicitous union of circumstances was it possible for the flattered author, the susceptible cosmopolite, the imaginative epicure, to acquire that strength of will and methodical discipline, wherein alone could self-respect be intrenched. He must either have met the problem of life on perpetual guard, conscious that vigilant resistance was his only safety, or retired from its blandishments with heroic self-abnegation; and to neither of these alternatives were his resolution and courage adequate. Hence his *qui vive* philosophy, his deliberate search for excitement, the habit of absorbing consciousness in variety of scene and outward enjoyment, the attempt to *waive off* all mundane annoyance, and even death itself.

So reduced, at one period, was Sterne, that he hired a pane in the window of a stationer's shop, and placed there advertisements offering his services to all who stood in need of pen-craft, from the indolent vicar desirous of an eloquent sermon, to the uneducated lover who would fain register his mistress' charms in an anagram. On another occasion, it is related that he stole forth at night, to solicit a loan from Garrick; but, hearing the sounds of festivity within, gently replaced the uplifted knocker rather than expose his shabby dress by appearing in gay company. Debt and neglect made his exit from the world forlorn; not a single friend ministered to his dying wants; and the very companions who had most frequently applauded his table-talk were interrupted in their mirth by the announcement of his decease. These anecdotes form a gloomy contrast to the hues in which Sterne loved to depict human life; for they are unrelieved by cheerfulness, and unsoftened by sentiment. Perhaps in all literary history there is not a more impressive instance of the inevitable consequence of that unnatural divorce between genius and character which turns the blessed promise of the former into a mockery. It is as painful in literature as in life to be charmed, and yet to feel obliged to question the spell; to experience a conflict between the sense of beauty and the moral judgment, and to condemn the man while we enjoy the author. Quite the reverse of the Oriental benediction, "May you die among your kindred!" was his confessed wish. "I certainly declare," he says, "against submitting to it [death] before my friends." In accordance with the vagrant humor and casual sentiment that gave a charm to his writing and a recklessness to his character, he desired to close his existence away from home, and to receive the last offices of humanity from strangers; and thus it happened. While hirelings were endeavoring to restore circulation to his feet, as he lay in his lodgings in Old Bond street, he expired; not, like Scott, surrounded by awed and weeping relatives and dependents; nor, like Cowper, with a smile of "holy surprise;" nor, like Johnson, with the friends of years tearfully awaiting the sad event. His ties, with one or two exceptions, had all been convivial and "sentimental," to use his favorite word, rather than affectionate; no grand sincerity of feeling or noble self-devotion had enshrined him in the hearts of those who were amused by his wit, or softened by his pathos; and the man who, of all English authors, made emotion the staple of his writings, and chiefly sought to apply literary art to the expression of sentiment, passed away with the paltriest oblation, and owed his monument to public charity.

It is usual to regard the private correspondence of an author as the best test of his disposition. We have ample means of this nature to aid our judgment. There are domestic letters to his wife and daughter, business letters to Foley his banker, friendly letters to Garrick, his cousin, and several London and Paris acquaintances, and love-letters to Mrs. Draper. In them we discover his social relations, his opinions, private life, and tone of mind, and can easily perceive the sprightliness and geniality that captivated such men as the Baron d'Holbach and Lord Bathurst. His letters confirm our theory of his character; they exhibit the extremes of animal spirits, the constant trials of an invalid, the caprices of a sensitive and the recklessness of an excitable mind; yet with these defects appear, in equally strong colors, devoted parental love, cheerful philosophy, a conscientious regard to the claims of family and friends, candor, kindliness, and a sense of the beautiful and the true. How variable in his moods, how much a creature of mere temperament and sensibility, how prone to artificiality in the midst of natural emotion, was this singular compound of the man of the world and the sentimental epicure, clearly appears in his off-hand epistles. The manner in which he meets the arguments of judicious friends, who urged him to suppress objectionable parts of Tristram Shandy, shows conclusively that he was deficient in what may be called the instinct of the appropriate. It was the fashion in his day for both the aristocracy and the literati to indulge in table-talk which now would scarcely be tolerated in a barrack; and it is evident that he calculated upon the popularity of an obscene joke, without any adequate notion of the defilement it cast on a printed work designed for general perusal. In those letters which are addressed to the last object of his sentiment, there is displayed an anxiety for her comfort and welfare which betokens genuine disinterestedness; and, during the few weeks preceding his death, a most affectionate solicitude for his child is apparent. A few random extracts will best illustrate these diverse traits of his correspondence.

"She made me stay an hour with her; and in that short space I burst into tears a dozen different times."

"Heaven forbid the stock of chastity should be lessened by the life and opinions of Tristram Shandy! I can assure you that the very passages and descriptions you propose that I should sacrifice in my second edition, are what are best relished by men of wit, and some others whom I esteem as sound critics."

"I never knew what it was to say or write one premeditated word in my whole life."

"Till I have the honor to be as much maltreated as Rabelais and Swift were, I must continue humble. I care not a curse for the critics."

"Lyd has a pony which she delights in. 'T is a very agreeable ride out in a chaise I purchased for my wife. Whilst they take these diversions, I am scribbling away at my Tristram. So much am I delighted with my Uncle Toby's character, that I am become an enthusiast."

"I Shandy it away fifty times more than I was ever wont."

"We are every night fiddling, laughing, and singing, and cracking jokes."

"We live all the longer for having things our own way. This is my conjugal maxim."

"Write, dear Lydia, whatever comes into your little head."

"I am but this moment returned from Scarborough, and have received marvellous strength, had I not debilitated it as fast as I got it, by playing the good fellow with Lord Granby and Co."

"I set out to lay a portion of it out (money derived from Tristram and Sermons) in the service of the world, in a tour round Italy; where I shall spring game, or the deuce is in the dice."

"Almost all the nobility of England honor me with their names."

"After all this *badinage*, my heart is innocent; and the sporting of my pen is equal, just equal, to what I did in my boyish days, when I got astride of a stick, and galloped away."

"Praised be God for my sensibility! Though it has often made me wretched, yet I would not exchange it for all the pleasures the grossest sensualist ever felt."

"Since I got home to quietness, and temperance, and good books, and good hours, I have mended; and am now very stout."

"There is so little true feeling in the herd of the world, that I wish I could have got an act of parliament, when the books first appeared, that none but wise men should look into them."

"My girl cannot form a wish that is in the power of her father that he will not gratify her in. I am never alone. The kindness of my friends is ever the same; I wish, though, I had thee to nurse me. God bless thee, my child!"

"Dearest, kindest, gentlest, and best of women! may health, peace, and happiness, prove your handmaids! If I die, cherish the remembrance of me, and forget the follies which you so often condemned — which my heart, not my head, betrayed me into. Should my child, my Lydia, want a mother, may I hope you will (if she is left parentless) take her to your bosom?"

We cannot, with some of the wholesale censurers of Sterne, find merely the proofs of licentious intrigue, even in the most lover-like of these epistles, — those addressed to the wife of an Indian nabob. The lady appears to have been one of the most fragile of beings, and to have possessed that ethereal grace of character so often coïncident with delicate organizations. Sterne takes infinite pains to convince her that he is not captivated by her beauty, but inspired by her truth, refinement, and social talents. She affects him in so genial a way that he wishes he could write under the immediate influence of her presence. His advice to her is excellent. It is directed against the too easy and frank disposition usually found in combination with such beautiful traits of character. "Reverence thyself," is his constant and wise monition. He proposes to her a visit to his wife and daughter, and promises that their friendship and care shall alleviate her physical sufferings; buys an arm-chair and other comforts as for an invalid, and begs her to avoid her newly-painted cabin when about to embark for the East. In short, the candor and solicitude of a tender and undisguised interest, which he evidently wishes his family and intimates to share, appear in the midst of his most sentimental outpourings.

In presenting a new volume of his sermons to an intimate

friend, Sterne declared that they were dictated by his heart, while his other writings came from his head. The style of these discourses is fluent, clear, and sometimes elegant; they are, however, more ingenious than impressive, and their eloquence is didactic rather than glowing. It is easy to recognize the author of Tristram Shandy even in the most chastened of his homilies. They indicate a knowledge of the world; Shakspeare is quoted; the text is sometimes opposed, by way of more effectually clinching the argument at last; a parable of Scripture narrative is often gracefully elaborated, and there is constant allusion to, and defence of, the compassionate virtues. In view of the limits prescribed to this species of writing, and compared with the average sermons of the Establishment in his day, they may be justly declared to possess uncommon interest in both matter and expression; but their tone is too much subdued, and the preacher hovers too near the brink of the humorous and the colloquial, for earnestness. He is most at home in eulogizing affection and sympathy, and in reproducing Bible stories, of one of which he says, "Like all others, much of it depends upon the telling." His two characteristics—frankness and susceptibility—are advocated with zest. "Be open," he remarks, in allusion to marriage, "be honest; give yourself for what you are; conceal nothing; varnish nothing; and, if these fair weapons will not do, better not to conquer at all than conquer for a day." And elsewhere, "Let the torpid monk seek heaven comfortless and alone. God speed him! For my own part, I fear I should never so find the way; let me be wise and religious, but let me be a man."

In our restless times, the perpetual digressions of Sterne excite impatience; yet, in the contemplative mood which genuine reading demands, this fragmentary and desultory style has its advantages. We seem to participate in the authorship, to enter into the process of the book; and, if sympathetic, we soon catch the spirit of leisure and speculation, the random and capricious taste of the writer, surrendering, at last, according to his wish, the reins of imagination into his genial hand. This is especially requisite to enjoy Sterne. He does not rely upon strong outlines and remarkable incidents, but upon the atmosphere of his narratives and lucubrations. Much of his material is but the transcript of vague musing. He deals with no improbabilities, and calls himself "a small hero," and "the sport of fortune;" but his pages, wrought as they are chiefly out of common experience, win over readers by their familiarity of detail and their candor. He seems to be minutely observant under the inspiration of a passionless ideality. There is, too, a vagrant humor in both his thought and his style, which has a peculiar charm, especially to the unadventurous dreamer. To read Tristram Shandy is like comparing notes with a kindly, eccentric, philosophical good fellow, somewhat of a scholar, but more of a human creature, who "loves a jest in his heart," can rail good-naturedly at the world, and is consoled by wit and animal spirits for its neglect. We soon, therefore, accede to his purpose, honestly avowed, and let "familiarity grow into friendship."

The then recent battles of Marlborough, and his own recollections of barrack and transport, naturally filled Sterne's mind with the technicalities and the enthusiasm of the soldier's profession reproduced so quaintly in Uncle Toby and Trim. His attainments were quite limited, but, as with the majority of belles-lettres authors, a taste for miscellaneous reading, and an aptitude for seizing on available materials, whether found in books or in life, supplied him with the needful resources from which to elaborate his wit and humor. All that he required was a nucleus for imagination, a starting-point for random cogitation and sentiment; and this he found at one moment in an historical anecdote, at another in a domestic incident, now in a logical proposition, and again in a Parisian shop, or a Calais inn-yard.

It detracts nothing from Sterne's originality, that the prototypes of his characters have been, in many instances, identified. It is the coloring, rather than the invention, of his writings, in which consists their peculiar charm. As in the plots of Shakspeare, and the travels of Byron, what of mere incident occurs is chiefly important as a nucleus for his idiosyncrasies. It is the treatment, and not the theme, that wins our sympathies. To use a chemical figure of speech, the scenes and personages to which he introduces us serve mainly to precipitate the humor and sentiment of the author. The papers on Sterne by Dr. Ferriar, preserved in the Transactions of the Manchester Society, are but curious literary researches, and throw comparatively no light on the real genius of Yorick. However largely he was indebted to old Burton and Rabelais, the individuality of his conceptions remains. Take away the plot, the scholarship, and the anecdotical episodes, and we have still a fund of quaint generalization, a special vein of pathetic and humorous sentiment, which constitutes the real claim of Sterne as an author. The delight which Dr. Ferriar derived from him was quite independent of his borrowed plumes; it came from the cleverness of his satire, and the power of inducing a mood of quiet emotion and gentle mirth; and especially from a suggestive faculty, in which no English author excels him.

He opened to the mass of English readers that attractive domain in literature, which Rousseau in France, and Richter in Germany, made popular; though in him, unfortunately, it was not linked with aspirations for social amelioration, as in Jean Jacques, nor with deep-hearted sympathies, as in Jean Paul. Sterne was organized to feel and to evolve, but not to hallow and realize, those beautiful emotions of the soul in which so essentially consist its glory and its bane. In his hands the work degenerated too often into "the art of talking amusing nonsense;" it was debased by indecency, and made contemptible by caprice. Burns declared that he put himself on the regimen of admiring a fine woman, in order to secure inspiration. Sterne said that he had been in love with some Dulcinea, all his life, because it "sweetened his temper." He was an amorous jester, a sentimental epicure, and his theory was to make the most of life by adroitly skimming its surface. The tender passion was a means of casual luxury, not a serious experience. He protested against gravity, and, as Goldoni fought off the spleen by habitually standing on his guard like a wary fencer, Sterne adopted mirth as a panacea, clutching at the straws on the tide of sorrow with the childish impulse of desperation. "I am fabricating them" (the last volume of Tristram Shandy), he says, "for the laughing part of the world; for the melancholy part of it, I have nothing but my prayers."

There was a decided taste in Sterne's day for those colloquial treatises, lay sermons, and minor speculations, which, under the name of the British Essayists, form a department of literature peculiar to England; and this taste was united in the uneducated with a love of narrative and fiction, to which De Foe, and other *raconteurs*, ministered. The two were admirably combined in Sterne; his writings are made up, in about equal proportions, of speculation and description — now a portrait, and now a reverie; on one page ingenious argument, on the next, humorous anecdote. Thus something seems provided for every literary palate; and his desultory plan, or want of plan, became a chief source of his popularity. That he was conscious of an original vein, notwithstanding the abundant material of which he availed himself, may be inferred from his self-complacent query, "Shall we forever make new books, as the apothecaries make new mixtures, by pouring only out of one vessel into another?"

Perhaps the absence of constructive art increased the popularity of Sterne. To many readers there is a charm in the boldness which sets rules at defiance; and the author of Tristram Shandy not only braved that sense of propriety which is an instinct of better natures, but seemed to take a wanton delight in writing a book without any regard to established precedents, either in its arrangement or the development of its subject. He was the reverse of careless, however, in his habits of composition, and, running through all his apparent indifference of mood, there is obvious a trick of art. It is in the use of his materials, rather than in style, that he violates the order of a finished narration. Gathering from the storehouse of a tenacious memory what he had heard of fortifications, camp life, obstetrics, and foreign countries, and linking them together with curious gleanings of erudition, he gave vitality and interest to the whole by the introduction of several original and well-sustained characters, and occasional passages of skilful dialogue and pathetic story. The result was a *mélange*, whose fragmentary shape and indecent allusions were counterbalanced, though by no means atoned for, by felicitous creations, and the graphic limning of still-life. He has candidly given us his own theory of authorship. "Digressions," he says, "are the sunshine; they are the life and soul of reading." Instead of apologizing for an episode, he calls it "a master stroke of digressive skill." "To write a book," he elsewhere observes, "is for all the world like humming a song; be but in tune with yourself, 't is no matter how high or how low you take it."

The best illustration of these traits is the "Sentimental Journey," the author's last, most finished, and most harmonious work. Borrow traversed Spain to distribute the Bible, Inglis to trace the footsteps of Don Quixote; Addison explored Italy for classical localities, Forsyth to investigate her architecture; Beckford revelled in the luxuries of art and climate; English travellers in America have applied microscopic observation to republican defects; some tourists have taken for their *spécialité* geology, others prison-reform, others physical geography, — some gossip, and some ridicule; but Yorick alone, so far as we are informed, has chased in foreign regions the phantom of sentiment, and sought food for emotion. The very idea of the book combines the humorous and the pathetic, in that conscious, playful way which individualizes Sterne among English authors. To set out upon one's Continental travels predetermined to enfold all experience, however familiar and commonplace, with an atmosphere of sentiment, and to note the sensations, moods, tears, sighs, and laughs, which beset a susceptible pilgrim, has in it a comic element, while there was just enough of reality in the states of mind recorded to banish the notion of a mere fancy sketch. "My design in it," said Sterne, "was to teach us to love the world and our fellow-creatures better." He is too little in earnest, — too sentimental, in the present acceptation of that word, — to have succeeded in this purpose as a man of deeper and less capricious feelings might have done; but, on the other hand, his book, considered as a literary experiment and a personal revelation, is a psychological curiosity. It admirably shows the difference between a man of sentiment and a sentimental man. The latter character is depicted to the life. Incorrigible to the last in the matter of *equivoques* and innuendoes, he has deformed this otherwise dainty narrative with indecencies that offer a remarkable contrast to the delicacy of perception and style which has rendered the work a kind of classic in the library of English travels. "What a large volume of adventures may be grasped within this little span of life by him who interests his heart in everything!" This is the text of the "Sentimental Journey," and it is founded on a genuine idiosyncrasy. Human nature boasts of more generous, permanent, and profound sensibilities than have to do with such a cosmopolitan and superficial heart; yet its exhibition forms one of those odd and suggestive chapters in life that aid our study of character. The design of the work once approved, no one can complain of the execution, always excepting the violations of propriety in certain of the episodes. A monk asking alms, a widow, servants on holiday, a dwarf whose view of the opera is interrupted by a tall soldier, a man lamenting his dead ass, an imaginary captain, a polite beggar, a crazed beggar-girl, an impoverished knight of St. Louis selling *patés*, — these, and similar by-way children of misfortune, are the subjects of the wanderer's compassion and reveries, with occasional memories of Eugenius and Eliza, and of his wife and daughter, who serve as permanent resources upon which his emotion falls back when no fresh object presents itself. In the hands of an ordinary writer these would prove ineffective materials; but Sterne has made distinct and rich pictures of them all. If the feeling smacks of affectation, wit embalms and redeems it. We are constantly disposed, as we read, to echo the Count de B——'s exclamation when Yorick talked him into procuring a passport, — "*C'est bien dit;*" so easy, colloquial, and often most nicely balanced, is the style. The short chapters are like cabinet pictures, neatly outlined and softly tinted; we carry from them an impression which lingers like a favorite air. How often have authors taken from this work a valuable hint, and, avoiding its exceptionable qualities, elaborately imitated its word-painting and its atmosphere! It modified the literature of travel, which previously bore marks of utter carelessness, by indicating the artistic capabilities of a species of books that had been deemed mere vehicles of statistical and circumstantial information.

Sterne often quotes Sancho Panza, and invokes the "gentle spirit of sweetest humor, who erst did sit upon the easy pen of his beloved Cervantes;" and it is probable that Don Quixote suggested the "Sentimental Journey." As "the Knight of the Rueful Countenance" went forth, with a peasant for a squire, in pursuit of chivalric adventures, so the author sets out, with a

French valet, on a crusade of sentiment. The Don saw everything through the lens of knight-errantry, and the susceptible pilgrim beholds the world through the medium of an exaggerated tenderness. The relations of Sancho and La Fleur to their masters are parallel, however diverse their characters. The incidents which Sterne arrays in an imaginative guise are as commonplace in themselves as those which Cervantes uses as materials for his hero's enthusiasm. What the windmill and the way-side inn are to the one, the Remise door and the glove-shop are to the other. In its effect, too, upon the reader's mind, this exaggerated contact of sentiment with every-day life is as humorous as that of ancient chivalry with modern utilitarianism; an equally salient contrast and a like quaint vein are opened. Speculation, anecdote, the high and the low, the vulgar and the ideal, blend their associations, both in the Spanish romance, and the "Sentimental Journey;" but all are enveloped in an atmosphere of harmonious feeling, and clothed in graceful language. This analogy is increased by the fact, that, as the readers of Don Quixote are enlightened as to the knight's habits by the garrulous squire, so to the valet of the sentimental pilgrim are we indebted for the little authentic information extant regarding Sterne's real state of mind. La Fleur, indeed, was as much an original in his way as his master. A native of Burgundy in the humblest circumstances, he followed the occupation of a drummer for six years, in order to see the world; and an officer of the regiment to which he was attached obtained for him the situation of a *valet* to a *Milord Anglois*, in which capacity he was afterwards employed by Sterne. His wife ran off with an actor, and he felt so much at home in England, that, during the latter part of his life, he was often employed as a courier, and was sent on repeated missions across the Channel. He used to surprise his master in fits of profound melancholy, whence, upon being observed, he would suddenly rouse himself with some flippant expression. He declares that the sight of misery usually affected Sterne to tears; that he was charitable, and used to make frequent notes of his daily experience; and that his conversation with women was "of the most interesting kind, and left them serious, if it did not find them so." The incidents so daintily recorded in his travels, La Fleur likewise authenticated; and through him we know that his master busily collected materials for a work on Italy during his tour in that country, although he never could succeed in speaking Italian.

In the history of English literature, there is, now and then, a writer who seems to have caught his tone from the other side of the Channel. The Gallic school was imitated by Pope and Congreve, though in the former it is exhibited rather in style than in range of thought. Brilliancy, artistical refinement, and graceful expression, are the characteristics of this class of writers; they deal rather in manners than in passions; fancy usurps with them the place of imagination, wit that of reflection; animal spirits, instead of soul-felt emotions, seem to inspire their muse; they are not often in earnest except in the desire to please; and, more ingenious than profound, with more tact than elevation, they offer an entire contrast to the manly, intense, frank utterance of Queen Elizabeth's dramatists, and the pure love of nature of the modern bards. Sterne partakes largely of the light graces and the vivacious tone of the best French writers; and one reason of his popularity is the refreshment his countrymen always derive from the less grave and more sprightly attractions of their Continental neighbors. "They order this matter better in France," was a maxim which Sterne's taste and temper made applicable not only to the economy, but to the philosophy, of life, of which his view was the opposite of serious. The foreign perversion which was introduced into English literature during the licentious era of the Restoration was casual and temporary. The writers then so fashionable are nearly all forgotten, while those of the age of Elizabeth and Anne maintain their just and clear supremacy. In a few instances, however, the influence of French taste moulded works on the English side of the Channel which the genius of the authors redeemed from neglect, in spite of an element alien to the Saxon mind; and such was the case with Sterne's writings.

This Continental affinity is still more obvious in his love of the old French *raconteurs*. Dr. Ferriar traces his manner directly to Marivaux; and it is equally significant that no English writer has been more completely domesticated on the Continent. Though we find cheap editions of Young and Dr. Franklin in the book-stalls of Paris and Florence, the gloomy speculation of the one and the practical wisdom of the other are but vaguely appreciated in France and Italy, while the sentimental refinements and genial musings of Sterne adapt themselves readily to their more susceptible and imaginative minds. It is true that the usual absurd mistakes occur which seem inevitable in the French interpretation of English literature,— one critic accepting Tristram Shandy as a veritable biography, and another classifying its author with the social innovators and daring thinkers of the revolutionary era; yet, on the other hand, very faithful translations of Sterne, especially in Italian, are not only obtainable, but have become the favorite reading of that large class who delight in Foscolo.

A recent critic * denies to Sterne all exact proficiency in the French language, and cites many errors to prove his incorrectness; as, for instance, *c'est tout egal* for *c'est egal*, *M. Anglois* instead of *M. l'Anglois*, etc. La Fleur, in speaking of a horse, is made to say, *C'est un cheval le plus opiniâtre du monde*, and it is argued that a good French scholar would never have applied the word *opiniâtre* to a horse, nor substituted the article *un* for *le.* In the chapter on "The Passport," also, *ces Messieurs les Anglois* should be *Messieurs les Anglois.* The correct French in the Drummer's letter, it is declared from internal evidence, is not Sterne's. Colloquial blunders, however, do not invalidate the Gallic pretensions of this author, whose natural affinity with his mercurial neighbors across the Channel is self-evident. French criticisms of English literature are proverbially superficial, and often ludicrous. Voltaire talks of Shakspeare, Chateaubriand of Milton, and Guizot of modern British poets, in terms of vague generalization, which show that at best they have only appreciated the tone, without penetrating to the deep significance and individual genius, of these authors. It is otherwise with such a writer as Sterne, although some amusing errors have occurred in the French estimate of his aims and character. The qualities which rendered him popular and eccentric are quite as well recognized by the nation he loved so dearly as at home.

* Notes and Queries.

Bayle describes him as "uniquement occupé à etudier ses sensations, ses gouts, ses penchants particuliers, à rendre un compte exact et minutieux des emotions qu'il eprouve et des hasards qui les font naître." He calls him "malin, pathetique," notes his "simplicité," his "sensibilité exquise et douce," his "expression fine, plaisante et moquese qu'indique un esprit vif, brillant, et caustique." "Sa conversation," he observes, "etait animée et spirituelle; son caractere jovial mais capricieux et inegal, consequence naturel d'un temperament irritable et d'un mauvais état de santé habituelle," and he declares him a "*plagiare*" who arranged "*sa mosaique avec tant d'art.*"* A more discriminating and true portrait of Sterne by a foreign critic can scarcely be imagined.

The vagrant boyhood of Sterne, as the offspring of an army officer, his school-days in Yorkshire, followed by the academical training of Cambridge, and twenty years of clerical life, such as it was in his day, when desultory reading, field sports, and gossip, occupied more time than priestly functions, afford sufficient materials for the kind of culture and the knowledge of life which his writings display; and if to these resources we add the ordinary incidents of Continental travel and the habit of *amateur* exercises in music and painting, we can easily trace the external elements that constitute the framework or ingredients of his books. Their real interest was altogether derived from the idiosyncrasies of the author. These were at first inappropriately confined to a profession for which he was singularly unfitted; and it is one of the most remarkable facts in his career, that not until past middle life did he achieve a literary reputation. His tendencies of character, as well as of mind, were utterly opposed to the office which, according to the irrational, not to say impious, system of dispensing church livings, was, for reasons altogether factitious and worldly, bestowed upon a man who, as one of the *coterie* of wits about town, of courtiers, politicians, or in any lay vocation, might have left a reputation comparatively free from blame. His profession was a continued reproach to his levity, and has caused him to be judged by subsequent moralists with severity; while his name

* Biographie Universelle.

has become a standard example of the insincerity of authors and the illusions of sentiment — the prototype and representative of the class who weep over the corpse of a donkey and at the same time maltreat their wives.

All incomplete characters must undergo an analytical sifting to separate the chaff from the wheat; and a like process is requisite in literature, where the superiority of a writer in certain particulars is modified by great defects in others. To no English author is the careful separation of gross alloy from pure metal more indispensable than in the case of Sterne. Time, which shapes reputation as well as the less abstract interests of humanity to "a perfect end," has already effected this result. A few genuine characters, episodes of true pathos, sketches of life drawn with exquisite art, phases of delicate sentiment, pictures traced and mellowed with remarkable tact and beauty, — these have survived whole pages of equivocal morality and pedantic display. Such are "the Story of Lefevre," and "Maria," and the characters of Uncle Toby, Trim, Obadiah, Dr. Slop, and Shandy. It is the originality of characterization, and finished bits of humor and of sentiment, that redeem both the writings and the fame of Sterne. What is indecorous and obscure is rejected by the literary gleaner; and the tedious digressions, the stolen erudition, the violations of good taste, and the artificial expedients, are forgotten in the occasional triumphs of art and nature which the genius of the author produced in his better moments. This partial success, this obscure glory, is a striking instance of the truth of Pope's trite maxim, that "want of decency is want of sense."

Not a little of our interest in Sterne is historical. The vein he opened has been more deeply worked by subsequent authors. Compared with the later essayists, his didactic passages want sustained glow and point; compared with succeeding novelists, his characters are deficient in variety and impressiveness; but in his speculations and his pictures he has produced studies of characterization. Artistically speaking, few English authors have proved more suggestive. Without elaborate finish, he furnishes perfect hints. His writings are to others of the same order which have since appeared, as the cartoons of the old masters are to the historical pictures of their followers. In the long array of the novelist's creations, "the beings of the mind and not of clay," from those of Fielding to those of Dickens, we linger before the few but well-defined originals of Sterne with a peculiar sense of their human significance. Unideal and unimpassioned, yet distinct and natural, they have the rare merit of exciting an interest without any extraordinary traits of adventures; they embody the genius of humor, reality made attractive by its consistent, habitual, minute exhibition; they are like the best Flemish paintings, mellow in tone, familiar in subject, and marvellous in execution,—true to Nature in her quips and fantasies, in her whims and everyday phases, rather than in deep or wonderful crises. In his way, Sterne is Shakspearian; and, although superseded to a great degree, he keeps a hold upon intelligent sympathy by the originality of his manner, which is constantly reproduced in popular literature.

Indeed, if a constant though unacknowledged and perhaps often unconscious reference to an author's scenes and ideas, and the frequent imitation of his style by subsequent aspirants for literary distinction, may be considered as a reliable test of originality and success, Laurence Sterne, notwithstanding the blots on his escutcheon, occupies a permanent niche in the temple of fame. Indirect memorials of his genius abound. Ball Hughes modelled the delectable group of Uncle Toby and the Widow Wadman; and Leslie's delicate pencil traced Yorick at the Glove-Shop. Travellers who land at Calais daily think of the "Sentimental Journey" as the porters on the quay vociferate "*Hôtel Dessein;*" and advocates, when hard pressed to combat testimony, allude magnanimously to the impracticable witness by quoting the incident of Uncle Toby and the fly. "There is room enough for thee and me," is the most convenient of philanthropic evasions. The schoolboy early learns to regard Sterne as a master of the pathetic, through familiarity with the story of Lefevre in his well-thumbed reader. An American bishop is said to have consumed whole evenings in searching the Bible for the sentence he proposed to use as a text for his next sermon, "God tempers the winds to the shorn lamb," and to have blushed when he was informed that the author of that gentle and endeared saying was no other than the most indecorous genius of his own order; and a celebrated New York medical professor of the old school quoted Tristram Shandy so habitually in his lectures, that country students used to ask, at the bookstores, for "Dr. Sterne's Midwifery." "Shandean" long ago became an adjective as significant and common as "Pickwickian" is to-day.

Among the popular writers who have either directly followed the vein of Sterne, or profited by his style, are Mackenzie, Irving, and Dickens. Many favorite volumes of "Reveries," by bachelors and others, now in vogue, are of his identical model. The desultory and quaintly simple yet learned production of Southey, "The Doctor," is essentially the same in plan as Tristram Shandy; Curran imitated Sterne in his letters; while a still more remarkable evidence of the popularity of our author's manner may be found in the fact that, after Sir Bulwer Lytton had run through the entire scale of the intense school of novel-writing, he surprised his admirers, and won over a new and previously antagonistic circle, by producing in "My Novel" a work of fiction so palpably imitated from Sterne as, in many passages, to have the effect of prolonging the key-note of his sentiment and exhibiting a *rifacimento* of his style.

In one noble mansion in London is his bust by Nollekens, and in another the famous portrait of him by Reynolds, copies of which have long been favorite illustrations with the disciples of Lavater and Gall. In Old Bond street, No. 41, now a cheesemonger's, but known in his day as "The Silk Bag-shop," are the lodgings whence are dated many of his letters, where, according to tradition, he finished the "Sentimental Journey," and where occurred his melancholy death. In the burial-ground fronting Hyde-Park, on the road to Bayswater, about the centre of the western wall, is the headstone that marks his grave, set up, as the best of London guide-books truly declares, "with an unsuitable inscription," by a "tippling fraternity of Freemasons."

The most interesting problem involved in his career as an author is the rank he holds as an expositor of sentiment. Critics have viewed him, in this regard, at the two extremes of hypocrisy and sincerity, of artifice and of truth. In order justly to estimate Sterne with reference to this, his most obvious claim and purpose, we must consider the true relation between human feeling and its written expression.

Sentiment, as an element of literature, is the intellectual embodiment of feeling; it is thought imbued with a coloring and an atmosphere derived from emotion. Its reality, duration, and tone, depend in books, as in character, upon alliance with other qualities; and there is no fallacy more common than that which tests its sincerity in the author by the permanent traits of the man. It may be quite subordinate as a motive of action, and altogether secondary as a normal condition, and yet it is none the less real while it lasts. In each artist and author, sentiment exists in relation to other qualities, which essentially modify it while they do not invalidate its claim. To say that a man who writes an elegy which moves us to tears, and at the same time displays the most heartless conduct in his social life, is therefore a hypocrite, is to reason without discrimination. The adhesiveness, the conscience, and the temperament, of each individual, directly influence his sentiment; in one case giving to it the intensity of passion, in another the sustained dignity of principle, now causing it to appear as an incidental mood, and again as a permanent characteristic. United to strength of will or to earnestness of spirit, it is worthy of the highest confidence; in combination with a feeble and impressible mind, or a lightsome and capricious fancy, or a selfish disposition, it is quite unreliable. In either case, however, the quality itself is genuine; its type and degree only are to be questioned. Thus regarded, the apparent incongruity between its expression and its actual condition vanishes.

Sentiment in Burns was essentially modified by tenderness, in Byron by passion, in Shelley by imagination; meditation fostered it in Petrarch, extreme susceptibility in Kirke White. In the French Quietists it took the form of religious ecstasy. In the Old English drama it is robust, in the Spanish ballads chivalric, in Hamlet abstract and intellectual, in "As You Like It" full of airy fancifulness. Miss Edgeworth and Jane Austen exhibited it as governed by prudence and common sense; Mrs. Radcliffe, as rendered mysterious by superstition. Scott delighted to interpret it through local and legendary accessories, under the influence of a sensuous temperament. In the Dantesque picture of Francesca da Rimini it is full of tragic sweetness, and in Paul and Virginia perverted by artificial taste. In Charles Lamb it is quaint, in Hood deeply human, in Cowper alternately natural and morbid, in Mackenzie soft and pale as moonlight, and in Boccaccio warm as the glow of a Tuscan vintage. Chastened by will, it is as firm and cold as sculpture in Alfieri, and melted by indulgence, it is as insinuating as the most delicious music in Metastasio. Pure and gentle in Raphael, it is half savage in Salvator and Michael Angelo; severely true in Vandyke, it is luscious and coarse in Rubens. And yet, to a certain extent and under specific modifications, every one of these authors and artists possessed sentiment; but, held in solution by character, in some it governed, in others it served genius; in some it was a predominant source of enjoyment and suffering, and in others but an occasional stimulus or agency. Who doubts, over a page of the Nouvelle Heloise, that sentiment in all its tearful bliss was known to Rousseau? The abandonment of his offspring to public charity does not disprove its existence, but only shows that in his nature it was a mere selfish instinct. The history of philanthropic enterprise indicates the same contradiction. Base cruelty has at times deformed the knight, gross appetites the crusader, hypocrisy the missionary, and the men whose names figure in the so-called charitable movements of our day are often the last to whom we should appeal for personal kindness and sympathy. The same inconsistency is evident in that large class of women in whose characters the romantic predominates over the domestic instincts. "Confessions" form a popular department of French literature, and are usually based on sentiment. Yet their authors are frequently thorough men of the world and intense egotists. It is this want of harmony between expression and life, between the eloquent avowal and the practical influence of sentiment, patriotic, religious, and humane, which gave rise to the invective of Carlyle, and the other stern advocates of fact, of action, and of reality. Meanwhile the beauty, the high capacity, the exalted grace of sentiment itself, is uninvaded. We must learn to distinguish its manifestations, to honor its genuine power, to distrust its rhetorical exaggeration.

The truth is, that Sterne's heart was more sensitive than

robust. It was like "wax to receive," but not like "marble to retain," impressions. Their evanescence, therefore, does not impugn their reality. Perhaps we owe the superiority of their artistic expression to this want of stability. Profound and continuous emotion finds but seldom its adequate record. Men thus swayed recoil from self-contemplation; their peace of mind is better consulted by turning from than by dwelling upon their states of feeling; whereas more frivolous natures may dally with and make capital of their sentiment without the least danger of insanity. We have but to study the portrait of Sterne in order to feel that a highly nervous organization made him singularly alive to the immediate, while it unfitted him for endurance and persistency. That thin, pallid countenance, that long, attenuated figure, the latent mirth of the expression, the predominance of the organs of wit and ideality, betoken a man to "set the table in a roar,"— one who passes easily from smiles to tears, from whose delicately strung yet unheroic mould the winds of life draw plaintive and gay, but transient music; — a being more artistic than noble, more susceptible than generous, capable of a shadowy grace and a fitful brilliancy, but without the power to dignify and elevate sensibility. His fits of depression, his recourse to amusement, his favorite watchword, "*Vive la bagatelle*," his caprice and trifling, his French view of life, his alternate gayety and blue devils, attest one of those ill-balanced characters, amusing in society, ingenious in literature, but unsatisfactory in more intimate relations and higher spheres.

THE LITERARY STATESMAN.

MASSIMO D'AZEGLIO.

It is seldom that the noble aims and benign sentiments of the genuine artist find development in life. His efficiency, however refined and graceful in itself, rarely can be traced to a practical issue; his dominion is usually confined to the vague realms of thought, and his name is familiar only to those who explore the world of fancy and ideas. A rare and beautiful exception to this abstract career of the artist in literature was recently visible in the case of Massimo d'Azeglio, the late secretary of state of Sardinia. It became his fortunate destiny to realize in action the dreams of his youth; to administer, to a certain extent at least, the principles which previously found only written expression; and to be the agent of some of the political and social ameliorations, which, at a less auspicious era, he could but suggest, illustrate, and prophesy. We can hardly imagine a more elevated satisfaction to a generous mind than the privilege of thus making tangible what was once ideal, carrying into affairs the results of deliberate study, and giving social embodiment to long-cherished and patiently-evolved truths. To feel the interest and realize the significance of such a career, we must compare the first work of the gifted novelist with the last discourse of the minister of foreign affairs; and trace his identity of opinion and sentiment, from the glowing patriotism of "Niccolò de' Lapi" and "Ettore Fieramosca," to the reforms which have rendered Sardinia the most free and progressive of the Italian states.

It is through his genuine patriotism, indeed, that D'Azeglio is both a popular writer and a liberal statesman; his fictions are derived from the same inspiration as his public acts; he is a man of the people, and an efficient and honored citizen of Italy, by virtue of a love of country not less remarkable for intelligence than for sincerity. This is his great distinction. Neither to the circumstances of his birth, education, nor experience, is he indebted for the independence, wisdom, and zeal of his national feeling, but altogether to the promptings of a noble heart and vigorous understanding. This eminent trait both of his character and his genius, his intelligent patriotism, is exhibited with beautiful consistency, first in an artistic, then in an argumentative, and finally in an administrative manner. It pervades his life, as well as his books, now finding utterance in the fervid words of an ancient Tuscan patriot, now in a direct and calm appeal to the reason of his contemporaries, and again in the salutary projects and unfaltering purpose of the ministerial reformer.

In the history of Sardinia there are obvious facts and tendencies indicative of a liberal destiny; vistas, as it were, of light athwart the gloom of despotic rule, and low and interrupted yet audible breathings of that spirit of liberty and national progress now evidently becoming more permanent and vital. The nucleus of the monarchy was Savoy, around which were grouped the fragments of several states, — the old kingdom of Burgundy, and remains of the Carlovingian and Frankish empire; but towards the end of the thirteenth century its individuality was fixed by the will of Count Asmodeus the Sixth; and by the peace of Utrecht it became a state of Europe. Although the power of the crown was unlimited, the government was administered by three ministers, and the succession confined to the male line, the assent of the Estates was requisite for the imposition of new taxes, and, while the nobility formed a large class, it was not exempt from taxation. The traveller who visits the church of La Superga, at Turin, and muses over her buried kings, will recall traits of royal character not unworthy of the superb mausoleum. In the forty-three years of his reign, Charles Emanuel the Third, both as a civic and military ruler, preserved a high character. In his disputes with the Pope, he successfully maintained the right of the state to make all ecclesiastical appointments; and the concordat was confirmed by Benedict the Fourteenth, in 1742. The new code of 1770 was in advance of the times, and the country flourished under its provisions. But these incidental advantages were not sufficient to modify the natural influence of despotism upon the character of the people; and the acknowledged superiority of the Sardinians in vigor and breadth of nature is, perhaps, not less owing to local and social circumstances. Among these we are disposed to reckon the variety of elements that constitute the state; it combines interior plains with mountains and sea-coast — the fertile levels of Asti and Alessandria, and the distant island of Sardinia; while Piedmont, as its name suggests, lies at the foot of the Pennine Alps (in which are the Great Saint Bernard on her north), and of the Grecian and Cottian Alps, including Mont Blanc and Mont Cenis, towards France and Savoy; in the direction of the south are the Maritime Alps, separating her from Genoa and Nice.

Another propitious influence that distinguishes Piedmont is the existence of a large body of Protestants, whose contests with the Catholic power early broke up the monotony of prescriptive opinion, and tended to enlighten and invigorate the adjacent people. Milton's noble sonnet to the Waldenses of Piedmont is a familiar memorial of their heroism and sufferings. Protected by their mountain barriers, they defeated the army of the Pope, who lost not less than seven hundred men in the struggle. The actual effect, however, of so complete a despotism as that which originally invested the territory, has been described in a vivid and graphic manner by another poet. Alfieri, in his ingenuous autobiography, gives us a melancholy picture of an education under royal authority. His fame is one of the redeeming associations that beguile the traveller at Turin.

In 1798, Charles Emanuel the Fourth ceded his whole territory to the French, with the exception of the island of Sardinia; and, four years subsequently, abdicated in favor of his brother, who, upon his return after the peace of Paris, in 1815, restored the old constitution as far as practicable, reädmitted the Jesuits, subscribed to the Holy Alliance, and established a rigorous censorship. The next year, harassed by the occupation of his kingdom by the Austrians, he also resigned in favor of his brother, Charles Felix. The Congress of Vienna, in 1822, provided for the evacuation of foreign troops; but, before three years had elapsed, the usual enactments of arbitrary power crushed whatever germs of a liberal policy remained. By a royal edict, such of the inhabitants as were not possessed of at least four hundred dollars were forbidden to acquire the first elements of learning; and only those having a certain investment in the funds were allowed to enter the university. Translations of Goëthe, Schiller, Wieland, and other authors, were prohibited. From time to time, formidable conspiracies against a government so tyrannical were discovered; the most important, that of 1821, was not without temporary success, since the regent, Charles Albert, was compelled to swear to the Spanish constitution. The spirit of the age and the lessons of experience were not altogether lost upon this prince, whose real character seems but recently to have been appreciated. We can desire no better evidence of his sincere love of country, and benign projects, than the fact that, many years since, when comparative tranquillity prevailed in Europe, he was accustomed to hold long and confidential interviews with our representative at his court, for the purpose of eliciting information as to the means and method of gradually ameliorating the institutions not only of Sardinia, but of Italy.

He long cherished the hope of giving her national unity, of combining from all her states an efficient army, and thus expelling the Austrians from the soil. This he believed to be the first step towards a constitutional government; popular education and military training he more or less encouraged in his own dominions, with this great ultimate object in view; and he certainly possessed the most efficient native troops, and the best-founded popularity, among the Italian princes. Since his death, impartial observers concur in deeming him far more unfortunate than treacherous; a reäction has justly taken place in the public estimation of his motives and career; and no candid inquirer can fail to recognize in him a brave ruler, who gave a decided impulse to liberal ideas, advanced the Italian cause, and became one of its involuntary martyrs.

"Yea, verily, Charles Albert has died well;
  And if he lived not all so, as one spoke,
The sin passed softly with the passing bell.
  For he was shriven, I think, in cannon smoke,
And, taking off his crown, made visible
  A hero's forehead. Shaking Austria's yoke,
He shattered his own hand and heart. 'So best.'
  His last words were, upon his lonely bed,
'I do not end like popes and dukes at least,—
  Thank God for it.' And now that he is dead,
Admitting it is proved and manifest
  That he was worthy, with a discrowned head,
To measure heights with patriots, let them stand
  Beside the man in his Oporto shroud,
And each vouchsafe to take him by the hand,
  And kiss him on the cheek, and say aloud,
'Thou, too, hast suffered for our native land!
  My brother, thou art one of us. Be proud!'" *

Into this amphibious country,—as Piedmont is quaintly called by the Italian tragic poet,—into this kingdom composed of the fragments of shattered dynasties, the scene of religious persecution, the heritage of a long line of brave and despotic kings, who adorned it with magnificent temples of religion by taxes wrung from an ignorant people and extorted from a pampered nobility,—into this romantic land, crowned with Alpine summits and indented with emerald vales,—a region memorable for many a hard-fought field, and which boasts the home of Rousseau, Alfieri, and Pellico,—Massimo d'Azeglio was born, on the second of October, 1798. His family was both ancient and noble; his native city was Turin, a capital so near the confines of France as to be more exposed to the influx of Continental ideas than any other metropolis of the land. A more vigorous and intelligent race tread its streets, and a bolder peasantry dwell amid the mountains around, than belong to the sickly Campagna or the Lazzaroni shores; the soldier has a manlier bearing, and the priest a franker aspect; while in society, not only the language, but the enlightenment, of the French prevails. At the *cafés* you find

* Mrs. Browning's "Casa Guidi Windows."

more foreign journals, in the *salons* a less antediluvian tone; the mellow atmosphere of the past which broods over the more southern districts is here scarcely perceptible, and a certain modern air and freshness of life immediately strike the traveller from that direction, as he enters the Sardinian capital.

Here Azeglio's early education was strictly private; he then passed through the usual college tuition, entered the militia, and soon became an army officer. His natural tastes, however, were for art and politics. Accordingly, when sent minister to Rome, at a subsequent period, we find him assiduously cultivating the fine arts; and in a short time he became a skilful landscape painter. Here his latent and instinctive taste and capabilities genially unfolded; the impressive ruins, the treasures of the Vatican, and the companionship of artists, continually informed and inspired his mind, which rapidly and gracefully developed in an atmosphere so accordant with its original bias. We frequently have occasion to remark the affinity between the fine arts and certain departments of literature; and seldom can this relation be traced with more charming effect than in the writings of D'Azeglio. The clearness of design, the felicitous adaptation of the atmosphere to the outline, the grouping, scenic descriptions, and fidelity to those laws of historical perspective, which are so analogous to the same principles in painting, all unfold themselves to the critical reader of his masterly narratives. We feel, as we read, that the best preparation for that species of literary art is the discipline of the accomplished draughtsman; for an historical romance, in its true significance, is like an elaborate picture, subject to the same conditions of light and shade, truth to fact and nature, and harmonious conception.

D'Azeglio delineates in language with a patient attention to details, a wise regulation of color, and a constant eye to unity of effect, which we at once refer to his studies in the Roman Academy and galleries, and his familiarity with the pencil and palette. It was not, however, until the maturity of his powers that his genius found scope in language. Before he had acquired fame as a novelist, the intrinsic qualities of the man won him an exalted place in the estimation of a circle of friends, including the most illustrious names of Lombardy. On his removal to Milan, in

1830, his urbanity of spirit, fluent expression, manliness, and evident intellectual ability, had thus gained him numerous admirers; and Rossi and Manzoni were among his most intimate and attached companions. It is an interesting coincidence, that the destined successor of the first of Italian novelists became his son-in-law. D'Azeglio espoused the daughter of Manzoni; and somewhat of the domestic pathos which gives a melancholy charm to his principal work is doubtless the reflection of his own sad experience, for but a single year of conjugal happiness followed his marriage, his bride having died soon after giving birth to a daughter.

The social character of Milan is rather literary than artistic; and it seems a natural inference, that, when the embryo statesman and clever landscape painter exchanged the Eternal City for the Lombard capital, and found himself in the centre of a distinguished group of patriotic men of letters, the chief of whom was bound to him by ties of family as well as sympathy of taste, he should catch the spirit of authorship, and seek to embody in that form the knowledge acquired in another field, and the aspirations that craved more emphatic utterance than could be expressed by the silent canvas. In 1833, therefore, appeared "Ettore Fieramosca, or the Challenge of Barletta," the best Italian historical romance since the "Promessi Sposi." Its easy and copious style, its truth of description and distinct characterization, the simplicity of its plot, and, above all, the thoroughly Italian nature of the argument, instantly established its popularity. The incident upon which the story is founded is as familiar to the historical reader as it is memorable in the annals of Italy; — that of a drawn battle between thirteen Italian and the same number of French knights, occasioned by the challenge of the former, for an imputation cast upon their national bravery by one of the latter. Sanctioned as was the encounter by the leaders of both armies, witnessed by a large concourse, including citizens and soldiers of France, Spain, and Italy, — the ferocious zeal of the combatants, the duration of the struggle, the patriotic as well as individual sense of honor involved, and, finally, the signal triumph of the Italian arms, combine to render the scene one of intense interest.

D'Azeglio availed himself of this episode in the early wars of his country, to revive that sentiment of national unity which so many years of dispersion and tyranny had obscured, but not extinguished, in the Italian heart. From the records of the past he thus evoked the spirit so requisite to consecrate the present. Ettore Fieramosca is the ideal of an Italian knight; his unfortunate but nobly-cherished love, his prowess, beauty, and fiery enthusiasm for his country, his chivalric accomplishments and entire self-devotion, beautiful and attractive as they are, become more impressive from the strict historical fidelity with which they are associated. The games, laws, costume, turns of thought and speech, and military and popular habits of the era, are scrupulously given. Among the characters introduced are Cæsar Borgia and Vittoria Colonna, names that eloquently typify the two extremes of Italian character, — the integrity of which, in its villany and its virtue, is admirably preserved; the ecclesiastic, the inn-keeper, the man-at-arms, the gossiping citizen, and the prince of that day, are portrayed to the life. Many of the local scenes described have the clearness of outline and the vividness of tint which make them permanent reminiscences to the contemplative reader, and have associated them in the minds of his countrymen with the hero of D'Azeglio's romance and the sentiment of national honor.

In 1841 appeared "Nicolò di Lapi," the work which established D'Azeglio's fame as a literary artist and a man of decided genius. The same patriotic instinct guided his pen as in his previous enterprise; but the design was more elaborate and finished, and the conception wrought out through more extensive research and a higher degree of feeling. The time chosen is that terrible epoch when Florence defended herself alone against the arms of Clement the Seventh and Charles the Fifth. In his account of the siege of 1529–30, he follows Varchi in regard to the prominent external facts; but into the partial and imperfect record of the historian he breathed the life of nature and tradition. For this purpose, the documents of the age were assiduously collated; the monuments, walls, and towers of Florence interrogated; the bastions of Saint Miniato, the palaces of the Medici and Pazzi, the Bargello, the piazza, ancient private dwellings — the courts and staircases, the portraits and legends — every tradition and memorial of the period, examined, to acquire the requisite scenic and local material, which are wrought up with such authentic minuteness as to form a complete picture, and one which the observation of every visitor to the Tuscan capital at once and entirely recognizes.

Nor has he bestowed less care upon the spirit and action of his romance. The people, as they once existed, in all their original efficiency and individual character, are reproduced, as they then lived, thought, suffered, and battled, after three hundred years of internal agitation and wars, proving themselves adequate to cope at once with both Emperor and Pope, and falling at last rather through treachery than conquest. The very atmosphere of those times seems to float around us as we read. The republic lives in its original vigor. We realize the events of history reänimated by the fire of poetic invention. Niccolò is the ideal of an Italian patriot, as Fieramosca is of a knight. There is a Lear-like solemnity in his vehement passion and religious self-control, a Marino Faliero dignity in his political ruin. The consistent earnestness of his character, the wisdom and majesty, the fierce indignation and holy resignation, the high counsels and serene martyrdom of the venerable patriot, are at once exalted and touching. Depressed by existing degeneracy, D'Azeglio seems to have evoked this noble example from the past to revive the dormant hopes and elevate the national sentiment of his countrymen. Around this grand central figure he has grouped, with rare skill and marvellous effect, a number of historical personages and domestic characters, whose words, acts, and appearance, give distinct reality and dramatic effect to the whole conception. It is enough to mention Savonarola, Feruccio, and Malatesta,— the reformer, the soldier, and the civic ruler,— all reproduced with accuracy, and their agency upon the spirit of the age and the course of events suggested with consummate tact.

From the intensely exciting scenes enacted in the camp, around the walls of the besieged city, on the bastions, in the cabinet, and at Volterra, we are suddenly transported to the home of Lapi, and witness the domestic life of the age. The family portraits are exquisitely discriminated; Lisa and Laodamia are two of those finely contrasted and beautifully conceived female characters which, like Scott's Minna and Brenda, leave a Shakspearian identity of impression on the reader's mind. Lamberto is a fine type of the youth of Tuscany; Troilo, of Italian duplicity; and Bindo, of a younger son, beloved and brave; while the struggle between monastic and martial impulses, so characteristic of the epoch, is vividly depicted in Fanfulla. Selvaggia is, also, a representative, both in her wild career and her genuine penitence, of a species native to the soil.

As Ruskin studied the architecture of Venice to fix dates and analyze combinations, D'Azeglio appears to have scrutinized the art, literature, and monuments, of Florence, to gather the varied and legitimate elements which compose this work. He catches the voice of faction, and prolongs its echo; he paints the edifice until it stands visibly before the imagination or the memory. He reveals the mood of the patriot and the lover, so that we share its deep emotion, and leads us, as it were, through the streets of the besieged city, to the bedside of the tender maiden and the vigil of the anxious citizen, till the objects and spirit of the age and people become, through sympathy and observation, like conscious realities. Among the incidental merits of this work may also be reckoned its philosophic insight, exhibited not only in a fine study of the laws of character, but in the influence of political opinion upon domestic life, the conflict between patriotic and personal sentiment, the local agency of institutions, and the mutual relation of military and religious enthusiasm. Nor can we fail to perceive, throughout, the singular advantages enjoyed by the historical novelist in Italy, finding in her works of art, her temples, palaces, and libraries, the most significant, and, at the same time, authentic hints and glimpses of the life of the past. Many exquisite touches of picturesque or suggestive limning, such as mark the patient explorer and the observant artist, occur in "Niccolò de Lapi." But if to these characteristics the work owes much of its immediate popularity, and not a little of its intrinsic interest, the standard literary value attached to it is, in no small degree, derived from the style. The language of D'Azeglio is terse, flowing, and appropriate. He writes in a calm though fervent spirit; his tone is chastened and intense;

and he uses words with a keen sense of their meaning and delicate adaptation. He has drawn a picture of the age, not only alive with moral sentiment and warmed by patriotic emotion, but so managed as to excite profound respect as well as earnest sympathy; to blend in harmonious contrast the office of historian and poet.

Indeed, D'Azeglio's great distinction is a certain moderation, judgment, and rational view of the prospects and needs of his country, rarely found in unison with so much zeal and genius. He early manifested this trait in habits of study and investigation, and has since and always been true to himself in this regard as a man of action. It is on account of his excellent sense, logical power, and reverence for truth, that he has so eminently succeeded both as an artist and a statesman. No better proof of his superiority to the mass of revolutionists can be desired, than the sentiments and arguments of his well-known political essay induced by the occurrences in Romagna in the autumn of 1845. He there states, without the least fanaticism or exaggeration, the real state of the case, and points out clearly and justly the reforms necessary in the Pontifical States. He rebukes all premature and ill-considered measures on the part of the oppressed people, as only calculated to postpone their enfranchisement and prejudice their cause. He wisely advocates gradual enlightenment, and eloquently describes the fatal consequences of rash and ignorant movements.

He gives a plain and authentic statement of facts to show the utter impolicy, as well as inhumanity, of secret prosecutions, of resort to foreign arms, base espionage, a contraband system, censorship, and an inconsistent and unreliable code, and all the other flagrant evils of papal sway; and while thus effectively reproaching the government, he is equally indignant and impartial in his condemnation of reckless agitators and precipitate heroes, who not only vainly sacrifice themselves, but bring into fatal disrepute more judicious patriots. D'Azeglio comprehends the inevitable agency of public sentiment as a means of national redemption. He understands the Italian character, and points out the difference between animal and civic courage. He thinks fools as dangerous as knaves to the cause of freedom; shows the need of political education; pleads for a due regard to time, opportunity, and means, in order to secure permanent advantage; and declares that the great lesson his countrymen have to learn is to avoid the two extremes of reckless despair and inert resignation, to improve, to hope, to prepare the way, and thus gain moral vigor, the world's respect, and God's favor; and, while he demonstrates the injustice of the Papal government, he would not have its victims imitate the madman, who, in flying from an insect, ran over a precipice.

He gives instances, on the one hand, of the decadence of the towns of Romagna in consequence of misrule, and, on the other, of the concessions of despotic governments to the consistent and enlightened appeal of their subjects. In his strict justice, he even praises Austria for her administration of law, compared with the Roman tyranny, that makes the judge and accuser one; and selects from his own state an example of treachery with which to contrast the self-devotion of those who fought at Barletta. This able pamphlet, entitled, "Ultimi Casi di Romagna," is one of the most candid and thoughtful expositions of actual political evils, and the only available means of overcoming them, which a native writer has produced. No one can read it without sympathy for the oppressed, indignation against the government, and respect for the reasoning of D'Azeglio. It is not less intelligible than philosophic; and subsequent events have amply proved the soundness of its arguments and the correctness of its inferences.

If, in view of the many abortive revolutions, the want of unity, the influence of Jesuitism, the interference of France and Austria, and all the other antagonistic conditions that environ the intelligent votaries of Italian independence and nationality, we seek a clue by which to thread the dark labyrinth of her misfortunes, and find a way into the light of freedom and progress, what rational plan or ground of hope suggests itself? Only, as it seems to us, the practical adoption in some section of the land of those political and social reforms which, once realized, will inevitably spread; the successful experiment in a limited sphere, which, by the force of example and moral laws, will gradually extend. Let the capacity for self-government, the advantages of liberal institutions, be demonstrated in one state, and they cannot fail to penetrate the whole nation. A few years since, Rome seemed the destined nucleus for such a change, and subsequently

30*

Tuscany; but the bigotry of ecclesiastical power in the one, and the grasp of Austrian power in the other, soon led to a fatal reäction. The course of events and the facts of to-day now indisputably designate Sardinia as the region whence the light is to emanate. Favored, as we have seen, by the character of her people, her local position, and the traits of her past history, the very disaster that checked her army has tended to concentrate and develop the spirit of the age and the elements of constitutional liberty within her borders. The loss of the battle of Novara, and the abdication of Charles Albert, though apparently great misfortunes, have resulted in signal benefits. After securing peace from their adversaries chiefly by a pecuniary sacrifice, the king and citizens of Piedmont turned their energies towards internal reform with a wisdom and good faith which are rapidly yielding legitimate fruit.

Public schools were instituted, the press made free, the Waldenses allowed to quit their valleys, build churches, and elect representatives, the privileges of the clergy abolished, and the two bishops who ventured to oppose the authority of the state, tried, condemned, and banished, the Pope's interference repudiated, the right of suffrage instituted, railroads from Turin to Genoa and from Alessandria to Lago Maggiore constructed, the electric telegraph introduced, liberal commercial treaties formed, docks built, and cheap postal laws enacted. In a word, the great evils that have so long weighed down the people of the Italian peninsula — unlimited monarchical power, aristocratic and clerical immunities derived from the Middle Ages, the censorship of the press, the espionage of the police, and intolerance of all but the Catholic religion — in a great measure, no longer exist in Sardinia. Regarding the constitution of Charles Albert as a sacred legacy, his son and people resolved to uphold and carry out its principles; and they have done so, with scarcely any violence or civil discord. Accordingly, an example is now before the Italians, and within their observation and sympathy, of a free, progressive, and enlightened government; and this one fact is pregnant with hope for the entire nation. Only fanatics and shallow adventurers behold the signs of promise without grateful emotion. The wise and true friends of Italy, at home and abroad, welcome the daily proofs of a new era for that unhappy land afforded by the prosperity and freedom now enjoyed in Piedmont.

It would be manifestly unjust to ascribe all these propitious changes to the personal influence of D'Azeglio; but he deserves the credit of projecting and successfully advocating many of the most effective ameliorations, and of having been the consistent and recognized expositor of the liberal policy of the state. The accession of Pius IX. was greeted by him with all the delight the hopeful dawn of his career naturally inspired among the Italian patriots. He published a letter full of applause and encouragement, and had a long and satisfactory interview with the new Pope; and when the bitter disappointment ensued, he carried out, in his official capacity, the sentiments he professed, and to which Pius IX. was shamelessly recreant. Like Henry Martyn, in England, he proposed the emancipation of the Jews in Piedmont, and his philanthropy is manifested in the establishment of public baths and fires for the poor. He took a bold and decided stand against the Pope, and originated the treaty with England. In his address to the Sardinian parliament, on the 12th of February, 1852, he expresses the noblest sentiments and principles, in language of simple and earnest vigor; repudiating what are called reasons of state, maintaining that the same morality is applicable to governments and individuals, that integrity has taken the place of astuteness, that good sense and good faith are all that the true statesman requires to guide him, and that the press and facility of intercourse which enable Turin, Moscow, and Edinburgh, to feel simultaneously the force of public opinion, have emancipated rulers from the narrow resource of subtlety, and induced among all enlightened governments reliance on the absolute power of truth and fidelity. He attributes, in this masterly discourse, the peaceful achievement of so much permanent good in the state, to the virtue of the people, the prudence of the legislature, and the loyalty of the king.

How long Sardinia will be permitted to carry on within her own limits the progressive system, that now so happily distinguishes her from the other continental governments, is extremely doubtful. The asylum she gives to political refugees, the unpleasant truths her free press announces, and the operation of her free-trade principles, occasion the greatest annoyance to Austria, and excite the sympathetic desires of less-favored states. She has incurred the permanent enmity of the Papal see by suppressing the monasteries and sheltering Protestants; and Count Cavour's plea to the allied Congress for the people of Rome and Naples, only riveted the bonds of despotic sympathy between their cruel and bigoted rulers. It is scarcely to be expected that interference of a more active kind than has yet taken place will not be attempted. Meantime, however, it is but just to recognize the noble example she has set of an enlightened self-government, and to award the highest praise to the generous and judicious statesman at the head of her policy. It will prove a remarkable coïncidence if the enterprise recently broached in New York, of a line of steamers between that city and Genoa, is realized; thus uniting by frequent intercourse the commercial emporium of the New World with the birthplace of her discoverer, and opening a direct and permanent communication between the greatest republic of the earth and the one state of Italy which has proved herself sufficiently intelligent, moral, and heroic, to reform peacefully an oppressive heritage of political and social evils.

The efficacy of D'Azeglio's patriotic zeal is, as we have endeavored to show, derived from his knowledge and judgment. Years of exile have not caused him to lose sight of the actual exigencies of the country. Having lived alternately at Turin, Florence, Genoa, Milan, Lucca, and Rome, and visited all parts of the peninsula, he is quite familiar with the condition of the people of the respective states, the special local evils of each administration, and the available resources of the nation. Thoroughly versed in the art, literature, and history of Italy, enjoying the intimacy and confidence of her leading spirits, and practically acquainted with diplomatic life, his views are not random speculations, but well-considered opinions, his aims distinct and progressive, and the spirit in which he works that of a philosopher. The beautiful emanations of his study and genius have awakened, far and wide, the pride and affection of his countrymen. In 1845 he commenced, in the "Antologia Italiana," a new romance, founded on the Lombard league, which the cessation of that journal and the claims of official life have obliged him to suspend. In 1848 he fought in Lombardy; and early in the succeeding year an unostentatious but select and cordial banquet was given him in Rome by his admirers and friends, to congratulate one another on the new hopes of Italian regeneration which events then justified. Of late he has retired from the cares of office and the pursuit of literature, to devote himself, with eminent success, to his original vocation — historical painting.

Through all the chances and changes of the times, the noble author, and statesman, and artist, has serenely maintained his faith and wisely dedicated his mind to his country, emphatically giving utterance to truth and reason, both to fanatical patriots and despotic rulers; to the one demonstrating the inutility of spasmodic efforts, of guerillas, of inadequate resistance and inopportune action; and to the other calmly proving the absolute folly, as well as wickedness, of a total disregard of the spirit of the age and the claims of humanity. The present condition and prospects of his native state justify his arguments and realize his dearest hopes; and it is her peculiar glory to have had at the head of her administration not only a liberal and wise statesman, but one of the most gifted and patriotic of her own sons.

THE GENIAL CHURCHMAN.

SYDNEY SMITH.

THE memoirs and correspondence of a man who, for twenty years, was prominent in London society, and pointed out to strangers as eminently noteworthy, must give a desirable insight not only into his personal gifts and character, but into the tendencies and the traits of the circle in which he held so conspicuous a place. In both regards the volumes edited by his daughter justify the anticipation they excite. Here we see portrayed, without exaggeration, the best side of the Churchman, — one of the highest places open to clerical ambition in England, — its lustre enhanced by intelligence, its exclusiveness redeemed by geniality, and its validity vindicated by uprightness and public spirit. We recognize the influence and the happiness that may be attained by a kindly, conscientious, fearless, candid dignitary of the Establishment, whose nature is leavened by a rich and persuasive humor, whereby his office, conversation, letters, and presence, are lifted from technicality and routine into vital relations with his fellow-beings and the time. Pleasant and suggestive is the record, full of amenity, and bright, cheerful traits. It is refreshing to meet with so much life, so much liberality, so much humane sentiment, where the conventional and the obsolete so often overlay and formalize mind and manner. Yet there is a distinct limit to this satisfaction. The vantage-ground which ecclesiastical *prestige* gave to Sydney Smith, his talents and agreeability confirmed; but his sympathies, with all their free play, had a conservative rebound. Those who would derive a complete idea of the modern English development from these memorials, err. He moved in a circle of the most active, but not of the highest intellectual range. We should never discover from this chronicle that Coleridge also talked, Carlyle reasoned, Lamb jested, Hazlitt criticized, and Shelley and Keats sang, in those days. Within the sensible zone of English life, as that term is usually understood, Sydney lived. He often ignored what was boldly original and radically independent. His scope was ever within the Whig ranks in politics and the Established Church pale in religion. What could be beheld and experienced therein, we see, but much that excites admiration without, is unrevealed. The iron horizon of caste is the framework of this attractive picture. The charm it offers is the manliness which a true soul, thus environed, exhibits. To us transatlantic lovers of his rare humor, it is the man rather than the priest, the companion rather than the prodigy, that wins attention.

We have seen, again and again, genius utterly perverted by self-love, usefulness marred by fanaticism, wit poisoned by malevolence, health shattered, existence abridged, vanity pampered, confidence destroyed, by the erratic, unprincipled, weak use of intellectual gifts. This tragic result is the staple of literary biography, so that prudent souls have blessed the fate which consigned them to harmless mediocrity. The rare and sweet exceptions to so general a rule are therefore full of satisfaction and redolent of hope. In the case of Sydney Smith we witness the delightful spectacle of a mind that bravely regulates the life which it cheers and adorns. Humor was the efflorescence of his intellect, the play that gave him strength for labor, the cordial held by a kindly hand to every brother's lips, the sunshine of home, the flavor of human intercourse, the music to which he marched in duty's rugged path. By virtue of this magic quality, he redeemed the daily meal from heaviness, the needful journey from fatigue, narrow circumstances from depression, and prosperity from materialism. He illustrated simultaneously the power of content and the beauty of holiness. Did Portland stone, instead of marble, frame his hearth? Innocent mirth and a clear blaze made those around it oblivious of the defect. Must a paper border take the place of a cornice? Laughing echoes hung the room with more than arabesque ornament. Were the walls destitute of precious limning? He knew how to glorify them with sunshine. Did he lack costly furniture? Children and roses atoned for the want. Was he compelled to entertain his guest with rustic fare? He found compensation in the materials thus furnished for a comic sketch. Did the canine race interfere with his comfort? He banished them by a mock report of law damages. Was his steed ugly, slow, and prone to throw his rider? He named him "Calamity" or "Peter the Cruel," and drew a farce from their joint mishaps. Was his coach lumbering and ancient? Its repairs were forever suggestive of quaint fancies. Was a herd of deer beyond his means? He fastened antlers on donkeys, and drew tears of laughter from aristocratic eyes. Did the evergreens look dim at Christmas? He tied oranges on their boughs and dreamed of tropical landscapes. Was a lady too fine? He discovered a "porcelain understanding." Was a friend too voluble? He enjoyed his "flashes of silence." Were oil and spermaceti beyond his means? He illuminated the house with mutton lamps of his own invention. A fat woman, a hot day, a radical, a heavy sermonizer, a dandy, a stupid Yorkshire peasant, — people and things that in others would only excite annoyance, — he turned instinctively to the account of wit. His household at Foston is a picture worthy of Dickens. Bunch, Annie Kay, Molly Miles, — heraldry, old pictures, and china, — in his atmosphere became original characters and bits of Flemish still-life, which might set up a novelist. He turned a bay-window into a hive of bright thoughts, and a random walk into a chapter of philosophy. To domestic animals, humble parishioners, rustic *employés*, to the oppressed, the erring, the sick, the market-woman, and the poacher, he extended as ready and intelligent a sympathy as to the nobleman and the scholar. He was more thankful for animal spirits and good companionship than for reputation and preferment. He reverenced material laws not less than the triumphs of intellect; esteemed Poor Richard's maxims as well as Macaulay's rhetoric; thought self-reproach the greatest evil, and occupation the chief moral necessity of existence. He believed in talking nonsense, while he exercised the most vigorous powers of reasoning. He gave no quarter to cant, and, at the same time, bought a parrot to keep his servants in good humor. If warned by "excellent and feeble people" against an individual, he sought his acquaintance. His casual *bon-mots* wreathed the town with smiles, and his faithful circumspection irritated the officials at St. Paul's. He wielded a battle-axe in the phalanx of reform, and scattered flowers around his family altar. He wakened the sinner's heart to penitence, and irradiated prandial monotony; educated children, and shared the counsels of statesmen; turned from literary correspondence to dry an infant's tears, and cheered a pauper's death-bed with as true a heart as he graced a peer's drawing-room. It is the human, catholic range and variety of such a nature and such a life, that raises Sydney Smith from the renown of a clever author and a brilliant wit to the nobler fame of a Christian man.

In his biography we have another signal instance of the effect of blood in determining character. The Gallic element permeated Sydney's Anglo-Saxon nature; and in him it was the vivacity of Languedoc that quickened the solemn banquets of the Thames. By instinct, no less than from principle, he encouraged cheerfulness. He thoroughly appreciated the relation of mind and body, and sought, by exercise, gay talk, and beneficent intercourse, while he avoided self-reproach and systematized business, to lessen the cares and to multiply the pleasures of daily life. The minor felicities were in his view as much a part of human nature as the power of reasoning and the capacity of usefulness. In his endeavor to make the most of life as a means of enjoyment, he was thoroughly French; in loyalty to its stern requirements and high objects, he was no less completely English. In practical wisdom he resembled Dr. Franklin; in the genuine benignity of his spirit, Bishop Berkeley; and in the power of colloquial adaptation, Burke. He sublimated Poor Richard's prudence by tact and wit; and called himself an "amalgam," from the facility with which his genial tone fused the discordant or reserved social elements around him. "Some sulk," he observes, "in a stage; I always talk." He was no abstract scholar or isolated sage, but read and wrote in the midst of his family, undisturbed by children, servants, or visitors. His idea of life and duty was eminently social; and in this also we recognize the influence of his French descent. The names of friends, acquaintances, and correspondents, in these volumes, include a remarkable variety of illustrious characters: first, the famous Edinburgh *coterie* — Playfair, Stewart, Brougham, Scott, Alison, Jeffrey, Horner, and their associates; then the authors and statesmen he knew so intimately in London, such as Lord Holland, Lord Grey, Mackintosh, Rogers, and Moore; then his Continental friends, Madame de Staël, Pozzo di Borgo, Talleyrand, the King of Belgium, and many more; besides the domestic and clerical associates incident to his position and family connections. Imagine a good, cheerful, wise, and endeared man, for thirty years, mingling in such spheres, dispensing words of cheer and humor, yet always in earnest as a divine, and always faithful as a reformer, and you have a picture of intellectual usefulness and enjoyment, of a healthy, active mind, which suggests a living worth but inadequately described in these volumes. Scotchmen and Quakers have been staple themes with the English wits for a century; Dr. Johnson and Charles Lamb were memorably comical about them; and Sydney Smith continued the merry warfare with credit. In each of the coteries represented by these idols of society, we find that the "mutual admiration" principle, so natural to special fraternities, holds sway. Johnson over-estimated, while he browbeat, his literary *confrères;* Lamb betrays a childlike devotion to Coleridge and his disciples; and Sydney Smith praises Jeffrey's articles, Horner's character, and Mackintosh's talk, with like partiality. This is but the instinct of the love and honor drawn out by intimate association; but such verdicts, in a critical point of view, are to be taken with due allowance, — not so much in regard to the merits of the individuals thus warmly regarded, as of contemporaries not belonging to the same clique, yet, in an intellectual aspect, having equal and often superior claims upon the lover of genius and worth.

As a representative man, Sydney Smith was more endeared for his liberal, frank, and mirthful nature, than for its refinements. He lacked that profound sense of beauty, and that patient love of art, which constitute poetical feeling. He felt no interest in Wordsworth, thought Madame de Sévigné's letters beneath their reputation, and declared himself satisfied with ten minutes of Talma's acting, and fifteen of observation at the Louvre. His passion for roses seems to have been rather a keen sense of their vital freshness, than a delicate perception of their beauty. They were precious in his sight chiefly as emblems of the spontaneous grace of nature. He delighted in transitions both of scene and of employment. He read with great rapidity, skimming, with hasty glances, the cream of literature. He had the ingenuous want of artificial elegance so often noticed as characteristic of manly genius. "Sydney," said one of his friends, "your sense, wit, and clumsiness, always give me the idea of an Athenian carter."

The combination "most devoutly to be wished" is an alert mind and an easy temperament; but the two are seldom found together. Quickness of conception and aptness of fancy are often embodied in a mercurial frame; and the nervous and sanguine quality of the body is a constant strain upon vital force, and tends to produce the irritability of a morbid or the grave errors of an animal enthusiasm. Hence the most famous wits have seldom proved equally satisfactory as intimate companions and judicious allies in a serious enterprise. Imprudence, impulse, and extreme sensitiveness, thus united to uncommon gifts of mind, are liable to make the latter more of a bane than a blessing; while the same endowments, blended with a happy organization, are the prolific source of active usefulness and rational delight. Seldom have these results been more perfectly exhibited than in Sydney Smith — a pioneer of national reforms without acrimony or fanaticism; prompt to "set the table in a roar," yet never losing self-respect, or neglecting the essential duties of life; capable of the keenest satire, yet instinctively considerate of the feelings of others; familiar with the extremes of fortune, yet unhardened by poverty and unspoiled by success; the choicest of boon companions, yet the most impressive of clergymen; the admired guest, and the recipient of permanent and elegant hospitality, yet contented in domestic retirement; born to grace society, and, at the same time, the idol of home; feasted and honored in the highest degree, yet true to his own axiom, that the secret of felicity is to "make the day happy to, at least, one fellow-creature;" with a deep-seated "disgust at hypocrisy," while recognized as the bravest advocate of Christian charity in the church; impatient to the last degree of the irksome and commonplace, yet unwearied in his endeavor to assimilate the discordant and to enliven the dull. In him, the soul and the body, the family and the fête, labor and pastime, criticism and hilarity, wit and wisdom, virtue and intelligence, priesthood and manhood, the pen and the life, the friend and the disputant, the mysteries of faith and the actualities of experience, "worked together for good."

Though comprehensive and facile as an intellectual man, he had the insular stamp, — the honest alloy of British prejudice, — frankly confessing that he thought no organized form of Christianity worthy to be compared with the Establishment, no beauty or genius equal to that which the best London circle includes, no physical comfort like a good fire, no restorative like a walk, and no talkers superior to Mackintosh, Macaulay, and the rest of his own coterie. His praise of good edibles and well-written books, his thorough honesty, his manly self-assertion, his want of sympathy with foreign associations, his keen appreciation of dinner, tea, argument, and home, mark the genuine Angloman. Yet he had a clearer sense than most of his countrymen of native peculiarities. "Have you observed," he asks, "that nothing can be done in England without a dinner?" And elsewhere he observes, "Mr. John Bull disdains to talk, as that respected individual has nothing to say." With the courage of his race he "passed his life in minorities," and, on principle, fought off the spleen. "Never give way to melancholy," he writes to a friend; "resist it steadily, for the habit will encroach."

His love of knowledge was strong and habitual; and he sought it, with avidity, in social intercourse, observation, and books, reproducing what he gleaned with ease and acuteness. His style partakes of the directness of his whole nature; he goes at once to his subject, whether the exposition of religious truth, a definition in moral philosophy, a business epistle, or "a word spoken in season." Without circumlocution, and with the prompt brevity of a man of action, the thing to be expressed is given out, interrupted only by some merry jest or humorous turn of thought — never by an elaborate or discursive episode. His letters are singularly brief and to the point; they indicate character by their kindly spirit and quaint vein, frank opinions, and excellent sense, but are valuable rather as glimpses of his manner of living and thinking, of his associations and objects, than as a complete illustration of the man. There is a marked individuality in the most casual note. He does not write with the rhetorical finish of Macaulay, the quaint introversions of Carlyle, the voluble knowledge of De Quincey, the smart ebullitions of Jeffrey, or the classic elegance of Landor; but he writes like an honest, sensible, prosperous, affectionate, witty Englishman, whose views, tastes, and principles, are fixed, and who desires, without waste of time or words, to meet every duty and every pleasure in an intelligent, self-sustained, and generous mood. The clerical and literary, the political and culinary, the friendly and professional interests of his life, come out in singular juxtaposition through his correspondence. Now it is a state question, and now the receipt for dressing a salad; one day, to acknowledge a present of game, and another, to criticize a new number of the Edinburgh; this letter describes a dinner-party, and that a plan for church organization; one proposes an article, and another chronicles a tour; the whole conveying a vivid idea of a most busy, social, amicable, cheerful existence. After dwelling on the entire picture, we can readily believe, with his little daughter, that "a family does n't prosper without a papa who makes all gay by his own mirth;" and that a dinner without him appeared to his bereaved wife unutterably solemn. He declares that a play never amused him; neither would it half the world, if there were more Sydneys in social life, to make every day's talk "as good as a play." He speaks of the "invincible candor of his nature," and this trait is the crystal medium through which we so thoroughly recognize him.

Notwithstanding the deserved rebuke he administered to our national delinquency in his American letters, he vindicates his claim to the title of Philo-Yankeeist. No British writer has better appreciated the institutions and destiny of the United States. He recognized cordially the latent force of Webster, the noble eloquence of Channing, and the refined scholarship of Everett.

"I will disinherit you," he playfully writes to a fair correspondent, "if you do not admire everything written by Franklin."

Perhaps the choicest lesson of his life is his practical cheerfulness. He was no willing polemic, but delighted in "peaceable bigotry." One is constantly lured, by this memoir, to speculate on the relation of humor to sensibility and caution; for its subject was as prudent and methodical in affairs as he was vagrant and lawless in fancy, and as keenly alive to sympathy and care for others as to comfort, society, and fun. "I have," he says, "a propensity to amuse myself with trifles." "The wretchedness of human life is only to be encountered on the basis of beef and wine." And, elsewhere, "If, with a pleasant wife, three children, a good house and farm, many books, and many friends who wish me well, I cannot be happy, I am a very silly, foolish fellow, and what becomes of me is of very little consequence." This disposition was not merely a background in the landscape; it made him a light-hearted, though none the less earnest worker. The sermon inculcating the deepest truth, the essay demolishing a time-hallowed error, the plea for some victim of oppression or indigence, the letter designed to counsel or cheer, the speech in behalf of civil reform, in fine, the entire intellectual activity of the man, was unalloyed by discontent and bitterness. He could wrestle with wrong, and smile; he could attack without losing his temper; he could sow the pregnant seeds of melioration, and, at the same time, scatter flowers of wit along the rugged furrows. Swift fought as bravely, but he lacked the *bonhommie* of Sydney to make the battle gay and chivalrous. Sterne diverted, with like ease, a festal board; but he wanted the consistent manhood of Peter Plymley to preserve the dignity of his office in the midst of pastime.

Literature has gradually merged the courageous in the artistic element. Style, instead of being the vehicle of moral warfare and practical truth, has degenerated into an ingenious means of aimless effect. To elaborate a borrowed or flimsy idea, to exaggerate a limited and unimportant experience, and to minister exclusively to the sense of amusement, have become the primal objects of popular writers. They have, in numerous instances, ignored the relation of thought to action, of integrity to expression, and of truth to eloquence. They have dreamed, dallied, coquetted on paper exactly as the butterflies of life do in society, giving no impression of individuality or earnestness. To divert a vacant hour, to beguile, flatter, puzzle, and relieve the ennui of thoughtless minds, appears the height of their ambition. The conventional, the lighter graces, the egotistic inanities of self-love, so predominate, that we gain no fresh impulse, receive no mental *stimuli*, behold no veil of error rent, and no vista of truth opened as we read. The man of letters is often, to our consciousness, not a prophet, an oracle, a hero, but a juggler, a pet, or, at best, a graceful toy. We realize the old prejudice, that to write for the public amusement is a vocation based on unmanly pliancy — a mercenary pursuit which inevitably conflicts with self-respect, deals in gossip, and trenches on the dignity of social refinement. Personal contact not seldom destroys whatever illusion taste may have created. We find an evasive habit of mind, an effeminate care of reputation, a fear of self-compromise, a dearth of original, frank, genial utterance. Our ideal author proves a mere *dilettante*, says pretty things as if committed to memory for the occasion, picks ingenious flaws to indicate superior discernment, interlards his talk with quotations, is all things to all men, and especially to all women, makes himself generally agreeable by a system of artificial conformity, and leaves us unrefreshed by a single glimpse of character or one heartfelt utterance. We strive to recognize the thinker and the poet, but discover only the man of taste, the man of the world, the fop, or the epicure; and we gladly turn from him to a fact of nature, to a noble tree, or a sunset cloud, to the genuine in humanity,— a fair child, an honest mechanic, true-hearted woman, or old soldier,— because in such there is not promise without performance, the sign without the thing, the name without the soul.

It is from the salient contrast with these familiar phases of authorship that the very idea of such a man as Sydney Smith redeems the calling. In him, first of all and beyond all, is manhood, which no skill in pen-craft, no blandishment of fame or love of pleasure, was suffered to overlay for a moment. To be a man in courage, generosity, stern faith to every domestic and professional claim, in the fear of God and the love of his kind, in loyalty to personal conviction, bold speech, candid life, and good fellowship,—this was the vital necessity, the normal condition, of his nature. Thus consecrated, he found life a noble task and a happy experience, and would have found it so without any Edinburgh Review, Cathedral of St. Paul's, or dinners at Holland House; although, when the scope and felicities they brought to him came,—legitimate results of his endowments and needs,—they were, in his faithful hands and wise appreciation, the authentic means of increased usefulness, honor, and delight, and chiefly so because he was so disciplined and enriched, by circumstances and by natural gifts, as to be virtually independent, self-sustained, and capable of deriving mental luxury, philosophic content, and religious sanction, from whatever lot and duty had fallen to his share. Herein lie the significance of his example and the value of his principles. Like pious and brave old Herbert, he found a kingdom in his mind which he knew how to rule and to enjoy; and this priceless boon was his triumph and comfort in the lowliest struggles and in the highest prosperity. It irradiated the damp walls of his first parsonage with the glow of wit; nerved his heart, as a poor vicar, to plead the cause of reform against the banded conservatives of a realm; hinted a thousand expedients to beguile isolation and indigence of their gloom; invested his presence and speech with self-possession and authority in the peasant's hut and at the bishop's table; made him an architect, a physician, a judge, a schoolmaster, a critic, a reformer, the choicest man of society, the most efficient of domestic economists, the best of correspondents, the most practical of political writers, the most impressive of preachers, the most genial of companions, a good farmer, a patient nurse, and an admirable husband, father, and friend. The integrity, good sense, and moral energy, which gave birth to this versatile exercise of his faculties, constitute the broad and solid foundation of Sydney Smith's character; they were the essential traits of the man, the base to that noble column of which wit formed the capital and wisdom the shaft. In the temple of humanity what support it yielded during his life, and how well-proportioned and complete it now stands to the eye of memory, an unbroken and sky-pointing cenotaph on his honored grave!

THE SUPERNATURALIST.

CHARLES BROCKDEN BROWN.

THE memoirs of distinguished men suggest to the philosopher the idea of a natural history of the human mind; so like the laws of instinct is the process of development in each species of character. The influence of climate, education, and political and social institutions, do not apparently modify the essential identity of genius. There is always a certain similarity in its experience, and a moral verisimilitude in its life; and the imprisoned poet of Ferrara, the domesticated bard of Olney, and the solitary cultivator of imaginative literature in America, as they are revealed to us in their familiar letters, and the anecdotes preserved of their habits and feelings, are distinguished by the same general characteristics. Thus, with each, life began in vague but ardent dreams, intensity of personal consciousness, and indications of ability which induced those in authority to assign them the law as a career; in each case, their gentle and earnest spirits revolted from its technical drudgery and tergiversation. They alike were beset by Giant Despair in the form of bitter self-distrust and profound melancholy; and equally owed their temporary emancipation to mental activity and the indulgence of the affections. Love and fame contended for the empire of their hearts, and finally achieved a kind of mutual victory, and established a holy truce. Their difference in renown is indeed great, but aspiration, insight, and the love of beauty, dwelt in each of their souls, and found unequal but powerful expression. The contest with fortune, the unswerving assertion of individuality of purpose, the life of the mind and the loyalty of the heart, distinguish these widely-severed beings, as they do the nobility of nature in all times and places.

It is an affecting reminiscence to look back half a century upon the enthusiastic American litterateur, delving at his self-imposed tasks alone, in the midst of a community absorbed in the pursuit of material well-being; throwing off his books with scarcely a breath of popularity to cheer his labor, and finding in the vocation for which his mind was adapted a satisfaction that required not the spur of laudation to prompt habits of industry. We perceive in his writings germs, which, under more cherishing influences, would have expanded into glorious fruits, scintillations of an eclipsed dawn, breathings of a premature spring, the pledge and the promise, as well as the partial realization, of original intellectual achievement.

Charles Brockden Brown was the first American who manifested a decided literary genius in a form which has survived with anything like vital interest. His native fondness and capacity for literature is not only shown by his voluntary adoption of its pursuit at a time and in a country offering no inducement to such a career, but they are still more evident from the unpropitious social circumstances and local influences amid which he was born and bred. He was the son of a member of the Society of Friends in Philadelphia — a class distinguished, indeed, for moral worth, but equally remarkable for the absence of a sense of the beautiful, and a repudiation of the graces of life and the inspiration of sentiment, except that of a strictly religious kind.

It is obvious that Brockden Brown could have found little that was favorable to literary aspirations in his early years. Calm, prescriptive, and monotonous, was the environment of his infancy, except that it richly yielded the gentle and sweet ministries of domestic ties and youthful companionship. Sustained by these, he seems to have fallen back upon his individuality with the singleness of purpose characteristic of genius. He was a devoted student; and mental application soon made inroads upon his delicate constitution. By the counsel of his teacher, he acquired the habit of making long pedestrian excursions; and in alternating between books and walks his youth was passed. His ramblings, however, were usually without a companion; and thus, in the solitude of nature, he was led to commune deeply with his own heart, indulge in fanciful reveries, and accustom himself to watch the action of the outward world upon his consciousness. He also became, from the same causes, abstracted in his habits of mind; and when the exigencies of practical life roused him from tasteful studies and romantic dreams to grapple with the perplexities and arid details of the law, he recoiled from the profession with the ardent feelings of a youth accustomed only to the agreeable fields of literature. He, however, persevered, and found consolation in the rhetorical exercises of a debating club, and those branches of the study, commenced at sixteen, that gave scope to his ingenuity and philosophical taste. To the disappointment of his friends, however, when admitted to the bar, he abandoned the idea of practice in disgust. Conscious, perhaps, of inconsistency and waywardness, yet tenacious of his obligation to follow the instinctive direction of his mind, the inactivity and hopeless prospect incident to such an entire change in his plan of life occasioned, for a while, the most painful depression of spirits.

Both his talents and sensibilities demanded a sphere, and their unemployed energy preyed upon his health and conscience. He sought relief in change of scene, and visited many parts of his own and the neighboring states. Under a calm exterior and an apparent indifference of mood, he at this time suffered the most acute and despairing chagrin. His kindred and companions disapproved of his course, and vainly remonstrated with him; and thus he not only failed to please those he loved, but was thoroughly dissatisfied with himself. In 1793 he visited New York, in order to unite with two fellow-students, between whom and himself there existed a strong attachment. With them he formed a pleasant home; and soon joined the Friendly Club, of which Dunlap, Dr. Mitchell, Bleecker, Kent, and other choice spirits of the metropolis, were active members. In their society his literary tastes revived, and his mental energies expanded. Sympathy quickened his confidence in his own resources, and he regained his cheerfulness and activity of spirit.

"Wieland" was published in 1798. It was the first work in

the department of imaginative literature of native origin, possessing indisputable tokens of genius, which appeared in the United States. Its author died on the twenty-second of February, 1810, having just completed his thirty-ninth year. His subsequent fictions were unequal both to each other and to the first; but all contain traits of reflective power and invention that enlist the sympathies of the intellectual reader. They constitute, however, but a modicum of his literary labor. When he commenced authorship the discussions incident to the French Revolution were rife; and his active mind soon became excited on the subject of politics and social philosophy. His first published work — if we except occasional contributions to periodicals — was a Dialogue on the Rights of Woman, said to have been unsuccessful, though ingenious; then followed the Memoirs of Carwin — the basis of his fictitious compositions and fame in that branch; but in the mean time, throughout his brief career, he was incessantly engaged in some kind of literary toil; editing the old American Monthly, the first American Review, the original Literary Magazine, and the American Register; compiling an elaborate geography; preparing architectural drawings; investigating various subjects; corresponding, translating Volney's work on the United States, and writing a series of political pamphlets. Although many of the questions thus treated have lost their significance and interest, the knowledge, logic, good sense, and general ability, manifest in the political writings of Brockden Brown, are thought by some, not incompetent judges, to be as remarkable, in view of the period and circumstances, as his novels. It is certain that the two exhibit a rare combination of practical and imaginative capacity; and evince a mind disciplined and prolific as well as versatile. He could reason comprehensively and acutely on affairs as well as on emotion; and discuss the interests of commerce and government with as clear and full intelligence as the mysteries of love, remorse, and superstition. But it requires the consummate literary art of a Burke and a Godwin to preserve the carelessly-strewn jewels of such a mind in enduring caskets.

So deficient, indeed, in constructive design and unity of purpose, are his writings, that, with the exception of his essays and other argumentative papers, they resemble the sketches that litter an artist's studio more than elaborate and finished works. His fictions might aptly be designated as studies in Romance. He left many fragmentary narratives, scenes and dialogues — some founded upon history, some upon observation, and others apparently the result of an inventive mood. At one time he had no less than five novels commenced, sketched out, or partially written. Architecture, geography, politics, and belles lettres, by turns, occupied his attention.

There is often in his letters a curious detail; and he possessed the art of making the recital of trifles interesting; while the logician and grave practical thinker, as well as the sincere and ardent patriot, are revealed by his spirited treatment of public questions. "Wieland" was the most powerful story that had appeared in the country; and the American Register, projected and commenced by Brown, was the most useful and appropriate literary undertaking of its day. Like most gifted men, he won and retained affections with ease; he was the idol of the domestic circle, and loyal as well as magnanimous in friendship; he stood manfully by his comrades during the fearful ravages of the yellow fever; and his letters, while they aim to elicit the inmost experience and outward fortunes of those he loves, are remarkably self-forgetful. He lived wholly in his mind and affections; from a child devoted to books and maps, and, as a man, congratulating himself upon that fragility of body that destined him to meditative pursuits. Reading, clubs, pedestrianism, journalizing, and earnest reflection, were the means of his culture and development. Like the author of the "Seasons," he was silent in mixed companies, but alert and expressive under genial mental excitement. An Utopian, he indulged in the most sanguine visions of the amelioration of society; a deep reasoner, he argued a question of law or government with subtlety and force; a devotee of truth, he ardently sought and carefully recorded facts; a wild dreamer, he gave the utmost scope to his fancy and the most intense exercise to his imagination; careless as to his appearance, unmethodical in affairs, intent upon the contemplative rather than the observant use of his faculties, he yet could summon all his powers at the call of love, duty, or taste, and bring them into efficient action. He describes his sensations at the first sight of the sea with the enthusiasm of Alfieri, and sums up an imaginary case, as president of a law society, with the grave reasoning of a Blackstone. The remarkable feature in his intellectual character was this union of analytical with imaginative power. So contented was he when his literary and domestic tastes were entirely gratified, as was the case during the last few years of his life, that he writes to one of his friends that the only thing which mars his felicity is the idea of its possible interruption. He fell into a gradual decline; and his wife declares that "he surrendered up not one faculty of his soul but with his last breath."

A prolific English novelist expressed his surprise at the discovery of what he called a tendency to supernaturalism in our people, having always regarded the American character as exclusively practical and matter-of-fact. It seems, however, that both individuals and communities are apt to develop in extremes; and that there is some occult affinity between the achieving faculty and the sense of wonder. Shakspeare has inwrought his grand superstitious creation amid vital energies of purpose and action, and thus brought into striking contrast the practical efficiency and spiritual dependence of our nature. The coïncidence is equally remarkable, whether it be considered as artistic ingenuity or natural fact; and probably, as in other instances, the great dramatist was true to both motives. The more strictly utilitarian the life, the more keen, it would appear, is a zest for the marvellous; from that principle of reäction which causes a neglected element of the soul to assert itself with peculiar emphasis. No class of people are kept in more stern and continuous alliance with reality than sailors and the poor Irish; and yet among them fanciful superstition is proverbially rife. There is, therefore, no absolute incongruity between the most literal sagacity in affairs and outward experience, and a thorough recognition of the mysterious.

The theological acumen and hardy intelligence of the New England colonists did not suffice against witchcraft and its horrible results; seers flourished among the shrewd Scotch, and gypsy fortune-telling in the rural districts of England. The faculty or sentiment to which these and other delusions appeal, in our more cultivated era, finds scope and gratification in the revelations of science; and so nearly connected are the natural and supernatural, the seen and the unseen, the mysterious and the familiar, that a truly reverent and enlightened mind is often compelled to acknowledge that a sceptical and obstinate rationalism is as much opposed to truth as a visionary and credulous spirit. There is an intuitive as well as a reasoning faith; and presentiments, dreams, vivid reminiscences, and sympathetic phenomena, of which introspective natures are conscious, indicate to the calmest reflection that we are linked to the domain of moral experience and of destiny by more than tangible relations. Hence the receptive attitude of the highest order of minds in regard to spiritual theories, the consolation found in the doctrines of Swedenborg, and the obvious tendency that now prevails to interpret art, literature, and events, according to an ideal or philosophical view.

It is a curious fact, in the history of American letters, that the genius of our literary pioneer was of this introspective order. If we examine the writings of Brown, it is evident that they only rise to high individuality in the analysis of emotion, and the description of states of mind. In other respects, though industrious, wise, and able, he is not impressively original; but in following out a metaphysical vein, in making the reader absolutely cognizant of the revery, fears, hopes, imaginings, that "puzzle the will," or concentrate its energies, he obeyed a singular idiosyncrasy of his nature, a Shakspearian tendency, and one, at that period, almost new as a chief element of fiction. The powerful use made of its entrancing spell by Godwin was the foundation of his fame; and it has been stated, upon good authority, that Brown's mind was put upon the track by "Caleb Williams," and also that Godwin has been heard to allude to Brown as a suggestive writer in the same vein. The consciousness of the former was the great source of his intensity. He was one of those sensitive and thoughtful men who found infinite pleasure in the study of his own nature; and traced the course of a passion or the formation of a theory with a zest and acuteness similar to that with which a geologist investigates fossils and strata — delighting in that which suggests limitless relations, and touches the most expansive circle of human speculation. Mrs. Radcliffe understood how to excite the superstitious instinct, but it was by melo-dramatic and scenical rather than psychological means. In the process of Brown there is a more rational mystery. He bases his marvellous incidents upon some principle of truth or fact in science, and keeps interest alive by the effect on the sympathies or curiosity of his personages. He identifies himself with the working of their minds, and, by casting his best descriptions in autobiographical form, makes them more real through the personality of the narrative. He has been called an anatomist of the mind; and the peculiar nature of his genius may be inferred from the kind of influences under which he loved to depict human nature — such as the phenomena of Pestilence in "Ormond" and "Arthur Mervyn," Somnambulism, in "Edgar Huntley," and Ventriloquism, in "Wieland."

This love of the marvellous, as it is called, in its ordinary aspects, and recognition of the spiritual, as its higher phase may be defined, is common to the least cultivated and the most gifted of human beings. Whoever has considered the speculations of Shelley on dreams, the theories of Coleridge in regard to the action and reäction of life and the soul, or heard Allston tell a ghost story, must have been convinced that there is a natural provision for wonder as well as for reason in select intelligences. The art of dealing with this feeling, however, is one of the most subtle of inventions, that fatal step from the sublime to the ridiculous being constantly imminent. One reason that Brockden Brown succeeded was, that a self-possessed intelligence, a reflective process, goes on simultaneously before the reader's mind with the scene of mystery or horror enacting; he cannot despise as weak the spectator, or the victim that can so admirably portray his state of feeling, and the current of his thoughts at such a crisis of fate. Witness the description of the scene with a panther, and the defence of Wieland.

There is an association of the marvellous recorded by Dunlap, the friend and biographer of Brown, which links itself readily to this vein of the weird and adventurous he delighted to unfold. It appears his name of Brockden was derived from an English progenitor, who nearly lost his life in consequence of overhearing a conspiracy, when a boy, against Charles the Second, and was sent to America to avoid the consequences; and there is manifest in the only lineal descendant of the novelist the same passion for experiment in actual life which inspired the latter in the world of opinion and fancy. The vigor, directness, and energy, of Brown's mind, increased with discipline; for, although his last novel is inferior to its predecessors, his last pamphlet is marked by great cogency and eloquence. His stock of knowledge, his range of observation, and his benign projects, expanded with his years; and no judicious and kindly reader can examine his literary remains, and ponder the facts of his brief career, without sharing the grief of those who lamented his early death as a public not less than a personal misfortune.

Crudity seems the necessary condition of a nascent literature; and a large amount of excellent material exists, in a printed form, which is destined to be recast, in a vital and artistic shape, by the American author. Style is the conservative element of ideas and traditions; and the hasty manner in which many of our writers have produced even their best works, the absence of a high and nice standard of taste, as well as of inspiring literary sympathy, accounts for the incomplete, unlabored, and fugitive shape in which the national mind has chiefly developed. The exceptions to this general rule do not invalidate its prevalence; and the high finish which Irving, Longfellow, Hawthorne, and other American writers, have bestowed on their productions, is in striking contrast with the unequal, careless, and fragmentary character of the average issues of the press.

In the case of Brown we have to regret the absence of careful revision and sustained labor. He opened a mine from which others have wrought images of more enduring beauty. Not anticipating any great result, conscious of toiling in an isolated field, and deprived of the encouragement to assiduous and refined toil which only warm and intelligent recognition affords, we cannot be surprised that he was satisfied to give utterance to his inventive talent, and indulge his personal taste, without striving to perpetuate their emanations. He wrote with great rapidity; his delicate organization forbade the prolonged endurance of mental glow; and, therefore, in almost every instance, his pages give indications of weariness towards the close. Many of his works were written and printed simultaneously; he did not apparently realize that the vein of fiction in which he excelled could be worked up into a standard value, or interest; but gave it vent without pausing to correct verbal inaccuracies, or condense and polish the style.

He was capable of giving to his theme the unity and finish of "The Sketch Book," the "Idle Man," or the "Scarlet Letter;" but he lived and wrote at a time and under influences in which such genial care received little praise; and we must look to the elements and not the form of his genius in order to do justice to his memory. The same kind of moral diagnosis, if we may use the phrase, which gives to Balzac's creations their singular hold upon the imagination, under the impulse of literary art, would have enshrined the name of the American novelist; he possessed as decided a love of exploring the very sources of affection, and dissecting character through all the convolutions of appearance. No one can read his novels without feeling that Brown was a psychologist, as well as a scholar; and the critic of judgment and candor must admit that his perception of the intricate in mental processes, and the profound and the conflicting in human emotion, if embodied in a choice dramatic or elaborate narrative form, would have continued to interest like the tragedies of Joanna Baillie and the romances of Scott. As it is, we turn to our countryman's writings with that peculiar interest which belongs only to what is initiative; full of promise, and significant of beauty, truth, and power, in a transition or inadequately developed state. We trace the footsteps of genius ere they move with entire confidence, follow them in wayward paths, and turn, with curious sympathy, from the works of more fortunate, though not more richly-endowed writers, to these early and original specimens.

THE PAINTER OF CHARACTER.

SIR DAVID WILKIE.

THE characteristic is an essential principle of art, and one that is never attained without original ability, and then rarely managed with tact. It possesses singular attraction, in modern times, from the uniformity of manners, induced by high civilization. The peculiar zest with which an epicure enjoys game, and a naturalist or poet explores a primeval and uninvaded scene, is experienced, in a degree, by every vigorous and healthful mind, in finding the characteristic effectively depicted in literature and art, or individualized in society. The interest awakened by the advent of a "lion" in the circles of Edinburgh, London, or Paris; the pleasure with which we encounter, in travel, a sequestered village, where the language, costume, or habits of the people, have retained their individuality; and the earnest praise we lavish upon the author who succeeds in creating a fresh, consistent, and memorable character, are familiar evidences of the natural love of what is characteristic as an element of universal taste. Yet this obvious truth has been comparatively seldom acknowledged, and rarely acted upon. Conformity to a classical type, the dominion of a prescriptive standard of taste, and the tyranny of fashion, have combined to elevate imitation above originality; and genius of a high and energetic kind has alone proved adequate to obtain recognition for the latter.

Shakspeare gave it sanction and nurture in England, and to him we ascribe, in no small measure, the bold individuality of achievement and taste, so remarkable in the history of art and letters in Great Britain. It is this which accounts for the otherwise anomalous taste that unites such opposite extremes of appreciation as Walpole and Gray with Burns, Crabbe, and Dickens, in literature; and in art, Turner, West, and Lawrence, with Moreland, Hogarth, and Wilkie. There exists, indeed, an interminable dispute between the votaries of the classic and the characteristic. Only by slow degrees and most unwillingly do the votaries of the former yield their ground. Accustomed to look at nature through the lens of antiquity, they dislike to admit that she can be directly viewed,— that her features may be seized and embodied, and her spirit infused, without the intervention of that style which the miracles of ancient art have consecrated. But when an original artist perfects himself in the details of this culture, as a means of expression, and then uses it to illustrate nature and manners as they actually exist, these devotees of antiquity are somewhat bewildered. In such a case the charge of ignorance or vulgarity is inadmissible. The execution proves high knowledge and acquaintance with standard models; but the familiarity of the subjects chosen, and the fact that, instead of beauty according to the abstract classical idea, nature in her characteristic significance is the essence of the work, disturbs the artistic creed of these ultra conservatives. The delight which all classes take in the sight of these adventurous efforts, the instant and genuine sympathy they awaken, and the extraordinary power they unquestionably display, "puzzle the will" of the elegant representatives of classicism; and they can only reïterate the arguments adduced in the old controversy in regard to the Shakspearian and Racine drama; or have the magnanimity to acknowledge that the sphere of art is infinitely more extensive and versatile than they had imagined, and cannot be limited by any theory which a single touch of genius may forever annihilate.

The career of Wilkie affords, perhaps, the most striking and certainly the most interesting illustration of these views. He began to be an artist from instinct, and seldom has the tendency been less modified by adventitious influences. Excepting a print of a Highland chief sent to his father's manse, the exercise of the artistic faculty was not even suggested to him by any visible example of its results; yet, on the floors and walls of his boyhood's frugal home, on the smooth stones of the field, on the sand of the brook-side, and on his slate at school, he continually sketched human faces, animals, and every picturesque object that caught his eye; no sooner was the visitor's back turned, than something, so near a likeness that it was immediately recognized, appeared in chalk or charcoal; groups of schoolboys surrounded his desk for "counterfeit presentments;" he preferred to cover the margin of the page with designs, to committing its text to memory; and to stand, with his hands in his pockets, and mark the pictures his comrades unconsciously made at their sports, to engaging in them himself; and it was his boast that he could draw before he knew how to read, and paint before he could spell.

That love of the characteristic was his chief inspiration, while thus spontaneously exercising the language of art, is evident from the subjects he chose and the kind of observation in which he delighted. His improvised drawings usually aimed at a great significance or whimsicality; mere imitation of uninteresting objects he abjured. On his way to school he loitered to sketch a gypsy wife or a maimed soldier, a limping sailor or a mendicant fiddler, and to observe groups of ploughmen; while it is remembered of him that his attention was often absorbed in watching a sunbeam on the wall, and the *chiaro 'scuro* effect of a smithy at night. He courted the society of good story-tellers, and displayed, under a demure exterior, the keenest relish of drollery and mischief. Like the Duke of Argyle, his heart "warmed to the tartan," though for its picturesque rather than its patriotic associations; and the two memorable experiences of his boyhood were the sight of the sea and a review of cavalry. Nerved by habits of simplicity, and practised in the observation of nature; sagacious, honest, candid, and poor, but wholly inexperienced in the technicalities and refinements of art — with this native sense of the characteristic, and a decided genius for embodying it, he left the manse of Cults, at the age of fourteen, to study art in Edinburgh.

Habits of incessant application, and a resolution to proceed intelligently, and never, by obscure steps, according to his fellow-pupils, distinguished him at the Trustees' Academy. He would not copy the foot or hand of an ancient statue without first knowing its law of expression, and accounting scientifically for the position of each muscle; he was thorough and constant, and therefore made visible progress in facility and correctness of drawing. He took a prize in a few months, and the intervals of his practice were given to his favorite sphere of observation; ever in pursuit of character, he frequented trysts, fairs, and market-places. David Allan, a kind of Scotch Teniers, was the only precursor of Wilkie that seems to have proved suggestive; they had a natural vein in common, though essentially different; and this appears to have been the exclusive source of his early education in art.

An imperturbable good-nature and love of quiet fun endeared Wilkie to his comrades; but his form grew thin and his cheek pale, from the life of assiduous routine that filled the cycle of his youth. Anxious not to invade, more than necessity compelled, the narrow resources of his family, he earnestly sought that command of art that would enable him to render it lucrative; and, on his return home, he began at once to seek, and permanently represent, the characteristic phases of life and manners in his native district, where, in boyhood, he had grown familiar with them, and whither he had returned with power to do justice to his conceptions.

The history of his first attempt, in the peculiar sphere for which nature so obviously adapted him, is one of those pleasing and impressive episodes in the uneventful career of genius, which confirm our faith in its natural resources and inevitable destiny. With an old chest of drawers for an easel, and a herdboy for a lay-figure, he began to put upon canvas a village fair. The scene of the picture was the adjacent hamlet of Pitteslie, the site of which, and its local features, he first carefully sketched. His groups and figures were gleaned on a market-day, and consisted of old women and bonnie lassies, venders of poultry, shoes, eggs, and candy, a travelling auctioneer, a ballad-singer, a gayly-decked recruiting sergeant; and the grave forms of ministers and elders whose portraits he transferred to a blank leaf of his Bible from the unconscious congregation at the kirk. Thus directly from life and nature every trait of the picture was derived. Its variety of character and dramatic style charmed the uninitiated, and the impressive originality of its conception won the favor of tasteful and unprejudiced observers. The number of the latter, however, was too limited at home for him to expect there the encouragement he needed; and while he made studies in the vicinity which proved of great future use, and sketched outlines of village and rustic life which became the means of many subsequent triumphs, his chief resource in Scotland was portrait-painting.

With the gains of several months' labor in this field, and means cheerfully advanced by his father and neighbors to the best of their slender ability, he went to London, like many an adventurous genius, with a gift of nature to develop, upon the recognition of which his prosperity wholly depended. We may imagine the feelings of the sagacious but demure young Scot, as he exchanged the familiar landscape of moor and mountain for the English coast, the ship-covered Thames, and the smoky canopy of London. Undaunted by the multitudinous life around him, with a modest but determined soul, he isolated himself, and patiently toiled. For nine long months he lived in humble lodgings, dined for thirteen pence a day, drew from his own limbs as models, and blacked his own shoes for economy. Illness as well as poverty beset him; but his studies at the academy, his observations in the streets, and his labors at the easel, were unremitted. He placed his pictures in a shop-window, and groups would cluster round and enjoy them; they found ready purchasers at six guineas each, but distrust of their own taste prevented many from acknowledging the merit they could not but feel; and Wilkie corresponded with his father on the subject of returning to the manse and renouncing his dream of metropolitan success.

True to his domestic attachments, he sought with his first earnings to procure a piano-forte for his sister; and at the shop of a distinguished manufacturer he excited curiosity, which led to an examination of his portfolio, and, at length, to the exhibition of Pitteslie Fair to the Countess of Mansfield, a patroness of the instrument-maker. Lord Mansfield ordered a picture of Wilkie, selecting his sketch of "The Village Politician" as the subject. The first idea of this work seems to have arisen from a popular ballad, but the excitement of the French Revolution, as it operated in rural districts upon the village gossips, over the ale-house Gazette, rendered it an epitome of the times; while in its details, as in the former instance, the painter followed nature with graphic authenticity.

An incidental discussion between several artists of distinction, which resulted in a visit to Wilkie's humble studio, contributed, at the same moment, to draw attention to his merits; and the exhibition of the "Village Politician" at the Royal Academy was an epoch in the history of English art. Although Lord Mansfield, in his pecuniary arrangement with Wilkie, did not emulate the liberality for which patrons of art are renowned in Great Britain, yet the artist's manly behavior on the occasion, and the fame of the picture, had the immediate effect of establishing him in public estimation. Thenceforth his reputation was fixed as an original painter; in him the characteristic found its legitimate exponent; and although Northcote sneered at his subjects as belonging to the "pauper school," and Haydon, in his admiration of the grand style, disputed with him as to the claims of his sphere of art, he calmly pursued his course; and the Auroras and Calypsos of the exhibition were neglected, in their artificial beauty, while the iron-railing about Wilkie's homely but true and natural creations, was constantly surrounded by eager throngs of all classes, whose looks of wonder, mirth, or tenderness, bore witness to their genuine emotion.

The effect of Wilkie's success upon the people of his native place formed a striking contrast to their original misgivings as to his career. The ominous shake of the head, with which the narrow but worthy presbyters had listened to what they deemed his profane intent, gave place to the reluctant confession that he was an ingenious lad; the old villagers, who had been most offended at finding their respectable faces transferred to the picture of a Fair without their knowledge and consent, now called at the manse, to thank the young artist for the enduring honor bestowed by his miraculous pencil; the rustic satirist, who had declared of one of his early sketches that it was more like a flounder than a foot, was now voted a simpleton; and the old dame, whose prophecy of the boy David, that he would live to be knighted, had been ridiculed, now won quite a reputation for second-sight, especially as the prediction was soon literally fulfilled.

Next to the patronage secured by his fame, its most valuable result was social advancement. He immediately gained the friendship and confidence, and, in many instances, the habitual society, of the leading men of rank, genius, and character, in the kingdom, and preserved the benefit first obtained through artistic genius, by his rich humor, unalloyed simplicity, and candid good-nature. Indeed, no better evidence of the solid nature of Wilkie's gifts and acquirements could be afforded, than that shown in the manner of receiving what has been justly called "this gust of fame." His enthusiasm remained calm as before, his habits of application unchanged, his assiduity in the study and representation of the characteristic increased; he seemed only confirmed, by the public response to his aspirations, in their essential truth and efficacy; no symptom of elation appeared; and it soon became evident to all that Wilkie's modesty was equal to his originality.

It is impossible to follow his subsequent career without acknowledging the peculiar value of individual patronage to the cause of art. We have seen that long and careful observation, repeated experiment, and patient study, are essential to the production of such works as those adapted to his genius. To toil thus upon a doubtful subject, to create instead of ministering to taste of this kind, or to sacrifice a sphere so original and attractive for portrait-painting, are equally undesirable alternatives; it is needful that the artist should be cheered by a reliable destination for his work, that he should devote himself to it with confidence, and a spirit of freedom, hope, and self-possession, such as can never be realized when the disposition and recompense of this labor is wholly precarious.

Accordingly, we deem Wilkie's successive admirable efforts the legitimate fruits of tasteful individual encouragement; the commission of Lord Mansfield was immediately followed by one from Lord Mulgrave, and others from the Duke of Gloucester and Sir George Beaumont. The latter gentleman may be considered the ideal of an artist's friend. Thoroughly versed in the principles, history, and practice of art, and only excluded from a high share of its honors by a want of executive facility, he not only ordered a picture with a tasteful wisdom that enlisted every true artist's gratitude, but watched its progress with an appreciative enthusiasm that awakened the best sympathies of the painter; his tact and liberality were equal to his intelligence and taste. His letters to Wilkie are beautiful illustrations of character, as well as evidences of artistic knowledge and zeal. His home was the favorite resort of the fraternity, and his visits and letters cheered the labors and the lives of a class of men who need more and receive less recognition than any other.

Wilkie continued to illustrate the subjects that from the first arrested his mind; usually they were tinged with his own experience, and had a distinct national association; and always the graces of execution were made to elucidate the characteristic in expression. "The Blind Fiddler," "The Letter of Introduction," "The Reading of the Will," "The Penny Wedding," "The Card Players," "The Newsmonger," "The Unexpected Visitor," "The Cut Finger," "Guess my Name," "The Parish Beadle," "Rent Day," and "The Rabbit on the Wall," are pictures, the very names of which at once suggest the genius of Wilkie, the originality of his sphere, and the causes of his popularity. Except to professional readers, the description of a picture is usually tedious and vague; the general character of those of Wilkie may be inferred from their names; while the inimitable skill and effect of their execution have been made familiar by the excellent engravings of the originals so widely distributed on both sides of the ocean. Like the poems of Burns, they speak directly to the heart and fancy, to the sense of humor and humanity; and, humble as is their apparent aim, few works of art breathe so universal a language; for it is derived from and addressed to our common nature, with only such local and individual modification as give it significance and personality.

The "Reading of the Will" is said to have been suggested by Bannister, the comedian; it is one of the most characteristic not only of Wilkie's pictures, but of the school to which it belongs; it is a kind of sublimated Hogarth, a genuine scene in life's drama, expressive, true, and having that fine mixture of nature, irony of observation, and skill, which forms the excellence of the domestic style of art. The business air of the attorney, the snuffling boy with his marbles, the pensive coquetry of the bouncing widow, the gallant devotion of the stalwart officer, and the flustering, indignant movement of the piqued dame, are eloquent exhibitions of character. For unity of design artists give the preference to the "Blind Fiddler;" the old man's complacent look at the sight of the children's pleasure, the boy imitating the musician with a pair of bellows, the leaping of the infant, and the mother's sympathetic delight, form a family scene, under the influence of music, at once sweet, natural, and harmonious.

Probably no single work exhibited at the Royal Academy ever produced the immediate effect of "The Waterloo Gazette." From the women leaning out of the windows to drink in the thrilling news, to the oyster suspended on the half-raised fork of the entranced listener, every figure and object indicates the effect of the tidings, and this so vividly as to absorb and infect spectators of every class.

The English school of painting is admirably illustrative of English life and character. It is essentially domestic, and often so when professedly historical. Its landscapes, family groups, rural manners, or characteristic subjects, depicted with elegance, nicety, expression, and truth, one would instantly infer were destined to become familiar and endeared to vigilant eyes in the privacy of home. Grandeur of design, and exaltation of sentiment,— the pictorial generalization of the old masters, intended to adorn cathedrals and princely walls,— would be singularly out of place in domestic retreats. A consciousness on the part of the artists that they thus minister to the individual and the family seems to chasten, refine, and genially inspire their labors. There is something almost personally attaching in some of these limners, as there is in the household writers of Britain; and we feel towards Gainsborough, Leslie, and Wilkie, as we do towards Thomson, Goldsmith, and Sterne. Yet one can scarcely imagine a greater variety of style than the renowned painters of England include; few contrasts in art being more absolute than those between Moreland and Turner, West and Leslie, or Reynolds and Lawrence.

In the works and artistic opinions of Wilkie there is more

intelligence than imagination; good sense, clear reasoning, and thoughtfulness, form the basis of his genius; and these are the very qualities which distinguish the English from the Italians and Dutch, — the former having sense as the main element of their artistic activity, the second imagination, and the latter imitation. "Art," says Wilkie, "is only art when it adds mind to form." Elsewhere he speaks of Turner's "glamour of color," and observes: "With a certain class of subjects it is necessary to put in much that is imaginary, or without authority, and to leave out much unadapted for painting."

Few artists uniformly had a better reason for the faith that was in them than Wilkie; and his memory and observation were equally characterized by this intelligent spirit. Jerusalem recalled to his mind the imagination of Poussin, and seemed built for all time; while he recognized in the works of Titian, Paul Veronese, and Piombo, the closest resemblance to the Syrian race, and ascribed it to the constant intercourse between Venice and the East. From his comprehensive style, he saw that Michael Angelo's prophets and sibyls resembled the Jews of the Holy City; while Raphael and Da Vinci recalled nature. He seems justly to have understood himself, and never painted well except when self-impelled to a subject. He declined a commission to execute a picture of the death of Sydney, from a conviction of his inaptitude for the particular style required; and all Sir Walter's counsel to him, in behalf of certain picturesque and memorable localities in Scotland, was thrown away upon the artist, who, meanwhile, was busy in his own manner, collecting pictorial data, and providing what his friends called "relays of character," — working up his inimitable conceptions, and, at intervals, replenishing his purse by limning a portrait. In the latter department, his most elaborate works are the Queen and her Council, Wellington, O'Connell, and Scott's family at Abbotsford.

In one of his felicitous speeches, Wilkie remarked of his native country: "Bleak as are her mountains, and homely as are her people, they have yet in their habits and occupations a characteristic acuteness and feeling;" and these he seemed as much inspired to embody and preserve as Scott the historic associations or Burns the rustic sentiment of the land; and his eminent success is chiefly attributable to the possession, in a high degree, of the traits of his nation — sagacity, perseverance, and a kind of implicit faith in the understanding as the guide to truth. His habit of interrupting conversation whenever he did not clearly understand what was said, and insisting on an explanation, his comments on art, and his patient experiments, both observant and executive, in order to arrive at the actual reflection of nature, evince a self-reliance and intelligent persistency that insured an ultimate triumph. He was usually an entire year in producing a work; it first existed vaguely in his mind for a long interval, and around the primitive conception were gradually clustered hints caught from experience; and, when at last on the easel, repeated changes brought it slowly to perfection. It indicates unusual perspicuity in his teacher at Edinburgh that he wrote the elder Wilkie that there was something of Correggio's manner in his son's drawing, and that "the more delicacy required in the execution the more successful would he be." He also prophesied his ability for the higher range of art, founded on this truth, and exactitude in the treatment of humble subjects. Yet, when Wilkie first presented himself with the Earl of Leven's introduction to the Trustees' Academy, he was refused admission on the ground of his technical ignorance. The deficiency in imitative skill, which he had enjoyed no adequate opportunity to gain, was thus suffered to blind the professor to his originality of conception — the rarest and most valuable gift of the artist. When culture and experience had given him a control of the vocabulary of art, his genius unfolded into what has been aptly called "the skill of Hogarth, and the glow without the grossness of Teniers." There is always a moral as well as a graphic power in his works, a lesson of humanity, a glimpse of universal truth, which exalt the homeliest details, and give significance to every casual touch.

Wilkie's artist-life was chiefly diversified by social recreation and travel. On his journeys to the Continent, his constant attention was given to pictures, and his letters abound in wise, just, and independent criticism. In Germany he enjoyed the satisfaction of finding two of his best works held in great estimation, — "The Reading of the Will," and "The Toilet of a Bride;"

the possession of the former having been amicably disputed by the kings of England and Bavaria.

He revelled in the examination of the Correggios at Parma, gazed with interest on Rembrandt's house at Antwerp, was reminded of Cuyp at Nimeguen, and studied Michael Angelo with reverence in Italy. He took the Sultan's portrait at Constantinople, and was honored by a public dinner at Rome, at which the Duke of Hamilton presided, and all the artists of distinction in the Eternal City were present. His last pilgrimage was to the East; and the record of his impressions overflows with a keen yet holy appreciation of its scenes and history. With his portfolio enriched by sketches of the landscape, costume, and physiognomy, in which that memorable region abounds, his views of art enlarged, and his fancy teeming with new subjects, on his way home, his life prematurely closed on board an oriental steamer in the harbor of Gibraltar.

His views of art were both acute and comprehensive. He recognized the spiritual aim of Correggio, and the detailed fidelity of the Dutch painters, and, in his last manner, more perfectly united them than any previous limner. "Take away simplicity from art," he writes, "and away goes all its influence;" yet elsewhere he declares that the "power of stirring deep emotion, and not of overcoming difficulties, is her peculiar glory." He considered art a language to be used wisely, and sought his own material among the pipers and deer-stalkers of Athol, in the byway hovels of Ireland, in Jew's Row, London, in projecting gables, in byway incidents, in the sagacity of mind and kindliness of heart of the aged, in the mirth of the Lowlands, in the figures at the public bath on the Danube, in the old scribe at the mosque door, and in the incidental groups, brilliant harmony of color, and effective light and shade, which nature and life afforded. He appealed to the immediate; selected themes of national interest, and made noble pictures out of familiar materials. Hence the ardent recognition and unbounded popularity he enjoyed. "From Giotto to Michael Angelo," he remarks, "expression and sentiment seem the first things thought of, while those who followed seemed to have allowed technicalities to get the better of them." In Wilkie's happiest efforts the desirable proportion between these two elements of art is completely realized.

An ingenious work has been published to show the effect of different mechanic trades upon the animal economy; a curious branch of the inquiry might include the influence of special kinds of mental action upon the brain and nerves. We have seen that Wilkie's superiority consisted in the minutiæ of expression attained by intense study. After thus executing several renowned works, he seems to have felt great cerebral disturbance; the power of sustained attention was invaded; when his mind became fixed upon a sketch or a conception, suddenly a mist would rise before his eyes, his ideas would grow bewildered, and only after an interval of repose or recreation could he again command his faculties. The discriminating reader of his own account of the process by which he worked out his artistic ideas cannot fail to recognize in the assiduous concentration of thought upon the details of expression, if not the proximate cause, at least an aggravation of this tendency to cerebral disease. A succession of domestic bereavements and pecuniary difficulties, consequent upon the failure of his bankers, increased these symptoms in Wilkie, induced his Eastern tour, and doubtless occasioned his apparently sudden demise.

Perhaps, too, the mental necessity of a change of habit led him at first to modify his style, and seek, in his last pictures, more general effects. From whatever cause, he certainly astonished even his admirers by the graceful ease with which he, all at once, rose to the dignity of historical subjects, and a more exalted dramatic expression. It is true that Wilkie is thought to have wholly failed as an ideal artist, but this opinion is probably owing to the comparative superiority of his character pictures. Hints of another phase of his genius he had, indeed, given at an early date, in the beautiful sentiment of the scene from the Gentle Shepherd, — one of his first works, — and subsequently in the picture of "Alfred the Great in the Neatherd's Cottage;" but the feeling and power displayed in the "Chelsea Pensioners," the "Maid of Saragossa," and "Knox Preaching the Reformation," proved that Wilkie could soar, at will, into the higher spheres of art, and carry his principles of execution into the noblest class of subjects. These and other pictures of the kind, besides possessing his usual merit of being eminently characteristic, were not less remarkable for their comprehensive spirit. The "Peep o' Day" tells in two figures the whole story of Ireland's wrongs; the "Chelsea Pensioners" is the most pathetic tribute to patriotic valor ever put upon canvas; sailors and soldiers, with their wives and children, wept over it at the exhibition.

The "Spanish Posada" is an epitome of modern Spain, grouping, as it does, with such truth to fact and nature, a Guerilla council of war, a Dominican, a monk of the Escurial, a Jesuit, a patriot in the costume of Valencia, the landlady serving her guests with chocolate, a mendicant student of Salamanca, with his lexicon and cigar, whispering soft things in her ear, a contrabandist on a mule, an armed Castilian, a dwarf with a guitar, a goatherd, the muzzled house-dog, the pet lamb, and the Guadarma Mountains in the background. Wilkie's picture and Byron's verses have made the Maid of Saragossa familiar to the civilized world; but perhaps no single work combines the excellence of Wilkie in a more impressive manner than "Knox." The still-life is as exact as if painted by a Flemish master, and as suggestive as if designed by Hogarth; all the faces are authentic portraits; — the expression of the stern and eloquent reformer, and the effect of what he says upon the different persons assembled, are absolutely and relatively characteristic. The whole scene is, as it were, thus redeemed in vital significance from the past. Wilkie explored the palace at Holyrood, the portraits of the leaders of that day, and attended the preaching of Chalmers and Irving, to obtain the materials of this inimitable work, in which the highest graces of the Flemish and Italian schools seem united. Calm, observant, persevering, and acute, Wilkie thus won successive victories in art, and proved his faith in its conservative worth by embodying memorable national events, until he fairly earned the praise of being the "most original, vigorous, and varied, of the British painters." He continued, as he advanced, to bear his honors meekly, from the freedom of his native town to the order of knighthood, the *éclat* of an exhibition of his collected works, the friendship of the noble, the gifted, and the powerful, to the annual enthusiasm excited by his contributions to the academy. His birth was registered in an obscure Scotch parish, and his death in the log-book of a Mediterranean steamer; yet, within the fifty-two years thus included, how richly did he contribute to art, win fame, and vindicate genius!

THE LAY PREACHER.

JOSEPH ADDISON.

There is not a name in the annals of English literature more widely associated with pleasant recollections than that of Addison. His beautiful hymns trembled on our lips in childhood; his cheerful essays first lured us, in youth, to a sense of the minor philosophy of life; we tread his walk at Oxford with loving steps; gaze on his portrait, at Holland House or the Bodleian Gallery, as on the lineaments of a revered friend; recall his journey into Italy, his ineffectual maiden speech, his successful tragedy, his morning studies, his evenings at Button's, his unfortunate marriage, and his holy death-bed, as if they were the experiences of one personally known, as well as fondly admired; and we muse beside the marble that designates his sepulchre in Westminster Abbey, between those of his first patron and his most cherished friend, with an interest such as is rarely awakened by the memory of one familiar to us only through books. The harmony of his character sanctions his writings; the tone of the Spectator breathes friendliness as well as instruction; and the tributes of contemporaries to his private worth, and of generations to his literary excellence, combine with our knowledge of the vicissitudes of his life, to render his mind and person as near to our sympathies as they are high in our esteem. Over his faults we throw the veil of charity, and cherish the remembrance of his benevolence and piety, his refinement and wisdom, as the sacred legacy of an intellectual benefactor.

This posthumous regard is confirmed by the appreciation of his coëvals. Not only did Addison find a faithful patron in Halifax and a cordial recognition from the public, but these testimonies to the merit of the author were exceeded by the love and deference bestowed on the man. Sir Richard Steele, with all his frank generosity, was jealous of Tickell's place in the heart of their common friend, Tickell's elegiac tribute to whom has been justly pronounced one of the most feeling and graceful memorials of departed excellence in English verse. When Budgell, a contributor to the Spectator, became a suicide, he endeavored to justify the rash act by the example and reasoning of Addison's Cato. When Pope turned his satirical muse upon the gentle essayist, he polished the terms and modified the censure, as if involuntary respect chastened the spirit of ridicule. Dryden welcomed him to the ranks of literature, and Boileau greeted him with praise on his first visit to France. Throughout his life, the distinction he gained by mental aptitude and culture was confirmed by integrity and geniality, of character. Even party rancor yielded to the moral dignity and kindliness of Addison; and his opponents, when in power, respected his intercession, and would not suffer difference of opinion to chill their affection. Lady Montagu thought his company delightful. Lord Chesterfield declared him the most modest man he had ever seen. When he called Gay to his bedside and asked forgiveness, with his dying breath, for some unrecognized negligence with regard to that author's interest, the latter protested, with tearful admiration, that he had nothing to pardon and everything to regret. Swift's jealousy of Addison is an emphatic proof of his merit; — the literary gladiator, unsatisfied with his triumphs, obviously turned a jaundiced eye upon the literary artist, whose object was social reform and intellectual diversion, instead of party warfare and intolerant satire. "I will not," says the cynical dean, "meddle with the Spectator, let him *fair sex* it to the world's end." The allusion to the improvement of women, to which this new form of literature so effectually ministered, is unfortunate, as coming from a man who, at the very time, was ruthlessly trifling with the deepest instincts of the female heart. Woman is, indeed, indebted to Addison and his fraternity, for giving a new impulse to her better education, and a more generous scope to her intellectual tastes. So much was this aim and result of the Spectator recognized, that Goldoni, in one of his comedies, alludes to a female philosopher as made such by the habitual perusal of it. Johnson's observations on Addison are reverent as well as critical; he pays homage to his character, and advises all, who desire to acquire a pure English style, to make a study of his writings. Nor have such tributes ceased with the fluctuations of taste and the progress of time. Of all the eloquent illustrations of English literary character which Macaulay's brilliant rhetoric has yielded, not one glows with a warmer appreciation, or more discriminating yet lofty praise, than the beautiful essay on Addison's Life and Writings, prefixed to the American edition, which is the most complete and best annotated that has yet appeared.

The tranquil and religious atmosphere of an English parsonage chastened the early days of Addison; and although a few traditions indicate that he was given to youthful pranks, it is evident that the tenor of his character was remarkably thoughtful and reserved. During his ten years' residence at Oxford he was a devoted and versatile student, and it is to the discipline of classical acquirements that we owe the fastidious correctness of his style. The mastery he obtained over the Latin tongue revealed to him the nice relations between thought and language; and he wrote English with the simplicity, directness, and grace, which still render the Spectator a model of prose composition. Seldom has merely correct and tasteful verse, however, been so lucrative as it proved to him. His Latin poems first secured his election to Magdalen College; his translations of a part of the Georgics, and their inscription to Dryden, drew from that veteran author the warmest recognition; his poem to King William obtained for him the patronage of Lord Somers, Keeper of the Great Seal, to whom it was addressed. His poetical epistle to Montagu from Italy was but the graceful acknowledgment of the Chancellor's agency in procuring him a pension of three hundred pounds. His poem of "The Campaign," written at the request of Lord Godolphin, to celebrate the victory of Hochstadt, gained him the office of Commissioner of Appeals; and thenceforth we find him appointed to successive and profitable offices, from that of Keeper of the Records in Birmingham's Tower, to that of Secretary of State, from which he retired with a pension of fifteen hundred pounds. Besides official visits to Hanover and Ireland, soon after his literary qualifications had won him the patronage of Halifax, he made a tour abroad, remained several months at Blois to perfect himself in French, mingled with the best circles of Paris, Rome, and Geneva, and surveyed the historical scenes of the Italian peninsula with the eyes of a scholar. These opportunities to study mankind and to observe nature were not lost upon Addison. He was ever on the alert for an original specimen of humanity, and interested by natural phenomena, as well as cognizant of local associations derived from a thorough knowledge of Roman authors. We can imagine no culture more favorable to the literary enterprise in which he subsequently engaged, than this solid basis of classical learning, followed by travel on the Continent, where entirely new phases of scenery, opinions, and society, were freely revealed to his intelligent curiosity, and succeeded by an official career that brought him into responsible contact with the realities of life. Thus enriched by his lessons of experience, and disciplined by accurate study, when Addison first sent over from Ireland a contribution to his friend Steele's Tatler, he unconsciously opened a vein destined to yield intellectual refreshment to all who read his vernacular, and to ally his name to the most agreeable and useful experiment in modern literature.

Never did the art of writing prove a greater personal blessing than to Addison. His knowledge, wit, and taste, were not at his oral command, except in the society of intimate friends. The presence of strangers destroyed his self-possession; and, as a public speaker, he failed through constitutional diffidence. Yet no one excelled him in genial and suggestive conversation. The fluency and richness of his colloquial powers were alike remarkable; but the world knew him only as a respectable poet and scholar, and a faithful civic officer, until the Spectator inaugurated that peculiar kind of literature which seemed expressly made to give scope to such a nature as his. There he talked on paper in association with an imaginary club, and under an anonymous signature. No curious eyes made his tongue falter;

no pert sarcasm brought a flush to his cheek. In the calm exercise of his benign fancy and wise criticism, he made his daily comments upon the fashion, literature, and characters of the day, with all the playful freedom of coffee-house discussion, united to the thoughtful style of private meditation. Thus his sensitive mind had full expression, while his native modesty was spared; and the Spectator was his confessional, where he uttered his thoughts candidly in the ear of the public, without being awed by its obvious presence. Taste, and not enthusiasm, inspired Addison; hence his slender claim to the title of a poet. His rhymes, even when faultless and the vehicles of noble thoughts, rarely glow with sentiment. They are usually studied, graceful, correct, but devoid of poetic significance; and yet, owing to the dearth of poetry in his day, and the partialities incident to friendship and to faction, Addison enjoyed an extensive reputation as a poet. There are beautiful turns of expression in his "Letter from Italy," — usually considered the best of his occasional poems. The famous simile of the angel and some animated rhetoric redeem "The Campaign" from entire mediocrity; and scholars will find numerous instances of felicitous rendering into English verse in his translations. Yet these incidental merits do not give Addison any rank in the highest department of literature to readers familiar with Burns and Byron, Coleridge and Wordsworth. He was an eloquent rhymer, but no legitimate votary of the Muse. It is the dying soliloquy of "Cato" alone that now survives; and yet few English tragedies, of modern date, were introduced with such éclat, or attended by more tributary offerings. Pope, Steele, and Dr. Young, sounded its praises in verse; the Whig party espoused it as a classic embodiment of liberal principles; and its production has been called the grand climacteric of Addison's reputation. On the night of its first representation, we are told that the author "wandered behind the scenes with restless and unappeasable solicitude." So far as immediate success may be deemed a test of ability, he had reason to be satisfied with the result. The play was acted at London and Oxford for many nights, with great applause. "Cato," writes Pope, "was not so much the wonder of Rome in his days, as he is of Britain in ours." What revolutions in public taste have since occurred; and how difficult is it to reconcile the admiration this drama excited with the subsequent appreciation of Shakspeare! Even as a classic play, how inferior in beauty of diction, grandeur of sentiment, and richness of metaphor, to the Grecian theme which the lamented Talfourd vitalized with Christian sentiment, and arrayed in all the charms of poetic art! Neither the fifty guineas that Bolingbroke presented to the actor who personated Cato, nor the Prologue of Pope, could buoy up this lifeless though scholarly performance on the tide of fame. The whole career of Addison as a writer of verse yields new evidence of the inefficacy of erudition, taste, and even a sense of the beautiful, and good literary judgment, where poetry is the object. There must be a divine instinct, a fervor of soul, "an idea dearer than self," or the mechanism of verse is alone produced.

Addison was not a man of ardent feelings. The emotional in his nature was checked and chilled by prudence, by discipline, and by reflection. We can discover but one native sentiment that glowed in his heart to a degree which justified its poetical expression, and that is devotion. Compare his hymns — evidently the overflowing of gratitude, trust, and veneration — with his frigid drama and his political verses. There is a genuine and a memorable earnestness in these religious odes. They were the offspring of his experience, prompted by actual states of mind, and accordingly they still find a place in our worship and linger in our memories. "The earliest compositions that I recollect taking any pleasure in," says Burns, in a letter to Dr. More, "were 'The Vision of Mirza,' and a rhyme of Addison's, beginning 'How are thy servants blest, O Lord!' I particularly remember one half-stanza, which was music to my boyish ear:

'For though in dreadful whirls we hung
High on the broken wave.'"

The hymn referred to was suggested by the writer's providential escape during a fearful storm encountered on the coast of Italy.

An able critic remarks that the love-scenes are the worst in "Cato;" and there is no rhymer of the time who exhibits so little interest in the tender passion. In "The Drummer" and

"Rosamond" there are indications of a playful invention and fanciful zest, which, like the most characteristic passages of the Spectator, evince that Addison's best vein was the humorous and the colloquial. In this his individuality appears, and the man shines through the scholar and courtier. We forget such prosaic lines as

> "But I've already troubled you too long,"

with which he closes his "Letter from Italy," and think of him in the more vivid phase of a kindly censor and delightful companion.

The "Dialogues on Medals" is the most characteristic of Addison's works prior to the Spectator. The subject, by its classical associations, elicited his scholarship and gratified his taste. Regarding "medallic history" as "a kind of printing before the art was invented," he points out the emblematic and suggestive meaning of coins with tact and discrimination, and illustrates the details of numerous medals by reference to the Latin poets. In the style we recognize those agreeable turns of thought and graces of language which soon afterward made the author so famous in periodical literature. His contemplative mind found adequate hints in these authentic memorials of the past, and it was evidently a charming occupation to infer from the garlands, games, costume, ships, columns, and physiognomies, thus preserved on metal, the history of the wars and individuals commemorated. His numerous translations, political essays, and letters, are now chiefly interesting as illustrative of the transitions of public opinion, and the studies and social relations of the author. In his "Remarks on Italy" there are curious facts, which the traveller of our day may like to compare with those of his own experience. The tone of the work is pleasant; but its *specialité* is classical allusion, and to modern taste it savors of pedantry. The comparative absence of earnest poetical feeling is manifest throughout. The reader who has wandered over the Italian peninsula with Childe Harold or Corinne finds Addison rather an unattractive *cicerone.* It is remarkable that he was so rarely inspired, during the memorable journey, by those associations which the master-spirits of Italian and English literature have thrown around that classic land. At Venice he is not haunted by "the gentle lady wedded to the Moor," nor does the noble Portia rise to view; he passes through Ferrara without a thought of Tasso or Ariosto; and at Ravenna he does not even allude to the tomb of Dante. He seems to have looked upon Fiesole oblivious of Milton, and passed through Verona heedless of Juliet's tomb. The saints and Latin authors won his entire regard. He copied a sermon of St. Anthony, at Bologna, and a letter of Henry VIII. to Anne Boleyn, in the Vatican. His observations on local characteristics, however, are intelligent; he was the first English writer to describe San Marino; and, to appreciate this work, we should remember that it was published before the age of guide-books and steam, and in accordance with the taste for classical learning and the need of information then prevalent.

To the majority of readers, at this day, the Spectator is doubtless a tame book. They miss, in its pages, the rapid succession of incidents, the melodramatic display, and the rhetorical vivacity, which distinguish modern fiction and criticism. Life is more crowded with events, and the world of opinion more diversified, society is more complex, and knowledge more widely diffused, than at that day, and therefore a greater intensity marks the experience of the individual and the products of literature. But it is in this very direction that popular taste is at fault; the over-action, the moral fever and restlessness of the times, have infected writers as well as readers. Both are dissatisfied with the natural and the genuine, and have recourse to artificial stimulants and conventional expedients; and these are as certain to reäct unfavorably in habits of thought and in authorship, as in scientific and practical affairs. It is to this tendency to conform the art of writing to the standard of a locomotive and experimental age that we ascribe the tricks of pen-craft so much in vogue.

Constable, the painter, used to complain of the *bravura* style of landscape, — the attempt to do something beyond truth, — and he defined the end of art to be the union of imagination with nature. This is equally true of literature. It is now faint praise to apply such epithets as "quiet," "thoughtful," and "discriminating," to a book; but is it not the very nature of written thought and sentiment to address the contemplative and emotional nature through the calm attention of the reader? Can we appreciate the merits even of a picture without a long and patient scrutiny; or enter into the significance of an author without abstracting the mind from bustle, excitement, and care? A receptive mood is as needful as an eloquent style. Paradise Lost was never intended to be read in a rail-car, nor the Life of Washington to be written in the form of a melodrama.

An author or reader whose taste was formed on the Addisonian or even the Johnsonian model, would be puzzled at the modifications our vernacular has undergone. The introversion of phrases, the coining of words, the mystical expressions, the aphoristic and picturesque style adopted by recent and favorite writers, would strike the novice, as they do every reader of unperverted taste, as intolerable affectations, or mere verbal inventions to conceal poverty of ideas. The more original a man's thought is, the more direct is its utterance. Genuine feeling seeks the most simple expression. Just in proportion as what is said comes from the individual's own mind and heart, is his manner of saying it natural. Accordingly, the verbal ingenuity of many popular writers of the day is a presumptive evidence of their want of originality. Truth scorns disguise, and an author, as well as any other man, who is in earnest, relies upon his thought, and not its attire. The priceless merit of Addison is his fidelity to this law of simplicity and directness of language; and those who cannot revert to his pages with satisfaction may justly suspect the decadence of their literary taste. The true lover of nature, when released a while from the crowd and turmoil of metropolitan life, rejoices, as he stands before a rural scene, to find his sense of natural beauty and his relish of calm retirement unimpaired by the pleasures and the business of the town. His mind expands, his heart is soothed, and his whole self-consciousness elevated, by the familiar and endeared, though long-neglected landscape. Thus is it with books. If we have remained true to the fountains of "English undefiled" amid the glaring and spasmodic allurements of later authors, the tranquil tone, the clear diction, and the harmonized expression of Addison will affect us like the permanent effulgence of a star when the flashing curve of a rocket has gone out in darkness. There are in the style of writing, as well as in the economy of life, conservative principles; and the return to these, after repeated experiments, is the best evidence of their value. Already a whole group of writers of English prose, whose books had an extraordinary sale and a fashionable repute, are quite neglected. When libraries are founded, or standard books desired, the intelligent purveyor ignores these specimens of galvanized literature, and chooses only writings that have a vital basis of fact or language. This quality is the absolute condition of the permanent popularity of books in our vernacular tongue. There is a certain honesty in its very structure which recoils from artifice as the presage of decay. The manliness, the truth, and the courage, of the Anglo-Saxon race, exact these traits in their literature. Coarseness such as deforms De Foe's graphic stories, elaborate phrases like those that give an elephantine movement to Dr. Johnson's style, fanciful conceits such as occasionally dwarf the eloquence of Jeremy Taylor, are all defects that are referable to the age or the temperament of the respective authors, and do not, in the least, affect the reality of their fame, which rests on a sincere, original, and brave use of their mother tongue; but when inferior minds attempt to perpetuate commonplace sentiments or borrowed thoughts in a harlequin guise made up of shreds and patches of the English language, joined together by a foreign idiom, or a mosaic of new and unauthorized words, the experiment is repudiated, sooner or later, by the *veto* of instinctive good taste.

Addison commenced writing when literature was mainly sustained by official patronage — in the age of witty coteries, of elegant dedications. Chiefly in political and scholarly circles were the votaries of letters to be found. The Spectator widened the range of literature, rendering it a domestic enjoyment and a social agency; it organized a lay priesthood, and gradually infused the elements of philosophy and taste into conversation. Although the Observator of L'Estrange, the Rehearsals of Leslie, and De Foe's Review, preceded the Tatler, those pioneer essays at periodical writing were mainly devoted to questions of the hour, and to the wants of the masses; they did not, like the work which Addison's pen made classic, deal with the minor morals, the refinements of criticism, and the niceties of human character.

No literary enterprise before achieved exerted so direct an influence upon society, or induced the same degree of individual culture. Its singular adaptation to the English mind is evinced not more by its immediate influence, than by the permanent form of instruction and entertainment it initiated. It was the prolific source of the invaluable array of publications which reached their acme of excellence in the best days of the Edinburgh Review and Blackwood's Magazine, and which continue now, in the shape of Household Words, and of the choicest monthly and quarterly journals, to represent every school of opinion and class of society, and to illustrate and modify the ways of thinking and the style of expression of two great nations. No works have ever gone so near the sympathies of unprofessional readers, or reflected more truly the life and thought of successive eras; none have enlisted such a variety of talent, or more genially tempered and enlightened the common mind.

When the Spectator flourished, the stern inelegance of the Puritan era, and the profligate tone which succeeded it, yet lingered around the written thought of England; while the French school represented by Congreve, the coarseness and spite of Swift, and the unsparing satire of Pope, frequently made literary talent the minister of unhallowed passions and depraved taste. To all this the pure and benign example of Addison was a delightful contrast. His censorship was tempered with good feeling, his expression untainted with vulgarity; he was familiar, without losing refinement of tone; he used language as a crystal medium to enshrine sense, and not as a grotesque costume to hide the want of it; he was above the conceits of false wit, and too much of a Christian to profane his gifts; in a word, he wrote like a gentleman and a scholar, and yet without the fine airs of the one or the pedantry of the other. He first exposed the lesser incongruities of human conduct, which no law or theology had assailed; he discussed neglected subjects of value and interest; and gave new zest to the common resources of daily life by placing them in an objective light. Then, too, by giving a colloquial tone to writing, he brought it within the range of universal sympathy, and made it a source of previously unimagined pleasure and instruction.

Addison's relation to Steele was one of mutual advantage; for, although the improvidence of "poor Dick" gave his virtuous friend constant anxiety, on the other hand, Sir Richard's easy temper and frank companionship lowered his classic Mentor from stilts, and promoted his access to their common readers. It is obvious that the social tone of the Spectator is as much owing to Steele as its grace and humor are to Addison. Indeed, their friendship, like those of Gray and Walpole, Johnson and Goldsmith, and, as a more recent instance, Wilkie and Haydon, was founded on diversity of character. Steele's vivacious temperament and knowledge of the world supplied the author of Cato with the glow and aptitude he needed, while the latter's high principle and rigid taste felicitously modified his companion's recklessness. If the one was a fine scholar, the other was a most agreeable gentleman; if the one was correct, the other was genial; if the one had reliable taste, the other had noble impulses; — so that between them there was a beautiful representative humanity. Macaulay attributes the execution which Addison levied on Steele's house to resentment at his ungrateful extravagance; but the editor of the new edition, before noticed, justly modifies, in a note, the extreme language of the text. We think, with him, that Addison's severity, in this instance, was more apparent than real; for he declared that his object was to "awaken him [Steele] from a lethargy which must end in his inevitable ruin." That no alienation occurred is evident from the preface that Steele wrote for his edition of "The Drummer," which is eloquent with love and admiration for his departed friend.

In that delectable creation of Addison, Sir Roger de Coverley, we recognize, as it were, the first outline or cartoon of those studies of character which have since given their peculiar charm to English fictions and essays. In no other literature is discoverable the combination of humor and good sense, of rare virtue and harmless eccentricities, which stamp the best of these productions with an enduring interest. Before the advent of Sir Roger delicate shades of characterization had not been attempted, satire was comparatively gross, and the excitement of adventure was the chief charm of narrative. But Addison drew, with a benignant yet keen touch, the foibles and the goodness of heart of his ideal country gentleman, and thus gave the precedent whereby the art of the moralist was refined and elevated. Compared, indeed, with subsequent heroes of romance, Sir Roger is a shadowy creature; but none the less lovable for the simple *rôle* assigned him, and the negative part he enacts. He is the legitimate precursor of Squire Western, Parson Adams, the Man of Feeling, and Pickwick. In the portrait gallery of popular English authors we gratefully hail Addison as the literary ancestor of Fielding, Sterne, Mackenzie, Lamb, Irving, and Dickens. The diversity of their style and the originality of their characters do not invalidate the succession, any more than Leonardo's clear outline and Raphael's inimitable expression repudiate the claims, as their artistic progenitors, of Giotto and Perugino. It is a curious experiment, however, to turn from the brilliant characters which now people the domain of the novelist, and revert to this primitive figure, as fresh and true as when first revealed at the breakfast-tables of London in the reign of Queen Anne. Addison thus rescued the lineaments of the original English country gentleman, and kept them bright and genuine for the delight of posterity, ere their individuality was lost in the uniform traits of a locomotive age. It is surprising that features so delicately pictured, incidents so undramatic, and sentiments so free from extravagance, should thus survive intact. It is the nicety of the execution and the harmony of the character that preserve it. Walpole compares Sir Roger to Falstaff, doubtless with reference to the rare humor which stamps and immortalizes both, however diverse in other respects.

We seem to know Sir Roger as a personal acquaintance, and an *habitué* of some manorial dwelling familiar to our school-days; there is not a whim of his we can afford to lose, or a virtue we would ever cease to honor and love. His choice of a chaplain who would not insult him with Latin and Greek at his own table, and whose excellence as a preacher he secured by a present of "all the good sermons that had been printed;" his habit of prolonging the psalm-tune a minute after the congregation were hushed, of always engaging on the Thames a bargeman with a wooden leg, of talking pleasantly all the way up stairs to the servant who ushered him into a drawing-room, of "clearing his pipes in good air" by a morning promenade in Gray's Inn Walks, of inquiring as to the strength of the axletree before trusting himself in a hackney-coach, of standing up before the play to survey complacently the throng of happy faces,— these, and many other peculiarities, are to our consciousness like the endeared oddities of a friend, part of his identity, and associated with his memory. Gracefully into the web of Sir Roger's quaint manners did Addison weave a golden thread of sentiment. His relations to his household and tenants, his universal salutations in town, and his "thinking of the widow" in lapses of conversation, are natural touches in this delightful picture. We see him alight and take the spent hare in his arms at the close of a hunt,— shake the *cicerone* at the Abbey by the hand at parting, and invite him to his lodgings to "talk over these matters more at leisure,"— chide an importunate beggar, and then give him a sixpence, — order the coachman to stop at a tobacconist's and treat himself to a roll of the best Virginia, — look reverently at Dr. Busby's statue because the famous pedagogue had whipped his grandfather. These anecdotes give reality to the conception. It would not be thoroughly English, however, without a dash of philosophy; and we are almost reconciled to Sir Roger's ill-success in love with "one of those unaccountable creatures that secretly rejoice in the admiration of men, but indulge themselves in no further consequences," by its influence on his character. "This affliction in my life," says Sir Roger, "has streaked all my conduct with a softness of which I should otherwise have been incapable." We envy the Spectator the privilege of taking this "fine old English gentleman" to the play, and enjoying his "natural criticism;" we honor Addison for his veto upon Steele's attempt to debauch this nobleman of nature, and deem it worthy of a poet to resolve upon his hero's final exit, rather than submit to so base an alternative; and we feel that it would have been quite impossible to listen, at the club, unmoved by the butler's epistle describing his tranquil departure, from the moment he ceased to be able "to touch a sirloin," until the slab of the Coverley vault closed over his remains.

The zest of this favorite creation of Addison is increased by the remembrance we have of a tendency to more spirited life in youth, when Sir Roger went all the way to Grand Cairo to take the measure of a pyramid, fought a duel, and kicked "Bully Dawson." This lively episode brings into strong relief the long years of quiet respectability, when his chief pastime was a game of backgammon with the chaplain, and his architectural enthusiasm was confined to admiration of London Bridge, and a bequest to build a steeple for the village church. His habits are so well known to us, that, if we were to meet him in Soho Square, where he always lodged when in town, we should expect an invitation to take a glass of "Mrs. Trueby's water;" and, if the encounter occurred under those trees which shaded his favorite walk at Coverley Hall, we should not feel even a momentary surprise to hear him instantly begin to talk of the widow. If Steele gave the first hint, and Tickell and Budgell contributed part of the outline, the soul of this character is alone due to Addison; his delicate and true hand gave it color and expression, and therefore unity of effect; and it proved the model lay figure of subsequent didactic writers, upon which hang gracefully the mantles of charity and the robes of practical wisdom. Sir Roger in the country, at the club, the theatre, or at church, in love, and on the bench, was the herald of that swarm of heroes whose situations are made to illustrate the varied circles of society and aspects of life in modern fiction.

It was in the form and relations of literature, however, that Addison chiefly wrought great improvement; and there is reason for the comparative want of interest which his writings excite at the present day, when we pass from the amenities of style to the claims of humanity and of truth. A more profound element lurked in popular writing than the chaste essayist of Queen Anne's day imagined; and since the climax of social and political life realized by the French revolution, questions of greater moment than the speculations of a convivial club, a significance in human existence deeper than the amiable whims of a country gentleman, and phases of society infinitely higher than those involved in criticism on points of manners and taste, have become subjects of popular thought and discussion. Accordingly, there is more earnestness and a greater scope in periodical literature. Minds of a lofty order, sympathies of a deep and philosophic nature, have been enlisted in this sphere. Carlyle, Stephens, Foster, and De Quincey, have given it a new character. The copious knowledge and eloquent diction of Macaulay, the rich common-sense and ready wit of Sydney Smith, the brilliant analysis of Jeffrey, the subtile critiques of Hazlitt and Lamb, the exuberant zest of Wilson and a host of other writers, have rendered the casual topics and every-day characters of which the Spectator often treats unimpressive in the comparison. It is therefore mainly as a reformer of style, and as the benevolent and ingenious pioneer of a new and most influential class of writers, that we now honor Addison.

It was at first his intention to enter the clerical profession; but all of aptitude for that office he possessed found scope and emphasis in his literary career. He ministered effectually at the altar of humanity, not indeed to its deepest wants, but most seasonably, and with rare success. The license and brutality of temper were checked by his kindly censure and pure example; the latent beauties of works of genius were made evident to the general perception; manners were refined, taste promoted, the religious sentiment twined into the daily web of popular literature; while spleen, artifice, vulgarity, and self-love, were rebuked by a corps of lay preachers, whose lectures were more influential, because conveyed under the guise of colloquial and friendly hints rather than sermons. Addison gave to literature a respectability which it seldom possessed before. He became the ideal of an author. His studies, observation, and benevolence, were turned into a fountain of usefulness and entertainment open to the multitude. He helped to dig the channel which connects the stream of private knowledge with the popular mind, across the isthmus of an aristocracy of birth, of education, and of society; thus creating the grand distinction between the Anglo-Saxon and the Southern European nations, as to intelligence, activity, and the capacity of self-government. It is in this historical point of view, and as related to the improvement of society and the amelioration of literature, that Addison deserves gratitude and respect. He was not a profound original thinker; he did not battle for great truths; timid, modest, yet gifted and graceful, his mission was conservative and humane, rather than bold and creative; yet it was adapted to the times and fraught with blessings.

Addison, therefore, illustrates the amenities, and not the heroism, of literature. The almost feminine grace of his mind was unfavorable to its hardihood and enterprise. Both his virtues and his failings partook of the same character; kindliness, prudence, and serenity, rather than courage and generosity, kept him from moral evil, and won for him confidence and love. He was reserved, except when under the influence of intimate companions, or "thawed by wine;" could ill bear rivalry or interference, and even when consulted, would only "hint a fault and hesitate dislike;" and thus in letters and in life he occupied that safe and pleasant table-land unvexed by the storms that invade mountain heights and craggy sea-shore. Such a man, at subsequent and more agitated epochs in the history of English literature, would have made but little impression upon the thought of the age; but, in his times, an example of self-respect and gentleness, of refinement and Christian sentiment in authorship, had a peculiar value. There are two excellences which have chiefly preserved his influence,—his rare humor, and the peculiar adaptation of his style to periodical literature. Lamb traces the latter, in a degree, to Sir William Temple; but Addison declared that Tillotson was his model. The description of Johnson is characteristic and just: "He is never feeble, and he did not wish to be energetic; he is never rapid, and he never stagnates; his sentences have neither studied amplitude nor affected brevity; his periods, though not diligently rounded, are voluble and easy." It is, however, the colloquial tone, fusing these qualities into an harmonious whole, that renders Addison's style at once popular and classic. His conversation was not less admirable than his writing; and when we consider how large a portion of time was given by the English authors of that day to companionship and talk, we can easily imagine how much the habit influenced their pen-craft. Both the humor and the colloquialism of the Spectator were fostered by social agencies. Addison, says Swift, gave the first example of the proper use of wit; and, as an instance, he remarks, "it was his practice, when he found any man invincibly wrong, to flatter his opinions by acquiescence, and sink them yet deeper into absurdity."

Even partisan spite could ascribe to Addison no greater faults than fastidiousness, dogmatism, and conviviality; and for these circumstances afford great excuse. The oracle, as he was, of a club, referred to as the arbiter of literary taste, conscious of superior tact and elegance in the use of language, and impelled by domestic unhappiness to resort to a tavern, we can easily make allowance for the dictatorial opinions and the occasional jollity of "the great Mr. Addison;" and when we compare him with the scurrilous and dissipated writers of his day, he becomes almost a miracle of excellence. There was in his character, as in his writings, a singular evenness. In politics a moderate Whig, prudent, timid, and somewhat cold in temperament, his kindliness of heart and religious principles, his wit and knowledge, saved from merely negative goodness both the man and the author. Yet a neutral tint, a calm tone, a repugnance to excess in style, in manners, and in opinion, were his characteristics. He lacked emphasis and fire; but their absence is fully compensated by grace, truth, and serenity. It is not only among the mountains and by the sea-shore that Nature hoards her beauty, but also on meadow-slopes and around sequestered lakes; and in like manner human life and thought have their phases of tranquil attraction and genial repose, as well as of sublime and impassioned development.

THE AMERICAN STATESMAN.

GOVERNEUR MORRIS.

THERE is an efficiency of character which, like the latent forces of nature, is made visible only by its results. It collects with the quietude of the electric fluid, and is silently diffused again or rapidly discharged, with no lingering traces of its energies but such as thoughtful observation reveals. Unlike the author or the artist, men thus endowed build up no permanent memorial of their renown, no distinctive and characteristic result of their lives, like a statue or a poem; neither are their names always associated with a great event or sacred occasion, like those which embalm the warrior's fame. Having more self-respect than desire of glory, their great object is immediate utility; their thought and action blend with and often direct the current of events, but with an unostentatious power that conceals their agency. As the dew condenses and the snow-flakes are woven, as the frost colors and the night-breeze strips the forest, they accomplish great changes in human affairs, and exert a wide and potent sway, without any parade of means, and by a process that challenges no recognition. It is only when we attentively mark the effect and consider the method, that we realize, in such instances, what may be called the genius of character.

The essential difference between this species of greatness and that which is tangibly embodied is to be traced to the fact that in the former direct utility, and in the latter abstract taste, is consulted; a sense of truth, of right, of efficiency, is the inspiration of the one, and a sense of beauty of the other. The superiority that is wholly intellectual or moral, when developed in action, and to meet the exigencies of society, incarnates itself too widely, sends forth too liberal ideas, and is too variously active, to provide for its own glory. There is an essential disinterestedness in the position and spirit of such greatness. Unconscious of self, absorbed in broad views, and as zealous in public spirit as ordinary men are in private interest, this rare and noble class of beings exercise a genial supervision and providential wisdom, with a dignity, confidence, and good faith, that as clearly designate them to be legitimate counsellors in national affairs, as the appearance of a great epic shows the advent of a poet, or the spontaneous apotheosis of a hero indicates the ordained leader. The American Revolution elicited a wonderful degree of this species of character. To its prevalence, at that epoch, has been justly ascribed the ultimate success of the experiment; for all the valor displayed in the camp would have been inadequate had it not been sustained by equal wisdom and firmness in the council. The mind of the country was enlisted in the struggle not less than its bone and muscle; and moral kept alive physical courage. The undismayed spirit of the people was, in a great measure, owing to a sublime trust in the integrity and intelligence of their leaders; and these qualities were sometimes embodied in an unambitious, devoted activity, more versatile, responsible, and unpromising, than ever before engaged the gifted spirits of a nation. The services thus rendered were often utterly devoid of any scope for distinction. They seldom gave any vantage-ground to the desire for brilliant results, and were often barren even of the excitement of adventure. They were grave, matter-of-fact, and discouraging toils, involving more personal discomfort than peril, demanding more prudence than zeal, and more patience than ingenuity; and yet essential to the great end in view, the prospect and hope of which were their exclusive motive. To this kind of fidelity the triumph of American principles is to be ascribed; and, instead of seeking their origin in men of extraordinary genius, we must look for them to the philosophy of character.

Few American civilians offer so noble an example as Governeur

Morris. One of his ancestors is said to have been distinguished as a leader in Cromwell's army. Weary of military life, he embarked for the West Indies, and thence came to New York, where he purchased three thousand acres of land with manorial privileges in the vicinity of Haerlem, an estate still known as Morrissiana. The descendants of this colonist took an active part in public affairs. A vein of eccentricity, often the accompaniment of originality of mind and independence of spirit, seems to have always marked the family.

Governeur Morris was born on the paternal domain, January 31, 1752. His boyhood was devoted to rambling over his father's extensive farm, and he then indulged a taste for rural freedom and enjoyment, to which he returned in later years with undiminished zest and entire contentment. He was placed, when quite young, with a French teacher at New Rochelle, and thus acquired the facility in that language which proved so useful to him during his long residence in France. His college life was unusually brilliant, chiefly on account of the rhetorical ability to which it gave scope and impulse; and he was eminent for his attainments in Latin and mathematics. Graduating with honor at a very early age, he entered with zeal upon the study of law, and was just rising to professional distinction when the diffi ulties between Great Britain and her American colonies broke out. He was soon deeply involved in the responsible toils of the Revolution; subsequently removed to Philadelphia, and successfully practised at the bar; went abroad, and was appointed minister to France; travelled extensively after being freed from official duties, and returned home to close his honorable and useful career in the home of his childhood. Such is an external outline of the life of Governeur Morris; but the details abound with facts seldom equalled in interest and value, in the merely civic life of a republican. As a legislator, financier, political essayist, ambassador, orator, and private gentleman, Governeur Morris coöperated with the leading spirits of a revolutionary age rich in eminent characters; greatly influenced the councils which ruled the destinies of an infant nation; grappled, with bold intelligence, the chaotic but pregnant elements of society and government; set a noble example of integrity and candor as an ally and a patriot;

and infused a philosophic spirit and an efficient wisdom into every interest and sphere with which he came in contact.

His life was a scene of versatile activity. He carried on his law practice, congressional duties, secret embassies, and extensive correspondence, with assiduity, during the whole American war; while abroad, he engaged in large mercantile speculations, prosecuted private claims, was an *habitué* of the best society, and faithfully discharged absorbing diplomatic obligations.

His diary in France, a collection of hasty data, evinces an uninterrupted and efficient activity, calling for the constant exercise of sagacity, wisdom, and reflection; while he used to declare that the multiplicity of his duties at home, during the seven years succeeding the Declaration of Independence, notwithstanding habits of method and application, prevented his keeping any notes of his own remarkable experience.

The American traveller in Europe is struck with the frequency of inscriptions, on public works, announcing the prince or pontiff to whose benevolent zeal any local improvement is attributable. To perpetuate, in every manner, the memory of national benefactors, is one of the conservative features of hereditary rule. With us it is quite otherwise. The process of national growth seems to go on, in republics, like the development of nature; a constant alternation of forces, each destined to be absorbed in the other; the deeds of one generation to fertilize the arena of the next; and the future to be so exclusively contemplated as to shut out of view the past. It is on this account that literature should attest departed worth, with authentic and careful emphasis. in a republic; and especially strive to do justice to those unpretending yet essential merits which result from character rather than genius, and, like the strains of great vocalists, leave no record but that which lingers in the souls they have warmed and exalted. A brief synopsis of the public life of Governeur Morris will give but an inadequate idea of its utility; but it may serve to illustrate its scope and aim. At the age of eighteen he began to enlighten the minds of his countrymen on a subject of vital moment to their interests, but in regard to which their provincial experience had afforded them little insight. Political economy was then a science in embryo, and finance a branch very imperfectly understood; questions relating to the principles of trade, debt and credit, exchange, and a circulating medium, were rife in the different states, when the adventurous stripling astonished his elders by the original views, the acute reasoning, and the thorough knowledge, with which he discussed them in the journals of the day. These, and subsequent financial essays, both instructed and influenced public sentiment, and prepared the way for whatever liberal and enlightened policy on this and kindred subjects was adopted.

The reputation of Governeur Morris, by these precocious writings, and several eloquent pleas to juries, was thus very early established in the colony. He was accordingly chosen a member of the first Provincial Congress; and regularly afterwards took his seat in the various assemblies there originated, under the names of Convention, Committee of Safety, and Congress, until he was duly elected to the Continental Congress. In these bodies his abilities were continually tasked, as a parliamentary orator, a private counsellor, and an efficient agent. He passed the hours between eleven and three in the House, despatched, at intervals, his professional affairs, and transacted the business of three committees of which he was chairman — those on the commissary, quartermaster's, and medical departments of the army, which was in a condition that rendered these duties of the most onerous description.

When the committees of correspondence were formed, he was appointed to Westchester county, and the gallant Montgomery to Dutchess. He devised a feasible and judicious plan to defray the expenses of the war, when the plan that he proposed for a reconciliation with England proved abortive. When the commander-in-chief approached, on his way to join the army at the north, Governeur Morris was one of those appointed to meet him at Newark, and there commenced the mutual esteem and entire confidence between them that never diminished. His speech in favor of independence, in the first Congress, was as remarkable for logical force as that of Patrick Henry for rhetorical fire. He was soon after sent on a mission to the Congress assembled at Philadelphia, appointed a commissioner to organize the new government, and sent to confer with General Schuyler, at Fort Edward, "on the means to be used by the state in aid of his plans of defence or resistance."

We next find him a delegate to Massachusetts in a convention to arrange "currency and prices;" a mission which was precluded by a more peremptory call to Washington's head-quarters. He was one of the five delegates, elected on the dissolution of the New York convention that formed the constitution of the state, to represent her in the mean time. In that terrible crisis when the army was encamped at Valley Forge, and all was confusion, foreboding, and privation, Governeur Morris was chosen as the bearer of encouragement and counsel to the army, and proved a most judicious and acceptable coädjutor with his beloved chief, in reducing it to something like order and comfort. His pen was then employed to draw up instructions to General Gates, and an account of the existent state of public affairs for the use of Congress.

His views on the appointment of foreigners to military office, on providing for the army, and other exigencies of the times, are impressively unfolded in his correspondence with Washington. He drafted an able and timely address to the American people on the prosperous crisis attending the French alliance; and wrote, for Dr. Franklin to lay before the French ministry, "Observations on the Finances of America." In February, 1779, we find him chairman of the committee "to consider the despatches from the American Commissioners abroad, and communications from the French minister in the United States" — "in its character and consequences," it has been said, "perhaps the most important during the war." In 1780, during the great fiscal depression, he published, in a Philadelphia journal, a series of methodical, condensed, and intelligent papers on the subject of continental currency and finance, and was soon after appointed assistant-financier to Robert Morris. With General Knox, he was delegated by Washington to consult with the agents of Sir Henry Clinton on an exchange of prisoners. He corresponded with the French minister on the trade with the West Indies, and induced desirable modifications of our commercial treaties.

While residing at the French capital, and mingling with more curiosity than sympathy in its social circles, he was appointed by Washington a Commissioner to England. Although his ill-success in effecting any immediate arrangement of the pending difficulties has been ascribed to the abrupt manner which characterized his interviews with Pitt and the Duke of Leeds, and also to a breach of diplomatic courtesy, to which a high sense of honor impelled him, in communicating to the French minister, then resident in London, the terms of the proposed treaty; it seems, on the other hand, to be generally conceded that the policy of the English government, at this epoch, was delay, in order to await the issue of the continental troubles before making definite terms with the United States. On his return to Paris, Governeur Morris received intelligence of his appointment as minister to France. He held the office at a terrible political crisis, discharged its varied duties with eminent fidelity, and, although restrained, by the delicacy of his position, from taking an active part in the affairs of the kingdom, he exercised a brave humanity in sheltering refugees, preserving the funds of the royal family, and transmitting them to the exiles, using every available means to obtain the liberation of Lafayette, securing the lives and property of his own countrymen, and maintaining the dignity of the nation he represented.

The interval between his retirement from this office and his return home was passed in visiting Switzerland, Germany, and other parts of Europe. During this tour his observant mind was constantly engaged — not, however, upon the objects that usually attract cultivated travellers from America; for art and antiquity his taste was not so evident as for those aspects and interests of national life which he esteemed of more practical importance. He collected information on political and commercial topics, and in regard to manufactures and agriculture. Society, however, was his chosen field, and conversation his favorite resource — "the dumb circle round a card-table" being his aversion. In Vienna, Berlin, and other capitals, he seems to have been regarded from two entirely opposite points of view — the boldness and originality of his thoughts, and the manner of expressing them, giving offence to some, and delight to others. His return home, after a wearisome voyage, was cordially welcomed. He immediately rebuilt the old homestead, and adorned his ancestral domain; was elected to Congress, where his speeches on the Louisiana question, and other topics of the day, several orations delivered in New York, and his successful advocacy of the Erie Canal, attest the continuance of his public spirit. Occasional journeys, an extensive correspondence, the care of his estate, and a liberal hospitality, agreeably diversified the remainder of his life.

The foresight which seems so natural to enlarged views was a prominent trait in Governeur Morris. His opinions were not the sudden conjectures of a heated fancy, nor the daring speculations of an undisciplined intellect. He looked calmly on a question, espoused a cause with his judgment not less than with his heart, and, having done so, knew how to abide the issue with tranquil manliness. There was nothing fanatical in his sentiments; they were generous, bold, and ardent; but they were also well-considered, reliable, and modified by reason and experience. Accordingly, he looked beyond the limits of party, and disdained the cant of faction; on broad, solid, and elevated ground he loved to stand and survey his country and the world. To his mental vision, therefore, "coming events cast their shadows before;" for his gaze was not absorbed in the details of adjacent life, but ranged far and wide, quickened by a spirit of enlightened curiosity, and genuine patriotic sympathies.

Many instances might be cited of the prescience of Governeur Morris. His consistent faith in the measures of Washington, and the intelligent support he uniformly yielded him, under all circumstances, was the instinctive adherence of a kindred spirit. Before the Revolution broke out he saw the natural unity of the American States, and advocated a plan for "uniting the whole continent in one grand legislature." At the very outset of the French Revolution, he anticipated the course of the people, and justly defined the true policy of the court. His letter to Lafayette distinctly presages the result to which he was unconsciously advancing, and breathes the genuine counsel of enlightened affection. One of the first to perceive the necessity of active intercourse between the seaboard and the interior of America, he broached in conversation the idea of the Erie Canal at a time when it was deemed chimerical, steadfastly advocated the project, and greatly contributed to its achievement. The broad avenues which now intersect the metropolis of New York, and constitute its redeeming feature, were first successfully advocated by Governeur Morris.

At a period when the municipal authorities proposed to save the expense of a marble facing to the back of the City Hall, on the ground that it would never be seen except from the suburbs, unmoved by the sneers of narrow-minded incredulity, he urged that the city should be laid out as far as Haerlem. The present American coinage is based upon his plan, although modified from the original scheme; and he originated the first bank in the country, upon principles the utility of which experience has amply proved. Instead of dating American liberty from the Stamp Act, he traced it to the prosecution of Peter Zenger, a printer in the colony of New York, for an alleged libel; because that event revealed the philosophy of freedom, both of thought and speech, as an inborn human right, so nobly set forth in Milton's treatise on "Unlicensed Printing." He derived the superiority of American nautical architecture from the Indian canoe — "its slender and elegant form, its rapid movement, its capacity to bear burdens and resist the rage of the billows and torrents." His criticism on his own portrait was sagacious: "The head is good," he remarked, "but the hands and face *tell a different story.*" It was this habitual reversion to first principles, this testing of every question by the dictates of his own understanding, rather than by the watchwords of prejudice, that marked Governeur Morris as a superior man even in an age of great and active intelligence. He was a philosopher rather than a politician.

Averse to the separation of the colonies, except on the principle of self-preservation, he was among the most able champions of conciliatory measures; but, when they proved ineffectual, he engaged with all his mind and will in the struggle for independence — at an almost entire sacrifice of private interest and feeling, being unsustained by his family and some of his earliest friends. Yet he was no undiscriminating republican. In the habits, character, and prospects, of his own countrymen, he recognized a natural aptitude for the form of government under which they have so greatly advanced and prospered; but in France the case presented itself to his mind in quite a different light; there he told Lafayette, with prophetic wisdom, that he was "opposed to democracy from regard to liberty." Upon the same conviction, that the welfare of France was most secure under legitimate monarchical rule, were founded the sentiments of his oration on the return of the Bourbons, yet memorable in New York for the offence it gave to many of his fellow-citizens, and the bold eloquence it developed in the orator. He was equally misjudged for maintaining the expediency of consolidating the public debts after the war — a measure regarded with a jealous eye by the ardent upholders of state rights, but one espoused by Governeur Morris, for the sake of the more liberal and wise policy of combining their interests and fostering the new-born and unconfirmed national sentiment. Thus, in all contingencies, he anticipated the future greatness of the country to whose welfare the flower of his youth was devoted. He saw the majestic tree in the swelling germ.

It was the habit of his mind to elicit the universal from the special, and to seize on the central idea and essential principles, instead of occupying himself with the incidental and temporary. Thus, when the charges against Silas Deane were discussed in Congress, upon the authority of Thomas Paine, Governeur Morris argued for the latter's removal from his office, on the ground that the honor due to the nation's ally was involved, while the incumbent had no social or personal claims, but was an adventurer. This was a statement of the case as it would appear to a European spectator, at a time when few in our country's councils had the perspicacity to take such a view. Personal ill-will, growing out of a newspaper controversy, has, indeed, been charged upon the legislator in this instance; but this does not correspond with the efforts he subsequently made in France for Paine's liberation, when the latter was far more degraded, and in peril of his life.

Although, as we have seen, the views of Governeur Morris were comprehensive, they were also eminently practical. He was one of those efficient philosophers who understand the actual worth of abstract truth, and know intuitively how far it can be applied to human affairs with utility and satisfaction. In our day there has been exhibited a mischievous fanaticism which advocates the realization of what is abstractly right and true, without any regard to existent circumstances. Similar principles, carried out by violence, occasioned the most dreadful results of the French Revolution; and there are always disciples enough of any doctrine, the espousal of which secures notoriety, however obviously detrimental it may be to the welfare of humanity, and the permanent interests of liberty or truth. The practical wisdom of Governeur Morris was early manifested in his financial essays, and appears conspicuously in his revolutionary writings and speeches; it induced him to warn Lafayette of Mirabeau, to suggest the basis of a popular constitution to Louis, and to coöperate with Clinton in his grand plans of internal improvement, upon which rest the prosperity of their native state. Time has proved the feasibility of his large practical conceptions, political and commercial. His genius for affairs has seldom been surpassed, and its evidences are yet apparent, though comparatively unacknowledged.

With this breadth of purpose and fertility of thought, there, however, blended a peremptory manner, which sometimes led Governeur Morris to check garrulity with a lofty impatience, and also imparted a somewhat dictatorial tone to his intercourse. With his frankness, too, there was united a certain love of discipline and courtly dignity, that were not always pleasing to the ultra democratic among his countrymen. With the local prejudice and social conformity of New England he had no sympathy, but seems to have inherited the dislike of Yankee customs and modes of feeling, which induced his father to prohibit his children, by will, a New England education. The elements of humanity were liberally dispensed to him. He did not live exclusively in his intellect and public spirit; but was a genuine lover of ease and pleasure, had a natural taste for elegance and luxury, and knew how to enjoy as well as how to work. Throughout the most active part of his life, however, he never allowed the one function to infringe upon the other.

It has been justly said of him that "he never shrunk from any task, and never commenced one which he left unfinished." Indeed, his faculty consisted mainly in a rare power of concentration. He could converge the light of his mind and the force of his emotions, at will; and, therefore, whether business or pleasure enlisted him, the result was never equivocal. His moral power was integrity; he was direct, open, sincere, a thorough, uncompromising, and zealous devotee of truth in philosophy, social relations, and life. Hence his courage, self-respect, and simplicity, rendering him altogether a fine specimen of a republican gentleman. His commanding figure, expressive features, and strong, emphatic articulation, combined as they were with superior intellectual gifts, justify Madame de Staël's remark to him: "*Monsieur, vous avez l'air tres imposant.*"

He was equally at home when absorbed in abstruse inquiries and conviviality, amusement and study, utility and agreeableness; and possessed that completeness of nature which is essential to manhood. His generosity was evinced in numerous and unostentatious services to the unfortunate; and his letter to a Tory friend, who desired to return to America, breathes the true spirit of magnanimity. He drafted the Constitution of the United States. Never being solicitous for the credit due to his patriotic labors, many services are claimed in his behalf, by his friends, which nominally belong to those with whom he was associated in public life. He often expressed the conviction that his own mind was more indebted for lucid and reliable principles of judgment and action to Robert H. Morris than to any other friend. Having married a niece of John Randolph, the latter was often his guest, and the keen encounters which would naturally occur between two such emphatic yet opposite characters may readily be imagined.

The manner in which his marriage occurred is an instance of that eccentricity to which we have alluded as indicating the originality and independence which marked his private not less than his public life. He had invited a large number of his relatives to a Christmas dinner, and, having greeted them all with his usual hospitality, left the room, and soon returned with his intended bride, and a clergyman who instantly performed the marriage ceremony, to the astonishment of all the guests, and the disappointment of those among them who expected to inherit the estate.

His behavior when the accident occurred by which he lost his leg was equally characteristic. While in attendance upon Congress, in Philadelphia, his horses having taken fright in consequence of some disturbance in the street, he was thrown from his phaeton, and so severely injured in the knee-joint, that amputation of the lower limb was deemed necessary. He conversed not only with calmness but with humor over his misfortune; and told the experienced surgeons that they had already sufficient reputation, and he preferred giving the operation to a young medical friend, that he might have the credit of it to advance his practice. When abroad he tried several very artistic substitutes for his lost member; but, naturally impatient of deception, even in costume, he continued to use a stump attached to the fractured leg, and managed to accommodate his locomotion to this inconvenience without in the least impairing the dignity of his movements. Indeed, it served him an excellent purpose on one occasion, for the cry of "Aristocrat!" being raised against him in the streets of Paris, for appearing in his carriage, when no such vehicles were allowed by the mob, he was surrounded by a bloodthirsty crowd, who threatened his life; but he coolly thrust his wooden leg out of the window, and cried out, "An aristocrat? Yes; who lost his limb in the cause of American liberty!" The reäction was instantaneous; he was not only allowed to proceed, but vehemently cheered on his way.

He had an old-fashioned but impressive manner of expressing himself, which, though at this day it might be considered somewhat ostentatious, accorded with the large canes and buttons, the broad-skirted coats and stately air, in vogue when Copley's portraits truly represented the style of character and taste in dress that prevailed. A genuine Knickerbocker, in whose now ripe memory Governeur Morris is the ideal of an American civilian, imitates with great effect the tone, at once significant and dignified, with which he asked a pretentious literary aspirant, who apologized for being late at dinner by stating that he had been engaged in forming a philosophical society, "Pray, where are your philosophers?" and his reply to a friend who asked his son, then a boy of four years old, if he had yet read Robinson Crusoe and Jack the Giant Killer, "Tell the gentleman, no; but that you are acquainted with the lives of Gustavus Adolphus, and Charles of Sweden,—the Twelfth."

There was a vein of what has been called Johnsonese in the

rhetoric of Governeur Morris, but it was underlaid by so much strong natural sense, and, in his deliberate efforts, vivified by such true enthusiasm, that it seemed quite appropriate to the man. He had all the requisites to sustain daring oratory. With a taste formed chiefly upon the French pulpit eloquence in its palmy days, his indulgence in personification, as when he invoked the shade of Penn in a speech in Philadelphia, and especially in the apostrophes of his funeral orations, in a man of less natural dignity and impressiveness would have been in imminent danger of gliding from the sublime to the ridiculous; but there was a singular unity of effect in the elocution of Governeur Morris. Intelligent crowds hung in silent admiration upon his eloquence; and servants stopped open-mouthed, dish in hand, to catch his table-talk. His social privileges were not less rich than various; and he enjoyed the signal advantages of that companionship with superior natures which is quickened and sustained by mutual duties and genuine intellectual sympathy. It was his rare fortune to be intimate with the leading spirits of two nations, at epochs of social and political convulsions which brought to the surface and into action the gifts and graces, as well as the passions, of humanity. At home the esteemed associate of Schuyler, Greene, and the other brave chiefs of the army; of Hamilton, Clinton, and all the eminent civic leaders of his time; the correspondent of public characters, embracing every species of distinction, from that of Paul Jones to that of Thomas Jefferson; and abroad, on terms of the frankest intercourse with Necker and his gifted daughter, Marmontel and the family of Orleans,—he had the best opportunity to estimate the comparative benefits of fortune, rank, genius, society, form of government, modes of life, and principles of nature.

His relation to Washington was of a kind that affords the best evidence of his worth. Their correspondence evidences the highest degree of mutual respect and confidence; their views on public affairs are developed with an intelligent frankness and unanimity of sentiment pleasing to contemplate; while the geniality of friendship incidentally appears in the "pigs and poultry" sent from Morrissiana to Mount Vernon; the commission Washington gave his former counsellor to purchase him a watch; and the candid letter of advice he wrote him on his appointment as minister to France. There was something kindred in the tone of both, however dissimilar in their endowments and career; and in form so much were they alike that Governeur Morris, when in Paris, stood for the figure of Houdon's statue of Washington. Notwithstanding the florid style of portions of the eulogy delivered on his beloved chief, at the public funeral in New York, Governeur Morris drew his character with great discrimination.

It is said that at a convivial party to which Washington was invited, his remarkable traits were the subject of earnest discussion among the company; and it was insisted that no one, however intimate, would dare to take a liberty with him. In a foolish moment of elation Governeur Morris accepted a bet that he would venture upon the experiment. Accordingly, just before dinner was announced, as the guests stood in a group by the fire, he induced a somewhat lively chat, and in the midst of it, apparently from a casual impulse, clapped Washington familiarly on the shoulder. The latter turned and gave him a look of such mild and dignified yet grieved surprise, that even the self-possession of his friend deserted him. He shrunk from that gaze of astonishment at his forgetfulness of respect; and the mirth of the company was instantly awed into silence. It is curious, with this scene fresh in mind, to revert to a passage in the eulogy to which we have referred: "You all have felt the reverence he inspired; it was such that to command seemed in him but the exercise of an ordinary function, while others felt that a duty to obey — anterior to the injunctions of civil ordinance or the compulsions of a military code — was imposed by the high behests of nature."

The quality which all history shows to be the basis of character is self-reliance. United with generosity and remarkable intelligence, this trait gives directness, force, and authority, to the manner, word, and thought. We trace to this combination much of the energy of Governeur Morris, and not a little of his social influence. Although, at times, his confidence in his own opinion and moods degenerated into complacency, and even offensive dogmatism, these were the extreme phases of an invaluable quality. The very same trust in his own resources and the deliberate convictions of his understanding, in the hour of earnest and momentous discussion, gave a profound emphasis to his discourse, that won his audience; and, in the hour of baffled endeavor and mortified hope, enabled him to impart vital encouragement to the desponding adherents of a glorious cause. In the society of rank and genius, it also endowed him, as the representative of liberal principles, with a dignity that met unawed the gaze of an opponent, and enabled him to estimate at their just value the grandeur and blandishments that subdue or captivate those not thus fortified.

The men who thus exert a great and benign personal influence usually combine will, intellect, and disinterestedness, in their characters; the two former in various proportions, but the latter always in an eminent degree. It is to such a union of high qualities that we ascribe the accurate and extensive insight for which such men are remarkable. Selfish instincts are proverbially short-sighted, and the first requisite for comprehensive views is a position elevated above the level of private interest; it is thus that the love of knowledge in the man of science, and the enthusiasm for beauty in the poet and artist, lift them into a region where what is petty, commonplace, and material, vanish in a limitless perspective. The same result is born of wide and intelligent sympathies, enlisting the feelings in enlarged social enterprises, the will in noble social reforms, and the mind in contemplations that embrace the welfare of nations and the good of humanity. In a field of action so often perverted to mere aggrandizement as that of politics, the presence of a thoroughly honest, wise, and ardent humanitarian, like Governeur Morris, is a spectacle that exalts our common nature. It affects us like an acted poem, and realizes in life the moral romance of history.

THE ITALIAN MARTYR.

SILVIO PELLICO.

Early on a January morning of the year 1854, a small funeral *cortége* passed from beneath one of the arcades that line so many of the streets of Turin. At that hour they were almost deserted; and the silence made doubly impressive the aspect of the few priests who walked beside the bier, and the little group of mourners that followed it to the tomb. On the summit of the mountain range that girdles the Sardinian capital, masses of snow rested, here and there touched with a glittering hue by the first pale beams of a winter sun; prominent, on one lofty slope, rose the church of La Superga, where the monarchs of the kingdom lie buried; yonder is the street Alfieri, reminding the stranger that here the tragic poet of Italy consumed a miseducated youth, whose trials he has bitterly recorded in the memoir attached to his dramas; near by is the palace within whose walls are so many gems of art; and not far distant the new church erected by the Waldenses, so long banished to the valleys of Piedmont, but now allowed "freedom to worship God" in the capital of a reformed and progressive state. From the associations this scene awakens, if one turn to the modest obsequies first noted, they also yield an historical lesson. The body thus unostentatiously carried to the sepulchre is that of one known far beyond these mountains, and whose name is identified with patriotism, with genius, and with suffering — three charms to win and to hold the love of mankind. It is the funeral of Silvio Pellico. "Fra due o tre ore," he said, a little while before his death, "sarò in paradiso. Se ho peccato, ho espiato. Vedete, — quando ho scritto Le Mie Prigioni, ho avuto la vanità de credermi un grand uomo, — ma poi ho veduto che non era vero, e mi sono pentito della mio vanità." * Thus meekly, yet confident in his faith, he expired; and thus, without public honors, he was buried. But his life was too remarkable to be concluded without a glance at its leading facts; and he wrote and suffered in a spirit and to an end which challenge, at least, a grateful reminiscence.

Born in Piedmont, in 1788, Silvio Pellico went, in early youth, to Lyons, and returned to Milan to enter upon the career of a man of letters and a teacher of youth. In the former vocation he became favorably known as the author of several tragedies. The example of Alfieri had given a new impulse to this form of literature, and it became the favorite vehicle of patriotic feeling. There is often a winning grace of diction, and a nobility as well as refinement of sentiment, in Pellico's tragedies, but they lack the concise vigor and suggestive intensity of his great prototype. He is evidently subdued by, instead of rising above, the trammels of dramatic unity; we but occasionally recognize a perfectly free and glowing utterance; the mould seems too rigid and precise for the thought, and, despite his casual success, it is evident that this was not the legitimate sphere for Pellico's genius. Yet there is much skill, taste, and emotion, as well as scholarship, in his plays. We have been brought into so much nearer contact with his mind, through its less studied and artificial expression, that these writings do not appear to do full justice or give entire scope to his powers. The subjects are mainly historical; characterization is secondary to plot and language; of the latter, Pellico had a poetical mastery. The scene of *Ester d'Engaddi* is laid in the second century, about fifty years after the destruction of Jerusalem; it is elaborated from Hébrew annals and tradition. *Iginia d'Asti*, which enjoyed, at one time, a considerable

* "In two or three hours I shall be in paradise. If I have sinned, I have also atoned. When I wrote 'My Prisons,' I had the vanity to believe myself a great man; but then I saw it was not true, and repented of my conceit."

degree of popularity, illustrates a local story of the thirteenth century. *Eufemio di Messina* is founded on the invasion of Sicily by the Saracens in 825. In each drama the story is used as the medium to exhibit some great truth or natural sentiment, and in this respect he resembles Joanna Baillie. Thus, *Erodiade* indicates the moral beauty of a fearless annunciation of truth; *Leoniero*, the misfortunes attendant on civil discord, as shown in the history of the Middle Ages, and the social necessity of human fellowship; in *Gismonda* is portrayed a woman of magnanimous soul battling with strong passions. *Tomaso Moro* is the most interesting of Pellico's tragedies, to the English reader. It traces, with effect, and a certain sympathetic insight, the career and martyrdom of Sir Thomas More; the last scenes, with the exception of an unfortunately tame line, are effective, and, throughout, the authentic and familiar biographies are followed. But the most popular of Pellico's tragedies, and undoubtedly the best, is *Francesca da Rimini.* Upon this theme he worked under signal advantages. It was already endeared and glorified to the hearts and the imaginations of his countrymen, by the memorable episode of the *Inferno* — one of the few instances where Dante combines his wonderful intensity of expression with a profound tenderness of sentiment, and thus seizes, at once, upon the very soul of the reader. The subject also gave scope to love and patriotism — feelings then dominant and glowing in the author's breast. With but four characters, he gives a dramatic version of the story that accords with the spirit in which it is so impressively hinted in the *Divina Commedia.* The simplicity of the plot and the directness of the interlocutors make the mere outline of this drama superior to any of its predecessors; but the earnest and beautiful language, and the depth of sentiment that warms and colors the whole, give it an harmonious and deep interest. It is, in fact, a graceful elaboration of the Dantesque episode which constitutes its appropriate introduction. One passage from the lips of Paolo always thrills an Italian audience:

"Ho sparso
Di Bizanzio pel trono il sangue mio,
Deballando citta ch' io non odiava,
E fama ebbi di grande e d'onor colmo

Fui dal clemente imperador: dispetto
In me facean gli universali applausi
Per chi di stragi si macchio il mio brando?
Per lo straniero. E non ho patria forse
Cui sacro sia de cittadini il sangue?
Per te, per te, che cittadini hai prodi,
Italia mia, combatterò, se oltraggio
Ti moverà la invidia. E il piu gentile
Terren non sei di quanti scalda il sole?
D' ogni bell' arte non sei madre, o Italia?
Polve d' eroi non é la polve tua?
Agli avi miei tu valor desti e seggio.
E tutto quanto ho di piu caro alberghi!" *

Notwithstanding the popularity of this work, Pellico, in the preface to his collected *Tragedie e Cantiche* (the latter best introduced by him into Italian literature), speaks of them with a self-distrust which evinces his consciousness of more efficient literary powers. Many of them were written, he says, during seasons of intense anxiety, and when the natural vivacity and freedom of his mind were baffled by painful circumstances. His little treatise, *Dei Doveri degli Uomini*, is a lucid address to youth on morality, in which good precepts are clearly enforced, and the obligations of religion and virtue defined. The author's name and style gave it sanction in Italy, where works of the kind are rare.

The interest of his dramatic writings was soon eclipsed by the tragedy of his own life. Let any one compare the formal and prescriptive style of utterance in one of these scholarly dramas with the angelic simplicity and soul-bred pathos of *Le Mie Prigioni*, and he will realize anew, and most vividly, the difference between the genuine and the conventional in literature. To write from inventive skill and from consciousness, to paint imaginary and real woes, to draw inspiration from the dry annals of the past and from the living, conscious, actual, present, — how diverse the process and the result! The genius of Pellico, the very elements of his nature, appear in the record of his imprisonment; there he speaks without art, and from the depths of moral experience; the utterance is childlike, earnest, direct, and therefore inexpressibly real and affecting. His articles in the *Concil-*

* *Francesca da Rimini*, Act I., Sc. v.

iatore, a Liberal journal established at Milan, occasioned his arrest. The origin of this periodical is due to Pellico, who acted as secretary of the associated writers, comprising some of the best minds of Italy in each department: in literature, Manzoni, Berchet, who has been styled the Italian Tyrteus, Camillo Uzoni, a profound critic, Pietro Borsieri, Ludovico de Marchesi de Breme, Giovanni Scalvini, Sismôndi, and Pellegrino Rossi — although the two last resided at Geneva; for political science, Gioja, Romagnosi, Count Giovanni Arrivabene e Dal Pozzo, the Marquis Hermes Visconti; for the exact sciences, Carlini, Mosetti, and Plana. Pellico narrates the event of his arrest with brief simplicity: "*Fu arrestato alle ore* 3 *pomesì diane del giorno* 13 *Octobre*, 1820." But another describes the climax of this infamous act more indignantly: "A young man, pale but calm, surrounded by *sbirri*, descended the Giant's Staircase in Venice, and, crossing the piazza of San Marco, mounted the scaffold. That young man, attenuated, manacled, beside malefactors, was the author of 'Francesca;' it was thou, child of Italian genius, dragged to the block between files of foreign soldiers and of police guards — thou, Silvio, a lamb of expiation!" Thenceforth, until the day of his release, a period of several years, his story is told by himself, in a prose-poem, which the world knows by heart.

Few political combinations in history are more justifiable than that identity with which caused his imprisonment. The leaders were not rash experimentalists, or ambitious malecontents, but men who deliberately sought to check a tide of reäction which threatened the best interests of humanity. The good they craved had been in a measure realized, and then wrested from their grasp; a dawn had broken upon their benighted country, and quickened its latent civic life and moral resources, only to be succeeded by the eclipse which an ignorant despotism initiated. It was like withdrawing the draught from lips parched with thirst just as they were moistened, — excluding the air of heaven from one accustomed to range the mountains and the sea, — or quenching the household fire at the instant its genial warmth penetrated the chilled frame of the northern wanderer. We are too apt to imagine the revolutionists of the early part of this century as restless fanatics, seeking a utopian boon, and to confound the movements of the southern nations, after the fall of Napoleon, with the ultra radicals of the first French convulsion. It is not enough remembered that the Italian Liberals of 1820 had experienced the beneficent effects of more free institutions and a comprehensive policy, under the arbitrary but comparatively enlightened sway of Europe's modern conqueror. When he crossed the Alps, he carried new principles into the heart of Italy; a thousand time-hallowed abuses vanished before the code he instituded; feudalism gave way, for the time, to progress; entails, titles, sacerdotal tyranny, monopolies, absurd laws, and many other social evils, disappeared, or were essentially mitigated; petty states were merged into one confederacy; the palsied arm of industry was active in effecting local improvements of vast public utility; capitalists found profitable investments; an avenue was opened for men of action, and men of thought uttered and published the ideas they had long cherished in secret; military enthusiasm was awakened by the prospect of advancement, and the certain reward which followed merit; in a word, a fresh and infinitely higher and more productive life, civic, social, and individual, followed the Italian campaigns. The Emperor's rule was despotic, but he was then abreast with the spirit of the age, and, so far as it was possible without interfering with his own political authority, he promoted social progress and national feeling in the beautiful land which his victories had won from a score of bigoted and narrow rulers, whose despotism combined mean intrigue with blind cruelty. To the large middle class of the Peninsula, and especially to the educated youth, a return to the old state of things from this vital and progressive experience was intolerable. The division of the country between Bourbons, archduchesses, and popes, and into minute states, with the resumption of the base system of espionage, secret trials, onerous taxes, impeded navigation, ecclesiastical privileges, and censorship, was alone sufficient to goad a patriotic mind into revolt or exile; but when Austrian bayonets enforced this retrograde and tyrannic rule, and the mental development, as well as the personal rights, of citizens, were invaded by brute force, upon the slightest pretext, it may easily be imagined that indignant protest was soon followed by a secret compact to overthrow, by the gradual formation of an efficient public sentiment, — to vent itself, when mature, in united action, — the dynasties which thus strove to bind, inexorably, the living frame of an awakened nation to the corpse of an obsolete and unsanctioned rule. Even the passing traveller sympathized with the regrets of the inhabitants, harassed as he was, at every frontier, by passport and custom-house regulations; and, on every occasion when a good road, a handsome bridge, or any other rare sign of intelligent enterprise, met his eye, referred to the *tempo di Napoleone* as the era of the improvement.

Like a mystical web, therefore, Carbonarism spread over Europe. Doubtless the association included many incapable of appreciating the grand results aimed at by the more intelligent and generous; many united themselves to the league from motives of selfishness; and even the leading spirits committed the fatal error of seeking the alliance of kings and nobles, whose pledges were as hollow as their patriotism. Yet, among the innumerable disciples of this secret and extensive combination were some of the noblest and most gifted men of the age; and no class evinced more constancy, good faith, and self-sacrifice, than the band of Italian youths who fell victims to the despotic cruelty of Francesco I. It was, however, partly in self-defence that he adopted the extreme course, towards these brave and patriotic men, which brought upon his rule the condemnation of the Christian world. He saw the growing conspiracy, and beheld, with well-founded apprehension, his brother princes give in their allegiance to a body whose real purpose was the utter destruction of thrones. To secure his own, by striking terror into the ranks of these mysterious allies, he determined to leave no means untried to discover the secrets of the fraternity, and to make a fearful example of those upon whom he could plausibly fix the charge of complicity. Hence the system of terrorism, the inquisitorial examinations, the long suspense, the jesuitical espionage, and, finally, the condemnation to scaffold and prison, which render the experience of these martyrs often as piteous as that of the early Christians, and as horribly mysterious as the victims of the Spanish Inquisition, or the Venetian Council, in their most palmy days. It is this refinement of cruelty which has rendered infamous the Austrian government. The political offenders of Lombardy, in 1820, were subjected to the examination of commissioners notoriously venal and cruel. No opportunity was allowed them to prove their innocence; the slightest pretext sufficed to arouse suspicion, and, when this occurred, the arrest followed. Henceforth the prisoner was allowed no intercourse with his family; his papers were seized, his companions threatened; he was thrown into a slimy dungeon, or under burning leads; allowed only inadequate food; and when sleep, brought on by the exhaustion consequent on these cruelties, came to his relief, he was suddenly aroused at midnight, and urged, while in a state of half-somnolency, to confess, to give up the name of a comrade, or to sign a paper which would prove his ruin. Sometimes his sentence was announced, and he was told to prepare for death; at others, promises of freedom and office were held out on condition of betraying a friend; false news of painful import was conveyed to him, in order to induce despair or turpitude; and thus for months, and sometimes years, he was basely tortured before his real fate was made known; and at last, when tyranny had exhausted her wiles, he was led out to die, or secretly conveyed to a distant and living tomb.

As the dead face of Caraccioli reäppeared on the surface of the Bay of Naples, and, with ghastly reproach, seemed to confront the great English admiral who so infamously lent himself to the sacrifice of an Italian patriot, Pellico's record of his imprisonment, translated into every language, seemed to rise, by virtue of its own elevated and tender sentiment, to the view of Christendom. He became a representative man. Through his revelations, sympathy for the political martyrs of his country was universally awakened; the dark deeds of Austria came to light, and the names of her noble victims were, thenceforth, passports to the hospitality of every land where they found refuge. This service is enough to consecrate the name of Silvio Pellico; and, to excuse him, in the sight of more ardent and less afflicted comrades, for keeping aloof, during the few years that remained to him, from the controversies that divided even his own party, and the hopeless experiments which continued to send annually new devotees of freedom to prison and the scaffold. There was another reason for this inactivity. All the readers of *Le Mie Prigioni* must remember how strong in the author's heart was filial devotion. The tie which bound him to his parents was of singular tenacity, and it was rendered more binding by years, not only of separation, but of entire non-intercourse. Accordingly, when the hour of liberation came, it was as a son that the poor captive most earnestly once more took up the broken thread of social life. To devote himself to his parents was his first and sacred duty, and one which he fulfilled. The danger of another forcible separation from them was imminent; for a long period after his release, he was subject to vigilant espionage; he therefore gratefully accepted the office of librarian to a benevolent and noble lady of Turin, and divided his time between his parents and his books. In this retirement honors often reached him. Few living authors have derived such literary celebrity and personal affection from a single production. The Academy of Sciences did not admit him to their ranks; but Gioberti dedicated his principal work to the gentle martyr of Spielberg. A highly flattering invitation was extended to him, with the promise of emolument, to make France his residence. Foscolo desired that he might be buried under the shadow of the same cross. Lord Byron would have satirized Monti had not Pellico disarmed him by relating several noble acts of his brother poet. And scarcely a month passed that some admiring traveller did not solicit the pleasure of grasping his hand, in testimony of the love his sufferings, and his resignation, and his genius, had inspired. Nor let it be supposed that he had grown indifferent to his country. On his death-bed he said to a friend: "S'ingannano quelli, che ritengono che io non amo più l'indipendenza italiana; io solo mi ritirai dagli uomini, che vi avevano una parte attiva dal momento che vidi immischiarvisi il Mazzinismo, il quale sempre vorrà turbare quella santa impresa. Il mio carattere non si affaceva alla doppia lotta." * He felt deeply the misrepresenta-

* "They deceive themselves who hold that I do not love Italian independence. I only withdrew myself from men who had taken an active part, from the moment I saw them mingle themselves with Mazzini-ism, which always seeks to disturb that holy undertaking. My character will not admit of this double struggle."

tion of his political critics. "I left Spielberg," says one of his letters, "to suffer another martyrdom in my own country — calumny, desertion, and scorn, which have stripped all earthly illusion from life."

It is not uncommon to regard sense and sentiment as antagonistic; the great truth, that they blend in the highest natures, is not sufficiently recognized. The effect produced by *Le Mie Prigioni* is a valuable illustration of this fact. The work is a truthful statement of an individual's experience, under the sentence of Austria for the honest exercise of an individual and natural right. There are no details given of the specific charge, the means used to extort evidence, or the facts of the trial; not a word of invective appears throughout. After the incident of the arrest, we are taken to the prisoner's cell, and admitted to his inmost consciousness; we hear him sigh, we behold his tears, watch his sleep, listen to his prayers, and become witnesses of the monotonous external, but vivid inward life, of those years of incarceration. The great idea derived from this memorial is, that a man of rare endowments, of the deepest sensibility, of the highest aspirations, and most pure aims, is forcibly separated from the world of nature and humanity, — his sacred birthright, — shut up with felons, invested with the livery of crime, denied communion with books, subjected to the greatest physical discipline and moral isolation; and, although the author of this great wrong is scarcely alluded to, we revert to him, for this very reason, with the deeper indignation, and follow the pen of the generous martyr with more profound sympathy. Vengeance could not have imagined, nor wit fashioned, a work so well adapted to operate on public opinion; and yet, so far from being the product of a shrewd or vindictive mind, it is the simple overflowing of a frank and benign spirit; and, by virtue of the very resignation, patience, love, and truth, it breathes, it became a seal of condemnation to the Austrian government, and an appeal for the Liberals of Italy throughout the civilized world! Even the censors of a jealous monarch were blind to its latent significance. The priests regarded it as a testimony to the efficacy of their creed; the Royalists thought it the confession of a penitent republican; and the Liberals hailed it as an eloquent picture of the cruelty of despotic rule. But while thus understood in Italy, the world at large was absorbed in the revelation it afforded, so clear, unstudied, and authentic, of the possible fate of a man of rare worth and genius, who dared to write and act for his country, in the state of Lombardy, and during the nineteenth century.

For several years Silvio Pellico has been regarded, even in the community where he dwelt, as dead to the world, — utterly withdrawn from the active interests of social life, and even indifferent to that great cause of political reform in behalf of which he so bravely suffered. It was in a resigned, and not in a misanthropic spirit, however, that he lived. His motto was, "*Leggo, penso, amo gli amici, non odio nessuno, rispetto le altrui opinioni e conservo le mie.*" This isolation was self-imposed in a degree, yet circumstances scarcely appreciated by the uninformed and enthusiastic, seem to us not only to render it excusable, but wise. The privation and moral anguish incident to a rigorous imprisonment, unalleviated by physical comfort, books, or the least knowledge of the external world, affect individuals according to their temperament and character. The resignation and self-control so remarkable in Pellico did not prevent the most terrible influence upon his organization; while, in the case of Foresti, a chronic disease of the digestive organs was induced by sparse nourishment and incarceration, and Maroncelli's limb mortified from the irritation of fever brought on by the same trials, Pellico, being of a highly nervous *physique*, experienced a cerebral attack; and, although the duration of his captivity was several years less than that of some of his companions, they, when released, in many instances, exhibited greater vigor of body and mind. No one, who has perused the affecting record of this gifted man's life in prison, need be informed that a more sensitive being has seldom lived. Of a delicate frame, with the keenest sense of beauty, a heart tender, loyal, and devoted, a mind imbued with the love of letters, and a natural piety which made him alive to all the teachings of human existence, who can wonder, that, suddenly deprived of home, friends, the scenes of nature, and the scope required by a healthy and cultivated intellect, his constitution received a fatal shock, which rendered him, when again restored to society, unfit to mingle in its bustle and festivities? Who can blame a man, thus organized and thus subdued, for retreating to a domestic nook, to watch over his aged parents, and avoid the excitement of outward life? Silvio Pellico's sufferings rendered him prematurely old. He could, with reason, plead for serenity as the only boon left. The harmony of his nature had been fatally disturbed by the wrongs he had suffered; mind and body no longer acted in effective concert; the pallor, born of a dungeon's shadow, rested on his high and smooth forehead; his sight was dimmed by years of twilight, his voice tremulous from the sighs of captivity. Instead of a stern indignation, a firm antagonism of mood, such as many of his comrades had maintained during their long imprisonment, Pellico sought to cherish a gentle, forgiving, and patient state of mind, beautiful in itself, but so destitute of the element of resistance that the iron of tyranny, if it did not so deeply enter his soul, more entirely prostrated his organism. Yet, to the last, he found comfort in his affectionate correspondence. "My health is gone," he wrote to Foresti, his fellow-prisoner, and so long the endeared Italian exile, and favorite teacher of his native tongue in New York, "and I with difficulty survive threatening suffocation. Yet life has its consolations. Never forget the gifts of intelligence and of feeling which developed in you during our common misfortune. I have learned that but little is needed to beautify existence, save the society of the loved and honorable."

The era of Pellico's early youth was not favorable to earnestness of character. He imbibed some of the ideas set afloat in the world of thought by the followers of Voltaire, and his first literary tastes were unavoidably tinged with the superficial views incident to the absence of faith which marked the era succeeding the French Revolution; but his nature was too pure and aspiring to succumb to these prevalent influences. Some of his contemporary authors were inspired by serious convictions; it was the epoch of Foscolo, and that gifted band of Italian poets and thinkers of which he was a central figure. At the house of the nobleman in Milan to whose children he was preceptor, Pellico associated with the best thinkers and writers of Lombardy. He there formed the acquaintance of many eminent persons — among them Count Porro, Byron, Brougham, Thorwaldsen, Schlegel, and Madame de Staël. His contributions to the *Conciliatore* were distinguished for the grace and elegance of their style, and at this period both the motive and the means of literary culture were fully enjoyed. The transition from such a sphere to a prison led him to reflect, with new zest, upon the discipline of life, the mysteries of the soul, and the truths of revelation. His latent religious sentiment was awakened. His heart, thrust back from the amenities of cultivated society and the delight of kindred, turned to God with a zeal and a singleness of purpose before unknown. He became devout, and experienced the solace and the elevation of Christian faith. There have been critics who pretend to see in this perfectly natural result only a proof of weakness, or an indication of despair. The candid utterance of pious feeling in his *Prigioni* was regarded, by the cynical, as evidence of a broken spirit and when he persevered in retirement and the offices of his faith, after emancipation, it was said that the wiles of Jesuitism had made him a victim and induced his political abdication. But no one can examine the writings of Pellico without feeling that he was evidently a man of sentiment. It was this quality, as contrasted with the severity of Alfieri, that first gained him popularity as a dramatic writer, that endeared him to family and friends, and that made him a patriot and a poet. Solitude, by the very laws of nature, where such a being is concerned, developed his religious sentiment; and to the predominance of this, united with physical disability, is to be ascribed his passive and hermit life. It should be a cause of praise, and not of reproach. He was true to himself; and in view alone of the sincerity and the consolation he obviously derived from religion, we are not disposed to quarrel with his Catholicism. The errors of that creed had no power over his generous and simple nature; it was hallowed to him by early association, and by parental sanctions; and there is no evidence that he accepted its ministrations with superstitious imbecility, but rather in a spirit above and beyond forms, and deeply cognizant of essential truth.

THE POPULAR POET.

THOMAS CAMPBELL.

When Burns was on his death-bed, he said to a fellow-member of his military corps, "Don't let the awkward squad fire over me." There is an awkward squad in the ranks of all professions, and most earnestly is their service to be deprecated on any occasions calling for solemnity or tenderness. Then we demand what is graceful, harmonious, and efficient. Yet it is the constant fate of genius to be tried by other arbiters than its peers, to be profaned by idle curiosity and malignant gossip. The "awkward squad" in literature not only fire over the graves of poets, but are wont to discharge annoying batteries of squibs at them while living. The penny-a-liners scent a celebrity afar off, and hunt it with the pertinacity of hounds; they flock in at the death like a brood of vultures; and often, without the ability either to sympathize with or to respect the real claims they pretend to honor, show up the foibles, mutilate the sayings, and fabricate the doings, of those whose unostentatious private lives, to say nothing of the dignity of their public fame, should protect them from microscopic observation and vulgar comment.

No modern English poet has suffered more from this kind of notoriety than Campbell. Unlike his brother bards, he neither sought rural seclusion nor foreign exile, but continued to haunt cities to the last; and it is refreshing to turn from the hackneyed sketches of him in the magazines to his own letters and the history of his early career, and revive our best impressions of his character.

To do this we must discard what is irrelevant, and contemplate the essential. The only demand we have any moral right to make upon the bard who has enlisted our hearts by his song, is that there exist in his actions and tone of feeling a spirit consistent with the sentiments deliberately advocated in his verse. There is no reason whatever to expect in him immunity from error; we are irrational to look for a beauty of feature, a majesty of life, and an evenness of temper, corresponding with the ideal created by the finish and exaltation of his poetry; but if baseness deface the behavior and indifference chill the intercourse of him who has eloquently breathed into the ear of the world noble and glowing emotion, we are justified in feeling not only disappointment, but almost scepticism as to the reality of these divine sympathies. Such an anomaly we do not believe possible in the nature of things. In spite of what is so often asserted of the discrepancy between authorship and character, literary biography demonstrates that "as a man thinketh so is he."

Milton and Dante, Goldsmith and Petrarch, were essentially what their works proclaim them, although the former occasionally exhibited asceticism, which is the extreme of that genius whose characteristic is will, and the latter sometimes displayed the weakness which, in our human frailty, attaches to the genius whose main principle is love. A touch of pedantry and hardihood slightly deforms the images of those august spirits who explored the unseen world, as vanity and egotism mar the serene beauty of the gentler minstrels who sung of the tender passion and the charms of domestic life. Were it otherwise, they would eclipse instead of representing humanity. There is a process of metropolitan decadence to which literary celebrities are liable, especially in London, for which we, whose privilege it is to look upon them over the grand perspective of the sea, should make just allowance. The most absurd whim of modern society is that of making what are called lions of authors, and especially of poets. No class of men appear to less advantage in a conventional position; and no two principles can be more radically adverse than that of mutual agreeableness, conformity, and display, of which society technically considered is the arena, and the spirit of earnestness, nature, and freedom, characteristic of poets. Idolized as they usually are, and with good reason, in the domestic circle and among intimate friends, the very qualities which are there elicited general society keeps in abeyance. Tact is the desideratum in the latter as truth is in the former; and though sometimes the natural dignity and manliness of genius successfully asserts itself in the face of pretence fortified by etiquette, as in the case of Burns at Edinburgh, the exception is too memorable not to have been rare. The consequence of this want of relation between the spirit of society and the poetic character is that a formal homage is paid its representatives on their first appearance, which, at length, becomes wearisome to both parties; and, if the time-honored guest has not the wisdom to anticipate his social decay and withdraw into honorable retirement, those upon whose memories the prestige of his original reputation does not rest are apt to fail in that recognition which habit has made almost necessary to his self-respect.

The admirers of dramatic and musical genius keenly regret the reäppearance of the favorites of their youth in public, only to awaken the unfeeling curiosity of a new generation; and somewhat of the same melancholy attaches to the prolonged, social exhibition of a man whose verse has rendered his name sacred to our associations and remembrance. That familiarity which breeds contempt denies the original glory of his presence. The name freely bandied at the feast comes to be repeated with less reverence at the fireside. The voice, whose lowest accent was once caught with breathless interest, is suffered to lose itself in the hum of commonplace table-talk; and the brow to which every eye used to turn with sympathetic wonder seems no longer to wear the mysterious halo with which love and fancy crown the priests of nature. And usually the victim of this gradual disenchantment is quite unconscious of the change, until suddenly aroused to its reality. Aware of no blight upon his tree of promise, inspired by the same feelings which warmed his youth, wedded to the same tastes, and loyal to the same sentiments, with a kind of childlike trustfulness he reposes upon his own identity, and is slow to believe in the precarious tenure upon which merely social distinction is held.

To a reverent and generous spectator this is one of those scenes in the drama of life, which is the more affecting because so few look upon it with interest. We sigh at the fragility of personal renown, and pity the enthusiasm that seems doomed to "make idols and to find them clay." Then how enviable appear those who "are gathered to the kings of thought, far in the unapparent,"—the young poet who died in the freshness of his life, and the aged bard who seasonably retreated to the sequestered haunts of nature, and breathed his last far from the busy world where the echo of his fame yet lingered! We are chiefly pained, in the opposite case, at the difficulty of associating the author with his works, the written sentiment with the ordinary talk, the poet with the man, when we are thus brought into habitual contact with the social effigy of genius. We are also mortified at the inconsistency of feeling which leads men to guard and cherish an architectural fragment, and yet interpose no wise and charitable hand to preserve from sacrilege "creation's masterpiece, the poet soul;" which expends such hero-worship upon the distant and the dead, but holds up no shield between the greatness at their side and the indifferent or perhaps malicious gaze of the world. Modern philanthropy has furnished asylums for almost all the physical and moral ills to which flesh is heir; but the award of celebrity apparently cancels the obligations of society towards the gifted. If improvident, as is usually the case, poverty and neglect are often their lot in age; and if prosperous in circumstances, but bereft of near and genial ties, they are homeless, and consequently reckless.

Instances of private sensibility to claims like these, not only felt but realized with beautiful zeal, are indeed recorded to the honor of our common nature; and such benefactors as Mrs. Unwin, the friend of Cowper, and the Gilmans, at whose house Coleridge died, will live in honor when more ostentatious almoners are forgotten. Let us congratulate ourselves that we are seldom among the witnesses of the social decadence of our favorite English authors. Freshly to us yet beams their morning fame; we know them only through their works, and death has but canonized what love had endeared. There is no dreary interlude between the glorious overture and the solemn finale. Their garlands, to our vision, press unwithered brows. The music of their names has never lost its spirit-stirring cadence; when uttered, memorable and eloquent passages recur, as "at the touch of an enchanter's wand." We think of Byron as he describes himself in his romantic pilgrimage, not as he appeared at Holland House and Drury. Shelley's memory is undimmed by the air of a chancery court, and remains as lofty, pure, and ethereal, as his funeral pyre; and Burns we never saw performing excise duties. But of all the modern poets of Great Britain, the one whose memory we could have least suffered to be desecrated was Campbell; and we rejoice to have known him as the bard of Hope, and not as Tom Campbell, especially as his correspondence exhibits his eminent title to poetical character as well as genius, and repudiates the shallow gossip which drew such superficial portraits of him in later years.

We find in these letters that Campbell the man was worthy of Campbell the poet; and that the ideal we had cherished of the author of Gertrude and Hohenlinden was essentially true to nature. The manner in which he has been dealt with, even by literary men, and especially by social detractors, is only another illustration of the humiliating truth that "Folly loves the martyrdom of Fame." Our view of the character of distinguished persons is three-fold: that derived from the deeds or writings upon which their fame rests, the report of contemporaries, and their own memoirs and letters. Between the first and last there is usually some essential harmony, but the intermediate link in the chain of evidence seldom coïncides with either. The decease of a renowned person is followed by the publication of his life, and recently it has been the wise and just custom to rely as far as possible on the testimony of the subject, rather than the opinions of the biographer.

The result is that the misrepresentations and partial glimpses afforded by rumor and ambitious scribblers give way before the direct and authentic revelation of facts and personal correspondence, and we enjoy the high satisfaction of reconciling the man and the author, and the assurance that the sentiment and tone which originally endeared to us the one were truly embodied in the other. How different is the view now cherished of Burns, Byron, Keats, and Lamb, from that prevalent before we were fully admitted to a knowledge of their trials, habits, temptations, and ways of feeling and acting, by the record of sorrowing friends, and the appearance of their familiar and confidential letters! In consideration of the inveterate tendency to exaggerate and distort the simple facts of a marked career, it would seem not only excusable but requisite for those who have won the peculiar sympathy or admiration of the world, to write an autobiography. Such a work, undertaken in the spirit and executed with the frank good-nature which belong to those of Cellini, Alfieri, Goldoni, and we may add, as a recent instance, the fragments of Southey and Haydon, are better portraits to bequeath than the formal and incomplete lives too often substituted by the zeal of friendship or the enterprise of authors.

Next to a good autobiography, however, the best service which can be rendered departed genius is to bring together and unite by an intelligent and genuine narrative such personal memorials as most clearly represent the man as he was. However unambitious, the task is one of sacred responsibility, due not less to the enthusiasm which cherishes, than to the gifts which hallow, posthumous renown. We can then trace the elements of character as developed in boyhood, estimate the influence of education and circumstances, and recognize the domestic and social life of those whose personal reputation may have appeared incongruous with their permanent fame; thus realizing the process and the principle of their eminence. It is not eulogy which we require; that, if deserved, is apparent in the deeds or words which have become a passport to glory; it is facts, sentiments, familiar illustrations, whereby to judge for ourselves of the man whose name is indissolubly associated in our minds with the inspiration of heroism and poetry. The characters of a poet and a man of letters are so often blended in literary memoirs as to appear identical, but their distinctness in nature is marked by inevitable traits. Seldom has the difference between the two been more clearly indicated than in the biography of Campbell; and the illustration is more emphatic from the fact that we are admitted to his experience and opinions through familiar correspondence.

The grand peculiarity of the poetic nature is faith in sentiment of some kind, obedience to its inspiration, delight in its utterance, and loyalty to its dictates. Neither time, nor interest, nor logic, suffice to exhaust or modify this vital principle. Where it fails to triumph over these, it is evidently inadequate to justify the title of bard, minstrel, poet, or whatever name we apply to those upon whose minds its influence is pervading and instinctive. To infuse the life of his own spirit, the glow of his personal emotion, into thought and language, is the characteristic of the poet. His words differ from those of other men chiefly by virtue and a magnetic quality. They appeal to consciousness rather than understanding, to the entire soul instead of the exclusive intellect. Hence they have power to stir the blood, linger on the ear, excite the imagination, and warm the heart. On the other hand, the man of letters can only grasp the technicalities of the art and wield the machinery of verse. As youth decays, as circumstances alter, as public taste varies, the enthusiasm which, at first, gave a temporary fire to his rhythmical writing, is subdued to such a degree as to render his so-called muse a very flexible and hackneyed creature—the mere effigy of what she once promised to be. The genuine poet, on the contrary, strives in vain to reconcile himself to the mechanical drudgery of the pen; is coy of an art whose real excellence he has too keenly felt to be satisfied with any "counterfeit presentment;" and lives on, wedded by an eternal affinity to the love of his youth, although he may have outgrown all relation to it but that of veneration and remembrance. The few gems of the latter outlive the mines opened by the former; scintillations of lyric fire, radiated from an earnest heart and generated by its native warmth, beam on like stars in the firmament; while the elaborate productions of tasteful and learned industry "fade into the light of common day." Only a felicitous passage, a theme accidentally enlivened by an impulse from individual life, redeems the ingenious and diffuse metrical composition from oblivion; but the spontaneous product of an inspired mind becomes a household and a national treasure.

Campbell's early life gave promise of this healthful endowment of the poetic faculty. He was a devoted student, and, although constantly bearing off prizes, won and retained the love of his companions. They once owed a holiday to his rhymed petition, and such instances of the loving exercise of his talents were of frequent occurrence. His success at college was eminent in Greek; and the temperament of genius was evinced in the extreme alternation of his moods. Although often in high spirits, when his deeper feelings became enlisted, gravity ensued. He made the most obvious progress both in facility and power of expression, as we perceive by the gradual improvement in the style of his letters and occasional verses. But the most satisfactory indication of his poetical gifts we find in the ardor, constancy, and generous faith, of his sentiments. In friendship, domestic intercourse, literary taste, and the observation of nature, there was evident, from the first, an enthusiasm and sensibility which gave the fairest promise as they brought him into vital relation with these sources of moral and sentient experience.

The early correspondence of few poets has a more truthful charm and graceful warmth. It reveals his heart and confirms the tenor of his poems. His visits to the Highlands — a residence of some months in Germany, and the study of the literature of the latter country, with the society of Edinburgh, all combined, at this most susceptible and enthusiastic period, to inform, excite, and chasten his mind. Thus enriched and disciplined, with the most limited pecuniary resources, and the greatest uncertainty as to what career he should adopt, the young poet was singularly exposed to the impressions of a period, when even the insensible and unenlightened were aroused to interest in public affairs, the welfare of society, and the progress of mankind. It was an epoch of war and of philanthropy, of revolution and experiment, of the most infernal tyranny and the noblest self-devotion. The overthrow of slavery was then first agitated; Poland and Greece heroically struggled, and the martyrdom of the former was achieved. The elements of civil society were deeply moved; the cause of truth and liberty inspired fresh championship, and the wrongs of humanity made themselves felt. At this time he meditated emigrating to America, where one of his brothers was already established.

It is a curious fact that several of the distinguished modern poets of England — among them Coleridge, Southey, and Keats — entertained similar views; and it is an equally curious speculation to imagine how such a course would have modified their writings and destiny. Campbell, also, with true poetical consistency, recoiled from the professions and commerce; and thus, by the force of circumstances as well as the promptings of genius, seemed destined for a literary life. This vague purpose was confirmed by the unprecedented success of his first poem. There is no instance, perhaps, in the annals of literature, of so instantaneous and complete a recognition of the advent of a poet as followed the appearance of the "Pleasures of Hope." It introduced him at once to fame and society; and it did this by virtue of the eloquent utterance it gave to feelings which then latently glowed in every noble heart. Like a bugle whose echoes speak the morning cheer which exhilarates the frame of the newly-roused hunter, it caught up, rendered musical and prolonged the strains of pity, hope, and faith, rife, though seldom audible, in the world.

It is essential to poetry of this nature that the sensibilities should be acted upon by some actual scene, person, or event; and accordingly we find that every successful composition of Campbell has a personal basis. To this, indeed, we may ascribe that spirit of reality which constitutes the distinction between forced and spontaneous verse. His muse, when herself, is awake, magnetic, and spirited; the sense of beauty, or the enthusiasm of love and freedom, being naturally excited, utter themselves in fervid strains. Thus the apostrophe to Poland, and the protest against scepticism, the appeal to the disappointed lover, the description of mutual happiness, and, in fact, all the animated episodes in the "Pleasures of Hope," grew directly out of the events of the day or the immediate experience of the poet. "Lochiel's Warning" embodies a traditionary vein of local feeling derived from the land of his nativity; the "Exile of Erin" consecrates the woes of a poor fellow with whom he sympathized on the banks of the Elbe; the "Beech Tree's Petition" was suggested by an interview with two ladies in the garden where it grew; the "Lines on a Scene in Bavaria" are a literal transcript from memory; "Ye Mariners of England" expresses feelings awakened by the poet's own escape from a privateer. It is a singular coïncidence that the draft of this famous naval ode, which was found among his papers, was seized, on his return from Germany, on the suspicion that his visit had a treasonable design. In the freshness of youth he witnessed a battle, a retreat, and the field upon which the night-camp of an army was pitched; and the vivid emotions thus induced he eloquently breathed in "Hohenlinden" and the "Soldier's Dream." His dramatic tastes are finely reflected in the address to John Kemble, and his classical in the ode to the Greeks. We also trace the relation between the very nature of the man and whatever appealed to the sense of the heroic or the beautiful in his letters. The State Trials excited his deepest youthful sympathy. It is natural that to him the memorable experiences of life were such incidents as to hear Neukomm play the organ, and to stand with Mrs. Siddons before the Apollo Belvidere. The "Turkish Lady" was written while his mind was full of a project to visit the East; and his subsequent intention of joining his brother in America, with whom he kept up a regular correspondence, accounts for his choice of "The Valley of Wyoming" as the scene of Gertrude.

A critic, whose taste and organization fit him to seize upon the vital spirit of works of genius, says that in this poem there is "the best got-up bridal" in the whole range of English poetry. The zest and truthful beauty of the description is drawn from the bard's own experience of the conjugal sentiment. His biographer describes Miss Sinclair, who became his wife, as one of those women who unite great vivacity of temperament with a latent tenderness and melancholy — the very being to captivate permanently a man at once ardent and tasteful, like Campbell.

Even his defects point to the same impressible temper. Quickly aroused to anger, of which several curious instances occur in his memoirs, he as quickly yielded to the reäction of generous and candid feeling. The transition was as childlike as it was sincere, and in perfect accordance with the poetical character. The same is true of his alternate relish of severe intellectual labor and the most luxurious self-indulgence. Campbell by nature was a patriot and a philanthropist, a lover and a friend, an enthusiast and a scholar; impulsive and fastidious at the same time, generous and vain by turns, with sensibility and culture, now fagging and now soaring; and, thus constituted, we may imagine the effect upon him of being doomed to write in the prime of his life, "My son is mad, my wife dead, and my harp unstrung." Yet, like nearly all the gifted men of his age, he was so singularly blessed with social privileges, that we are forcibly reminded of Scott's declaration that these constituted his real obligations to literature. In the course of Campbell's letters, we find him at different periods enjoying the society, first of Dr. Burney, Mrs. Inchbald, Dr. Gregory, Dugald Stewart, and the leading spirits of the past century; then of Klopstock, Schlegel, and Humboldt; and, on his return from his first continental visit, of Currie, Roscoe, Sydney Smith, Mackintosh, Rogers, and the habitués of Holland House in its palmy days; while Madame de Staël, Mrs. Siddons, Scott, and the last bright galaxy of British writers, were familiar associates.

In regard to the form of Campbell's poetry, we are immediately struck with his delicate and true feeling for the harmony of language. He knew instinctively how to follow Pope's rule, and cause the sound to be an echo to the sense. When a boy he expressed keen disappointment at not being able to make a lady appreciate the meaning of Homer by the sound of celebrated passages. We know of few specimens of English verse comparable to the best of Campbell's for effective rhythm. Contrast the spirit-stirring flow of the song of the Greeks with the organ-like cadence of "Hohenlinden," or the pathetic melody of "Lord Ullin's Daughter" with the deep-flowing emphasis of the "Battle of the Baltic." It is remarkable that this fine musical adaptation belongs to all his genuine pieces — we mean those naturally inspired; while his muse is never whipped into service, as in Glencoe and Theodric, without betraying the fact in her stiff or wayward movement. This only proves how real a poet Campbell was.

We demur, however, to the opinion frequently advanced that his poetic fire died out long before his life. One of his noblest compositions, lofty and inspiring in sentiment, and grandly musical in rhythm, is "Hallowed Ground," and one of his most striking pieces, "The Last Man;" both of which were late productions.

The personality so characteristic of genuine feeling is not only evident in the obvious inspiration, but in the verbal execution of his conceptions. Thus he constantly impersonates insensible objects. It is the bugles that sing truce, and he that lays himself beneath the willow; the glow of evening is like, not the cheek and brow of woman, but of her we love. Throughout the intensity of the feeling personifies the object described, and gives human attributes to inanimate things, exactly as in the artless language of infancy and the oratory of an uncivilized people. Such is the instinct of nature; it is what separates verse from prose, the diction of fancy and emotion from that of affairs and science.

If any one is preëminently entitled to the name of poet, in its most obvious sense, it is he who so emphatically represents in verse a natural sentiment that his expression of it is seized upon by the common voice, and becomes its popular utterance. This direct, sympathetic, intelligent, and recognized phase of the art has been the most significant and effective, from the days of Job and Homer to those of Tasso and Campbell. The vivid rhetorical embodiment of a genuine feeling prevalent at the time, or characteristic of humanity, is the most obvious and the most natural province of the bard. The ballads of antiquity, the troubadour songs, and the primitive national lyric, evince how instinctive is this development of poetry. The philosophic combinations of the drama, the descriptive traits of the pastoral, and the formal range of the epic, are results of subsequent culture and more premeditated skill. This is also true of the refinements of sentiment, the mystical fancies, and the vague expression, which German literature, and the influence of Wordsworth, Shelley, and Coleridge, have grafted upon modern English verse.

If we were to adopt a vernacular poet from the brilliant constellation of the last and present century, as representing legitimately natural and popular feeling with true lyric energy, such as finds inevitable response and needs no advocacy or criticism to uphold or elucidate it, we should name Campbell. He wrote from the intensity of his own sympathies with freedom, truth, and love; his expression, therefore, is truly poetic in its spirit; while in rhetorical finish and aptness he had the very best culture, that of Greek literature. Thus simply furnished with inspiration and with a style, both derived from the most genuine sources, the one from nature and the other from the highest art, he gave melodious and vigorous utterance, not to a peculiar vein of imagination, like Shelley, nor a mystical attachment to nature, like Wordsworth, nor an egotistic personality, like Byron; but to a love of freedom and truth which political events had caused to glow with unwonted fervor in the bosoms of his noblest contemporaries, and to the native sentiment of domestic and social life, rendered more dear and sacred by their recent unhallowed desecration. It was not by ingenuity, egotism, or artifice, that he thus chanted, but honestly, earnestly, from the impulse of youthful ardor and tenderness moulded by scholarship.

It is now the fashion to relish verse more intricate, sentiment less defined, ideas of a metaphysical cast, and a rhythm less modulated by simple and grand cadences; yet to a manly intellect, to a heart yet alive with fresh, brave, unperverted instincts, the intelligible, glowing, and noble tone of Campbell's verse is yet fraught with cheerful augury. It has outlived, in current literature, and in individual remembrance, the diffuse metrical tales of Scott and Southey; finds a more prolonged response, from its general adaptation, than the ever-recurring key-note of Byron; and lingers on the lips and in the hearts of those who only muse over the elaborate pages of those minstrels whose golden ore is either beaten out to intangible thinness, or largely mixed with the alloy of less precious metal. Indeed, nothing evinces a greater want of just appreciation in regard to the art or gift of poetry, than the frequent complaints of such a poet as Campbell because of the limited quantity of his verse. It would be as rational to expect the height of animal spirits, the exquisite sensation of convalescence, the rapture of an exalted mood, the perfect content of gratified love, the tension of profound thought, or any other state, the very law of which is rarity, to become permanent. Campbell's best verse was born of emotion, not from idle reverie or verbal experiment; that emotion was heroic or tender, sympathetic or devotional — the exception to the every-day, the common-place, and the mechanical; accordingly, in its very nature, it was "like angels' visits," and no more to be summoned at will than the glow of affection or the spirit of prayer.

That idleness had nothing to do with the want of productiveness of his muse, so absurdly insisted on, during his life, is evident from his letters. He was always busy; but unfortunately for

for the most part, in tasks of literary drudgery undertaken for subsistence; and deserves laudation instead of censure, for, having respected the divine art, he loved, too much to degrade it into the service of hackneyed necessity. He was in fact a singularly industrious man; in his youth, an assiduous student while performing the duties of tutor, clerk, and compiler; and, in manhood and age, always engaged upon some bookseller's undertaking, now making an abridgment and now a translation; at one time the editor of a magazine, and, at another, of a collection of the English poets; now writing notes for a classic, and now paragraphs for a journal, lectures for the Glasgow University, state papers for Lord Minto, the biography of Mrs. Siddons or Petrarch, letters from Algiers, — whatever, in short, offered in the way of literary work, that would give him bread. His correspondence lets us into the secret of his unostentatious and patient labor, his constant projects, the suggestions of others, and the encroachments of ungenial employment upon his sensitive organization.

One cannot but honor the kindly and philosophic manner in which he speaks of his disappointments in these familiar letters; and rejoice to perceive that the feelings which inspired his memorable lines consoled him under all reverses, so that the moment he was in contact with the attractions of nature, friendship, and domestic peace, joy revived within him. The genuineness of his poetic impulse is thus indicated by the tenor of his life. Instead of lazily reposing on laurels early won, he was eminently true to the faith and independence which make beautiful the dreams of his youth, — devoted to his kindred and friends with self-denying generosity, sympathizing, to the last, in the cause of freedom, cognizant, everywhere and always, of the intrinsic worth of the primal sentiments whose beauty he so fondly sung, and never forgetful of the duty and the privileges of amity, courage, and fame. Such is the evidence of the unstudied epistles collected by Dr. Beattie, the spontaneous record of his occupations, opinions, and feelings, throughout life. They are consistent, and worthy both of the man and the poet. They exhibit a career divided between books and journeys — each nourishing his mind; an episode of domestic happiness which realizes all that good sense would advocate and romance glorify, — intervals of great physical suffering, melancholy bereavements, and cheerless toil, ever and anon redeemed by delightful social intercourse, deserved honors, and felicitous moods. The death of his wife, the idiocy of his only son, the failure of his own health, his homeless life in London, and his death in forlorn exile,—these, and some of the natural consequences of such vicissitudes, throw a gloom over portions of his chequered life; but through them and beyond, now that they are passed, the poet rises benignly in the integrity of his sentiments and the beauty of his art.

THE AMERICAN PHILOSOPHER.

BENJAMIN FRANKLIN.

THE pervading trait of Franklin's character was allegiance to the practical. Few devotees of knowledge have so consistently manifested this instinct, the more remarkable because united to speculative tendencies which quickened his intelligence and occupied his leisure to the very close of his existence. For the intangible aims of the metaphysician, the vagaries of the imaginative, the "airy bubble reputation," he exhibited no concern; but the application of truth to the facts of nature and of life, the discovery of material laws and their conversion to human welfare, the actual influence of morals, economy, politics, and education, upon civil society and individual development, were problems upon which he never failed to think, read, talk, write, and experiment. A striking evidence of this was his youthful disdain of the muses (although he wrote quite a respectable ballad at the age of twelve), because "verse-makers generally make beggars;" and his preference, in maturity, for that circle abroad where the "understanding" found such exclusive recognition and utterance: "I believe Scotland," he wrote to Lord Kaimes, "would be the country I should choose to spend my days in." Accordingly the history of the man is that of some of the most pregnant of great external interests; and his entire devotion to them, to the exclusion of more ideal, vague, and purely intellectual subjects, arose chiefly from his peculiar mental organization, and also, in no small degree, from the transition period in government, society, and popular intelligence, during which he lived. He was so indifferent to literary fame that the indefatigable editor * of his works informs us that some of his most characteristic writings were never intended for the press, very few were published under his own supervision, and nearly all came forth anonymously. His object, like Swift's, was immediate effect. In youth he studied the art of perspicuous expression in order to act with facility upon the minds of others; but it was in order to disseminate useful knowledge, to enlarge the boundaries of science, to advocate political reform, and direct into expedient channels the enterprise, speculation, and party zeal of his day, rather than to build himself a monument in the library, or a shrine in household lore. What he achieved as a writer was incidental, not premeditated; for he valued the pen as he did time, money, and experience, for its direct tendency to diffuse knowledge, comfort, utility, and settled principles of inference and action. The most deliberate of his writings, that is, the one which seems inspired least by a definite purpose and most by the anticipated pleasure of the undertaking, is his famous autobiography; and even in this it is evident that the luxury of reminiscences was in abeyance to the desire of imparting, and especially to the young, the benefit of his own experience. For many years, indeed, the pen of Franklin was too variously employed, and dedicated too constantly to the advancement of immediate national interests, to admit of any well-considered, elaborate, and finished work. What his written and spoken word, however, thus lost in permanent value, it gained in vigor and in direct utility. If we glance at the subjects and occasions of his tracts, letters, reports, paragraphs, and essays, we shall find they embrace the whole circle of questions important to his country and his age, — morals, the economy of life, commerce, finance, history, and politics. We find in them the germs of ideas now triumphant; of principles, through his advocacy, in no small degree, since embodied in action, and brought to grand practical results. A parable wins men to toleration; a maxim guides them to frugality; a comprehensive argument initiates the plan of that federal union which has proved

* Jared Sparks, D.D., LL.D.

the key-stone of our national prosperity; the farmer or the mariner, consulting Poor Richard's Almanac to learn the fluctuation of weather or tide, finds, beside these chronicles of Nature's mysteries, advice which puts him unconsciously on the track of provident habits, temperance, and contentment; the patriot in the field is cheered by the wisdom of the judge in council; the shipwright, the horticulturalist, the printer, the lowly aspirant for self-improvement, as well as the statesman and the philosopher, find wisdom and encouragement from his "words spoken in season;" in the prudent household his name is associated with the invaluable heating-apparatus that saves their fuel and increases the genial warmth of the evening fireside; in the disconsolate crises of war his foreign diplomacy and judicious hints warm the heart of valor with the prescience of success; in the land of his country's enemies, his clear statement of grievances and his intrepid reproof of injustice conciliate the nobler spirits there, and vindicate the leaders at home; the encroachments of savage tribes are checked, the policy of colonial rule softened, the comforts of domestic life enhanced, the resources of the mind elicited, and, in a word, the basis of national prosperity laid on the eternal foundation of popular enlightenment, self-reliance, and foresight, by the oracles of the American philosopher, thus casually uttered and incidentally proclaimed.

But while official duty and patriotism gave Franklin occasion to propagate and actualize so many useful and requisite principles, — to become the thinker and advocate, the incarnated common-sense of his country and his time, — there was another sphere of mental activity, another range of sagacious enterprise, in which he expatiated with kindred success. This was the domain of science. When he was not required to apply reflection to conduct, and to deal with a great climax in the political world, he turned with alacrity to that of natural philosophy. This was his congenial element. "I have got my niche," he writes, exultingly, "after having been kept out of it for twenty-four years by foreign appointments." He was, by instinct, a philosopher; one whom Bacon would have hailed as a disciple, and to whom Sir Kenelm Digby would have delighted to unfold the merits of the "sympathetic powder," Sir Thomas Browne to lament "vulgar errors," and Bishop Berkeley to explain the law of optics and the merits of tar-water. Lord Brougham expresses the conviction that he would have promulgated the inductive philosophy had not Bacon anticipated him.

At the commencement of the seventeenth century the provincial town, built upon three hills on the coast of Massachusetts, was an excellent place for the education of circumstances. Among its inhabitants were the most enlightened of the English emigrants, who brought with them the industrious habits, the domestic discipline, the taste for reading, and the love of thrift and enterprise, which induce and sustain commercial prosperity and municipal order. Questions of church and state, the conservatism of an old and the innovations of a new country, — the meeting-house, the newspaper, the fireside, and the school-room, — were their elements of civilization. The arts of luxury, the venerable in architecture, and the beautiful in decoration, had not yet superseded more stringent provisions for utility and comfort. The back settlements of the continent were exposed to savage invasion. The mother country, with her rich historical associations, her time-hallowed precedents, her glorious trophies of literature, her royal prerogatives, and her ancestral graves, was to the colonists the grand and mellow perspective of life, to which their New England dwellings on those bleak hill-sides, and beside that rock-bound bay, were the rude foreground, where they were to realize great principles of religion and government, achieve individual prosperity, and eventually battle manfully for freedom and truth. Meanwhile honest subsistence, religious zeal, and the cause of education, employed their energies. Months of dreary winter, when roofs were white with snow and the harbor a sheet of ice, alternated with a brief season of heat more than tempered by a keen breeze from the east; so that only the hardy maize and tough grass yielded reliable crops. Orchards were their only vineyards, a good sermon their most available entertainment, and Fast and Thanksgiving days their festivals. The great event of the month was an arrival from England — usually a weather-beaten craft, often ten weeks on the voyage; and her epitome of London news, the colonial agent she brought, the original copies of Pope's verses, Addison's Essay, or De Foe's novel, the new fashion for the "gude dame" and her daughters, and the watch or shoe-buckles for her husband, made themes for the street and the hearthstone for many days. The isolation of such a community, the fact that nonconformity had driven their fathers thither, the providence and frugality incident to the climate, the demand for foresight and self-denial, the force of public opinion, the distinction yielded to character, the comparative dearth of temptation, and the rigorous observance of family, church, and municipal discipline, though unfavorable to the more graceful and tender, moulded the sterner elements of humanity into unusual rectitude of purpose. To the expanded intellect and free aspirations of youth, there might be too much of the Puritan inflexibility and narrowness in such an environment; but, as a means of acquiring the habit of self-dependence and self-control,— the vestibule of more enlarged and spontaneous development, — we cannot but recognize its inestimable value.

The early circumstances, physical and moral, of men who leave distinct and permanent influences behind them, are more significant than we imagine. It was no accidental coïncidence that reared the most fervent of false prophets in the arid vales of Arabia, the greatest of religious reformers among the cold heights of Germany, or the most fanatical of usurpers beside the monotonous fens of Huntingdon. How intimate was the connection of the civil strife in Tuscany with the shadowy and sharp features of Dante's muse, of the sunny lassitude of southern Italy and France with the amorous melody of Petrarch's numbers, of the fiery passions and stern hardihood of Corsican life with the indomitable will of Napoleon! And who that knows New England, — even as modified by a foreign population, by the facilities of modern intercourse, and the liberality of an advanced civilization, — does not recognize, in the sagacity, prudence, hardihood, love of knowledge, industry, practical consistency, and wisdom of Frankin, the vigorous training of that Spartan mother, — the self-reliant discipline of that hard soil and rigid climate?

If the prime of Franklin's life was the critical era of our national fortunes, it was no less a period of literary and political transition in Great Britain. It was the epoch when History assumed a more philosophical development under the thoughtful pen of Hume, when sentiment and humor grew bold and vagrant in expression through Sterne, when the greatest orator of the age recorded its events in the Annual Register, when humane letters rose in public esteem by virtue of Goldsmith's graceful style, when Garrick made the stage illustrious, when Methodism began its work, when the seer of Stockholm proclaimed spiritual science, and the bard of Olney sang the pleasures of rural and domestic life. Yet how diverse from them all was the renown their American contemporary won, and the method of its acquisition! It is the clear vista to a humble origin, and the gradual rise from the condition of a poor mechanic to that of a statesman and philosopher, opened by Franklin in his artless memoir of himself, which gave at once individuality and universality to his fame. Who can estimate the vast encouragement derived by the lowliest seeker for knowledge and social elevation from such a minute chart of life, frankly revealing every stage of poverty, scepticism, obscure toil, dissipation, on the one side, — and manly resolution, indefatigable industry, frugal self-denial, patient study, honest and intelligent conviction, through, and by means of which, the fugitive printer's boy, with no library but an odd volume of the Spectator and an Essay of De Foe's, translations of Plutarch and Xenophon, the treatises of Shaftesbury and Locke, an English Grammar and the "Pilgrim's Progress," trained himself to observe, to write, and to think, while earning often a precarious subsistence in Philadelphia and London by type-setting and pen-work? The play-house alternating with the club made up of vagabonds and steady fellows, both "lovers of reading," a swimming-match and experiments in diet, conversation with "ingenious acquaintances," hard work, constant observation, and the habit of "improving by experience," exhibit the youth as he develops into the man, who, with remorse for the "errata" in his life, goes on to reveal the process, available to all with self-control and understanding, whereby from a ballad-hawker and printer he became a shop-keeper, then a journalist, and subsequently launched into an unprecedented career of public usefulness and honor.

The example of Franklin is invaluable as a triumph of self-culture. His name was not only an honorable passport among the learned, but an endeared watchword to the humble. The lowliest laborer of the undistinguished multitude claims a part in his fame, as well as the great discoverer or the regal patron. Never dawned a self-reliant character more opportunely on the world; at home, illustrating to a new country what perseverance, honesty, observation, and wisdom, can effect with the most limited resources; abroad, proving to an ancient *regime* how independent a genuine man may be of courts, academies, and luxury; — both the most requisite lessons for which humanity thirsted, and both enforced with an attractive candor, a gracious consistency, a modest resolution, which no argument could attain, and no rhetoric enhance.

Let us glance at the variety of subjects, identified with human welfare and apart from political interests, which, from first to last, employed his mind, and elicited either sagacious conjectures or positive suggestions; — the causes of earthquakes and the art of printing, the circulation of the blood and the cultivation of grasses, theories of light and the treatment of fevers, the manufacture of salt by evaporation and the arrangement of musical glasses, a remedy for smoky chimneys and the tendency of rivers to the sea, husbandry and fireplaces, magnetism and water-spouts, the effect of oil on water, meteorology, the aurora borealis, toads, balloons, thermometers, and ventilation. He searches out the mossy inscriptions on the gravestones of his ancestors in Northamptonshire, and acquires proficiency in a foreign language after sixty. He is one of a commission to examine the claims of Mesmer's theory in France, and to protect St. Paul's from lightning in London. He could not watch a shooting star, glance at a metallic crystal, behold the flush of sunset clouds or the hectic on an invalid's cheek, note the ebb of the tide or the greeting of the wind, examine a proposed law of state or a vegetable product of the earth, hear a beetle hum or feel a quivering pulse, gaze on a petrifaction or a type, converse with a stranger or meet a committee, draft a plan or look at a machine, without feeling the plea of causality, striving to trace the origin of effects, and to infer a law applicable to the wants of his race, or the elucidation of truth. No experiment was too insignificant for his philosophy, no task too humble for his patriotism. Open his correspondence at random; here you find precautionary hints for a voyage, there a sketch of an English school; now observations on maize, and again remarks on paper currency; to-day he draws up a plan of union for the colonies, to-morrow a dialogue with the Gout; at one time he invents a letter from China, and at another counsels the settler beyond the Alleghanies; commerce one moment, and a *jeu d'esprit* the next; advice to a Yankee tradesman, and a bagatelle for a Parisian lady, seem equally genial themes; a state paper and a proverb, allegory and statistics, the way to save money and the way to form a government, an article for the "Busy Body," a fable for the Almanac, and an epitaph for himself, — health, finance, natural history, the story of "The Whistle," — a theory of water-spouts, and "Cool Thoughts on Public Affairs," alternately occupy his pen; and to determine how many valuable precedents were established, what useful principles were realized, and what impulse was given to individual minds and to social progress by his enlightened activity, were as hopeless a task as to define the respective influence of the elements in fructification. He benignly and opportunely scattered the seeds of popular knowledge and of experimental science; they took root in the virgin soil of a new civilization; and the tiller of the earth, the reader of the newspaper, the frugal housewife, the public-spirited citizen, the aspiring mechanic, the honest tradesman, the legislator, and man of science, — the worker, thinker, companion, writer, the baffled and the novice, the adventurous and the truth-seeking of America, caught gleams of wisdom, warnings of prudence, perceptions of law, moral and physical, from Franklin, which gave them a clue to prosperity, and a motive to culture.

Like all resolute intelligences thus spontaneously breasting the vast ocean of truth, vigilant for discovery, and intent upon deduction, his earnest confidence and patient search were rewarded by a signal triumph. Philosophy, thus loyally wooed, smiled upon her votary; and nature, ever indulgent to the heart that loves her, whether with scientific insight or poetic enthusiasm, opened one arcana to his vision. The history of Franklin's electrical experiments and discoveries is one of the most attractive, beautiful, and pregnant episodes in modern science. The grand simplicity of his theory, the familiar apparatus by which it was tested, the accuracy of his foresight, and the unpretending spirit with which he received the fame incident to so great a result, form together one of those memorable instances of the conquest of mind over matter, of human intelligence over the secret facts of nature, which add the cognizance of new laws to the domain of knowledge, and brighter names to the catalogue of her immortal disciples. However temporary in their *prestige*, or limited in their absolute use, may be the other fruits of his studies, Electricity is identified with Franklin. It is the common destiny of scientific discoverers to be forgotten in the very progress they initiate; the pioneer is superseded in his march by the advanced guard, and what is a brilliant novelty to-day becomes a familiar truth to-morrow. The modern chemist forgets the alchemist, who, amid his illusive researches, brought to light some of the very principles that subserve later and more useful inquiries. The astronomer, as he sees, through a telescope undreamed of by the Chaldeans, a new planet wheel into the fields of vision, bestows no thought upon the isolated and self-denying astrologer, who, in the fanciful task of casting nativities, systematized the first rude alphabet of the stars, which modern science has elaborated into that "poetry of heaven" whereby genius keeps vigil, and the trackless sea is navigated without perplexity. But it is otherwise with the initiation of an absolutely new branch of knowledge. When Franklin drew down the lightning, and identified it with electricity, he forever allied his name to a subtle element, whose every subsequent revelation is associated with the kite and key, the thunder and the conductor, the benign image and endeared name of the Boston printer, the Philadelphia sage, and the American patriot. The vista his experiments opened has never ceased to lead further and deeper into the undiscovered mysteries of the universe; and, at this moment, the element of natural science most prophetic of new wonders and subtle uses is electricity. The phenomena of consciousness and nervous sympathy point more and more to an intimate relation between the electric fluid and the vital principle. The most inscrutable of material forces, it appears to be the direct medium of sensation, emotion, and all the modes of interaction between material existences and the embodied human soul. By it has recently been invented the most brilliant and powerful light yet obtained. As the most intense agent for decomposing the latent affinities of matter, and unimagined forces of locomotion and intercourse, its wonders are but foreshadowed in the electric telegraph, the application of magnetism as a motive power, and its use as a curative agent, and a disintegrating element. And it is worthy of remark that the magnetic expression of the human countenance, especially of the eye, and the affinities of the individual temperament, are graduated by the moral as well as the physical condition, and are capable of apparent extinction through grossly material habits and perverted natural instincts,—facts which seem to confirm the near relation of the electric principle with life, emotion, and spiritual development, as exhibited in organic forms. The prevalence of this unseen but ever vital principle in nature, in the amber of the torrent's bed and the fur of the domestic animal, in the circumambient air, in our own consciousness of attraction and repulsion, of cheerfulness and depression, in the healthy and the morbid experiences of humanity, would seem clearly to indicate that the sphere, whose latent significance was first revealed by Franklin, is limitless in its resources of power, use, and beauty.

His varied aptitudes, offices, inquiries, and discoveries, secured for him a sphere of acquaintance and friendship embracing the widest range of human character, vocation, and renown. Among his early intimates were three colonial governors; Godfrey, the inventor of the quadrant; and Ralph, a writer of history and verse. He took counsel on national affairs with Washington, the Revolutionary leaders, and the framers of the constitution; confronted the inimical scrutiny of the British ministry and parliament; was the messenger to Lord Howe, after a foreign army had encamped on our shores; conferred with Gates, Schuyler, Adams, Hancock, Jay, Hopkinson, Morris, Jefferson, Livingston, and Quincy; corresponded or conversed with Colden and Bartram, on natural history; with Priestley and Sir Joseph Banks, on scientific questions; with Hume, on mental philosophy; with (and on a large diversity of subjects) Paine and Cobbett; with Lafayette and the Count de Vergennes, Foy and Mazzei, Whitfield and the Duke of Orleans, Lord Kaimes, the Abbe Morelli, and Dr. Stiles, Madame Brillon and Dr. Robertson, Voltaire and Houdon, Darwin, Lord Chatham, Dr. Fothergill, D'Alembert, David Hartley, Diderot, and Madame Helvetius. From republican America to aristocratic France, at Philadelphia, London, and Versailles, in the court and the congress, the laboratory and the saloon, he enjoyed the best facilities and the most intimate associations. It is because of his readiness and versatility, his self-possession and independence, that in his life and letters we seem to behold, although ever conscious of his identity, at one time a grave philosopher and at another a genial companion, a patriarch here and a man of pleasure there; the wary statesman to-day and the playful humorist to-morrow,— ever active, cognizant, alert, content, inventive, useful, wise, cheerful, self-sustained, provident, far-sighted,— the type of good sense and urbanity, of thoroughness and insight, of tact and aptness. Hence, too, the fecundity of anecdote to which his life gave birth. Nor was he insensible to these social privileges and considerations, which, in the retrospect of eminent lives, always seem the most desirable of their felicities. "The regard and kindness I meet with," he writes to his wife from London, "from persons of worth, and the conversation of ingenious men, give me no small pleasure;" and he adds, with that superiority to circumstances and tenacity of purpose so characteristic: "I am for doing effectually what I came about, and I find it requires both time and patience." He elsewhere speaks of society as being his "dearest happiness." He tells us of his youthful zest for improving association when a printer's boy; his image, costume, manner, sayings and doings, as a man of society, are among the traditions of the old French court.* One of the last written descriptions of him, dated in his

* A once popular print represents Franklin in homespun, yarn stockings, and thick shoes, in the midst of a brilliant court, kissing, Yankee fashion, the queen, and the king crying "*Encore!*" This is an exaggeration; the facts are stated thus in Madame Campan's Memoirs of Marie Antoinette:

"Dr. Franklin appeared at court in the costume of an American cultivator; his hair plainly brushed, without powder. His round hat and plain coat of brown cloth contrasted strongly with the powdered *coiffures* and the bespangled and embroidered coats of the perfumed courtiers of Versailles. His simple and novel yet dignified appearance charmed the ladies of the court, and many were the *fêtes* given him, not only for his fame as a philosopher, but in acknowl-

lifetime, is that of a benign and cheerful octogenarian, seated in pleasant discourse under a mulberry-tree, beside his dwelling, exhibiting to his attached grandchild a two-headed snake. In a letter to Washington, written the same year, he says:

"For my own personal ease I should have died two years ago; but, though those years have been spent in excruciating pain, yet I am pleased to have lived them, since they have brought me to see our present situation. I am now finishing my eighty-fourth year, and, probably, with it, my career in this life; but in whatever state of existence I am placed hereafter, if I retain any memory of what has passed here, I shall with it retain the esteem, respect, and affection, with which I have long been, my dear friend, yours most sincerely," etc.

Parallel with his devotion to scientific inquiry was a ceaseless activity for public good, wherein his career is eminently distinguished from that of the majority of modern philosophers. One of the earliest projectors of the conquest of Canada, he was also an efficient agent in raising troops for the unfortunate Braddock; we find him vigorously at work throughout the scale of official duty and volunteer patriotism, at home and abroad, through the press and in society; doing military service; initiating fire-companies; teaching "the way to wealth;" speaker of the Pennsylvanian Assembly; a postmaster;* on committees; promoting the culture of silk in America; enlightening the British public on colonial affairs; bringing from Europe the latest facts in science and polity for the benefit of his own countrymen; casting type at Passy for a Philadelphia journal; interceding for prisoners of war; planning maritime expeditions with Paul Jones; befriending Captain Cooke; exciting French sympathy for the American

edgment of his patriotic virtues, which led him to enroll himself among the noble supporters of the cause of liberty. I assisted at one of these entertainments, where the most beautiful from among three hundred ladies was designated to place a crown of laurel on the gray head, and to salute with a kiss each cheek, of the American philosopher."

* A century ago, as Postmaster-General of the American colonies, he set out, in his old gig, to make an official inspection of the principal routes; and eighty years since, he held the same office under the authority of Congress, when a small folio, now preserved in the department at Washington, containing three quires of paper, served as his account-book for two years.

cause, and baffling English prejudice; a signer of the Declaration of Independence; framing treaties of alliance for his native land; the counsellor of the exile; the adviser of the official; a commissioner to Versailles; a delegate to the convention which framed the Constitution of the United States; — a versatile and responsible series of occupations, enough to furnish alone the materials of a noble and distinguished life, and yet constituting but a single phase of the illustrious career of Franklin.

The silent dignity with which he was content, amid the inevitable attacks, and even insults, misrepresentations, and sneers, which attend success in every path and superiority of whatever kind, is one of the most admirable traits of Franklin's character, and one that was generously acknowledged by his opponents when the tide of prejudice and animosity ebbed. He met the caprices of delegated authority, the jealousy of his colleagues, the injustice of his political antagonists, the tirade of the solicitor-general of the crown, the attempts at bribery and intimidation, with a serene and undemonstrative resolution. "My rule is," he said, "to go straight forward in doing what appears to me right at the time, leaving the consequences to Providence. I wish every kind of prosperity to my friends, and forgive my enemies."

If there were no blemishes in this picture, it would scarcely be human; but they are casual, and, like flitting shadows, of vague import, while through and above them the bland and sagacious, the honest and wise lineaments, tranquilly beam. The spirit of calculation, the narrowness of prudence, the limits of a matter-of-fact vision, the gallantries tolerated by the social standard of the times, the absence of that impulse and *abandon*, that generous and ardent mood which seems inseparable from the noblest and most aspiring natures, sometimes render Franklin too exclusively a provident utilitarian and a creature of the immediate, to satisfy our loftiest ideal of character, or our sympathies with genius as spontaneously and unconsciously manifest. Gossip has bequeathed hints of amours that derogate somewhat from the gravity of the sage; partisan spite has whispered of a too selfish estimate of the chances of expediency; and there are those who find in the doctrine and practice of the American philosopher an undue estimate of thrift, and an illustration of the creed that man "lives by bread alone," which chills enthusiasm and subdues praise. But when we contemplate the amount of practical good he achieved, the value of his scientific discoveries, the uprightness, self-devotion, consistency of the man, the loyal activity of the patriot, and the interests he promoted, the habits he exemplified, the truths he made vital, and the prosperity he initiated, our sense of obligation, our admiration of his practical wisdom, and our love of his genial utility, merge critical objection in honor and gratitude. What is the flippant sarcasm of the queen, cited by Madame du Barry, that he eat asparagus like a savage, to intellectual Hume's assertion that "America has sent us many good things, gold, silver, sugar, indigo, etc., but you are the first philosopher"? If, on the one hand, his having embraced Voltaire in the presence of the French Academy be cited as proof of *persiflage*, on the other, his frank expression of religious convictions to Dr. Stiles, evidences a deliberate faith in things unseen and eternal. If the graphic pen of Mrs. Grant, in depicting the candid graces of colonial life in America, attributes the subsequent devotion to gain, to the economical maxims of Franklin, the sacred opinion of Washington affords a more just view of the legitimate rank their author held in the affections of his countrymen. "If to be venerated for benevolence, if to be admired for talents, if to be esteemed for patriotism, if to be beloved for philanthropy, can gratify the human mind, you must have the pleasing consolation to know that you have not lived in vain."

It must be confessed that the spiritual was not developed in Franklin's nature in proportion to the scientific element, and, as an inevitable consequence, religion was a grand social interest, or, at most, a private conviction rather than a matter of profession or of sentiment. It is probable that an early and not auspicious familiarity with the conflicts of sects confirmed his aversion to a merely doctrinal faith. He was familiar in his native town and in his adopted home respectively with the two extremes of prescriptive belief and strongly marked individualism, as displayed by the Puritans and the Quakers, and found enough of vital piety and moral worth in both to emancipate him from superstitious reliance on a positive creed. But there is ample evidence that he recognized those broad and eternal truths which lie at the basis of all religion. He seems to have profoundly felt his responsibleness to a higher than earthly power; everywhere he beheld a wise and beneficent Creator, in the operation of material and moral laws; always he sought the traces of Divine wisdom in the universe and in events. We find him advising his daughter to rely more upon prayer than sermons; recognizing the hand of Providence in the destinies of his country; moving a resolution for devotional services in the convention that framed the constitution; preparing an abridgment of the ritual; and, in his last days, enjoying those devotional poems which have so long endeared the name of Watts. It is not so much the comparative silence of Franklin on religious or rather sectarian questions, which has given rise to a vague notion of his scepticism and indifference, as the fact that he acknowledged deistical opinions in youth, and subsequently worked almost exclusively in the sphere of material interests, and was intimately associated with the infidel philosophers of France. Other affinities than those of speculative unbelief, however, allied him to a class of men whose names have become watchwords of infidelity; literature and science, government and philosophy, were themes of mutual investigation common to them and him; and if, in order to attest their sense of his intelligence and republicanism, they placed his bust upon the altar of the Jacobin Club with those of Brutus, Helvetius, Mirabeau, and Rousseau, it was chiefly because, with those friends of popular freedom and social reform, he had proved himself an independent thinker and a noble devotee of human progress, and because, to the vague though eloquent sentiment of social amelioration kindled by Jean Jacques, his practical sagacity had given actual embodiment. Few men, indeed, have lived whose time, mind, and resources were more wisely and conscientiously directed to the elevation of society, the enlightenment of the mass, and the improvement of human condition. He was indisputably one of the greatest benefactors of mankind.

Except in a scientific direction, however, it must be acknowledged that the spirit of Franklin's precepts and theories is not adapted to beguile us "along the line of infinite desires;" his wisdom was applicable to the immediate and the essential in daily and common life; he dealt chiefly with details; he advocated habits, ideas, and methods, based on positive utility; success as derived from patient and gradual but determined action, minute observation, careful practice, rather than from broad generalization, daring achievement, or the imagination and enthusiasm which so often prove intuitive means of triumph, which are indispensable in art, and constitute the difference between the process of genius and that of talent. There is nothing certain, he used to say, but death and taxes; happiness he believed the aggregate of small satisfactions, rather than the instant realization of a great hope; and fortune he regarded as the reward of assiduity and prudence, rather than of prosperous adventure or of daring enterprise. Compared with the ephemeral impulses, the obscure theories, the visionary and uncertain principles, in vogue elsewhere and before and since his day, there was incalculable value in his maxims and example. But it would be gross injustice to the versatile and comprehensive nature of man, to the aspirations of exalted minds, to the facts of spiritual philosophy, to the needs of immortal instincts, to the faith of the soul, the annals of genius, and the possible elevation of society, to admit that such views are more than the material basis of human progress, or the external conditions of individual development. What the ballast is to the ship, the trellis to the vine, health of body to activity of mind, such was Franklin's social philosophy to human welfare; all-important as a means, inadequate as a final provision; a method of insuring the coöperation of natural aids, of fostering intrinsic resources, whereby the higher elements may freely do their work, and man, sustained by favorable circumstances, and unhampered by want, neglect, and improvidence, may the more certainly enjoy, aspire, love, conceive, expand, and labor, according to the noblest inspiration and the grandest scope of his nature and his destiny.

If we compare the life of Franklin, as a whole, with that of other renowned philosophers, we find that the isolated self-devotion, the egotism and vanity, which too often derogate from the interest and dignity of their characters as men, do not mar the unity of the tranquil, honest, and benign disposition, which lends a gracious charm to the American philosopher. Archimedes invented warlike machines to overthrow the invaders of his country; but his heart did not warm like Franklin's, nor did his brain work to devise the means of elevating his poor and ignorant fellow-citizens in the scale of knowledge and self-government. Newton proclaimed vast and universal laws; but there was in his temper a morbid tenacity of personal fame, beside which the disinterested zeal of Franklin is beautiful. The scope of Franklin's research was limited in comparison with that of Humboldt; but unsustained, like that noble *savant*, by royal patronage, he sacrificed his love of science for half his lifetime to the cause of his country. Arago excelled him in the power of rhetorical eulogy of the votaries of their common pursuits; but while the French philosopher spoke eloquently to a learned academy, the American had a people for his audience, and disseminated among them truths vital to their progress and happiness, in a diction so clear, direct, and convincing, that it won them simultaneously to the love of science and the practice of wisdom.

When he was released from official care, his mental activity, though unremitted, was singularly genial; and to this characteristic of the philosophical temperament we attribute his self-possession, rational enjoyment, and consequent longevity; for, of all pursuits, that which has for its aim general knowledge and the discovery and application of truth, while it raises the mind above casual disturbance, supplies it with an object at once unimpassioned and attractive, serene yet absorbing, a motive in social intercourse, and a resource in seclusion. Just before Thierry's recent death, although he was long a martyr to disease, he remarked to a friend: "Had I to begin my life again, I would again set out in the path which has led me to where I am. Blind and suffering, without hope and without intermission, I may say, without giving testimony which can be suspected, there is something in this world better than material pleasure, better than fortune, better than health itself, and this is attachment to science." Of this good Franklin was a large partaker, and we cannot but imagine the delight and sympathy with which he would have followed the miraculous progress of the modern sciences, and of those ideas of which he beheld but the dawn. "I have sometimes almost wished," he writes, "it had been my destiny to be born two or three centuries hence; for inventions and improvements are prolific, and beget more of their kind." Had he lived a little more than another fifty years, he would have seen the mode of popular education initiated by the Spectator expanded into the elaborate Review, the brilliant Magazine, the Household Words, and scientific journals of the present day; the rude hand-press, upon which he arranged the miniature "copy" of the New England Courant, transformed into electrotyped cylinders worked by steam and throwing off thirty thousand printed sheets an hour; the thin almanac, with its proverbs and calendar, grown to a plethoric volume, rich in astronomical lore and the statistics of a continent; the vessel dependent on the caprice of the winds and an imperfect science of navigation, self-impelled with a pre-calculated rate of speed, and by the most authentic charts; and the subtle fluid, that his prescience caught up and directed safely by a metal rod, sent along leagues of wire — the silent and instant messenger of the world! With what keen interest would he have followed Davy, with his safety-lamp, into the treacherous mine; accompanied Fulton in his first steam voyage up the Hudson; watched Daguerre as he made his sun-pictures; seen the vineyards along the Ohio attest his prophetic advocacy of the Rhenish grape-culture; heard Miller discourse of the "Old Red Sandstone," Morse explain the Telegraph, or Maury the tidal laws! Chemistry, almost born since his day, would open a new and wonderful realm to his consciousness; the Cosmos of Humboldt would draw his entranced gaze down every vista of natural science, as if to reveal at a glance a programme of all the great and beautiful secrets of the universe; and the reckless enterprise and mad extravagance of his prosperous country would elicit more emphatic warnings than Poor Richard breathed of old.

There have been many writers who, in simple and forcible English, by arguments drawn from pure common sense and enlivened by wit or eloquence, interpreted political truth, and vastly aided the education of the people. But, in the case of Franklin, this practical service of authorship was immeasurably extended and confirmed by the *prestige* of his electrical discoveries, by the dawning greatness and original principles of the country of which he was so prominent a representative, and by the extraordinary circumstances of his times, when great social and political questions were brought to new and popular tests, which made the homely scientific republican an oracle in the most luxurious and artificial of despotic courts. When the intricate tactics of rival armies have been exhausted, the able general has recourse to a *coup de main*, and effects by simple bravery what stratagem failed to win. When a question has been discussed until its primary significance is almost forgotten in a multitude of side-issues, the true orator suddenly brings to a focus the scattered elements of the theme, and, by a clear and emphatic statement, reproduces its normal features, and, through a bold analysis, places it in the open light of truth, and heralds the bewildered council to a final decision. In like manner, when vital principles of government and society have been complicated by interest, speculation, and misfortune, when men have grown impatient of formulas and ceremonies, and aspire to realities, he who in his speech, dress, habits, writings, manners, and achievements, — or, in the exponent of all these, his character, — represents most truly the normal instincts, average common sense, and practicable good, of his race, is welcomed as an exemplar, an authority, and a representative. Such was the American philosopher at once in the eyes of a newly-organized and self-dependent nation, and in those of an ancient people, in its transition from an outgrown to an experimental *regime*.

He took his degree in the school of humanity before the technical honor was awarded by Oxford, Edinburgh, and the Royal Society. It was this preëminent distinction which led Sydney Smith to playfully threaten his daughter, "I will disinherit you if you do not admire everything written by Franklin;" and which enshrines his memory in the popular heart, makes him still the annual hero of the printer's festival, associates his name with townships and counties, inns and ships, societies and periodicals, — with all the arrangements and objects of civilization that aim to promote the enlightenment and convenience of man. The press and the lightning-rod, the almanac, the postage-stamp, and the free-school medal,* attest his usefulness and renown; maxims

* "I was born in Boston, in New England," — this is the simple language of his will, — "and owe my first instructions in literature to the free grammar

of practical wisdom more numerous than Don Quixote's garrulous squire cited gave birth under his hand to a current proverbial philosophy; and his effigy is, therefore, the familiar symbol of independence, of popular education, and self-culture. Those shrewd and kindly features, and that patriarchal head, are as precious to the humble as the learned; and in every land and every language Franklin typifies the "greatest good of the greatest number." Mignot rightly defines him as "gifted with the spirit of observation and discovery;" Davy calls his inductive power felicitous; Paul Jones augured success in his desperate sea-fights from the "Bon Homme Richard;" and the memorable epigraph of Turgot is the acknowledged motto of his escutcheon:

> "Erupuit cœlo fulmen
> Sceptrumque tyrannis."

schools established there." He added the bequest of a fund, of which the income should be annually applied, in silver medals, to be awarded to the most meritorious boys in these schools.

HISTORY.

Prescott.

HISTORY OF THE REIGN OF PHILIP II.

By William H. Prescott. With Portraits, Maps, Plates, &c Two volumes, 8vo. Price, in muslin, $2 per volume.

The reign of *Philip the Second*, embracing the last half of the sixteenth century, is one of the most important as well as interesting portions of modern history. It is necessary to glance only at some of the principal events. The War of the Netherlands — the model, so to say, of our own glorious War of the Revolution — the Siege of Malta, and its memorable defence by the Knights of St. John; the brilliant career of Don John of Austria, the hero of Lepanto; the Quixotic adventures of Don Sebastian of Portugal; the conquest of that kingdom by the Duke of Alba; Philip's union with Mary of England, and his wars with Elizabeth, with the story of the Invincible Armada; the Inquisition, with its train of woes; the rebellion of the Moriscos, and the cruel manner in which it was avenged — these form some of the prominent topics in the foreground of the picture, which presents a crowd of subordinate details of great interest in regard to the character and court of Philip, and to the institutions of Spain, then in the palmy days of her prosperity. The materials for this vast theme were to be gathered from every part of Europe, and the author has for many years been collecting them from the archives of different capitals. The archives of Simancas, in particular, until very lately closed against even the native historian, have been opened to his researches; and his collection has been further enriched by MSS. from some of the principal houses in Spain, the descendants of the great men of the sixteenth century. Such a collection of original documents has never before been made for the illustration of this period.

The two volumes now published bring down the story to the execution of Counts Egmont and Hoorn in 1568, and to the imprisonment and death of Don Carlos, whose mysterious fate, so long the subject of speculation, is now first explored by the light of the authentic records of Simancas.

HISTORY OF THE REIGN OF FERDINAND AND ISABELLA, The Catholic.

By W. H. Prescott. With Portraits. Three volumes, 8vo. Price, in muslin, $2 per volume.

"Mr. Prescott's merit chiefly consists in the skilful arrangement of his materials, in the spirit of philosophy which animates the work, and in a clear and elegant style that charms and interests the reader. His book is one of the most successful historical productions of our time. The inhabitant of another world, he seems to have shaken off the prejudices of ours. In a word, he has, in every respect, made a most valuable addition to our historical literature." — *Edinburgh Review.*

HISTORY OF THE CONQUEST OF MEXICO,

With the Life of the Conqueror, Fernando Cortez, and a View of the Ancient Mexican Civilization. By W. H. Prescott. With Portrait and Maps. Three volumes, 8vo. Price, in muslin, $2 per volume.

"The more closely we examine Mr. Prescott's work the more do we find cause to commend his diligent research. His vivacity of manner and discursive observations scattered through notes as well as text, furnish countless proofs of his matchless industry. In point of style, too, he ranks with the ablest English historians; and paragraphs may be found in his volumes in which the grace and eloquence of Addison are combined with Robertson's majestic cadence and Gibbon's brilliancy." — *Athenæum.*

HISTORY OF THE CONQUEST OF PERU;

With a Preliminary View of the Civilization of the Incas. By W. H. Prescott. With Portraits, Maps, &c. Two vols., 8vo. Price, in muslin, $2 per volume.

"The world's history contains no chapter more striking and attractive than that comprising the narrative of Spanish conquest in the Americas. Teeming with interest to the historian and philosopher, to the lover of daring enterprise and marvellous adventure, it is full of fascination. A clear head and a sound judgment, great industry and a skilful pen, are needed to do justice to the subject. These necessary qualities have been found united in the person of an accomplished American author. Already favorably known by his histories of the eventful and chivalrous reign of Ferdinand and Isabella, and of the exploits of the Great Marquis and his iron followers, Mr. Prescott has added to his well-merited reputation by his narrative of the Conquest of Peru." — *Blackwood.*

Mr. Prescott's works are also bound in more elaborate styles, — half calf, half turkey, full calf, and turkey antique.

Barry.

THE HISTORY OF MASSACHUSETTS,

By Rev. John Stetson Barry. To be comprised in three volumes, octavo. Volume I. embracing the Colonial Period, down to 1692, now ready. Volumes II. and III. in active preparation. Price, in muslin, $2 per volume.

Extracts from a Letter from Mr. Prescott, the Historian.

BOSTON, June 8, 1855.

Messrs. Phillips, Sampson, & Co.

Gentlemen, — The History is based on solid foundations, as a glance at the authorities will show.

The author has well exhibited the elements of the Puritan character, which he has evidently studied with much care. His style is perspicuous and manly, free from affectation; and he merits the praise of a conscientious endeavor to be impartial.

The volume must be found to make a valuable addition to our stores of colonial history.

Truly yours,

WILLIAM H. PRESCOTT.

Hume.

THE HISTORY OF ENGLAND,

From the Invasion of Julius Cæsar to the Abdication of James II., 1688. By David Hume, Esq. A new edition, with the author's last corrections and improvements; to which is prefixed a short account of his life, written by himself. Six volumes, with Portrait. Black muslin, 40 cents per volume; in red muslin, 50 cents; half binding, or library style, 50 cents per volume; half calf, extra, $1.25 per volume.

The merits of this history are too well known to need comment. Despite the author's predilections in favor of the House of Stuart, he is the historian most respected, and most generally read. Even the brilliant *Macaulay*, though seeking to establish an antagonistic theory with respect to the royal prerogative, did not choose to enter the lists with *Hume*, but after a few chapters by way of cursory review, began his history where his great predecessor had left off.

No work in the language can take the place of this, at least for the present century. And nowhere can it be found accessible to the general reader for any thing like the price at which this handsome issue is furnished.

These standard histories, Hume, Gibbon, Macaulay, and Lingard, are known as the *Boston Library Edition*. For uniformity of style and durability of binding, quality of paper and printing, they are the cheapest books ever offered to the American public, and the best and most convenient editions published in this country.

Macaulay.

THE HISTORY OF ENGLAND,

From the Accession of James II. By Thomas Babington Macaulay. Four volumes, 12mo., with Portrait. Black muslin, 40 cents per volume; red muslin, 50 cents; library style and half binding, 50 cents; calf, extra, $1.25.

"The all-accomplished Mr. Macaulay, the most brilliant and captivating of English writers of our own day, seems to have been born for the sole purpose of making English history as fascinating as one of Scott's romances." — *North American Review.*

"The great work of the age. While every page affords evidence of great research and unwearied labor, giving a most impressive view of the period, it has all the interest of an historical romance." — *Baltimore Patriot.*

Gibbon.

THE HISTORY OF THE DECLINE AND FALL OF THE ROMAN EMPIRE,

By Edward Gibbon, Esq. With Notes by Rev. H. H. Milman. A new Edition. To which is added a complete Index of the whole work. Six volumes, with Portrait. 12mo., muslin, 40 cents per volume; red muslin, 50 cents; half binding, or library style, 50 cents per volume; half calf, extra, $1.25.

"We commend it as the best library edition extant." — *Boston Transcript.*

"The publishers are now doing an essential service to the rising generation in placing within their reach a work of such acknowledged merit, and so absolutely indispensable." — *Baltimore American.*

"Such an edition of this English classic has long been wanted; it is at once convenient, economical, and elegant." — *Home Journal.*

Lingard.

A HISTORY OF ENGLAND,

From the first Invasion by the Romans to the Accession of William and Mary in 1688. By John Lingard, D. D. From the last revised London edition. In thirteen volumes; illustrated title pages, and portrait of the author. 12mo., muslin. Price, 75 cents per volume.

"This history has taken its place among the classics of the English language." — *Lowell Courier.*

"It is infinitely superior to Hume, and there is no comparison between it and Macaulay's romance. Whoever has not access to the original monuments will find Dr. Lingard's work the best one he can consult." — *Brownson's Review.*

"Lingard's history has been long known as the best history of England ever written; but hitherto the price has been such as deprived all but the most wealthy readers of any chance of possessing it. Now, however, its publication has been commenced in a beautiful style, and at such a price that no student of history need fail of its acquisition." — *Albany Transcript.*

Lamartine.

HISTORY OF THE FRENCH REVOLUTION OF 1848,

By Alphonse de Lamartine. Translated by F. A. Durivage and William S. Chase. In one volume, octavo, with illustrations. Price, in muslin, $2.25.

Same work, in a 12mo. edition, muslin, 75 cents; sheep, 90 cents.

A most graphic history of great events, by one of the principal actors therein.

"The day will come when *Lamartine*, standing by the gate-post of the Hotel de Ville, and subduing by his eloquence the furious passions of the thousands upon thousands of delirious revolutionists, who sought they knew not what at the hands of the self-constituted Provisional Government of 1848, will be commemorated in stone, on canvas, and in song, as the very impersonation of moral sublimity." — *Meth. Quarterly Review.*

"No fitting mete-wand hath To-day
For measuring spirits of thy stature, —
Only the Future can reach up to lay
The laurel on that lofty nature. —
Bard, who with some diviner art
Hast touched the bard's true lyre, a nation's heart."
James Russell Lowell, "To Lamartine."

www.ingramcontent.com/pod-product-compliance
Lightning Source LLC
LaVergne TN
LVHW020926110826
845150LV00004B/778

* 9 7 8 1 4 2 5 5 5 3 3 5 7 *